EYEWITNESS TRAVEL GUIDES

LOIRE VALLEY

Main contributor: JACK TRESIDDER

LONDON, NEW YORK,
MELBOURNE, MUNICH AND DELHI
www.dk.com

PRODUCED BY DUNCAN BAIRD PUBLISHERS, LONDON, ENGLAND
Project Editor Stephanie Driver
Editor Slaney Begley
Editorial Assistant Joanne Levêque
Designers Paul Calver, Jill Mumford
Design Assistant Christine Keilty
US EDITORS MARY SUTHERLAND, KATHLEEN KENT

PHOTOGRAPHERS
John Heseltine, Paul Kenward, Kim Sayer

ILLUSTRATORS
Joanna Cameron, Roger Hutchins, Robbie Polley,
Pat Thorne, John Woodcock

Reproduced by Colourscan (Singapore)
Printed and bound by L. Rex Printing Company Limited (China)

First American Edition, 1996

**Reprinted with revisions 1997 (twice), 1999,
2000, 2001, 2003, 2004**

04 05 10 9 8 7

Published in the United States by
DK Publishing, Inc., 375 Hudson Street,
New York, New York 10014

Copyright © 1996, 2004 Dorling Kindersley Limited, London

ISSN 1542-1554
ISBN 0-7894-9733-6

THROUGHOUT THIS BOOK, FLOORS ARE REFERRED TO IN ACCORDANCE WITH EUROPEAN
USAGE, I.E., THE "FIRST FLOOR" IS THE FLOOR ABOVE GROUND LEVEL

**The information in this
Dorling Kindersley Travel Guide is checked regularly.**
Every effort has been made to ensure that this book is as up-to-date
as possible at the time of going to press. Some details, however,
such as telephone numbers, opening hours, prices, gallery hanging
arrangements and travel information are liable to change. The
publishers cannot accept responsibility for any consequences arising
from the use of this book, nor for any material on third party
websites, and cannot guarantee that any website address in this
book will be a suitable source of travel information. We value the
views and suggestions of our readers very highly. Please write to:
Publisher, DK Eyewitness Travel Guides,
Dorling Kindersley, 80 Strand, London WC2R 0RL, Great Britain.

CONTENTS

Statue in La Lorie

INTRODUCING THE LOIRE VALLEY

**King Louis XIV portrayed as
Jupiter, conquering La Fronde**

The town of Argenton-sur-Creuse

Manoir du Grand-Martigny

Stained-glass portrait of Agnès Sorel

Young boys fishing at Pornichet marina in Loire-Atlantique

Cathédrale St-Etienne, Bourges

HOW TO USE THIS GUIDE

THIS GUIDE will help you get the most from your stay in the Loire Valley. It provides both expert recommendations and detailed practical information. *Introducing the Loire Valley* maps the region and sets it in its historical and cultural context. *The Loire Valley Area by Area* describes the important sights, with maps, photographs and illustrations. Suggestions for food, drink, accommodation, shopping and activities are in *Travellers' Needs*, and the *Survival Guide* has tips on everything from the French telephone system to getting to the Loire and travelling around the region.

THE LOIRE VALLEY AREA BY AREA

In this guide, the Loire Valley has been divided into six regions, each of which has its own chapter. A map of these regions can be found inside the front cover of the book. The most interesting places to visit in each region have been numbered and plotted on a *Pictorial Map*.

Each area of the Loire Valley can be quickly identified by its colour coding.

1 Introduction
The landscape, history and character of each region is described here, showing how the area has developed over the centuries and what it has to offer the visitor today.

A locator map shows the region in relation to the whole of the Loire Valley.

2 Pictorial Map
This gives an illustrated overview of the whole region. All the sights are numbered, and there are also useful tips on getting around by car and public transport.

Features and story boxes highlight special or unique aspects of a particular sight.

3 Detailed information on each sight
All the important towns and other places to visit are described individually. They are listed in order, following the numbering on the Pictorial Map. *Within each town or city, there is detailed information on important buildings and other major sights.*

4 Major Towns
An introduction covers the history, character and geography of the town. The main sights are described individually and plotted on a Town Map.

A Visitors' Checklist gives contact points for tourist and transport information, plus details of market days and local festival dates.

The town map shows all major through-roads as well as minor streets of interest to visitors. All the sights are plotted, along with the bus and train stations, parking, tourist offices and churches.

5 Street-by-Street Map
Towns or districts of special interest to visitors are shown in detailed 3D, with photographs of the most important sights, giving a bird's-eye view of the area.

A suggested route for a walk covers the most interesting streets in the area.

For all the top sights, a Visitors' Checklist provides the practical information you will need to plan your visit.

6 Top Sights
These are given two or more pages. Important buildings are dissected to reveal their interiors.

Stars indicate the works of art or features that no visitor should miss.

INTRODUCING THE LOIRE VALLEY

Putting the Loire on the Map

THE LOIRE VALLEY lies in central France, bordered by the regions of Brittany, Normandy and the Ile de France to the north, the Massif Central and Poitou to the south, Burgundy to the east, and the Atlantic Ocean to the west. The river itself, the longest in France, flows for 1,020 km (634 miles) from its source in the Cévennes to the Atlantic Ocean just south of Nantes at St-Nazaire. The region covers an area of 71,228 sq km (27,500 sq miles) and has a population of about 5.2 million.

KEY

- ☐ Area covered by this guide
- ⛴ Ferry service
- ✈ Airport
- ═══ Motorway / Motorway characteristics
- ─── Major road
- ─── Railway line

0 kilometres   100

0 miles   100

Satellite view of the River Loire and the large fields of its flood-plain

The Loire as it passes through Tours

A PORTRAIT OF THE LOIRE VALLEY

THE LOIRE VALLEY, *world-famous for its beautiful châteaux, has long been described as exemplifying* la douceur de vivre: *it combines a leisurely pace of life, a mild climate, mellow wines and the gentle ways of its inhabitants. The overall impression conveyed by the region is one of an unostentatious taste for the good things in life.*

In this central region of France, the people have neither the brisk, sometimes brusque, demeanour of their northern counterparts, nor the excitable nature of the southern provinces. They get on peacefully with their lives, benefiting from the prosperity generated not only by the region's centuries old popularity with French and foreign visitors alike, but also by a fertile soil and a favourable climate, which rarely succumbs to extremes of heat or cold.

The Loire as a region is far from being a cultural and historical anachronism, although the wealth of well-preserved historical monuments harks back to the past. Many local people are surprisingly proud of the nuclear power stations at Avoine-Chinon and at St-Laurent-des-Eaux near Beaugency, both symbols of the region's role in the technological revolution. The well-publicized (and successful) campaign in the mid-1980s to have the high-speed TGV train rerouted was based not on any intrinsic dislike of new-fangled schemes, but on alarm at the potential damage to the bottles of wine stored in their underground cellars close to the planned track.

Cyclist on the Ile de Noirmoutier causeway

The bridge across the Loire at Blois, one of several historic bridges in the region

◁ Berry village in the evening

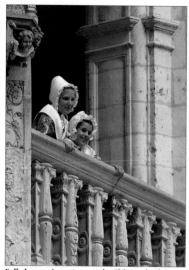
Folk dancers in costume at the Château de Blois

restaurants is assured. And in the towns and villages of Touraine and Anjou, conviviality is everywhere apparent. The many fairs, fêtes and festivals devoted to local wines and produce – garlic, apples, melons or even chitterling sausages – bear witness to the large part, even by French standards, that food and drink play in the social life of these old provinces.

They also play a major role in the region's economy: around 12 per cent of the local population is involved in agriculture or the food industry in some way. Many a *primeur* (early fruit or vegetable) in the markets and restaurants of Paris has been transported from the fertile fields and orchards beside the Loire, and the region's melons and asparagus are sold all over the country. So are the button mushrooms, known as *champignons de Paris* (Paris mushrooms), grown in tufa quarries near Saumur.

Colourful summer display

Although some local wines are reputed not to travel well, many of them do so very successfully, not only in France but also abroad, adding to the region's prosperity. In terms of the volume of production, the

Yet the way of life in the Loire Valley remains largely anchored to the traditional values of *la France profonde*, the country's conservative heartland – seeking to perpetuate a way of life that has proved its worth over the centuries. This is particularly true of the Berry, the easternmost region of the Loire covered in this guide. It is the geographical centre of the country – several villages claim the honour of being situated at "the heart of France" – and it seems to the visitor charmingly off the beaten track. It comes as no surprise to discover that folk traditions and, some say, witchcraft are still part of everyday life in some of these timeless villages. In November 2000, UNESCO made the Loire Valley one of its protected areas of natural beauty.

LOCAL ATTRACTIONS

The opportunity to stay in a private château is one of the many treats for visitors to the Loire Valley, where hospitality is a serious business. Even in Orléans, whose proximity to Paris has led to its reputation as a dormitory town, a warm welcome in hotels and

The Loire at Amboise, dotted with sandbanks

A walk along a river bank at Rochefort-sur-Loire, one of many country pursuits to enjoy

region ranks fifth in France and, although production is on a smaller scale than the famous wine giants of Bordeaux and Burgundy, the quality and popularity of Loire wines are both increasing. Sancerre and Muscadet are probably the best known, but others, such as Vouvray and Bourgueil, are also much in demand.

The restaurants and hotel dining rooms of the Loire Valley take full advantage of the excellent produce available locally – no wonder so many Parisian families have been attracted to the area. Just as once the nobility of France established their châteaux and stately homes in the area, now wealthy Parisians are flocking to the Loire Valley to buy *résidences secondaires*. The influx has been swelled in recent years with the advent of the TGV, which takes less than an hour to reach the region from Paris.

Sign offering wine-tastings

RECENT DEVELOPMENTS

In the west of the region, Nantes has adapted to changing economic times. The closure of its once-flourishing shipyards has led to a new focus on advanced technology and international business. In the mid-1980s a science park, the Technopole Atlantique, was built on the banks of the River Erdre, an electronic research institute opened and the city acquired a World Trade Centre *(Centre Atlantique du Commerce International)*. Yet here, too, the broad streets and avenues (formerly water-courses) create a feeling of spaciousness that helps to perpetuate the mood of *douceur de vivre* beside the new economic dynamism.

In the same way, Tours' chic new conference centre in the heart of the city does not seem to have detracted from the bustle of streets often thronged with foreign students. They have come to learn to speak what is alleged to be the purest French in France. By "pure", the experts mean well-modulated speech devoid of any strong accent – a fine symbol for a populace admired for being pleasant and relaxed.

Locally grown asparagus

From Defence to Decoration

OVER THE CENTURIES, châteaux in the Loire Valley gradually developed from feudal castles, designed purely as defensive fortresses, into graceful pleasure palaces. Once the introduction of firearms put an end to the sieges that medieval castles were built to withstand, comfort and elegance became key status symbols. Many defensive elements evolved into decorative features: watchtowers became fairy-tale turrets, moats served as reflecting pools and crenellations were transformed into ornamental friezes. During the Renaissance, Italian craftsmen added features such as galleries and formal gardens, and carved decoration became increasingly intricate.

Château d'Angers in 1550, before its towers were lowered

Slate and stone walls

Fortifications with pepper pot towers removed

Angers (see pp74–5) *was built between 1228 and 1240 as a mighty clifftop fortress, towering over the River Maine. Along its curtain wall were spaced 17 massive round towers. These would originally have been 30 m (98 ft) high before their pepper pot towers were removed in the 16th century.*

Slate roof

Postern

Ainay-le-Vieil (see p148), *dating from the 12th century, contrasts two styles. An octagonal walled fortress, with nine massive towers topped by pepper pot turrets and lit by arrow slits, was entered through a huge medieval postern gate across a drawbridge that crossed the moat. Inside, however, there is a charming, early 16th-century Renaissance home.*

Ainay-le-Vieil's delightful living quarters, hidden inside an octagonal fortress

Circular tower,
formerly defensive

Corbelled walkways,
once useful in battle

Chaumont (see p128) *stands on the site of a 12th-century fortress, destroyed in 1465 by Louis XI to punish its owners for disloyalty. The château was rebuilt from 1498 to 1510 in the Renaissance style. Although it has a defensive appearance, with circular towers, corbelled walkways and a gatehouse, these features have been lightened with Renaissance decoration.*

Chaumont's walls are carved with the crossed Cs of Charles II d'Amboise, whose family rebuilt the château.

Decorated
turret

Renaissance carved
windows

Decoration on the north façade of Azay-le-Rideau

Azay-le-Rideau (see pp96–7), *its elegant turrets reflected in a peaceful lake, was built from 1518 to 1527 and is considered one of the best-designed Renaissance châteaux. Its interior staircase, behind an intricately decorated pediment with three storeys of twin bays, is very striking.*

Dormer window

Cylindrical tower

Ussé (see p101) *was built in 1462 as a battlemented fortress. Later, the walls overlooking the main court-yard were modified during the Renaissance, with dormer windows and pilasters. In the 17th century the north wing was replaced by terraced gardens.*

Château d'Ussé, once a fortress, now an aristocratic château

Inside the Châteaux

Stone carving on staircase

THE TYPICAL LOIRE VALLEY château boasted several large, lavishly furnished reception rooms, adorned with luxurious tapestries and paintings and featuring decorative panelling and ceilings. The main rooms included the Grand Salon, often with an imposing fireplace, and an elegant dining room. The gallery was a focal point for host and guests to meet to discuss the events of the day, admire the views over the grounds or the paintings displayed on the gallery walls. The châtelain's private rooms, and those reserved for honoured (particularly royal) guests, were grouped in a separate wings, while servants were housed in the attics.

Apartments in one wing were for private use.

Grand Escalier (Grand Staircase)

Chairs *were often spindly – elegant but uncomfortable. The more comfortable models with armrests might be covered with precious tapestries, as with this one from Cheverny, upholstered in Aubusson.*

The Grand Escalier, *or Escalier d'Honneur (grand staircase), had richly carved balustrades and an elaborately decorated ceiling, such as this magnificent Renaissance staircase at Serrant (see p69). The staircase led to the owner's private suites, as well as to state guest bedrooms and rooms used on special occasions, such as the armoury.*

The Grand Salon, mostly used for entertaining, had a majestic marble fireplace carved with the owner's coat of arms, emblem or intertwined initials.

Main entrance

Galleries, *like this one at Beauregard (see pp130–31), were where owners and guests met to converse or to be entertained. They were often hung with family and other portraits.*

State dining rooms, *for receiving important visitors, were as sumptuously furnished and decorated as the other main reception rooms. This one in Chaumont (see p128) features Renaissance furniture.*

Château rooms were filled with costly tapestries, paintings and fine furniture, and attention was paid to detail. Decorative features, such as this French Limoges enamel plaque, or intricately carved wooden panelling were common. Even the tiles on stoves that heated the huge rooms were often painted.

The Salle d'Armes, or armoury, displayed suits of armour and weapons beside fine tapestries and furniture.

The east wing was reserved for important guests.

Dining Room

King's Bedroom

The King's Bedroom *was kept permanently ready for a royal visit. Under the* droit de gîte *(right of lodging), château owners were bound to provide accommodation to the king in return for a building permit. This room, at Cheverny (see p130), was used frequently.*

Gallery

Kitchen

CHEVERNY

A dignified Classical building in white tufa, Cheverny *(see p130)* has scarcely been altered since it was built between 1620 and 1634. The central section, containing the staircase, is flanked by two symmetrical wings, each consisting of a steep-roofed section and a much larger pavilion with a domed roof. The interior is decorated in 17th-century style.

Kitchens *were in the cellars, or separately housed. Huge spits for roasting whole carcasses were worked by elaborate mechanisms. Though often dark, the kitchens gleamed with an array of copper pots and pans, like these at Montgeoffroy (see p71).*

Churches and Abbeys

T HE LOIRE VALLEY is well-endowed with medieval
ecclesiastical architecture, ranging from tiny
Romanesque village churches to major Gothic cathedrals like Chartres and Tours. In the early Middle
Ages, the Romanesque style predominated, character-
ized by straightforward ground plans, round arches
and relatively little decoration. By the 13th century,
the rib vaulting and flying buttresses of Gothic architecture had emerged, enabling builders to create taller,
lighter churches and cathedrals. The Late Gothic style
in France, often referred to as Flamboyant Gothic,
features window tracery with flowing lines licking
upwards like flames.

LOCATOR MAP

① Romanesque architecture

⑨ Gothic architecture

ROMANESQUE FEATURES

Apse · Crossing · Transept

***The plan of St-Benoît-
sur-Loire*** *is typical of
Romanesque architecture,
with its cross shape and
rounded apse.*

Tunnel vault · Vaulted nave · Side aisle

***A section of La Collégiale de
St-Aignan-sur-Cher*** *shows
Romanesque tunnel vaulting.
The vaulted side aisles provide
added support for the high nave.*

Pointed bay · Rounded arch

***The round arches of
St-Aignan*** *are typically
Romanesque, while the
pointed nave bays
predict the Gothic style.*

GOTHIC FEATURES

Apsidal chapel · Apse · Nave

***The plan of Chartres
Cathedral*** *shows its very
wide nave, and its apse
ringed with chapels.*

Side aisle · Buttress · Flying buttresses

A section of St-Etienne *in Bourges reveals
its five divisions with two aisles on either
side of the nave. The building also has five
portals rather than the usual three.*

Triforium · Pointed arch

Pointed arches *withstand greater stress and
allow large windows, as
in the nave at Bourges.*

WHERE TO FIND ROMANESQUE ARCHITECTURE

① St-Maurice, Angers *pp72–3*
② L'Abbaye St-Vincent, Nieul-sur-l'Autise *pp182–3*
③ Notre-Dame, Cunault *p79*
④ L'Abbaye de Fontevraud *pp86–7*
⑤ St-Maurice, Chinon *pp98–9*
⑥ La Collégiale, St-Aignan-sur-Cher *p129*
⑦ St-Eusice, Selles-sur-Cher *pp24–5*
⑧ La Basilique de St-Benoît-sur-Loire *p140*

WHERE TO FIND GOTHIC ARCHITECTURE

⑨ St-Etienne, Bourges *pp152–3*
⑩ St-Louis, Blois *pp124–5*
⑪ St-Hubert, Amboise, *p110*
⑫ St-Gatien, Tours *pp116–17*
⑬ La Trinité, Vendôme *p123*
⑭ Notre-Dame, Chartres *pp172–5*
⑮ St-Julien, Le Mans *p166*
⑯ Asnières-sur-Vègre *p163*

Bell-tower
Machicolations
Tympanum

The west façade of Notre-Dame *at Cunault is simply decorated. Its machicolations and lateral towers give it a fortified appearance.*

Carved frieze
Tiered apse
Apsidal chapel

The east end of St-Eusice *in Selles-sur-Cher, with its three apsidal chapels, is decorated with friezes of carved figures.*

Stepped tower
Rose
Sculpted portal
Geometric window
Apse
Apsidal chapel
Pinnacle
Flying buttresses

The west façade *of St-Gatien in Tours has richly carved, Flamboyant Gothic portals.*

The east end *of St-Julien cathedral in Le Mans has a complex arrangement of paired flying buttresses, each topped by pinnacles.*

TERMS USED IN THIS GUIDE

Basilica: Early church with two aisles and nave lit from above by clerestory windows.

Clerestory: A row of windows illuminating the nave from above the aisle roof.

 Rose: Circular window, often stained glass.

Buttress: Mass of masonry built to support a wall.

 Flying buttress: An arched support transmitting thrust of the weight downwards.

Portal: Monumental entrance to a building, often decorated.

 Tympanum: Decorated space, often carved, over a door or window lintel.

Vault: Arched stone ceiling.

Transept: Two wings of a cruciform church at right angles to the nave.

Crossing: Centre of cruciform where transept crosses nave.

Lantern: Turret with windows to illuminate interior, often with cupola (domed ceiling).

Triforium: Middle storey between arcades and the clerestory.

Apse: Termination of the church, often rounded.

Ambulatory: Aisle running round east end, passing behind the sanctuary.

Arcade: Set of arches and supporting columns.

Rib vault: Vault supported by projecting ribs of stone.

 Gargoyle: Carved grotesque figure, often a water spout.

Tracery: Ornamental carved stone pattern within Gothic window.

Flamboyant Gothic: Carved stone tracery resembling flames.

 Capital: Top of a column, usually carved.

Writers and Artists of the Loire Valley

THE VALLEY OF THE River Loire is well known for its agricultural fertility, and it has also proved to be productive ground for literature, too. Over the centuries, internationally famous writers such as François Rabelais, the great lyrical poet Pierre de Ronsard and the novelists Honoré de Balzac and George Sand have lived close to the mighty river, often drawing inspiration from their native soil. Perhaps strangely, however, the pure light that so appeals to visitors to the region does not seem to have inspired as many of the country's greatest painters, although Claude Monet spent a fruitful period in the peaceful Creuse Valley.

Novelist Honoré de Balzac

Writer Marcel Proust, in a late 19th-century portrait by Jacques-Emile Blanche

WRITERS

ONE OF THE earliest authors to write in the "vulgar" French tongue was born in Meung-sur-Loire in the mid-13th century. Jean Chopinel, better known as Jean de Meung, produced the second part of the widely translated and influential *Roman de la Rose*, a long, allegorical poem about courtly love. While the first half of the poem focuses delicately on two young lovers and their affair, Jean de Meung's sequel undermines the idealistic conventions of courtly love, taking a more cynical view of the world.

During the Hundred Years' War, a century and a half later, aristocratic poet Charles, Duc d'Orléans was

Illumination from the *Roman de la Rose*

imprisoned by the English for 25 years. While in prison he was able to develop his considerable poetic skills. On his return he made his court at Blois a key literary centre. He invited famous writers and poets, among them François Villon, a 15th-century poet as renowned for the skill of his writing as for his highly disreputable lifestyle. While he was in Blois, Villon won a poetry competition with his work, *"Je Meurs de Soif auprès de la Fontaine"* ("I am Dying of Thirst by the Fountain").

François Rabelais, the racy 16th-century satirist and humanist, was born in 1483 near Chinon *(see pp98–9)* and educated at Angers. He became famous throughout Europe upon the publication of his *Pantagruel* (1532) and *Gargantua* (1535), huge, sprawling works full of bawdy humour and learned discourse in equal measure.

Pierre de Ronsard, born near Vendôme 30 years after Rabelais, was the leading

George Sand, the 19th-century novelist

French Renaissance poet, perhaps best known for his lyrical odes and sonnets to "Cassandre", "Hélène" and "Marie" (an Anjou peasant girl). Court poet to Charles IX and his sister Marguerite de Valois, he lived and died at St-Cosme Priory near Tours. Ronsard was also at the head of the Pléiade, a group of seven poets who were determined to revolutionize French poetry through the study of the classics. In the same group was Joachim du Bellay, an Anjou aristocrat and keen advocate of French literature. His *Defence and Illustration of the French Language* (1549) was a prose manifesto of the Pléiade doctrine.

Another famous native of the Loire Valley spearheaded a 17th-century intellectual revolution. Mathematician and philosopher René Descartes, born in Touraine and educated at the Jesuit college in La Flèche *(see p167)*, developed a new method of philosophical inquiry involving the simultaneous study of all the sciences. Starting with the celebrated "I think, therefore

I am," he developed the rationalist doctrine known as Cartesianism in his most famous work, the *Discourse on Method*.

France's most prolific 19th-century novelist, Honoré de Balzac, often referred to his native Touraine as his favourite province. Tours, Saumur and the Château de Saché feature as settings for some of his best-known novels, all of which are keenly observant of 19th-century French mores. The work of Balzac's contemporary, George Sand (the masculine pen name of Aurore, Baroness Dudevant), is rooted in the landscapes of her native Berry, which also inspired Alain-Fournier's magical *Le Grand Meaulnes*, a romantic vision of his childhood in the region.

The hawthorn hedges and peaceful villages near Chartres provided the unforgettable setting for the early passages of Marcel Proust's impressive sequence of novels, *Remembrance of Things Past*. At the mouth of the Loire, the city of Nantes saw the birth, in 1826, of the ever-popular Jules Verne *(see pp192–3)*, whose pioneering works of science fiction have been enormously influential.

ARTISTS

IN 1411, THE THREE Limbourg brothers became court painters to the Duc de Berry in Bourges. He commissioned them to paint some 39 miniatures for *Les Très Riches Heures du Duc de Berry*. This Book of Hours was to become the jewel in the duke's fabled manuscript collection and remains one of the finest achievements of the International Gothic style. Some of these intricate illustrations depict scenes from life in the Loire Valley.

Jehan Fouquet, born in Tours in about 1420, was officially appointed royal painter in 1474. His portraits

A miniature from *Les Très Riches Heures du Duc du Berry*

include the famous image of the royal mistress Agnès Sorel *(see p104)* posing as the Virgin Mary.

A century after Fouquet's birth, François I persuaded the elderly Leonardo da Vinci to settle in the manor house of Cloux (now called Le Clos-Lucé, *see pp110–11*) near the royal château of Amboise. Aged 65, Leonardo was no longer actively painting, although he is known to have made some sketches of court life which have not survived. However, he was engaged in scientific investigations and inventions, the results of which can be seen in a museum in the basement of the château.

At about the time of Leonardo's death in 1519, François Clouet was born in

Henri Rousseau, in a self-portrait that typifies his naïve style

Tours. He succeeded his father, Jean, as court painter to François I and produced a string of truly outstanding portraits. His sitters included François I himself, Elizabeth of Austria and Mary, Queen of Scots. François Clouet's style, which was typical of the French Renaissance, was perpetuated by the artists and artisans in his workshop.

Anjou's most celebrated sculptor is David d'Angers, who was born in 1788. His works include busts and medallions of many of the major historical figures of his day, including a memorial to the Marquis de Bonchamps, which can be found in the church at St-Florent-le-Vieil *(see p57)*.

François Clouet's portrait of Mary, Queen of Scots

Exactly a century later, the Impressionist painter Claude Monet spent several weeks in the village of Fresselines in the Creuse Valley, painting the river as it passed through a narrow gorge *(see p147)*. One of these canvases, *Le Pont de Vervit*, now hangs in the Musée Marmottan in Paris.

Henri Rousseau, the quintessential naïve painter, was born in the town of Laval in 1844. Although he never left France, his best-known works are stylized depictions of lush jungles, home to all manner of wild animals. Part of the château in Laval has been converted into a Museum of Naïve Art *(see p160)* in honour of the artist.

Themed Tours of the Loire Valley

FOR THOSE WHO WISH to travel independently of tour companies, or who have a special interest in the region, themed tours provide an attractive alternative. Local tourist offices produce information on routes visitors can travel in order to see the best sights on a given theme – including wine, churches, châteaux, historical buildings and beautiful botanical gardens and arboretums. Illustrated brochures and tourist maps describing each route, often in languages other than French, are available, and some of the routes are signposted along the way. Tourist office staff are also able to customize a route for your particular needs.

A la Recherche des Plantagenêts traces the lives of Henry Plantagenet, his wife, Eleanor of Aquitaine, and their sons (see p50). The evidence of their remarkable lives, including this fortress in Loches, can be seen throughout the region.

The Route Touristique du Vignoble (Wine Route) guides the traveller through some of the region's prettiest wine country, including the Coteaux de la Loire. Further information is available from the tourist offices in Angers, Nantes and Saumur.

The Route de la Vallée des Rois takes motorists to many former royal residences, such as Azay-le-Rideau, as well as to cathedrals and churches along the part of the Loire known as the Valley of the Kings. Information is available from tourist offices in Saumur, Blois, Gien and Orléans.

La Flèche
Angers
St-Cosme
Champtoceaux
Nantes
St-Florent-le-Vieil
Chalonnes
Cunault
Bour
Saumur
Clisson
Montreuil-Bellay
Ch
Vouvant
Fontenay-le Comte
Luçon
Nieul-sur-Autise
Maillezais

The Circuit Sud-Vendéen au Pays de la Fée Mélusine takes in the attractions of the south Vendée, including the Marais Poitevin, to give a selection of the varied sights in this area. The tourist office at La-Roche-sur-Yon provides details.

The Route Historique des Parcs et Jardins *takes visitors to Villandry and many other exquisite châteaux and manor house gardens, contemporary gardens, parks and arboretums in the region. Contact the tourist office in Tours.*

The Route Jacques Cœur *leads motorists through some picturesque towns as well as to memorable châteaux, including the Château de Maupas and the Palais Jacques-Cœur in Bourges (see p151), the former home of the wealthy merchant who gives the tour its name. Some of the private châteaux on the route take paying guests (see pp200–201). The tourist office in Bourges provides details of the route.*

0 kilometres   50

0 miles   50

The Route Historique François I *explores the châteaux, such as Valençay, constructed during the reign of François I (see p54), who held court in Chambord and Blois during the 16th century. Information is available from the tourist office in Romorantin-Lanthenay.*

KEY

▬	Circuit Sud-Vendéen
▬	Route Historique des Parcs et Jardins
▬	A la Recherche des Plantagenêts
▬	Route Historique François I
▬	Route Jacques Cœur
▬	Route de la Vallée des Rois
▬	Route Touristique du Vignoble

Walking in the Loire Valley

T HE BEST WAY to follow the "most sensual river in France," as Flaubert called it – to appreciate the transformation of the river as it flows through the Sologne forests, carves out the Valley of the Kings, and finally rushes into the ocean – is on foot. The *Grande Randonnée 3* (GR 3) is one of the longest marked walks in France, accompanying the Loire from its source at Gerbier de Jonc to its mouth. The route occasionally strays from the river bank in order to follow the most picturesque paths. For walks lasting a few hours, or several days, ramblers can follow a part of the *Grande Randonnée* or try the region's many shorter, often circular, routes. A Topo-Guide *(see p224)* is a useful companion for detailed information about your walk.

— Recommended walk

— Grande Randonnée de Pays

— Grande Randonnée

In the charming Alpes Mancelles, in the Parc Régional Normandie-Maine, there are four- to seven-day walks in the valleys of the Sarthe, the Mayenne and the Orne. *(Topo-Guide 039)*

The Folies-Siffait, *close to Le Cellier, 15 km (9 miles) northeast of Nantes, offers an unusual two-hour walk, leading visitors around a labyrinthine park.* (IGN 1323)

La Grande Brière (see p180) *contains three beautiful regional routes taking walkers through the reeds where thousands of birds build their nests.* (Topo-Guide 003)

Sille-le-Guillaume

Laval

Mayenne

Sarthe

Chateaubriant

Guérande

Le Cellier   Loire

Angers

Loire

Nantes

ANJOU

Saumur

Pornic

LOIRE-ATLANTIQUE AND THE VENDEE

St-Jean-de-Monts

La Roche-sur-Yon

Moutiers-les-Mauxfaits

0 kilometres   50

0 miles   50

Circuits de Promenade en Presqu'île Guérandaise

ROUTE MARKERS

All the walking routes are marked *(balisé)* with symbols painted onto trees or rocks along the paths. The different colours of the symbols indicate which kind of route you are taking. A red and white mark denotes a *Grande Randonnée* (GR) route, yellow and red are used for a regional route *(Grande Randonnée de Pays)*, and local routes *(Petites Randonnées)* are marked in a single colour (usually yellow).

	Grande Randonnée	Grande Randonnée de Pays	Petite Randonnée
Straight on			
Change direction			
Wrong way			

The Grande Randonnée 3, *one of the longest national pathways, follows the River Loire along its entire length.*

GRACQ, A WALKING WRITER

For French ramblers, it is difficult to walk beside the River Loire without thinking of Julien Gracq. One of the most famous contemporary French writers, Gracq lives in St-Florent-le-Vieil *(see p68)*, a village perched on the south bank of the river between Angers and Nantes. Many of his books entice the reader to explore the Loire Valley on foot. *La Presqu'île* is set in the Guérande region, and *Les Eaux Etroites* evokes the River Evre, which flows into the Loire at St-Florent. *La Forme d'une Ville* is a portrait of Nantes, where Gracq was a schoolboy and teacher, and where he met the Surrealist André Breton.

Julien Gracq

Les eaux étroites

josé corti

The Sancerrois (see p155), *where some of the best white wines in France are produced, is crossed by 30 small walks (Petites Randonnées) of between 9 and 32 km (5–20 miles) passing through Sancerre's vineyards.* (Topo-Guide 064)

The Sologne *is on the route of the GR 3C, a variation of the GR 3. The path leaves the Loire between Gien and Chambord and takes walkers on a five-day journey through this mysterious forest (see p141).* (Topo-Guide 362)

The Natural History of the Loire Valley

FRANCE'S LONGEST RIVER is fed by a number of tributaries, including the Loir, the Mayenne, the Sarthe, the Cher, the Indre, the Vienne, the Creuse and the Beuvron. Within easy reach of the central Loire Valley are four park areas *(Parcs Naturels Régionaux)*: Brière, Normandie-Maine, Marais Poitevin and La Brenne. The region is dotted with lakes and ponds that shelter birds and other wildlife, and the woods, forests, hills and plains are crossed with trails known as *Grandes Randonnées (see p26)*, ideal for walkers and cyclists.

European grey wolf

KEY

▭	Regional natural park
▭	Forest and woodland
↦	Lake
≈	Major river

0 kilometres   50

0 miles   50

The Sarthe flows southwest through Le Mans towards Angers, where it finally joins the Loire. This stretch of the river, which is navigable, passes through peaceful meadows, farmland and woodland.

Parc Naturel Régional de Normandie-Maine

Mayenne

Le M

Sarthe

Forêt de Gâvre

Forêt de Juigné

Le Croisic

Parc Naturel Régional de Brière

Erdre

Angers

Loire

Lan St

Nantes

Loire

Forêt de Beaulieu

Forêt de Brissac

Sau

Lac de Grand-Lieu

Sèvre Nantaise

Lac de Verdon

Forêt de Pays de Monts

St-Jean-de-Monts

Lac de Grand-Lieu

Vendée

Parc Naturel Régional du Marais Poitevin

*A **medieval mosaic** of canals, lakes, reed beds and flooded meadows makes the Parc Naturel Régional de Brière the second most significant wetland in France, after the Camargue in Provence.*

The Lac de Grand-Lieu covers 6,300 ha (15,600 acres), and is home to more than 230 species of bird, 500 species of plant and 50 mammal species. It has the largest colony of grey heron in the world.

***Landes St-Martin** is a vast wooded area north of the Loire. It includes the 250-ha (618-acre) Lac de Pince-maille, part leisure complex and part wetlands, home to wildfowl such as golden plovers, cormorants and peregrine falcons.*

***The Forêt des Pays de Monts** consists of mixed woodland bordering golden Atlantic beaches.*

Magnificent oaks, some more than 300 years old, flourish alongside horse chestnuts, pines and beech in the Futaie des Clos (see p168) part of the Forêt de Bercé. Bounded by the Veuve, Dinan and Loir rivers, the forest has seven straight "rides."

The Forêt d'Orléans is the second largest in France at 50,000 ha (124,000 acres). It is bisected by the canal d'Orléans and is rich in wild boar, deer and other game. Agricultural scenery alternates with wild woodland and pools.

Containing a wealth of botanical treasures, including orchids and alpine plants, the 300-ha (740-acre) Vallée de la Grande Pierre de Marolles et de Vitain lies 10 km (6 miles) north of Blois.

The Parc de Chambord is a game preserve covering 5,500 ha (13,600 acres) and surrounded by 33 km (21 miles) of wall, making it the largest "walled garden" in Europe. It is possible to observe resident wildlife (including deer, wild boar and badgers) from viewing platforms.

The park area between the rivers Indre and Creuse is known as the Pays des Mille Etangs, after its 1,270 lakes and pools. Two unusual residents are pond tortoises and wolves housed in a wildlife reserve in the Forêt de Preuilly, about 4 km (2½ miles) northwest of Azay-le-Ferron.

A little off the beaten track, the Sologne (see p141) covers 490,000 ha (1.2 million acres). The wooded landscapes of silver birch, oak, larch, spruce, pine and fir blend with marshland and heath. Its lakes attract many species of bird and other wildlife including pine marten, roe deer, and the black and yellow salamander.

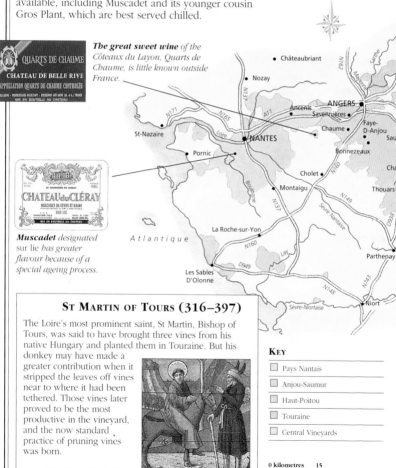

Winemaking and Vineyards

THE IMPORTANCE OF WINE to life in the Loire Valley is immediately apparent. Fields of vines stretch along both banks of the river, and roadsides are lined with signs offering *dégustations*, or wine tastings *(see p212)*. Stretching 300 km (186 miles) from Nantes to Pouilly-sur-Loire, the Loire Valley is the fifth largest wine-producing area by volume in France and offers an unprecedented range of wine styles. The white Sancerres have an excellent reputation *(see p155)*, as do some of the rosé wines of Anjou, the sweet and sparkling Vouvrays, the full-bodied reds of Chinon and Bourgueil, and the superb, dry *méthode champenoise* wines of Saumur. There are many more modest wines available, including Muscadet and its younger cousin Gros Plant, which are best served chilled.

Caricature of a wine maker in "costume"

Traditional vineyard cultivation

The great sweet wine of the Côteaux du Layon, Quarts de Chaume, is little known outside France.

Muscadet designated sur lie *has greater flavour because of a special ageing process.*

ST MARTIN OF TOURS (316–397)

The Loire's most prominent saint, St Martin, Bishop of Tours, was said to have brought three vines from his native Hungary and planted them in Touraine. But his donkey may have made a greater contribution when it stripped the leaves off vines near to where it had been tethered. Those vines later proved to be the most productive in the vineyard, and the now standard practice of pruning vines was born.

St Martin on his donkey

KEY

- Pays Nantais
- Anjou-Saumur
- Haut-Poitou
- Touraine
- Central Vineyards

0 kilometres 15
0 miles 15

KEY FACTS ABOUT LOIRE WINES

 Grape Varieties
The Muscadet grape makes simple, dry whites. The Sauvignon Blanc produces gooseberryish, flinty dry whites. Chenin Blanc is used for the dry and medium Anjou, Vouvrays, Savennières and Saumur, and the famous sweet whites, Vouvray, Quarts de Chaume and Bonnezeaux. Summery reds are made from the Gamay and the Cabernet Franc.

 Good Producers (west to east)
Muscadet: Château de la Bretesche, Marquis de Goulaine, Château de Chasseloir. *Anjou* (red): Domaine de Ste-Anne. *Anjou* (rosé): Robert Lecomte-Girault. *Anjou* (dry white): Domaine Richou. *Saumur* (sparkling): Bouvet-Ladunay, Ackerman-Laurance, Gratien & Meyer. *Saumur* (red): Château de Villeneuve. *Saumur* (white): Domaine des Nerleux,

Château de St-Florent. *Bourgueil* (red): Clos du Vigneau. *Chinon* (red): Domaine Réné Couly, Clos de la Dioterie. *Touraine* (white): Domaine Joel Delaunay. *Vouvray*: Clos du Bourg, Le Haut-Lieu, Chevreau-Vigneau, Alain Ferraud, Sylvain Gaudron. *Sancerre*: Domaine de St-Pierre, Domaine des Villots, Domaine Paul Prieur. *Crémant de Loire* (sparkling white): Château de Midouin, Perry de Maleyrand.

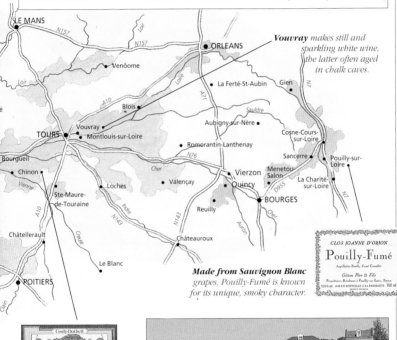

Vouvray *makes still and sparkling white wine, the latter often aged in chalk caves.*

Made from Sauvignon Blanc *grapes, Pouilly-Fumé is known for its unique, smoky character.*

Couly-Dutheil's Clos de l'Echo *is a beautiful, bright ruby wine made from Cabernet Franc grapes. The AOC wines of Chinon have an attractive, spicy aroma and age well.*

The Clos de l'Echo vineyard

A VIEW OF THE RIVER LOIRE

A NATURAL HIGHWAY to the centre of France, the Loire was travelled from the earliest days. The remains of prehistoric canoes have been found along the river; later evidence shows that Celtic tribes and the Romans used the river extensively as a major trade route. In fact, until the development of the railway network during the 19th century, the river was a key transportation route. The growth of the French canal network from the 17th to 19th centuries, connecting the port of Nantes with Paris and the north, enhanced the Loire's importance. **See pages 34–5**

The River Loire can be unpredictable and sometimes dangerous, and it was one of the first rivers that man tried to control. There is evidence that embankments were being built as early as the 12th century – and work continues – but the river remains essentially wild and is still subject to floods, freezes, shifting sands and dangerous currents. Today, the river is no longer used for commerce, except by tour boats giving visitors a unique view of the surrounding landscape. This makes an exploration of the River Loire all the **See pages 36–7** more pleasant.

Sailing boats, with their typical square sails, often travelled in groups of three or more.

Steamers would use powerful winches to dip their smoke-stacks, enabling them to pass under low bridges.

Amboise's bridge traverses the river and the Ile St-Jean.

Château d'Amboise is set on a promontory above the river, safe from possible flooding.

VUE D'AMBOISE
This painting by Justin Ouvrié, now kept in the vaults of the Musée de la Poste in Paris, was painted in 1847. The bustling river scene, which includes several types of vessel, gives an indication of the importance of the River Loire to life and trade in the region, before the railways came to dominate transportation later in the century.

Barges, known in French as *chalands*, did not always have sails – sometimes they were rowed.

***Everyday objects** were often decorated with river scenes, such as this 19th-century plate from the Musée de la Marine de Loire in Châteauneuf-sur-Loire.*

◁ **Orléans, with the imposing Cathédrale Ste-Croix, seen from across the river**

River View: St-Nazaire to Montsoreau

A pleasure barge on the River Loire

A S THE RIVER LOIRE leaves Touraine and heads through Anjou and the Loire Atlantique, it widens and flows faster, as though rushing towards the Atlantic Ocean. Its waters are also swelled by many tributaries. Some flow alongside, creating a multitude of islands big and small; other tributaries flow north and south through the surrounding countryside. This land is rich in ancient monuments, including the Bagneux dolmen, the largest Neolithic construction of its kind, as well as fortresses built during the Middle Ages.

Champtoceaux
The village of Champtoceaux, on a cliff 80 m (260 ft) above the river, offers panoramic views. A private Renaissance château now occupies the lower part of the bluff, where a medieval citadel once stood.

St-Nazaire
At the mouth of the River Loire, where it flows into the Atlantic Ocean, St-Nazaire (see p190) is the site of a major French industrial zone. Its graceful bridge is the westernmost river crossing.

Nantes' Cathédrale
St-Pierre et St-Paul is built in the Flamboyant Gothic style.

Ancenis

Nantes
Nantes was a prosperous port during the 18th and 19th centuries (see pp190–193), the meeting point between the ocean and the inland river transportation channels.

0 kilometres   20

0 miles   20

Péage Fortifié du Cul-du-Moulin
This toll station was one of many constructed in the 13th century to collect revenue from passing vessels. This is one of the few remaining river toll stations in France.

THE BRIDGES OF THE LOIRE

There have long been bridges across the River Loire – there was one at Orléans as early as AD 52, which was later destroyed by Julius Caesar's army. Now, with so many options for places to cross the river, it is difficult to imagine what it was like during the Middle Ages, when there were only five, or during the 15th century, when there were just 13. The bridges crossing the river today tell the story not only of the development of bridge building, but also of the region itself, its history and relationships.

St-Nazaire
At 3,356 m (11,000 ft), St-Nazaire is the longest bridge in France. The central, suspended section is 404 m (1,300 ft) long. It opened for traffic in 1975. Before then, the estuary was crossed by ferry, and the nearest bridge was at Nantes.

St-Florent

Once the church of a Benedictine monastery, the abbey on the promontory was the site of dramatic events during the Vendée Uprising (see p68). More than 40,000 Royalist troops and their supporters crossed the river here.

Montsoreau

Montsoreau, at the confluence of the Loire and Vienne rivers, has a 15th-century turreted château (see p85).

The Château d'Angers, with its massive towers and curtain walls, is on the River Maine, north of the Loire.

Angers

The Apocalypse Tapestries (see pp76–7), masterpieces of the 14th century, are displayed in the Château d'Angers.

Cunault

The impressive Romanesque church in Cunault (see p79) is home to this painted 15th-century statue of St Catherine.

Les Rosiers

Saumur

Saumur is famous for its cavalry school, whose fallen cadets are honoured by this memorial.

The Château de Saumur (see p82) rises above the town like a fairytale castle.

Ile Béhuard

This island (see p69) was once a pilgrimage site for sailors, who prayed to a sea goddess to help them navigate the sometimes treacherous waters of the River Loire. The present church was built by Louis XI who had nearly drowned here.

Chinon

Above the River Vienne, Chinon (see pp98–100) was home to Henry Plantagenet in the 12th century.

Ancenis

The suspension bridge at Ancenis opened in 1953, replacing one destroyed in 1940. As the town is at the border of Brittany and Anjou, two coats of arms adorn either end of the bridge, one with the three lilies of Anjou and one with the ermine of Brittany.

Les Rosiers

The bridge at Les Rosiers is one of the two that cross the Loire at this point. The river is particularly wide here and has an island in the middle. The island is connected to the banks at the towns of Les Rosiers and Gennes by two bridges.

River View: Tours to Nevers

Stained glass in Gien

THIS IS TRULY the royal Loire Valley. As the river flows through the regions of Touraine, Blésois and Orléanais, it passes beside many Renaissance châteaux. Some, like Chaumont, Amboise and Gien, show their fortress-like exteriors to the river, often concealing courtyard gardens and highly decorated façades. Others, like Sully, glory in their luxury. Throughout Touraine, vineyards gently slope towards the river, while in the west, the lands bordering the river are taken up by the forests that were once the hunting grounds of kings and princes.

Beaugency's massive keep *(see p136)* dates from the 10th century.

Beaugency

Langeais
In the town of Langeais, (see p92) high above the river, there is a massive 15th-century château, still furnished in keeping with its period.

Blois
On the north bank of the Loire, Blois (see pp124–7) was the seat of the counts of Blois, and then the residence of François I, whose salamander emblem decorates one fireplace.

Château d'Amboise
(see p110) is a 15th-century château, built by Charles VIII.

Pagode de Chanteloup
All that remains of a once-lovely château, this strange pagoda (see p111) is 44 m (145 ft) tall.

Tours
In the heart of the Loire Valley region, Tours (see pp112–17) was always a significant crossing point on the river. The lively place Plumereau, lined with 15th-century buildings, is in the Old Town.

Château de Chaumont
The great fortress of Chaumont (see p128) is softened by Renaissance touches and offers impressive views from its terrace.

Tours
When Tours' original 18th-century bridge was built, the rue Nationale, which links it to the centre of the city, became the major thoroughfare, in place of the road between the cathedral and the Old Town.

Blois
The bridge at Blois was built between 1716 and 1724, replacing a medieval bridge destroyed when a ship crashed into it. It was built to a very high standard, enabling it to survive floods and freezes.

Abbaye de St-Benoît *(see p140)* has one of France's finest Romanesque abbey churches.

Jargeau

An amateur fisherman, one of many attracted to the banks of the Loire

0 kilometres 15

0 miles 15

Château de Sully-sur-Loire
A magnificent 14th-century castle, Sully is set in a moat created from the diverted River Sange.

Briare Bridge-Canal
The elegant Pont-Canal de Briare (see p141) carries the Canal Latéral à la Loire across the river.

Orléans
Set strategically at the point where the Loire turns southwards, Orléans (see pp138–9) has been inhabited since the earliest times. It is famous as the town that was liberated by Joan of Arc during the Hundred Years' War.

Nevers •

Gien
Gien's 15th-century château (see p140) replaced an earlier fortress. The terraces give good views of the river and of the town's 16th-century bridge.

Beaucency
Beaucency's bridge is built in several different styles, because sections of the original 12th-century wooden structure were gradually replaced with stone. The earliest date from the 14th century.

Jargeau
The original bridge was replaced by a wooden suspension bridge in the 19th century. A steel bridge, built in the 1920s, was hit in World War II. The current bridge dates from 1988.

THE LOIRE VALLEY
THROUGH THE YEAR

SPRING AND EARLY SUMMER are often particularly beautiful in the regions bordering the River Loire. But it should not be forgotten that this is the "Garden of France", and that successful gardens need plentiful watering in the main growing season, so be prepared for showery days. In the sultry, humid heat of July and early August, the Loire is usually reduced to a modest trickle between glistening sand banks.· The châteaux can be very crowded in the summer. Perhaps the most pleasant season is autumn, when forests gleam red and gold in the mild sunshine, the restaurants serve succulent local game and wild mushrooms, and the grape harvest is celebrated in towns and villages with many colourful festivals. Music festivals are also very popular in the region. Concerts are staged all year round at the Abbaye de Fontevraud *(see pp86–9)*, and Amboise *(see p110)* holds its Summer Organ Festival between June and August. For more information about any of these festivals, contact the local tourist office *(see p227)*.

Spring asparagus

SPRING

MARCH SEES the reopening of many châteaux after their winter closure, often on the Palm Sunday weekend that marks the beginning of the influx of visitors from the rest of France and abroad. The spring flowers in the meadows, the flowing waters of the Loire and other rivers, swollen by winter rains, and the spring migrations of birds are particularly appreciated by nature lovers.

MARCH

Foire à l'Andouillette *(Palm Sunday & preceding Sat)*, Athée-sur-Cher (nr Chenonceau). This is one of many celebrations of local produce, in this case chitterling sausages. **Foire aux Vins** *(first weekend)*, Bourgueil (nr Chinon).

Wine fairs bring together many local producers to display their latest vintages, but drinking as well as tasting is the order of the day.

APRIL

Concours Complet International *(last week)*, Saumur *(pp80–82)*. This international horse-riding competition also signals the beginning of the famous Cadre Noir tattoo and equestrian displays, which continue until September.
Le Printemps de Bourges *(third week)*, Bourges *(pp150–51)*. This contemporary music festival starts off the long concert season in this music-loving region.
Carnaval de Cholet *(last week)*, Cholet *(p69)*. Cholet's grand carnival culminates in a night-time parade of multi-coloured floats.

Horse and rider from Saumur's Cadre Noir display team

MAY
Fête de Jeanne d'Arc *(week of 8 May)*, Orléans *(pp138–9)*. One of France's oldest fêtes, begun in 1435 to celebrate the routing of the English in 1429, this festival takes the form of a huge, colourful costume pageant.
Jours de Loire *(last week)*, Anjou and Touraine. This wide-reaching, informative and constantly moving festival illustrates and celebrates all aspects of life lived alongside the River Loire.
Le Printemps des Arts *(May and Jun)*, Nantes *(pp190–93)* and surrounding area. A Baroque dance and music festival, with concerts and shows held in churches and historic buildings in Nantes, Angers and other towns in the western Loire.

Farm workers in the fields around Bourgueil

AVERAGE DAILY SUNSHINE

Hours

Jan Feb Mar Apr May Jun Jul Aug Sep Oct Nov Dec

Sunshine Chart
The summer months are generally hot, with the hottest period in July. On the Atlantic coast, cool sea breezes often bring welcome relief from the heat but do not mean that sun-bathers are less likely to burn. In the spring and autumn, river areas can be misty in the mornings.

SUMMER

FRANCE's traditional mid-summer celebrations take place on or around the Feast of John the Baptist on 24 June, with fireworks, bonfires, live music and dancing. Towards the end of the month, most of the famous son et lumière *(see pp42–3)* performances begin again, although the long, light evenings of June and July are the peak time for these special events. Many of the small towns and villages hold local fêtes in July and the first half of August, the height of the French tourist season.

JUNE

Les 24 Heures du Mans *(second weekend)*, Le Mans *(pp164–7)*. One of France's most important events, this international 24-hour car race attracts enormous crowds.
Le Festival International des Jardins de Chaumont-sur-Loire *(Jun–Oct)*, celebrates the region's horticultural magnificence.
Foire aux Escargots *(last weekend)*, Loché-sur-Indrois (nr Azay-le-Rideau). Snails are served along with local wines in an open-air restaurant.

JULY

Bastille Day *(14 Jul)*.
The celebrations for the Fête Nationale, commemorating the Storming of the Bastille in 1789, are the high point of the year in many small communities, when visitors can join in the dancing, firework displays and wine-quaffing.

The beach at the popular Atlantic resort, Les Sables d'Olonne

Fêtes Musicales de Touraine *(two or three weekends)*, Tours *(pp112–17)*. Started by Sviatoslav Richter in 1964, this international festival of chamber music is held in a superb medieval tithe barn, called the Grange de Meslay.
Foire aux Champignons, *(first Sun)*, Ports-sur-Vienne (nr Richelieu). This fair celebrates mushrooms, a local speciality that contributes to the region's economy.
Foire au Vin, au Fromage et au Boudin *(last Sun)*, Richelieu *(pp102–3)*. The fair associates local cheeses and wine with *boudin*, one of the many delicious pork products created in the region.
Foire au Basilic et à l'Ail *(26 Jul)*, Tours. The headily-scented basil and garlic fair is held on the Feast of St Anne *(p117)*.

Folk dancers at a festival

Festival d'Anjou *(all month)*, Angers *(pp72–3)*. Plays are staged within the walls of the Château d'Angers.
Festival International d'Orgue *(Sun in Jul and Aug)*, Chartres Cathedral *(pp171–5)*. Famous organists come from all over the world to participate in this prestigious organ festival.

AUGUST

Marché Médiéval *(first weekend)*, Chinon *(pp98–100)*. A lively market takes over the whole of the little town, with stallholders dressed in period costume and medieval dishes served in outside taverns.
Foire aux Vins *(on or around 15 Aug)*, Montlouis-sur-Cher, Vouvray and other major wine-producing centres. The Feast of the Assumption is marked by numerous local festivities, with wine events predominating in the vine-growing areas.
Foire aux Sorcières *(first Sun)*, Bué (nr Sancerre). The Berry is often said to be a centre of witchcraft and sorcery. Children dressed as witches or ghosts parade through the village to a nearby field where crowds play games and watch folk groups performing.
Festival de Musique Baroque *(last weekend)*, Sablé-sur-Sarthe *(p162)*. Over a period of four days, musicians perform in churches and manor houses around Sablé.

AVERAGE MONTHLY RAINFALL

Rainfall Chart
Spring and autumn are the wettest times, with the amount of rainfall occasionally causing the River Loire and its many tributaries to break their banks. As you head inland from the coast, precipitation tends to increase. During the summer, rains and violent storms are common at night.

AUTUMN

THE GOLDEN DAYS of autumn attract large numbers of Parisians to the region for shooting weekends, especially to the forested eastern areas. This is also the season for the *vendanges*, or grape harvest, and the events and festivities associated with it, and for fairs celebrating the new season's produce.

SEPTEMBER

Fête du Pain *(second Sat)*, Montreuil-en-Touraine (nr Amboise). The humble bread loaf, often decorated with nuts and leaves to celebrate the arrival of autumn, becomes a work of art in the skilful hands of local bakers.
Foire aux Melons *(second Fri)*, Bléré. The fields around Bléré near Chenonceau are bright with golden and orange melons in autumn.
Foire aux Rillons *(29 Sep)*, St-Michel-sur-Loire (nr

Langeais). The Feast of St Michael is celebrated with a festival devoted to a delicacy of Touraine *(see p210).*
Journées du Patrimoine *(third weekend)*. For one weekend a year, châteaux and other historic buildings which are not normally open to the public can be visited, and numerous concerts, exhibitions and other cultural events are staged.
Festival International de Musique et Folklore *(second weekend)*, Angers *(pp72–3)*. Folk-music groups from many countries perform in the streets and squares of Angers during this four-day festival. The highlight is a concert held in the modern Centre des Congrès.

OCTOBER

Festival International du Cinéma Européen *(all month)*, La Baule. This informal and delightful festival that celebrates all things cinematic is growing in influence and reputation.

High-quality local produce on sale at the Saturday market in Saumur

Foire aux Pommes *(second Sun)*, Le Petit-Pressigny (nr Le Grand-Pressigny). Apple orchards yield their fruit this month, filling the markets with a wide variety of apples. Azay-le-Rideau holds its own Apple Fair during the last weekend of October.
Foire à la Bernache *(last Sun Oct or 1st Sun Nov)*, Reugny (nr Tours). Although it may be an acquired taste, the *bernache* (unfermented new wine) is very popular with the locals.
Foire aux Marrons *(last Tue)*, Bourgueil (nr Chinon). Chestnuts are the traditional accompaniment to new wine, and for this reason they feature in many guises here.
Concerts d'Automne *(each Sun)*, Saint-Cyr-sur-Loire (nr Tours). Autumn concerts are held in the Salon Ronsard in the Hôtel de Ville. Of the four events, three are recitals of chamber music, while the fourth may feature a more contemporary style of music, such as jazz.

Wine-tasting at Kerhinet in La Grande Brière

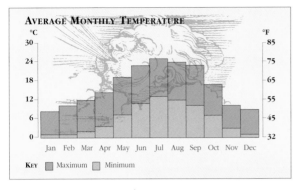

AVERAGE MONTHLY TEMPERATURE

KEY ■ Maximum ■ Minimum

Temperature Chart
It is rare for winter temperatures to fall below freezing in the Loire Valley. In the west, the sea moderates the climate, keeping it mild. Elsewhere, summer temperatures can reach over 30° C (86° F) in the middle of the day, but the evenings are usually cooler and perfect for eating outside on terraces by the river.

WINTER

WINTER IS THE QUIET season in the Loire Valley, when a damp chill rather than a frosty cold sets in, and many of the châteaux are closed. A few Christmas markets are held, but in general this is a time when local people prefer the pleasures of home.

DECEMBER

Foire de St-Nicolas (*Sat closest to 6 Dec*), St-Nicolas-de-Bourgueil (nr Chinon). The Feast of St Nicolas marks the beginning of the Christmas season, celebrated with fairs and markets selling toys and festive decorations.
Foire de Noël (*third weekend*), Richelieu (*p102–3*). This Christmas market sells gifts, decorations and seasonal food. In the evening, there is a son et lumière performance.
Foire des Chants de Noël (*first weekend*), Château de Brissac (*p78*). The members of the audience process through the château while carols are sung.

An old windmill in the Anjou countryside

JANUARY

Foire des Rois (*first or second Mon*), Richelieu (*pp102–3*). Epiphany is celebrated with a large craft and food market. The arrival of the Three Kings is celebrated here and throughout France with the *galette des rois*, a flat, round, flaky pastry confection filled with almond paste and containing a *fève*, a tiny gilt or ceramic figure.

FEBRUARY

Foire aux Vins (*first weekend*), Vouvray (nr Tours). Through the region, the winter period is enlivened by wine fairs. Another is held in Azay-le-Rideau on the last weekend of the month.

PUBLIC HOLIDAYS

New Year's Day (1 Jan)
Easter Sunday and Monday
Ascension (sixth Thursday after Easter)
Whit Monday (second Monday after Ascension)
Labour Day (1 May)
VE Day (8 May)
Bastille Day (14 Jul)
Feast of the Assumption (15 Aug)
All Saints' Day (1 Nov)
Remembrance Day (11 Nov)
Christmas Day (25 Dec)

A concert at the Abbaye de Fontevraud

Son et Lumière in the Loire

THE LOIRE VALLEY was the birthplace of son et lumière (literally "sound and light") shows, and some of the world's finest examples can be found here. The first performances, staged at Chambord in 1952, combined lighting effects and a soundtrack to emphasize the beauty of the building and to conjure up important historical figures. Today many of the shows use lasers and dramatic fireworks, as well as a cast of hundreds (often amateur actors drawn from the local community), to create a spectacular pageant. The following list includes the main regular shows, but it is worth keeping an eye open for posters advertising one-off events. Performance times may vary.

Actor at Amboise

Lighting effects bringing drama to the Château d'Azay-le-Rideau

TOURAINE

Amboise At the Court of King François (1½ hours). ☎ 02 47 57 14 47. 🕐 late Jun–Jul: 10:30pm Wed, Sat; Aug: 10pm Wed, Sat. 🎫 book in advance. **Translations** Eng.

This is a celebration of the life of François I, held at his favourite royal château *(see p110)*. The show is enacted by local residents and re-creates the court, with its sumptuous costumes, thrilling hunts, pleasure gardens and elaborate festivities.

Azay-le-Rideau The Fantasy of Azay-le-Rideau (1 hour). ☎ 02 47 45 42 04. 🕐 May–Jul: 10:30pm nightly; Aug: 10pm nightly; Sep: 9:30pm nightly. 🎫 under 12s free.

During this fascinating promenade production, all the spectators walk around the grounds of this elegant château *(see pp96–7)*, as they observe a succession of stage, sound and lighting effects.

Chenonceau In the Days of the Ladies of Yesteryear (45 mins). ☎ 02 47 23 90 07. 🕐 late-Jun–early-Sep: 10:15pm nightly. 🎫

The history of Chenonceau is the history of a series of remarkable women who in turn designed, improved and restored this beautiful royal residence *(see pp106–9)*. In the château's son et lumière production, a light show takes place in the garden designed by Diane de Poitiers, while a commentary tells the story of her life and that of the wife she usurped, Catherine de Médicis.

Loches Merlin l'Enchanteur (1½ hours). ☎ 02 47 91 82 82. 🕐 Jul: 10.30pm Fri, Sat; Aug: 10pm Fri, Sat. 🎫 **Translations** Eng, Ger, Ital.

Merlin l'Enchanteur (Merlin the Wizard) is staged in the château grounds *(see p104)*, with over 100 actors dressed in stunning costumes. The enchanted world of Lancelot and the Knights of the Round Table, King Arthur and Merlin is vividly enhanced by highly creative light effects.

BLÉSOIS AND ORLÉANAIS

Blois The Story of Blois (45 mins). ☎ 02 54 78 72 76. 🕐 8–31 May: 10:15pm nightly; Jun–Jul: 10:30pm nightly; 1–15 Aug: 10:15pm nightly; 16–31 Aug: 10pm nightly; 1–19 Sep: 9:30pm nightly. 🎫 under 6 yrs free. **Translations** Eng, Ger, Ital, Span.

Images of key moments in the history of the château *(see pp126–7)* are projected onto its façade. Included are the visit of Joan of Arc in 1429, the poetry contest between Charles of Orléans and François Villon, and the assassination of the Duc de Guise. Watch the show from the château's courtyard.

Cléry-Saint-André Dunois Jean Bâtard d'Orléans (1¼ hours). ☎ 02 38 45 94 06. 🕐 last 3 w/ends Jul: 10.30pm. 🎫

Over 200 thespians in period costume perform vignettes from the life of Jean d'Orléans, Count of Dunois (1402–1468), companion-at-arms of Joan of Arc. All the drama takes place at the foot of Basilique Cléry, which holds Dunois' tomb and is a spectacular backdrop for the illuminations. At night medieval feasts are served.

Faces from the past projected onto the walls of Château de Blois

Fireworks and lighting effects illuminate the château of Puy-du-Fou

BERRY

Valençay (2 hours). █ █ 02 54
00 04 42. ◯ late-Jul and Aug: 10pm
Fri, Sat. 🎫 book in advance.
Translations Eng, Ger, Ital, Span.

More than 200 elaborately-
costumed actors bring to life
the history of the château *(see
p146)*, which includes the
adventures of Bonaparte's
minister, Talleyrand, who
lived here for many years.
The finale is a superb
firework display.

Aubigny-sur-Nère

Different Franco-Scottish themes
(90 minutes). █ 02 48 81 50 07.
◯ Jul: 9.30pm Fri, Sat Sun. 🎫 book
in advance. **Translations** Eng.

Centuries of proud assocation
with the Stuart clan, including
a time in the 18th century
when Jacobite exiles made
their home at Aubigny *(see
p154)*, are reflected in this
Franco-Scot celebration. On
Friday night, over 100 costumed villagers enact the tale
of Mary, Queen of Scots, with
music, dance, fireworks and
fountains. On Saturday this
spectacle is complemented by
a feast in the gardens of the
château. On Sunday the event
culminates with a costumed
parade, other events in the
town, and Franco-Scottish
games and contests, culminating in the son-et-lumière,
a final open-air banquet and
fireworks.

LOIRE ATLANTIQUE AND THE VENDÉE

Le Puy-du-Fou Jacques
**Maupillier: a Peasant from the
Vendée** (110 minutes). █ 02 51 64
11 11. ◯ end May–Jul: 10:30pm Fri,
Sat; Aug–early Sep: 10pm Fri, Sat. 🎫
book in advance. **Translation** Eng.

The Château du Puy-du-Fou
(see p188) hosts the Cinéscénie, which is the largest
permanent water and light
show in Europe. More than
700 professional actors, 2,000
volunteers from the region,
50 horsemen and various
spectacular technical effects
combine to trace the turbulent history of the Vendée
from the Middle Ages to the
present day. The music for
the show was composed by
Georges Delerue.

THE MAGICIAN OF THE NIGHT

The master of the modern
son et lumière in France is
Jean-Claude Baudoin, who
is also known as *"le magi-
cien de la nuit"*. Since 1966
he has created the sets for
more than 150 musical pro-
ductions, held at
the châteaux of
Blois, Loches
Chambord and
Valençay, as
well as in St-
Aignan-sur-
Cher, Les
Sables
d'Olonnes
and Chartres.

**Producer
Jean-Claude
Baudoin**

The history of the Vendée re-enacted in the Cinéscénie at Le Puy-du-Fou

THE HISTORY OF THE LOIRE VALLEY

HE LOIRE's central role in French history is splendidly displayed in the breadth of its architectural styles, ranging from megalithic structures to royal and ducal châteaux.

Imposing prehistoric monuments testify to the existence of thriving Neolithic cultures as early as the third millennium BC. By the 1st century BC, the conquering Romans found sophisticated Celtic communities already established. Later, as Christianity spread, the ancient Celtic towns at Angers, Bourges, Chartres, Orléans and Tours became well known as centres of learning, and they remain vibrant cultural centres today.

A long period of territorial conflict began in the 9th century, first among local warlords and later between France and England, when Henry Plantagenet, count of Anjou and duke of Normandy and Aquitaine, inherited the English crown in 1154. Major battles between the two countries were fought in the region during the Hundred Years' War. The Loire also saw bloodshed during the fierce 16th-century Wars of Religion, which took place between the Catholics and the Protestant Huguenots. Later, the Vendée Uprising of 1793 was the most serious civil threat to the French republic after the 1789 Revolution.

Fleur-de-lys, the royal emblem

Yet the Loire was also the scene of outstanding cultural achievements and the home of many French kings. By the 17th century, France's political focus had shifted to Paris, although the River Loire remained a key transportation route until the advent of the railway in the late 19th century.

In the 20th century, the impressive architectural evidence of this rich history has led to the growth of the Loire's tourist industry. This balances with a diverse, well-established industrial base and thriving agriculture to make the valley one of the most economically stable regions of France.

16th-century views of Tours, with its cathedral, and Angers, with quarries of *ardoise* slate

◁ **A portrait of François I, the Renaissance king (reigned 1515–47), attributed to Jean Clouet**

Rulers of the Loire

IN THE COURSE of the Loire's history, the power of the
local nobility often rivalled that of the French throne.
The dukedoms of Anjou and Blois were established
when Charlemagne's territory was divided among his
sons upon his death in 814. Henry Plantagenet, count
of Anjou, duke of Normandy and king of England,
could trace his lineage to Charlemagne. The French
monarchy did not consolidate its authority until
Charles VII moved from the Loire back to Paris in
1436. Another local family, the royal house of Orléans,
saw two of its sons become kings.

KEY

French monarchs

Notable members of local dynasties

1151–89 *Henry Plantagenet*

1180 Philip Augu

879–81 Louis III

884–88 Charles II, the Fat

893–922 Charles III, the Simple

1040–60 *Geoffrey Martel*

447–58 Merovich

716–21 Childéric II

743–51 Childéric III

860–66 *Robert the Strong*

954–86 Lothaire

1031–60 Henri I

1067–1108 Philippe I

1189 *Rich the Lion*

458–82 Childéric I

840–77 Charles I, the Bald

768–814 Charlemagne

987–96 Hugh Capet

400	700	800	900	1000	1100
MEROVINGIANS	**CAROLINGIAN DYNASTY**		**CAPETIAN DYNASTY**		
400	700	800	900	1000	1100

721–87 Thierry IV

751–68 Pépin the Short

724–41 *Charles Martel*

711–16 Dagobert III

996–1031 Robert II, the Pious

987–1040 *Foulques Nerra*

986–87 Louis V

936–54 Louis IV, the Foreigner

888–98 Odo, Count of Paris

879–84 Carloman

877–79 Louis II, the Stammerer

814–40 Louis I, the Pious

1199–1216 *John Lackland*

1108–37 Louis VI, the Fat

1223– Louis VII

482–511 Clovis I

1137–80 Louis VII

1422–61
Charles VII,
the Victorious

1270–85 Philippe III

1285–1314 Philippe
IV, the Fair

1314–16 Louis X

1316–22
Philippe V,
the Tall

1322–28
Charles IV,
the Fair

1328–50
Philippe VI

1483–98
Charles VIII,
the Affable

1498–1515 Louis XII,
Father of the People

1515–47 François I

1547–59 Henri II

1559–60
François II

1643–1715 Louis
XIV, the Sun King

1774–92 Louis XVI

1804–14
Napoléon I

| 1300 | 1400 | 1500 | 1600 | 1700 | 1800 |

VALOIS DYNASTY **BOURBON DYNASTY**

| 1300 | 1400 | 1500 | 1600 | 1700 | 1800 |

1350–64
Jean II,
the Good

1430–80
*René I of
Anjou*

1461–83
Louis XI, the
Spider

1560–74
Charles IX

1574–89 Henri III

1814–24
Louis XVIII

1824–30
Charles X

1830–48
*Louis-Philippe I,
Duc d'Orléans,
King of the French*

1226–70
Louis IX
(St Louis)

1364–80
Charles V,
the Wise

1380–1422
Charles VI,
the Fool

1715–74
Louis XV

1852–70
Napoléon III

1589–1610 Henri IV

1610–43 Louis XIII

Neolithic and Roman Loire

NEOLITHIC CULTURE produced some of France's largest prehistoric tombs and sacred sites. Their builders had Central European roots, as did the Celts who established cities along the Loire in the Bronze and Iron Ages. Julius Caesar's conquest of the valley in 51 BC left the Celtic tribes under a light Roman rule, the basis of peace and prosperity for the next 300 years. The spread of Christianity coincided with Rome's military decline and the rise of kingdoms ruled by Visigoths to the south and Germanic Franks to the north. The Frankish king Clovis I converted to Christianity and took power in 507 by routing the Visigoths.

Baptism of Clovis
Frankish chieftain Clovis converted to Christianity at the start of the 6th century to legitimize his rule.

The entrance porch is a distinctive feature of Angevin dolmens.

Palaeolithic Remains
Flint tools made in the Loire basin were traded by Palaeolithic tribes at least 50,000 years ago.

Celtic Art
Celtic art was not dominated by the naturalistic ideals of the occupying Romans. This bronze statuette of a young woman dates from the 1st–2nd century AD.

BAGNEUX DOLMEN
This 5,000-year-old chamber tomb in Saumur is 21 by 7 m (69 by 23 ft). The nine massive uprights were levered onto loose stones, dragged to the site, tilted and sunk into ditches 3 m (10 ft) deep.

TIMELINE

c.2500 Loire dolmens with porches set new style of Neolithic burial chamber

c.800 Celtic Carnutes found settlements at Blois, Chartres and Orléans

57–6 Romans conquer western Loire tribes

51 Julius Caesar ends Gaulish uprising that began in Orléans

Julius Caesar, first to unite Gaul

2500 BC		100 BC	AD 1	AD 100

c.1200 Loire region exports bronze weapons made using local tin resources

Celtic helmet

31 Roman emperor Augustus sets framework for 300 years of Pax Romana (peace and prosperity) in the Loire

50 Loire Valley flourishes as border link between two Gallo-Roman provinces, Lugdenunsis and Aquitania

Celtic Armour
The warlike Celts were skilled armourers, as this bronze breastplate of 750–475 BC shows. The Romans found them formidable opponents.

WHERE TO SEE NEOLITHIC AND ROMAN LOIRE

Anjou is rich in Neolithic sights, mostly on the south bank of the Loire. The largest are at Saumur *(see pp82–3)* and Gennes *(p78)*. Gennes' amphitheatre and the walls at Thésée *(p129)* are two of the few surviving Gallo-Roman monuments. Museums at Orléans *(pp138–9)* and Tours *(pp114–15)* have major Gallo-Roman collections.

Gennes Amphitheatre
Roman gladiatorial combats were held in the amphitheatre at Gennes.

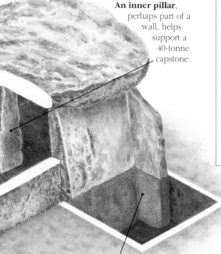

An inner pillar, perhaps part of a wall, helps support a 40-tonne capstone.

Orthostats (walls) were sunk in holes 3 m (10 ft) deep and filled with sand, which was then dug out.

Gallo-Roman Art
This beaten bronze stallion, displayed in the archeology museum in Orléans, was dedicated to Mars, bringer of war and god of agriculture.

Fresh Water by Aqueduct
Roman pillars near Luynes supported a 2nd-century aqueduct which carried spring water to baths in Caesarodunum (Tours).

St Martin, Bishop of Tours

250 Gatien, Bishop of Tours, among the first Christian evangelists in the Loire	**313** Emperor Constantine makes Christianity official Roman religion	**372** Martin, Bishop of Tours, leads monastic growth	**507** After converting to Christianity, Clovis defeats Visigoths near Poitiers / **498** Clovis I takes Orléans		**511** Clovis I dies; his sons divide his lands
200		**300**	**400**		**500**
250 Romans build amphitheatre at Gennes			**451** Visigoth kingdom of Toulouse helps repel Attila the Hun at Orléans	*Wine: an early Loire export*	
275 Emperor Aurelian gives Orléans independent status				**473** Visigoths capture Tours	**c.550** First record of wine production in the Loire region

The Early Middle Ages

Royal seal of Henry II

IN RAISING the massive keep at Loches, Foulques Nerra of Anjou was typical of the warlords who took power in the Loire after the 9th century. The chains of citadels they built laid the foundations for the later châteaux. The Plantagenets, who followed Nerra as rulers of Anjou, also claimed territory from Normandy to Aquitaine and then inherited the English throne. It was not until the 13th century that the French King Louis IX brought Anjou back under direct control of the crown. Throughout this period the Church was a more cohesive power than the French crown. Its cathedrals and monastic orders established schools and *scriptoria* (where manuscripts were copied and illuminated), and it was to the Church rather than the throne that feudal warlords turned to mediate their brutal disputes.

THE LOIRE AROUND 1180

☐ *French royal domain*
☐ *Other fiefs*

Gregory I codified the liturgical music sung during his reign as pope (590–604).

St Louis
Popularly called St Louis for his piety, Louis IX (1214–70) was the first Capetian monarch to inherit a relatively stable kingdom. A brave crusading knight and just ruler, he forced England to abandon claims to the Loire.

TIMELINE

687 Pépin II establishes the power of the "mayors" of the Carolingian dynasty, ancestors of Charlemagne, over Merovingian kings

732 Charles Martel drives Moors back from the Loire in decisive battle south of Tours

850 Normans lay waste to Loire Valley

866 Robert the Strong, ancestor of Capetian kir killed by Normans in A

911 Chartres repels Normans

| 600 | 700 | 800 | 90• |

Charlemagne, the Frankish king

768-84 Charlemagne conquers Brittany and all Loire

796 Charlemagne's mentor, Alcuin, makes Tours a centre of Carolingian art

Coinage of Charles the Bold

Carolingian Ivory
Ivory plaques, reliquaries and book covers are among the most beautiful Frankish decorative objects to survive Norman destructions of the 10th century. Carolingian art usually served a religious or utilitarian purpose.

Medieval musical notation showed variations in pitch (high and low notes). The length of each note depended on the natural rhythm of the text.

Monastic Arts
The development of the Caroline Minuscule style of calligraphy was led by the monks of Tours' Basilique St-Martin in the 9th century.

Fine Craftsmanship
Many of the finest surviving pieces of medieval craftsmanship are worked in metal. This 13th-century funerary mask was cast in copper from the effigy of a woman and then gilded.

ILLUMINATED MANUSCRIPT
This manuscript is the first page of a 13th-century gradual, a book of plainsong sung during mass. It is typical of the style of illuminated manuscripts that were produced by the abbeys of the Loire Valley. This collection of Gregorian chant was compiled by monks of the strict Cistercian Order (see p149).

WHERE TO SEE EARLY MEDIEVAL LOIRE
Early churches such as the one at Cunault (see p79) are charged with medieval atmosphere, as are abbeys such as Noirlac (p149) or at Solesmes (p162) and Fontgombault (p146), where you can hear Gregorian chant. Fortress châteaux such as the one at Loches (p104) and ruined towers at Lavardin (p122) or Montrichard (p128) tell grimmer feudal stories.

Romanesque Capitals
This Romanesque sculpture is on a capital in Cunault church.

Hugh Capet of Orléans
Hugh, depicted here being handed the keys to Laon, was elected king in 987, ending the Carolingian dynasty. He set a precedent for kings to seek refuge in the Loire in troubled times.

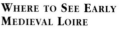

Hugh Capet of Orléans becomes first Capetian king of France

1101 Founding of Abbaye de Fontevraud
1096 First Crusade launched

1128 Marriage in Le Mans of Geoffrey Plantagenet and Matilda, daughter of Henry I of England
1189 Henry II's death leaves his son, Richard the Lionheart, as the Angevin rival to the French king

1000	1100	1200

Foulques Nerra

992 Bretons driven out of Anjou by Foulques Nerra

1154 Henry Plantagenet accedes to the English throne as Henry II
1125 Thibaut IV of Blois and Champagne rivals Capetian power
1214 Angevin empire ends with defeat of King John at Angers

The Hundred Years' War

14th-century knight

THE DESTRUCTIVE CLIMAX of the Middle Ages was war between the French and English crowns, flaring intermittently from 1337 to 1453. When the English besieged Orléans in 1428, the Loire region became the focus for a struggle that seemed likely to leave France partitioned between England and its powerful ally, Burgundy. Instead, the teenage heroine, Joan of Arc, inspired Orléans to fight off the English and brought the dauphin Charles VII out of hiding in Chinon. Her martyrdom in 1431 helped to inspire a French recovery. In spite of marauding soldiery and the more widespread disaster of the plague known as the Black Death, the Loire knew periods of peace and prosperity, during which medieval court life flourished.

THE LOIRE VALLEY IN 1429

☐ *French territory in the Loire*

▨ *English possessions*

The English longbow was a powerful weapon, requiring strong, skilled archers.

Charles VII

Joan of Arc's dauphin, often portrayed as a weakling, was in fact a crafty man in a difficult situation. Disinherited by the French royal family in 1420, he used Joan's charisma to rally support. However, he distrusted her political judgment.

Cannons could fire stone balls that weighed as much as 200 kg (440 lb).

Jousting Tournament

The sumptuous trappings of their warlike recreations display the wealth of the ruling class in the early 15th century. Jousting was dangerous – Henri II died from a lance blow.

TIMELINE

1341 English support John of Montfort against Charles of Blois in War of Brittany Succession

1346 English longbows defeat French knights at Crécy

1352 Loire begins recovery from four years of plague

Black Death depicted in a 15th-century illuminated manuscript

1325	1350	1375

1337 Philippe VI, first Valois king, confiscates English lands in Guyenne, starting Hundred Years' War

Portrait of Philippe VI

1360 Anjou becomes a duchy

Apocalypse
War and the plague made the end of the world a preoccupation of 15th-century art. In this tapestry from Angers (see pp76–7), St John hears the clap of doom.

WHERE TO SEE THE LOIRE OF THE 14TH AND 15TH CENTURIES

Guérande *(p180)* is a well-preserved, 15th-century walled town. Many others, such as Chinon *(pp98–100)*, have half-timbered houses. Orléans *(pp138–9)* has a replica of the house in which Joan of Arc lodged. Le Plessis-Bourré *(p70)* exemplifies the shift towards more graceful lifestyles after the end of the Hundred Years' War.

The halberd was a typical infantryman's weapon.

Siege tower

Joan of Arc
Although shown here in feminine attire, the real Joan (see p137) wore men's dress into battle.

Château de Chinon
This château is strategically positioned on a cliff above the River Vienne.

René, Duke of Anjou
René I (1409–80) loved tournaments but was also a painter, scholar and poet. To his people he represented the ideal 15th-century ruler.

THE SIEGE OF ORLÉANS

The English first besieged Orléans in November 1428, and they quickly established their position and built major siegeworks. In February 1429, a French attempt to cut English supply lines was defeated, and it was not until 30 April that Joan of Arc's troops were able to enter the city. Within a week the English were forced to abandon the siege.

1409 Birth of René I, Duke of Anjou	**1429** Joan of Arc visits the dauphin Charles at Chinon, ends English siege of Orléans and crowns him King Charles VII at Reims	**1453** War ends without a treaty, with English retaining only Calais	
1417–32 English occupy Chartres	**1418** Charles VI burns Azay-le-Rideau		**1461** Louis XI begins his reign
1400	**1425**	**1450**	
1392 Louis, Duke of Orléans, acquires Blois	**1415** Crushing English victory at Agincourt leads to alliance between England and Burgundy	**1428** English besiege Orléans	**1438** Jacques Cœur of Bourges becomes court banker and reorganizes France's tax system	*15th-century sporting crossbow*
		1435 Charles VII makes peace with Burgundy. Army reforms lead to French victories		**1470** Silk weaving in Tours begins

Renaissance Loire

Catherine de Médicis (1519–89)

THE ITALIAN WARS of Charles VIII, Louis XII and François I between 1494 and 1525 gave all three kings a taste for Italian art and architecture. At Amboise, Blois and Chambord they made the Loire a centre of court life, establishing the culture of the French Renaissance. François I patronized countless artists and craftsmen who worked in the Italian style, setting an example for the aristocracy throughout France. The Loire suffered 40 years of warfare when his son's widow, Catherine de Médicis, could not persuade Catholics, led by the Guise family, to live in peace with Protestants during the reigns of her sons, Charles IX and Henri III.

Fortress of Faith
The pope is besieged by Protestants in this portrayal of the Wars of Religion.

François I
France's strongest Renaissance king made the Loire his hunting playground. His great confidence is captured here by François Clouet of Tours (see p23).

Colonnades were a feature of the Classical Renaissance style.

The First Tank Design
Leonardo spent his last years at Le Clos-Lucé (see p111). This tank is a model of one of the inventions he worked on there.

THE IDEAL CHÂTEAU

From Charles VIII (1483–98) onwards, French Renaissance kings dreamt of creating the ideal château. The symmetrical vistas of this plan by Androuet du Cerceau display a late-Renaissance stylistic move towards Classical grandeur.

TIMELINE

Cellini's saltcellar for François I (1515–47)

Charles VIII, France's first Renaissance king

1484 Etats Généraux, a national assembly, meets at Tours

1493 Charles VIII redesigns his birthplace, the Château d'Amboise, in Italian style

1498 Duke of Orléans is crowned Louis XII and marries Anne of Brittany

1515 François I conquers Milan and invites Italian artists to the Loire

1532 Treaty binds Brittany and Nantes to France

1475

1500

1525

1508 Louis XII remodels Blois as Renaissance royal capital

1491 Marriage of Charles VIII to Anne of Brittany links autonomous Brittany to French crown

1519 François I begins building Chambord. Leonardo da Vinci dies at Le Clos-Lucé (see p111)

Henri IV
Brave, astute and likeable, Henri IV of Vendôme and Navarre skilfully reasserted the authority of the crown over a disintegrating kingdom within 10 years of his accession in 1589. Rubens (1577–1640) shows him receiving a betrothal portrait of Marie de Médicis.

WHERE TO SEE RENAISSANCE LOIRE

Fine Renaissance buildings can be seen throughout the region. Older châteaux that reflect the Italian influence include Amboise *(p110)* and Blois *(pp126–7)*. The most delightful achievements of the French Renaissance are Chenonceau *(pp106–9)* and Azay-le-Rideau *(pp96–7)*. Smaller examples, such as Beauregard *(pp130–1)*, are widespread. Undoubtedly the most spectacular is Chambord *(pp132–5)*.

Château de Chambord
This impressive château sits on the banks of the River Cosson.

High roofs and dormers show the persisting French influence.

Anne of Brittany's Reliquary
By marrying successively Charles VIII and Louis XII, Anne of Brittany, whose reliquary is in Nantes (see p191), welded her fiercely independent duchy to France.

An arcaded central courtyard formed the basis of 15th-century palaces in the Italian style.

Diane de Poitiers
The mistress of Henri II was flatteringly portrayed as Diana, the Roman goddess of the hunt.

1559 Death of Henri II begins power struggle between his widow, Catherine de Médicis, and anti-Protestant followers of the Duc de Guise	**1572** Court moves to Fontainebleau after St Bartholomew's Day massacre of Protestants	**1576** Henri, Duc de Guise, founds pro-Catholic Holy League. Meeting of Etats Généraux at Blois fails to find a peace formula	**1598** Edict of Nantes establishes Protestant rights of worship

1550 **1575**

1547 Henri II begins reign and gives Chenonceau to his mistress, Diane de Poitiers	**1562** Wars of Religion start with major battles and massacres along the Loire	**1588** Holy League virtually takes over government. Henri III has Duc de Guise and his brother murdered at Blois	**1594** Henri IV crowned at Chartres after becoming a Catholic to end the Wars of Religion

Coin of Henri IV "the Great"

Growth and Prosperity

THE LOIRE LOST ITS CENTRAL ROLE in French politics when the focus of court life moved to the Paris region at the end of the 16th century. The Vendée, however, was the centre during the French Revolution of a violent popular uprising against Republican excesses, including rising taxes, the persecution of priests and conscription. River trade remained important, especially for the increasingly wealthy port of Nantes. In the 17th century, work had begun on canals to connect Nantes and the Loire directly with Paris, of which Eiffel's bridge-canal at Briare was the aesthetic high point. Although industry grew slowly, the region remained predominantly agricultural.

19TH-CENTURY WATERWAYS

— *Rivers*

— *Canals built before 1900*

Cardinal Richelieu
As Louis XIII's chief minister between 1624 and 1642, Cardinal Richelieu helped to establish orderly government in France.

The 15 granite piers supporting the structure were bedded using early compressed-air techniques.

Winemaking in the Loire
Winemaking in the 18th century remained a pastime for the idle rich, who used badly paid peasants to harvest and press the grapes.

TIMELINE

1610–16 Regency of Henri IV's widow, Marie de Médicis, over Louis XIII

1617 Louis XIII banishes his mother to Blois. They are reconciled by Richelieu in 1620

1631 Richelieu starts building planned village and château in Touraine

1720s Loire again becomes a centre of country life for the nobility

1600

Louis XIII

1648–53 La Fronde: a series of French civil wars

1650

17th-century watch made in Blois

1700

1685 Saumur and other cities lose Huguenot population as these terrorized Protestants flee after the revocation of the Edict of Nantes

Vendée Hero
Bonchamps' plea to spare Republican prisoners (see p187) was depicted in stone by David d'Angers.

Loire "Inexplosibles"
Faced by competition from the railways, 19th-century steamboats were a last attempt to maintain the Loire's role as France's greatest trade route.

Graceful lamps above the wide pavements provide a Parisian boulevard touch.

Passage Pommeraye
The elegance of this 19th-century shopping arcade reflected the wealth of Nantes.

BRIARE BRIDGE-CANAL
Gustave Eiffel designed this 662-m (725-yd) bridge to carry canal traffic safely across the Loire. Opened in 1896, it completed a grand waterway system begun in the 17th century linking the Seine and Rhône rivers. The metal structure used new steel technology.

Steam Omnibus
In 1873, Amédée Bollée's l'Obéissante was the first car to be built in Le Mans.

1756 Royal College of Surgeons founded at Tours

1789 French Revolution

1793–4 Vendée Uprising

1846 Paris railway reaches Tours

1897 Opening of Eiffel's bridge-canal spanning the Loire at Briare

1852 Napoleon III crowned emperor

1856 Great flood of the Loire

*50 1800 1850

1770–90 Nantes reaches peak of mercantile wealth

1804 Napoléon makes La Roche-sur-Yon the capital of pacified Vendée and funds drainage of the eastern Marais Poitevin

1829 First Loire steamboat, *Le Loire*, travels from Nantes to Angers in 16 hours

The Vendée heart emblem **1863** Last Loire steamboat company closes

1870 Franco-Prussian War drives Napoléon III into exile

1873 Amédée Bollée begins manufacturing steam-driven cars at Le Mans

The Modern Era

Fruits of the Loire Valley

ALTHOUGH SHIP-BUILDING reached a peak at Nantes and St-Nazaire in the 1920s, and light industry expanded steadily around Orléans, Le Mans and Angers, the region did not become prosperous until after World War II. Its larger cities were occupied by the Germans in 1940 and many were bombed in 1944. Since the 1960s, when the recovery gathered momentum, tourism has supplemented the Loire's traditional strength as the "Garden of France". Private châteaux have been opened to the public, and the state has funded major restoration schemes, as at the Abbaye de Fontevraud.

Wilbur Wright
The pioneer US flying ace galvanized European aviation when he demonstrated this commercial prototype near Le Mans in 1908.

Dramatic fireworks
light up the night sky.

TGV Links
With stops at Vendôme, Tours, Angers and Nantes, the Loire is well served by France's TGV (Train à Grande Vitesse) network.

Orléans, 1944
Bridges across the River Loire were prime bombing targets at both the beginning and the end of World War II.

SON ET LUMIÈRE
Puy-du-Fou's Cinéscénie laser spectacle updates a tradition begun at Chambord in 1952 by Robert Houdin, son of a famous Blois magician. Evening performances draw thousands to Blois, Chenonceau, Cheverny and other great châteaux *(see pp42–3)*.

TIMELINE

1905 Loire farming in decline as falling wheat prices follow damage to vines from phylloxera

1908 Wilbur Wright stages test flights at Auvours near Le Mans

1920 Cheverny opens to the public

Cheverny (see p130), a privately-owned château

| 1900 | 1910 | 1920 | 1930 | 1940 |

Alain-Fournier (1886–1914)

1914 World War I begins. Among the first dead is the writer Alain-Fournier *(see p23)*

1923 First 24-hour race at Le Mans

1929 Town of La Baule builds promenade and becomes one of France's top beach resorts

1936 Renault opens Le Mans factory

1940 German advance forces temporary government to move from Paris to Tours

Earth Day Ecology Protests on the Loire
*Environmentally-aware locals are committed to
preserving the rich natural resources of the great river.*

Nuclear Power
*The Loire was an early
resource for cooling nuclear
reactors. Avoine, near
Chinon, opened in 1963.*

Computer-controlled lighting
effects, lasers and water jets
add a modern twist.

More than 2,000 local residents
volunteer as performers, security
patrols and guides at each
Cinéscénie evening.

Le Vinci
*The sensitive modernization of
Tours city centre shows how
old and new architectural
styles can be combined.*

Le Mans
*The renowned 24-hour race at Le Mans attracts
motor enthusiasts from around the world.*

44 Liberation
Loire cities
ds four-year
rman
cupation

1963 First French
nuclear power
station at Avoine
near Chinon

1970s Loire wine
exports, especially of
Muscadet, soar

1994 Government
dismantles dam at
Maisons Rouges on the
River Vienne to allow
salmon to reach
spawning grounds

1950	1960	1970	1980	1990

1952 First
son et lumière
performance
at Chambord

1959 André Malraux
made Minister of
Cultural Affairs. He
speeds up
restoration work on
Loire monuments

*Muscadet,
produced
east of
Nantes*

1989–90 Inauguration of
TGV Atlantique high-speed
services brings Angers
within 90 minutes of Paris

THE LOIRE VALLEY AREA BY AREA

The Loire Valley at a Glance

RICH IN HISTORY AND ARCHITECTURE, the Loire Valley is best known for its sumptuous Renaissance châteaux, such as Chambord and Chenonceau. But the region has also retained the wealth of earlier ages, from Bronze Age dolmens to medieval keeps, such as the Château d'Angers, and an impressive heritage of religious architecture, including the Gothic marvels of Chartres and Bourges cathedrals. Visitors who desire a break from the past can revel in the beauty of the landscape, which contains natural surprises such as the lush Marais Poitevin. In a region packed with delights, those shown here are among the very best.

The Gothic spires of Chartres Cathedral, which tower over an attractive town *(see pp172–5)*

The Château d'Angers, protected by its formidable curtain walls *(see pp74–7)*

NORTH OF THE LOIRE

Angers

ANJOU

Nantes

Cholet

LOIRE-ATLANTIQUE AND THE VENDEE

La Roche-sur-Yon

Abbaye de Fontevraud, the largest medieval abbey complex in France *(see pp86–7)*

0 kilometres   50

0 miles   50

The Marais Poitevin, a labyrinth of shady canals contrasting with rich fields of painstakingly reclaimed land *(see pp182–5)*

The memorable François I Renaissance staircase of the Château de Blois *(see pp126–7)*

Chambord, the largest royal residence in the Loire *(see pp132–5)*

Bourges Cathedral, a Gothic masterpiece *(see pp152–3)*

Chartres

ans

Orléans

BLESOIS AND ORLEANAIS

Blois

Tours

TOURAINE

BERRY

Bourges

Châteauroux

Chenonceau, stretching languidly across the River Cher *(see pp106–9)*

The graceful symmetry of Azay-le-Rideau *(see pp96–7)*

Villandry's spectacular reconstructed Renaissance gardens *(see pp94–5)*

ANJOU

THE LANDSCAPE OF ANJOU *is as gentle and pleasant as its climate and its people. The region's rolling plains are intersected by a network of rivers, which help to irrigate the already fertile land. North of the city of Angers, the confluence of the Sarthe, Mayenne and Loir rivers forms a great flood-plain in the winter months and is a regular port of call for thousands of migrating birds.*

The creamy limestone, or tufa, used to build the great châteaux of Anjou, combines with grey roof slates to give Angevin architecture its distinctive look. Tufa quarrying has created hundreds of caves. Many are now used for growing mushrooms, and others have been transformed into troglodyte dwellings, some of which are open to visitors.

Some of the Loire Valley's finest fruits and vegetables are grown here. Trees and flowers also flourish: white magnolias, mimosas and palms decorate the region's parks, and the rose gardens of Doué are legendary. The region's vines produce the sparkling wines of Saumur and St-Cyr-en-Bourg. Visitors can see the complicated process of the *méthode champenoise* firsthand by visiting the major wine houses around Saumur.

Anjou is steeped in the history of the powerful rival dynasties of medieval France. Then, as now, Angers, dominated by its barrel-chested fortress, was the centre of the region. The city was the feudal capital of the Plantagenets, among them Henry of Anjou, who became Henry II of England. Fifteen of the family, including Henry II, his wife, Eleanor of Aquitaine, and their sons, Richard the Lionheart and John Lackland, are buried at Fontevraud Abbey. Nearby, Saumur's château formed the fairy-tale backdrop to the "September" miniature in the 15th-century masterpiece, *Les Très Riches Heures du Duc de Berry*. Other impressive châteaux in this region include Brissac, the tallest château in the Loire, and Le Plessis-Bourré, a charming pre-Renaissance château.

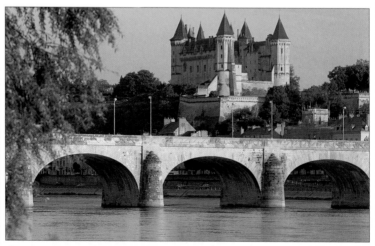

Château de Saumur, towering above the town and the River Loire

◁ **Cattle resting in an Anjou meadow**

Exploring Anjou

NORTHERN ANJOU IS CROSSED by the Mayenne, Sarthe and Loir rivers, flowing southwards to their convergence in the River Maine. Angers, the geographical and administrative centre of the region, straddles the Maine 8 km (5 miles) before it flows into the Loire. Anjou's most famous châteaux, antiquities and troglodyte sites are located around Angers and Saumur, 50 km (30 miles) up the Loire. But there are also dozens of lesser-known châteaux, clustered around Segré in the northwest and Baugé in the northeast.

Rennes

Laval

SEGRÉ ● ❶ CHÂTEAU DE LA L

LE LION-D'ANGERS

Nantes

❹ SERI

ST-GEORGES-SUR-LOIRE ●

Loire

BEHUA

ST-FLORENT-LE-VIEIL ❷

CHALONNES SUR-LOIRE

● CHAMPTOCEAUX

Eglise St-Maurille, Chalonnes-sur-Loire

BEAUPREAU ●

❸ CHOLET

La Roche-sur-Yon

0 kilometres   10

0 miles   10

The Loire in full flood in Anjou

GETTING AROUND

Angers is 90 minutes from Paris by TGV. *L'Océane* autoroute (A11) via Le Mans is the fastest road access from Paris. Between Tours and Angers, the D766 via Baugé is reasonably quick. The D751 from Saumur follows the south bank of the Loire and is the most pleasant drive towards Angers. It continues as the Corniche Angevine, providing splendid views of the Loire on the road to Champtoceaux. Leisurely boat cruises are available on the Oudon and Mayenne tributaries.

Le Mans

770

Sarthe

Loir

LE PLESSIS-BOURRE

N23

D766

D338

BAUGE

D766

ASSES
LLEES
EWINES

485 (E60)

D74

A11 (E501)

ANGERS

MOTGEOFFROY ⑦

D938

N147

D952

485 (E60)

BRISSAC ⑨

D751

GENNES ⑩

D10

⑪ CUNAULT

D761

ST-HILAIRE
ST-FLORENT

SAUMUR 485 (E60)

⑫

N152

Tours

TROGLODYTE TOUR ⑮

D960

D947

⑭ MONTSOREAU

DOUE-LA-FONTAINE ●

D751

N147

⑯ FONTEVRAUD-
L'ABBAYE

⑬ MONTREUIL-
BELLAY

Parthenay

KEY

▰ Motorway

▰ Major road

▰ Minor road

▰ Scenic route

▰ River

✲ Viewpoint

One of Angers' lively pavement cafés

St-Florent-le-Vieil's 18th-century church, on a hill above the old town

Château de la Lorie ❶

Road map B3. 🚌 *Segré, then taxi.*
C *02 41 92 10 04.* ⭘ *Jul–mid-Sep:*
Wed–Mon; groups by appt. 🖎

Elegant gardens in the 18th-century French style introduce this private, dry-moated château, 2 km (1 mile) southeast of the old town of Segré on the River Oudon. The original building, which is embellished by a statue of the Roman goddess Minerva over the central door, was built during the 17th century by René le Pelletier, provost-general of Anjou.

A century later, two wings were added to form a court-yard, together with an ornate marble ballroom. This *pièce de résistance* is crowned with a musicians' gallery located in an overhead rotunda. It was completed by Italian craftsmen in 1779, only a few short years

before the French Revolution put an end to these types of extravagant shows of wealth and personal power.

St-Florent-le-Vieil ❷

Road map B3. 🚶 *2,690.* 🚉
Varades, then taxi. 🚌 🛈 *Pavillon de la Mairie (02 41 72 62 32).* 🛒 *Fri pm.*
🎭 *Festival de Musique, Les Orientales (mid-Jun–Jul).*

A walk through the narrow streets of the old town, lined with buildings dating from the 16th to the 18th centuries, ends atop a hill on which stands a large, 18th-century church, the scene of dramatic events during the Vendée Uprising. The Uprising began in the square outside the church in March 1793, with a mass revolt against conscription into the Republican army.

Seven months later, the Royalist army, beaten at Cholet, crossed the Loire here with 40,000 troops and at least as many supporters. They planned to kill more than 4,000 Republicans held in the church, but were stopped by one of their leaders, the Marquis de Bonchamps, who cried, "Spare the prisoners," as he lay dying. Among those

---

THE CORNICHE ANGEVINE

One of the most scenic routes in the region, the Corniche Angevine (D751) curves along the cliffs above the south side of the Loire, offering lovely views of the islands that break up the river in this area, and of the opposite bank, with its fertile vineyards and beautiful manor houses. The road is never more than hilly and has a pleasantly rural feel as it runs alongside the Louet (a tributary of the Loire), passing though villages and flanked by vineyards and fields.

Chalonnes-sur-Loire, at the western end, is an ancient village with a graceful church, the Eglise St-Maurille, parts of which date back to the 12th century. The quay beside the church is a good place to stop for a picnic. Further along, La Haie Longue has particularly pretty views across the river. At the eastern end of the Corniche Angevine, the town of Rochefort-sur-Loire has a 15th-century bell-tower and a square of old turreted houses. Powerful fortresses once stood on outcrops of rock below the village, and the ruins of some of them can be explored.

The view across the river at La Haie Longue

saved was the father of the sculptor David d'Angers, whose marble statue of Bonchamps was placed in the church in 1825 *(see p57)*. Stained-glass windows in the chancel recount the story, as does the **Musée d'Histoire Locale et des Guerres de Vendée**.

�sz Musée d'Histoire Locale et des Guerres de Vendée

Place J et M Source. **(** 02 41 72 50 03. **○** Apr–Jun & mid-Sep–Oct: Sat & Sun pm only; Jul–mid-Sep: daily pm. ◪

Emile Boutigny's 1899 depiction of the Vendée Uprising in Cholet

Cholet ❸

Road map B4. ♟ 58,000. ⊞ ➡ ℹ pl de Rougé (02 41 49 80 00). ⊟ Sat. ⍟ Carnaval de Cholet (Apr); Festival de l'Arlequin (Apr–May); L'Eté Cigale (Jun–mid Sep). ⍵ www.ot-cholet.fr

CAPITAL OF THE Mauges region and second city of Anjou, Cholet was a thriving town until 1793 when it lost half its population in the Vendée Uprising *(see p187)*. Its revival was testimony to the strength of the area's

The tomb of the Marquis de Vaubrun in Serrant's chapel

textile industry. Cholet's red handkerchiefs with white borders are souvenirs of a crucial battle. The Vendée Uprising is commemorated in the portraits, battle scenes and models in the city's **Musée d'Art et d'Histoire**.

�sz Musée d'Art et d'Histoire

27 av de l'Abreuvoir. **(** 02 41 49 29 00. **○** Wed–Mon. ● public hols. ◪

Château de Serrant ❹

Road map B3. ❒ Angers, then taxi. ⛟ St George-sur-Loire. **(** 02 41 39 13 01. **○** Apr–Jun, Sep–Oct: Wed–Mon; Jul–Aug: daily. ◪ ◪

THE MOST WESTERLY of the great Loire châteaux, the privately-owned Serrant was begun in 1546 and developed in an entirely harmonious style over the next three centuries. Its pale tufa and dark schist façades, with massive corner towers topped by cupolas, create an air of dignity. Inside, the central pavilion contains one of the most beautiful Renaissance staircases in the region. The château also has a fine collection of 18th-

century furniture and Flemish tapestries, and a library of some 12,000 books.

Serrant's most famous owner was the Marquis de Vaubrun, whose death in battle (1675) is commemorated by a magnificent tomb in the chapel, sculpted by Antoine Coysevox. The Irish Jacobite family of Walsh, shipowners at Nantes, owned Serrant in the 18th century, and the château displays a painting of Bonnie Prince Charlie bidding farewell to Anthony Walsh, whose ship took the prince to Scotland.

In 1830 Serrant passed to the Duc de la Trémoille. His descendents still own it today.

A statue of the Madonna, set in the church wall at Béhuard

Béhuard ❺

Road map C3. ♟ 110. ➡ Baiche Maine, then taxi. ℹ Angers (02 41 23 51 11).

THE NARROW LANES of the medieval village on this delightful island in the Loire were made for pilgrims visiting a tiny church fitted into an outcrop of rock. Since pagan times, prayers have been offered on this site for the safety of sailors navigating the often treacherous river.

The church, moving in its simplicity, was built during the 15th century under the protection of Louis XI, who was himself saved from shipwreck on the Loire. The aisle that bisects the little nave is hollowed from the rock.

The south façade of Château de Serrant, with huge corner towers

Château du Plessis-Bourré ❻

Road map C3. 🚉 *Angers, then taxi.* 📞 *02 41 32 06 72.* ⏰ *Apr–Jun & Oct: Wed–Sun pm; Jul–Aug: daily.* ⬤ *Nov–Feb (except groups by appt).* 📷 ♿ *grd flr only.*

S ET IN A MOAT so wide it looks more like a lake, Château du Plessis-Bourré, with its silvery-white walls and dark slate roofs, seems to float on the water. Built in five years from 1468, this is the least altered and perhaps even the most perfect example of the work of Jean Bourré, whose home it was.

As advisor and treasurer to the king of France, Bourré also oversaw the creation of Langeais *(see p92)* and Jarzé and was influential in the transformation of Loire castles from fortresses into pleasure palaces. The Château du Plessis-Bourré itself is well defended, but its fortifications do not interfere with a design that is orientated towards gracious living. Its wonderful condition stands as a testament to the quality of the materials used in its construction and to the skills of the craftsmen who created it.

After crossing a long, seven-arched bridge, visitors enter the château's arcaded courtyard by one of two working

Ceiling of the Salle des Gardes

drawbridges, still shut by the owner at night. The state rooms are surprisingly light and airy, with finely-carved stone decoration. A superb painted ceiling in the Salle des Gardes depicts many allegorical and alchemical scenes, including a lively representation of the demon-wolf Chicheface, emaciated because she could eat only wives who always obeyed their husbands. Some furniture, mainly dating from the 18th century, is displayed. During the French Revolution, coats of arms on the library fireplace were defaced, and graffiti can still be seen.

Château du Plessis-Bourré, set in its wide moat

BIRD-WATCHING IN THE BASSES VALLÉES ANGEVINES

At the confluence of the Sarthe, Loir and Mayenne rivers, some 4,500 ha (11,100 acres) of land, the Basses Vallées Angevines, are flooded between October and May each year. Thousands of migrating birds visit the area, making it an exceptional bird-watching site.

Perhaps the rarest visitor is the elusive corncrake, which arrives in the grasslands during March. There are more than 300

breeding pairs in the area – more than anywhere else in Europe. Protection of this species is aided by enlightened local farming methods, such as late hay harvests.

Insects in the meadows, ditches and rivers attract swifts, hobbys, whinchats and yellow wagtails. In early summer the Basses Vallées resound with birdsong and in the evenings the strange call of the corncrake can be heard.

The flood-plains of Anjou at twilight

Château de Montgeoffroy ❼

Road map C3. 🚆 *Angers or Saumur, then taxi.* 🚌 📞 *02 41 80 60 02.* 🕐 *mid-Mar–mid-Nov: daily.* 📷 ♿ *restricted.*

MONTGEOFFROY is a masterpiece of late 18th-century style, built for the Maréchal de Contades by the architect Nicolas Barré between 1773 and 1775, and beautifully preserved by his descendants. The château is a model of balance, with subtle blue and grey harmonies of stone and paintwork, tall French windows and a lovely park.

The central building is flanked by flat-roofed pavilions, which connect two side wings to the main house. The wings are both rounded off with towers built in the 16th century. One tower houses a harness room smelling of fresh Norwegian spruce, leading to magnificent stables and a fine display of carriages. The chapel in the opposite wing is also 16th-century.

The symmetrical façade of the Château de Montgeoffroy

Next to the main house, the kitchen has a collection of 260 copper and pewter pots. The charming principal rooms are alive with pictures, tapestries and furniture made especially for the château. An innovation in the dining room is a porcelain stove fashioned in the shape of a palm tree, brought from Strasbourg where the *maréchal* (marshal) was governor. His crossed batons are used as a decorative motif

Hérault de Séchelles by Hubert Drouais

in the superbly positioned Grand Salon. The marshal's "friend", Madame Hérault, had her own rooms, where a portrait of their "natural" grandson, Marie-Jean Hérault de Séchelles, can be seen.

Montgeoffroy's stables, where the collection of carriages is housed

Snipe

Lapwing

BIRD SPECIES

Resident ducks, cormorants and coots can be seen all year round. In winter, they are joined by geese and swans at the margins and golden plovers in the fields. February sees the arrival of 30,000 black-tailed godwits. Pintail ducks, greylag geese, lapwings and black-headed gulls also appear for a time, as do waders such as ruff, snipe, redshank and dunlin.

Golden plover

BIRD-WATCHER'S CHECKLIST

Road map C3. 🚆 *Angers, then taxi or hire car.* ℹ️ *Ligue pour la Protection des Oiseaux, 84 rue Blaise Pascal, Angers (02 41 44 44 22).* 📅 *Day, night and weekend outings including special trips for children.* 📷 *Reservations are required for LPO programmes.*

Best viewing area (Feb–late Jul): confluence of Loir and Sarthe rivers, southwest of Briollay. Take the D107 from Angers to Cantenay-Epinard. Turn right just before the village and follow signs for Le Vieux Cantenay. Return to the D107 via Vaux. Continue north to Noyant, where all of the little roads across the meadows lead to the River Sarthe. Return to Noyant and head for Les Chapelles and Soulaire-et-Bourg. Then take the D109 to Briollay if the road is passable.

Angers

Angers Cathedral carving

SITUATED ON THE River Maine, only 8 km (5 miles) before it joins the Loire, Angers was once the power base for Foulques Nerra *(see pp50–51)* and the other notorious medieval counts of Anjou. By the 12th century, under the rule of the Plantagenets, Angers became the regional capital of an empire stretching as far as Scotland. Today, it is a thriving university town, with wide boulevards, beautiful public gardens and narrow older streets evocative of its long history.

Exploring Angers

Angers is divided into two sections by the River Maine. The oldest part is on the left bank of the river, guarded by the fortress-like 13th-century **Château d'Angers** *(see pp74–5)*. Shielded inside the château's massive walls are the Apocalypse Tapestries, the oldest and largest of France's tapestries, dating from the 14th century *(see pp76–7)*. The **Cathédrale St-Maurice** is just a short walk from the château.

Angers has 46 timber-framed houses, most of them found in the old streets near the cathedral. The best of these is the **Maison d'Adam**, at No. 1 place Ste-Croix. This 15th-century merchant's house is decorated with carved wooden figures of sirens, musicians and lovers tucked into every angle. The extravagant decoration was a display of the owner's prosperity. Maison d'Adam is now a centre for the textile industry, but its exterior is its principal charm.

On the right bank of the River Maine, the old quarter of **La Doutre** (*"d'outre Maine"*, or "the other side of the Maine") is well worth a visit. Formerly an area of tradesmen's establishments, inhabited only by the poor, the district has now been restored and contains a number of well-preserved timber-framed buildings.

A rewarding stroll from rue Gay-Lussac to place de la Laiterie passes many of La Doutre's historic buildings. Included among them are the elegant **Hôtel des Pénitentes** (once a refuge for reformed prostitutes), a 12th-century **apothecary's house** and the restored church of **La Trinité**, which adjoins the ruins of Foulques Nerra's Romanesque **Abbaye du Ronceray** – a Benedictine abbey reserved for daughters of the nobility.

🔓 Cathédrale St-Maurice

4 rue St Christophe.
📞 02 41 87 58 45. ⭕ daily.
This striking cathedral was built at the end of the 12th century, although the central lantern tower was added during the Renaissance period. The façade's Gothic

Maison d'Adam, the best of Angers' timber-framed houses

sculptures are still impressive, although they have become heavily worn over the years and are shell-pocked.

The elegant Angevin vaulting in the nave and the transept is one of the best, and earliest, examples of its kind, and gives a dome-like shape to the high ceiling. The interior is lit through glowing stained glass, which includes a stunningly beautiful 15th-century rose window in the northern transept.

🏛 Musée des Beaux Arts

10 rue du Musée. 📞 02 41 88 64 65.
⭕ for renovation until at least 2005.
♿
The municipal art collection of Angers is housed in a fine 15th-century mansion, the Logis Barrault, which is currently being restored. There is an intriguing display of religious antiquities on the first floor, including a lapidary Cross of Anjou; a beautiful 13th-century copper-gilt mask, taken from the effigy of a woman; and sceptres from the abbeys at Toussaint and Fontevraud *(see pp86–7)*.

Among the paintings in the upper galleries are a number of portraits, including one of Agnès Sorel, mistress of Charles VII *(see p104)*; still lifes by Jean-Baptiste Chardin; *Les Génies des Arts*, a vast and amusing work by François Boucher; and Jean-Auguste-Dominique Ingres' *Paolo Malatesta and Francesca da Rimini*, which illustrates a scene from Dante's *Inferno*.

One of the many beautiful public gardens in Angers

Cointreau

Angers, the city of Cointreau, produces some 30 million bottles of the famous liqueur every year. The distillery was founded in 1849 by the Cointreau brothers, local confectioners well known around Angers for their exotic, curative tonics. But it was Edouard, the son of one of them, who created the original recipe. The flavour of this unique colourless liqueur is artfully based on sweet and bitter orange peels.

Visitors' Checklist

Road map C3. 226,000. pl de la Gare. pl de Molières. pl Kennedy (02 41 23 50 00). Wed & Sat. Festival d'Anjou (Jul).

⋔ Galerie David d'Angers

33 bis, rue Toussaint. 02 41 87 21 03. mid-Jun–mid-Sep: daily; mid-Sep–mid-Jun: Tue–Sun. public hols.

The glassed-over ruins of the 13th-century abbey church of Toussaint are filled with plaster casts of the work of local sculptor Pierre-Jean David (1788–1856), known as David d'Angers. His idealized busts and figures were much in demand as memorials for people such as the Marquis de Bonchamps (see p57). Enhanced by the well-lit gallery, they are forceful examples of Academic art.

Sculpture by David d'Angers

⋔ Musée Jean Lurçat et de la Tapisserie Contemporaine

4 bd Arago. 02 41 24 18 45/48. mid-Jun–mid-Sep: daily; mid-Sep–mid-Jun: Tue–Sun. public hols.

A Gothic masterpiece in La Doutre, this graceful building functioned as a hospital until 1875, the oldest surviving one in France. It was founded in 1175 by Henry II of England, and the Plantagenet coat of arms is displayed with the Anjou heraldry just inside the entrance to the delightful grounds. A reconstruction of the dispensary occupies one corner of the Salle des Malades, and a chapel and 12th-century cloisters can be reached through a door at the far end of the gallery. The Hôpital St-Jean now houses the works of the 20th-century artist Jean Lurçat, namely Le Chant du Monde, his masterpiece, and many of his vivid tapestries which inspired a renaissance in the art form (see p77).

⋔ Musée Cointreau

Bd des Brétonnières. 02 41 31 50 50. daily: 10.30am, 2.30pm & 4.30pm. Jan & public hols.

From a walkway high above the alambics and bottling machines, visitors can observe the production processes involved in the creation of Cointreau, in this superbly re-designed museum (inaugurated in 1999, in celebration of 150 years of production). The 2-hour tour takes you round the distillery, in the St. Barthélémy district of Angers, ending up with a dégustation of the famous orange-flavoured liqueur. Thousands of objects, documents, photos, publicity posters and films illustrate the long history of the company and its famous square bottle.

Angers Town Centre

Cathédrale St-Maurice ③
Château d'Angers ②
Galerie David d'Angers ⑤
Musée Jean Lurçat et de la Tapisserie Contemporaine ①
Maison d'Adam ④
Musée des Beaux-Arts (Logis Barrault) ⑥

0 metres 500
0 yards 500

Key

🚌 Bus terminus

🅿 Parking

ℹ Tourist information

⛪ Church

Château d'Angers

THE HUGE DRUM TOWERS and curtain walls of this powerful feudal fortress were built on the site of Count Foulques Nerra's stronghold between 1228 and 1240. The work was begun at the behest of Blanche of Castille, the mother of Louis IX and regent during his youth. Within the 650-m (2,100-ft) perimeter, later nobles developed a château lifestyle in almost playful contrast to the forbidding schist and limestone towers. The last duke of Anjou, King René I, added charming buildings, gardens, aviaries and a menagerie. After several centuries as a prison, the citadel-château now houses France's most famous tapestries.

One of the deer living in the dry moat

The Logis du Gouverneur was built in the 15th century and modified in the 18th century.

Moat gardens

★ Moat Gardens
The dry moat, which is 11 m (36 ft) deep and 30 m (98 ft) wide, is now filled with geometric flower beds.

Fortress Towers
The 17 towers rise up to 60 m (200 ft) in height. They lost their pepper pot roofs and were shortened as a delaying tactic, following royal orders to demolish them completely during the 16th century.

Formal gardens have been planted in the great courtyard.

The drawbridge leading to the Porte de la Ville (Town Gate) is the entrance to the château.

TIMELINE

1230–40 Fortress built on a rocky spur, where counts of Anjou had built older castles

1410 Louis II and Yolande of Aragon reconstruct chapel and Logis Royal

Henry III

1945 Allied bombers damage fortress, in use as a German munitions base

1648–52 Louis XIV turns fortress into a prison

1200	1300	1400	1500	1600	1700	1800	1900

1360 Louis I of Anjou cuts doors and windows to relieve the grimness of the walls

1450–65 René I renovates interior, adding gardens and new buildings

1585 Fortress taken by Huguenots. Henri III wants towers demolished but governor merely lowers them

1875 Declared a historic monument

1952–54 Bernard Vitry builds gallery to house Apocalypse Tapestries

★ Apocalypse Tapestries
Bernard Vitry's modern Galerie de l'Apocalypse displays the Apocalypse Tapestries (see pp76–7).

The Roi Window depicts René I, king of Naples, and his wife, Jeanne de Laval, kneeling before the Virgin.

VISITORS' CHECKLIST

Prom du Bout du Monde. 🚌
📞 02 41 87 43 47.
🕐 May–Aug: 9:30am–6:30pm daily; Sep–Apr: 10am–5:30pm.
⬤ 1 Jan, 1 May, 1 Nov, 11 Nov, 25 Dec. 💷 📷
🌐 www.monum.fr

Walkways along the wide walls stretch for more than a kilometre (¾ mile). There are fine views of the town, as well as some beautiful gardens.

The towers are ascended by spiral staircases.

The Logis Royal is home to the beautiful Millefleurs tapestries *(see p77)*.

★ Ducal Oratory
The ducal oratory overlooks the Chapelle St-Geneviève. Equipped with a fireplace and decorated with statues of past owners of the château, it was used by the duke and members of his family.

★ Châtelet
Built in 1450 by René I, the gatehouse still retains its charming pepper pot roofs.

STAR FEATURES

★ Apocalypse Tapestries

★ Ducal Oratory

★ Moat Gardens

★ Châtelet

The Tapestries at Angers

THE APOCALYPSE TAPESTRIES, made in the 14th century for Duke Louis I of Anjou, illustrate the visions of St John from the Book of Revelation. In the turmoil of the French Revolution, the tapestries were thrown out, cut up and used for anything from bed canopies to horse blankets. Restoration began in the mid-19th century. Acclaimed as a masterpiece, the surviving sections of this work stretch for 103 m (338 ft) along a specially-built gallery in the Château d'Angers. Nearly 600 years after their creation, they inspired Jean Lurçat to design his own tapestry sequence, called *Le Chant du Monde*.

Detailed Work
Each of the devils devouring Babylon has a distinct character. The tapestries were woven so skilfully that the front and the back are almost mirror images.

An angel dictates to St John in one of the best-preserved scenes. Elsewhere, the green textiles have faded to beige.

St John appears as the narrator of each vision.

THE FALL OF BABYLON

The Apocalypse Tapestries were woven in 1375–83 in Parisian workshops. Designed by Hennequin de Bruges, who was inspired by Carolingian manuscript illuminations, they depict the end of the world and the coming of a New Jerusalem. The original 90 panels were arranged in 6 chapters, each with an introductory panel and 14 scenes. Scene 66 depicts the Fall of Babylon: "Babylon the Great is fallen, is fallen, and is become the habitation of devils" (Rev. 18:2).

Water is changed to poisonous wormwood at the blowing of the third trumpet in this cataclysmic scene.

Mille Fleurs Tapestries
Displayed in the Logis Royal, these late 15th-century Flemish tapestries are still vibrantly coloured.

Le Chant du Monde

Jean Lurçat (1892–1966)

THE VAST, VAULTED INTERIOR of the Musée Jean Lurçat *(see p73)* provides a stunning background to *The Song of the World*. This piece, which stretches for 79 m (260 ft) around three sides of the hall, was Lurçat's response to the Apocalypse Tapestries, which he saw for the first time in 1937. The ten panels are 4 m (13 ft) high and were woven from wool at workshops in Aubusson between 1957 and 1963. Thematically, the images move from the horrors of Nazi genocide and the bombing of Hiroshima to the conquest of space, conceived as the dawning of a new age.

"Ornamentos Sagrados" from Lurçat's *Le Chant du Monde* tapestry

The tumbling towers of Babylon reveal a nest of demons.

Blue backgrounds alternate with red, providing continuity through the series.

THE ART OF TAPESTRY

In medieval times, tapestries were a symbol of luxury, commissioned by royal and noble families to adorn châteaux and churches. Hung on the thick stone walls, they helped to keep the vast rooms warm by preventing drafts.

Medieval tapestry weaver

Paris and Flanders were the centres of tapestry work in the 14th century, where highly skilled weavers followed an artist's full-size drawing, called a "cartoon". Threads were stretched vertically (the warp) on a loom to the length of the finished piece, then coloured threads (the weft) were woven horizontally across them.

Tapestry-making declined from the 16th century, but the 20th century has seen a revival, with artists such as Pablo Picasso and Henri Matisse experimenting in the medium.

Coloured tapestry threads at the Manufacture St-Jean in Aubusson

Brissac's wine cellars

Château de Brissac ❾

Brissac-Quincé. **Road map** C3.
🚊 *Angers, then taxi.* 🚌 📞 *02 41 91 22 21.* ⏰ *Apr–Jun & Sep–Oct: Wed–Mon; Jul–Aug: daily; Nov–Mar: groups only by appt.* 📷 🅿️
🌐 *www.brissac.net*

THE CHATEAU of the dukes of Brissac, towering above the River Aubance 18 km (11 miles) southeast of Angers, is the tallest along the Loire, and is perhaps the grandest still in private hands. Ownership has passed down a line going back to Charles de Cossé, governor of Paris and marshal of France. His death in 1621 halted the completion of a programme to build a vast palace set upon on the ruins of an earlier fortress.

On the entrance façade, an ornate, 17th-century, domed pavilion soars to 37 m (120 ft) between two 15th-century towers. Ten of the 150 rooms are open to the public and are filled with furniture, paintings and tapestries. Among the most striking is the Salle des Gardes, which is 32 m (105 ft) long and is decorated with Aubusson tapestries and gilded ceilings. The room is lit through the distinctive paned windows that are a feature of architect Jacques Corbineau's work.

Other memorable rooms are Louis XIII's bedroom and an 1883 opera theatre, still used for concerts. In the château's picture gallery hangs a 19th-century portrait of Madame Clicquot, matriarch of the famous champagne house and a distant ancestor of the present duke. At the end of the visit, the duke's own wines can be tasted in cellars dating from the 11th century.

Gennes ❿

Road map C3. 🚊 *1,900.* 🚌 *Saumur or Les Rosiers-sur-Loire* 🚌 ℹ️ *square de l'Europe (02 41 51 84 14).* 🛍️ *Tue.*
🌐 *www.gennestourisme.com*

DURING THE Gallo-Roman period (*see pp48–9*) Gennes, on the south bank of the River Loire, was an important religious and commercial centre. The largest **amphitheatre** in western France was built on a hillside here more than 1,800 years ago and was used from the 1st to the 3rd centuries for gladiatorial contests. A restoration project, started in 1985, has revealed the sandstone walls and brick tiers of a stadium that seated at least 5,000 spectators and included changing rooms and an efficient drainage system. In front of the arena, which measures 2,160 sq m (2,600 sq yds), marshlands on the Avort river were probably flooded for aquatic combats and displays.

The area around Gennes is also very rich in Neolithic sites. Among the 20 ancient burial chambers and menhirs nearby is the **Dolmen de la Madeleine**, one of the largest in France. Used as a bakery

The medieval Eglise St-Vétérin in the town of Gennes

until recently, it can be found 1 km (1100 yds) east, past Gennes' medieval **Eglise St-Vétérin** on the D69.

An excellent panoramic view can be seen from the tower of **St-Eusèbe**, a ruined church dating from the 11th to the 15th centuries, sited on a knoll above the village. Beside the old nave is a moving memorial to cadets of the Saumur cavalry school (*see p83*) who died trying to prevent the German army crossing the Loire in June 1940.

A bronze statue of Mercury has been discovered on the hill, and this seems to suggest that a temple to the Roman god may have stood here in the Gallo-Roman period.

🏛 **Amphithéâtre**
📞 *02 41 51 55 04.*
⏰ *Jul–Aug: daily; Apr–Jun & Sep: Sun & public hols pm only.* 🅿️
🏛 **Dolmen de la Madeleine**
📞 *02 41 51 84 14.* ⏰ *daily.*
♿ *restricted.*

The Neolithic Dolmen de la Madeleine, near Gennes

Environs: At L'Orbière, 4 km (2½ miles) from Gennes, the sculptor Jacques Warminsky has created a monumental work, named *L'Hélice Terrestre (The Earth's Helix)*. Occupying a surface area of 875 sq m (1,050 sq yds), this spiralling labyrinth has been cut into the soft limestone hillside. Warminsky and his assistants have carved out a series of galleries, some reaching 14 m (46 ft) below the surface, which expand or contract into organic and mineral forms.

The helix continues its path out to the exterior, where it becomes a spiral assemblage of reversed forms. The two spaces are complementary and represent the universal philosophy of the artist.

🏛 **L'Hélice Terrestre**
L'Orbière, St-Georges-des-Sept-Voies. **Road map** C3. 🚉 Saumur. 🚌 Gennes, then taxi. 📞 02 41 95 92. ⬜ May–Sep: daily; Oct–Apr: daily pm only. 📷

Artist Jacques Warminsky at work on *L'Hélice Terrestre*

Cunault ⓫

Road map C3. 🏠 1,120. 🚌 Saumur. 🛈 pl Victor Dialand (02 41 67 92 55). 🎵 Les Heures Musicales (Jul–Aug: 5pm Sun), Mois de L'Orgue (May: Sun 5pm).

C UNAULT's pale limestone priory church, the **Eglise Notre-Dame**, has rightly been called the most majestic of all the Romanesque churches in Anjou, if not the whole of the Loire Valley. In the 12th century, Benedictine monks from Tournus in Burgundy built the church in this small village on the south bank of the Loire. They incorporated the bell-tower, dating from the 11th century, from an earlier building. A short spire was added in the 15th century.

Cunault is the longest Romanesque church without a transept in France. Inside, the first impression is of simplicity and elegance. The height of the pillars is impressive; they are topped with 223 carved capitals, decorated with fabulous beasts, demons and religious motifs, and are placed high enough so as not to interfere with the pure architectural lines. Binoculars are needed to see details.

Three aisles of equal width were made to accommodate the crowds of pilgrims who travelled to the church to see its relics, which include one revered as the wedding ring of the Virgin Mary, and the floor is deeply worn beside a 12th-century marble stoup at the foot of the entrance steps. Towards the chancel, the ambulatory is floored with scalloped terracotta tiles. Traces of 15th-century frescoes remain, including a figure of St Christopher.

Other treasures include some impressive furniture in oak and ash, a 13th-century carved wooden reliquary and a painted 15th-century statue representing St Catherine.

The central aisle of Cunault's majestic 12th-century church

CULTIVATED MUSHROOMS

Around 75 per cent of French cultivated mushrooms come from Anjou. The damp, dark caves in the tufa cliffs along the Loire are the perfect environment for the *champignons de Paris*, so called because they were first cultivated in disused quarries in the Paris region before production began in the Loire Valley in the late 19th century. Today, mushroom cultivation is a thriving business, employing around 5,000 people in the region. Growers have been diversifying in recent years, cultivating more exotic mushrooms such as *pleurottes* and *shiitake*, in response to demand from food-lovers.

Oyster mushrooms, known as *pleurottes*

Street-by-Street: Saumur ⓬

THE STORYBOOK CHATEAU is set on a hill high above the town, making it easy for visitors to locate Saumur's old quarter, which lies mainly between the château, the river and the main street running straight ahead from the central bridge over the Loire. The twisting streets that wind up and down the hill on which the château is built merit exploration. Saumur's modest size, which suits sightseeing on foot, is only one of the many charms of this friendly town.

Theatre
Saumur's theatre, which opened in the late 19th century, was modelled on the Odéon in Paris.

Rue St-Jean is the heart of Saumur's main shopping area.

The Hôtel des Abbesses de Fontevraud, at No. 6 rue de l'Ancienne-Messagerie, was built in the 17th century and has a marvellous spiral staircase.

Maison du Roi
This pretty Renaissance building at No. 33 rue Dacier once housed royalty but is now the headquarters of the Saumur Red Cross. In the courtyard is a plaque to the much-loved René I of Anjou, who often held court at Saumur.

RUE MOLIEE
RUE ST-JEAN
RUE CORNEILLE
RUE CANDRIÈRE
RUE DU MA
RUE DACIER
RUE DES PAIENS
RUE DU TEMPLE
GRANDE RUE
RUE DU PRECHE

STAR SIGHTS

★ **Château de Saumur**

★ **Eglise St-Pierre**

| 0 metres | 50 |
| 0 yards | 50 |

Hôtel de Ville
The town hall was originally a manor house forming part of the city's fortified river wall. Built in 1508, subsequent restorations and additions have been in keeping with its Gothic style.

VISITORS' CHECKLIST

Road map C3. 32,000.
av David d'Angers.
pl St-Nicolas. pl de la Bilange (02 41 40 20 60).
Sat. Carrousel Cavalry (Jul).

Place St-Pierre
Saumur's oldest half-timbered houses, dating from the 15th century, are situated in place St-Pierre (Nos. 3, 5 and 6).

★ Eglise St-Pierre
First erected in the 12th and 13th centuries, and completed during the 15th and 16th centuries, this church has a fascinating collection of tapestries.

Maison des Compagnons
is a 15th-century building at the top of La Montée du Fort, which has been restored by a guild of stonemasons whose apprentices can be seen at work.

★ Château de Saumur
Saumur's château is situated next to the Butte des Moulins, a small hill that was once covered with windmills. Views of the town and the Loire and Thouet rivers can be seen from the top of the watchtower.

KEY

– – – Suggested route

Exploring Saumur

Today, SAUMUR is best known for its sparkling wines, mushrooms and fine horse riders. It was once an important port and a centre of Protestant scholarship in the 16th and 17th centuries, until the revocation of the Edict of Nantes in 1685 forced many Protestants to leave. This rich legacy is easy to see during a walk through the attractive streets of the old quarter.

Panel from the 15th-century choir stalls in the Eglise St-Pierre

The old quarter

At the heart of Saumur's old quarter stands the **Eglise St-Pierre**, which was built in the late 12th century. Its treasures include the beautifully carved 15th-century wooden stalls in the choir, and the magnificent 16th-century tapestries of the lives of Sts Peter and Florent. The latter was an influential figure in the monastic history of the region. He is depicted being rescued from Roman

The façade of the Eglise Notre-Dame de Nantilly

persecution, slaying a dragon and founding a monastery.

Nearby, the **Grande Rue**'s limestone and slate houses reflect Saumur's prosperity in the late 16th century under Protestant rule. The "Huguenot Pope", Philippe Duplessis-Mornay, who governed the town between 1589 and 1621, owned the house at No. 45.

The oldest church in Saumur, **Notre-Dame de Nantilly**, was the town's principal place of worship for centuries. It too has a collection of 16th-17th-century tapestries, as well as carved capitals and an epitaph composed by the poet-king René I (*see p53*) to his childhood nurse inscribed on the third pillar on nave's south side.

🏛 Musée de la Figurine

Route de Montsoreau.
📞 02 41 83 13 32. ⭕ daily (Nov–Feb: ring to check visits). ● 25 Dec, 1 Jan. 🔲
Transferred from the gunpowder room of the Château, 10,000 lead figures from around the world have found new life within the caves of Gratien & Meyer, displayed imaginatively in cut-away barrels with glass fronts.

⚜ Château de Saumur

📞 02 41 40 24 40. ⭕ Apr–Sep: daily; Oct–Mar: Wed–Mon. ● 25 Dec, 1 Jan. 🔲
The famous miniature of this château in *Les Très Riches Heures du Duc de Berry* (*see p23*) shows a white fairy-tale palace. The château was built by Louis I, Duke of Anjou, in the second half of the 14th century. It was constructed on the base of an earlier fortification. The glittering mass of chimney

Skyline of the Château de Saumur

stacks and pinnacles was later simplified to a more sturdy skyline of shortened pencil towers, but the shape of the château remains graceful. In the ducal apartments, the window bays have romantic views of the River Loire. The powerful-looking outbuildings that surround the château recall its later, although less pleasant, roles as a Protestant bastion, state prison and finally army barracks.

The château houses two very different museums. The **Musée des Arts Décoratifs** is a collection formed by Count Charles Lair, a native of Saumur, who left it to the château in 1919. It includes paintings, many fine tapestries, furniture, statuettes and ceramics that date from the 13th up to the 19th century.

Statuette from the Musée des Arts Décoratifs

Horse-lovers will find a great deal to delight them in a second museum, the **Musée du Cheval**, housed beneath the timbered ceilings of the château's attics. Founded by a veterinarian at Saumur's cavalry school, its exhibits trace the development of the horse and its relationship with man from prehistoric times to the present day. They include a wonderful Russian carved sleigh and the skeleton of the unbeaten Flying Fox, winner of the 1899 Epsom Derby and sire of 20th-century French champions. There is also a collection of beautiful saddles from all around the world.

🏛 Musée des Blindés

1043 rte de Fontevraud. **(** *02 41 83 69 99.* ⬭ *daily.* ⬤ *1 Jan, 25 Dec.* 🏷 ♿

This barn-like museum houses hundreds of tanks. Owned by the Cavalry and Armoured Vehicles School, it has on display more historic tanks and armoured personnel carriers in working order than any other international military collection.

Beginning with a FT 17 Renault dating from 1917 and moving through the German World War II panzers to the monsters produced today, the museum offers a chance to see at close quarters these veterans of many conflicts.

⌂ Bagneux Dolmen

56 rue du Dolmen, Bagneux. **(** *02 41 50 23 02.* ⬛ *Saumur.* ⬭ *Thu–Tue.* ⬤ *24 Dec, 1 Jan.* 🏷 ♿

Saumur's main street leads to the suburb of Bagneux. Here, in a local bar's garden, one unexpectedly finds one of the most impressive Neolithic burial chambers in Europe. Visitors can sip drinks in the garden, absorb the impact of the dolmen and marvel at the massive sandstone slabs, some weighing 40 tonnes, that were dragged, tilted and wedged into position 5,000 years ago *(see p48–9)*.

A signpost for the Bagneux dolmen

ENVIRONS: The village of St-Hilaire-St-Florent, 2 km (1½ miles) northwest of Saumur on the D751, is well worth a visit for its museums and the famous Cadre Noir riding

A 1917 Renault tank in the collection of the Musées des Blindés

school. It also has a number of wine cellars where visitors can taste and buy the famous Saumur Brut, a sparkling wine that is produced by the *champagne method*. The chalky tufa stone, contained in the soil on which local grapes are grown, is said to add to the wine's natural tendency to sparkle.

🏛 Musée du Champignon

Route de Gennes, St-Hilaire-St-Florent. **(** *02 41 50 31 55.* ⬭ *Feb–mid-Nov: daily.* 🏷 ♿

This unique museum takes visitors through a network of limestone caves. Displays show how mushrooms that are grown from spores in bagged or boxed compost thrive in the high humidity and constant temperature of this environment *(see p79)*. The museum has an excellent collection of live mushroom species, as well as of fossils found during quarrying. On offer, and worth tasting, is a local speciality, *gallipettes farcies*. These are large mushrooms, stuffed with a variety of fillings.

🏛 Musée du Masque

Rue de l'Abbaye, St-Hilaire-St-Florent. **(** *02 41 50 75 26.* ⬛ ⬭ *Easter–Oct: daily; Nov–Easter: Mon–Fri pm only; groups by appt all year: phone 02 41 50 26 54 .* 🏷 ♿

Saumur is a leading producer of masks, and this museum, attached to the Jules César mask factory in St-Hilaire-St-Florent, is a delight. The factory specializes in film stars, royalty and politicians, making both caricatures and portraits. In the museum are fantasy tableaux showing costumed models in circus, carnival, stage and film masks, some dating from the 1870s.

Tintin in the Musée du Masque

🏛 Ecole Nationale d'Equitation

Terrefort, St-Hilaire-St-Florent. **(** *02 41 53 50 60.* ⬭ *Apr–Sep: Thu–Sat am; Oct–Mar: groups only, by appt. Mornings: show (except Aug) and buildings; afternoons: buildings only.* 🏷 ♿ ⓦ *www.cadrenoir.com*

The National Riding School, founded in 1814, is world famous for its team, known as the Cadre Noir because of the riders' elegant black and gold ceremonial uniforms. The Cadre Noir's horses are trained in a distinctive style of dressage, which was first practised in the 19th century. They are taught perfect balance and control and learn choreographed movements that show their natural grace.

During the summer months, visitors can enter the academy team's quarters and watch a training session. There are also regular performances of the spectacular show.

The 5,000-year-old Bagneux dolmen near Saumur

Montreuil-Bellay ⓮

Road map C4. 👥 *4,300.* 🚉
Saumur 🚏 ℹ *pl du Concorde (02 41
52 32 39.* 🛒 *Tue & Sun (May–Sep).*
🌐 *www.saumur-tourisme.com*

COMBINING an ancient
village and a fascinating
feudal château, Montreuil-
Bellay, 18 km (11 miles) south
of Saumur, is one of the most
attractive towns in Anjou. The
château complex occupies a
site which was first fortified in
the 11th century by Foulques
Nerra and besieged by Geoffrey Plantagenet during the
following century. In the 13th
century it was surrounded by
strong walls, with a grand tow-
ered entrance (known as the
Château-Vieux) and 11 other
towers. Inside the ramparts is
a collection of mainly late 15th-
century buildings, looking over

**Frescoes in the oratory of the
Château de Montreuil-Bellay**

landscaped terraces falling to
the pretty River Thouet.

The Château-Neuf is an
elegant Renaissance-fronted
building, begun in the late
15th century. The turret was
made famous by the infamous
French noblewoman, Anne
de Longueville (1619–79),
who rode her horse to the
top of its spiral staircase.

The interior of the château
is superbly furnished and has
a number of fireplaces in the
Flamboyant style as well as
splendid painted and carved
ceilings. Frescoes dating from
the 15th century, depicting
the Crucifixion and angelic
musicians, adorn the touch-
ingly beautiful, small oratory.
The medieval kitchens, with
much of their 18th-century
cooking equipment, are said
to be modelled on those of
the earlier Fontevraud Abbey
(see pp86–7).

♣ **Château de
Montreuil-Bellay**
📞 *02 41 52 33 06.* ⏰ *Apr–Oct:
daily; Nov–Mar: Wed–Mon.* ♿

Troglodyte Tour ⓯

CAVES, CUT INTO THE TUFA cliffs beside
the Loire and other limestone-rich
areas in Anjou, are used as dovecotes,
chapels, farms, wine cellars and even
homes. These so-called "troglodyte"
dwellings are extremely old, with some
dating back to the 12th century, and
have hardly changed over the
centuries. They are now
fashionable again as
résidences secondaires for
wealthy Parisians. Life in
and among these caves
is the subject of this
fascinating tour.

Dénézé-sous-Doué ⑥
In these underground
caves, carved by
Protestant stonemasons
during the 16th-century
Wars of Religion, more
than 400 figures are
chiselled into the walls,
floors and ceilings.

**Carved figures at Dénézé-
sous-Doué**

La Fosse ⑦
This inhabited troglodyte
farmhouse is open
to visitors.

GENNES

0 kilometres   3

0 miles   3

Rochemenier ⑤
This former troglodyte
farming community has
been turned into a
museum displaying
underground
farmyards, barns,
houses and a simple
rock chapel.

Doué-la-Fontaine ④
The rue des Perrières was
excavated from a stratum of shell
marl *(faluns)*; its "cathedral"
vaults were dug vertically from
the top. The town also has an
amphitheatre cut from the rock
and an outstanding zoo in the
old quarries.

Montfort

Troglodyte houses at Rochemenier

Château de Montsoreau ⑭

Road map C3. 🚉 *Saumur, then taxi.* 🚌 ☎ *02 41 51 70 25.* 🕐 *Apr–Oct: Wed–Mon.* 🌐 www.chateau-montsoreau.com

A FORBIDDING battlemented wall is all that remains of the four-sided château built in 1455 for Jean de Chambes and his wife, Jeanne Chabot, heiress to the village of Montsoreau. The view from within the château's former courtyard, however, is far from forbidding: a beautiful octagonal palm-vaulted staircase was added to the northeast of the courtyard around 1520. It carries a frieze, featuring monkeys labouring at its construction, under the heading, *Je le feray,* or, *I will make it.*

Château de Montsoreau on the River Loire

In Alexandre Dumas' novel, *La Dame de Montsoreau,* the jealous Count, Charles de Chambes, forces his wife to lure her lover, the governor of Anjou, Bussy d'Amboise, to the château, where he is brutally murdered. The story is true: the characters lived in the château de Montsoreau. The murder itself, however, took place at a château on the opposite bank of the river, now long-since vanished.

KEY

═══ Tour route

═══ Other roads

Souzay ①
East of Saumur, the little "château" at Souzay, like many local houses, projects from the cliff. Its back rooms are cut directly into the rock face.

The "château" at Souzay

SAUMUR

Distré

Varrains

D947

D93

D205

D9

D405

D162

D162

Turquant ②
A chapel, a restaurant and extensive wine cellars lie behind the smartly-cut façades at La Grande Vignolle.

St-Cyr-en-Bourg ③
The location of one of the few remaining active tufa quarries, this vast underground network of galleries is owned by the St-Cyr wine co-operative, which makes a full range of Saumur *appellations* in these caves.

TIPS FOR DRIVERS

Tour length: 52 km (32 miles) in one day, starting from Saumur.
Stopping-off points: Doué la Fontaine is a pleasant place to stop for lunch: Restaurant La France and Auberge le Bienvenue are excellent restaurants.

Abbaye de Fontevraud ⑯

Stained glass in church

FONTEVRAUD ABBEY, founded in 1101 by the hermit Robert d'Arbrissel for both women and men, is the largest and most extraordinary of its kind in France. It was run for nearly 700 years by aristocratic abbesses, almost half of them royal-born. They governed a monks' priory outside the main walls, and four distinct communities of nuns and lay sisters, ranging from rich widows to repentant prostitutes, as well as a leper colony and an infirmary. Ongoing restoration work is diligently removing traces of the ravages of the Revolution and the subsequent 150 years, when this "queen of abbeys" was used as a prison.

The grand refectory, with its Renaissance ribbed vaulting, is 60 m (200 ft) long.

Nursing sisters of the St Benoît order cared for invalids in this section of the abbey.

★ Chapter House Paintings
The paintings in the Chapter House date from the 16th century. However, some figures were added later.

★ Plantagenet Effigies
These four effigies (gisants), each a realistic portrait, are displayed in the nave of the abbey church.

Grand-Moûtier
The cloisters of the main convent are the largest, and possibly the finest, in France. They have Gothic and Renaissance vaulting and upper galleries built in the 19th century.

STAR FEATURES

- ★ Plantagenet Effigies
- ★ Chapter House Paintings
- ★ Romanesque Kitchens

THE RESTING PLACE OF THE PLANTAGENETS

The medieval painted effigy of Henry Plantagenet, count of Anjou and king of England (1133–1189), lies beside that of his wife, Eleanor of Aquitaine, who died here in 1204. With them are the effigies of their son, King Richard the Lionheart (1157–1199), and Isabelle, wife of his brother, King John. In all, 15 of the family are buried here.

Effigies of Eleanor of Aquitaine and Henry II

St-Lazare Priory
Built as a hospital for lepers, the priory is now a 52-room hotel. It has a Romanesque chapel and an elegant 18th-century staircase.

Former orangery in a wing of the Abbess's Palace

Central chamber

Fireplace

Original floor plan of the kitchens

★ Romanesque Kitchens
The medieval kitchen-tower originally had eight alcoves. The six visible today served as fireplaces, and the towers were used for smoking meat and fish.

Reception and information centre

TIMELINE

1119 Pope consecrates abbey church and blesses cemetery	**1177** Henry II founds dependent order in England	**1457** Marie de Bretagne begins abbey reforms	**1793** Revolutionaries destroy monks' priory	**1973** Centre Culturel de l'Ouest opens
	1204 Eleanor of Aquitaine dies in abbey and is buried there		**1561** Huguenots desecrate abbey	

1100	1300	1500	1700	1900

1115 First Abbess appointed to oversee each of the five orders	*17th-century abbess, Gabrielle de Rochechouart*		**1792** Order suppressed by Revolutionaries	**1804** Napoléon converts main buildings into state prison
1099–1101 Order of Fontevraud founded by Robert d'Abrissel (1047–1117)				**1963** Prison closed, restoration begins

TOURAINE

OURAINE IS KNOWN *chiefly for the magnificent white châteaux strung out along the broad Loire and its tributaries. Added to these are its rich history and fertile landscape, making it the archetypal Loire Valley region. The rolling terrain and lush forests that once attracted the kings and queens of France continue to work their charm over visitors from all around the world today.*

The feudal castles that still exist, at Loches and Chinon for example, remind visitors that this now tranquil region was once a battleground on which the warring counts of Blois and Anjou staged many an epic encounter. It was also here, at Chinon, that Joan of Arc managed to bully the future Charles VII into raising the army that she would lead to victory over the English.

François I brought the influence of the Italian Renaissance to France and set a fashion in architecture that produced the unforgettable châteaux of this region. The most magical – the delicate Azay-le-Rideau, the majestic Chenonceau, and Villandry with its extraordinary formal gardens – were built during this period. At the end of the 16th century, however, Touraine ceased to be a playground for the aristocracy, and its people then settled into the peaceful, unhurried routine that still prevails.

Tours, at the heart of the region, makes a natural base for visitors, who can enjoy its sensitively restored, medieval old town and marvel at the Cathédrale St-Gatien, a Gothic masterpiece.

The rolling terrain and gentle climate of Touraine encourage outdoor pursuits, including hiking, boating and fishing. The area is also famous for its *primeurs*, early fruit and vegetables, such as white asparagus, grown on its low-lying, fertile soils. Its many wines, including the well-known *appellations* of Bourgueil, Chinon and Vouvray, are the perfect accompaniment to the region's excellent cuisine.

A view of the Château de Chinon, on a cliff above the River Vienne

◁ The rooftops of Le Grand-Pressigny, as seen from high on the hill on which the town is built

Exploring Touraine

CRISS-CROSSED BY RIVERS great and small, Touraine sits regally at the heart of the Loire Valley. Châteaux are distributed along the paths of the rivers: Langeais and Amboise by the Loire itself; Ussé, Azay-le-Rideau and Loches by the gentle Indre; and Chenonceau gracefully straddling the Cher. Tours, the main town in the region, is also on the Loire. The Gâtine Tourangelle to the north of the river was once a magnificent forest but was felled progressively from the 11th century by local people in search of wood and arable land. However, small pockets of woodland remain, delightful for walking and picnicking.

Candes-St-Martin, with its 12th- to 13th-century church

KEY

▬	Motorway
▬	Major road
▭	Minor road
▬	Scenic route
▭	River
☀	Viewpoint

GETTING AROUND

Tours is the natural hub of the region. The TGV from Paris takes an hour to St-Pierre-des-Corps, followed by a five-minute shuttle service to the centre of Tours. It is possible to rent a car either from Tours or St-Pierre-des-Corps. The A10 is the fastest route from Paris by car. The N152, running east– west along the north bank of the Loire, is the easiest way to get across the region. The smaller D751 along the south bank passes through attractive countryside. The prettiest drives, however, follow the banks of the Indre.

One of Touraine's renowned vineyards

Le Mans

CHATEAU-LA-VALLIERE

Lac de Pincemaille

CHAMPCHEVRIER

LUYNES
3

CINQ-MARS-LA-PILE
2

LANGEAIS
1

4
VILLAN

BOURGUEIL

AZAY-LE-RIDEAU **5**

Angers

9 USSE
10
11 SAC
VILLAINES
LES-ROCH

8
CANDES-ST-MARTIN

6 CHINON

7 LA DEVINIERE

D760

12 RICHELIEU

Châtellerault

0 kilometres 10

0 miles 10

A field of poppies near Vouvray

Chapel of the Château de Langeais, with its curved, wood ceiling

Château de Langeais ❶

Road map D3. 🚆 📞 *02 47 96 72 60.* ⬜ *daily.* ⬛ *25 Dec.* ♿

THE FEUDAL Château de Langeais, looming up in the centre of the small town, was built for King Louis XI between 1465 and 1490 by his treasurer, Jean Bourré. It stands on the site of an earlier fortress built by the fearsome Foulques Nerra (*see p50*), of which only the rectangular keep remains.

Langeais' forbidding outer walls, towers, drawbridge and heavily machicolated sentry walk contrast strongly with its elegant interior courtyard. The whole has remained virtually unaltered over the centuries. Unlike many of the châteaux in the region, Langeais is largely furnished in keeping with its period, offering a fascinating picture of aristocratic life in the late Middle Ages and Renaissance. Its collection of 15th- and 16th-century furniture, paintings and tapestries was amassed in the late 19th century by its last private owner, the Alsace banker and philanthropist, Jacques Siegfried.

Among the treasures in the castle is the wedding chest brought by the 14-year-old Anne of Brittany when she married the tiny, hunchbacked Charles VIII here in the early hours of 6 December 1491. A waxwork tableau re-creates this clandestine event – both were already betrothed to others – and includes a copy of Anne's cloth-of-gold wedding gown, lined with 160 sable skins.

From the castle's parapets visitors can view the small town below, which has a good Sunday morning food market selling the delicious local melons in season.

The Gallo-Roman tower near Cinq-Mars-la-Pile

Château de Cinq-Mars-la-Pile ❷

Road map D3. 🚆 📞 *02 47 96 40 49.* ⬜ *Jul & Aug: Wed–Mon; 16 Sep–Oct, Mar–Jun: Sat & Sun.* ⬛ *2nd & 3rd wk Mar; 3rd & 4th wk Oct.* ♿

THE MOST FAMOUS inhabitant of the castle of Cinq-Mars was Henri Ruzé d'Effiat, Marquis de Cinq-Mars, and the eponymous hero of a novel by the Touraine writer Alfred de Vigny. The marquis, a favourite of King Louis XIII, rashly became involved in a plot against Louis' minister, Cardinal Richelieu, and was beheaded in 1642, aged 22. Richelieu ordered the castle at Cinq-Mars to be truncated – it is said that even the trees had their crowns chopped off. A pair of towers remain, each with three vaulted chambers, surrounded by an extremely wide moat. The château's fragrant, romantic gardens are adorned with topiary.

The *Pile* in the town's name refers to a strange Gallo-Roman brick tower, more

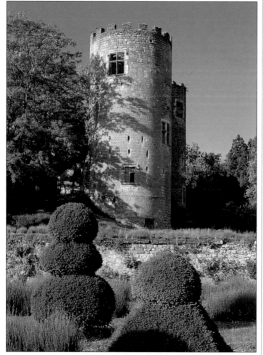

Towers of the Château de Cinq-Mars-la-Pile

Luynes' imposing château, dominating the village below

than 30 m (98 ft) high, on a ridge just east of the village. The south side of the tower, whose purpose and precise date are a mystery, was decorated with 12 multi-coloured brick panels, laid out in a geometric design, four of which are still intact today.

Luynes ❸

Road map D3. 🏠 4,800. 🚌 Tours, then bus. 🚍 **ℹ** 9 rue Alfred Baugé (02 47 55 77 14). 🛒 Sat.

Brooding over this pretty little village is a château, originally called Maillé after the noble owners who rebuilt it in the early 13th century. Not open to the public, it is still inhabited by descendants of the first Duc de Luynes, who bought it in 1619. With its stout towers, the château looks much as it did in the Middle Ages. The old town developed to the south of the château, and its 15th-century wooden market hall remains.

The remaining 44 arches of a **Gallo-Roman aqueduct** can be seen 1.5 km (1 mile) northeast of Luynes. Standing in isolation amid fields, they are a striking sight.

The wealthy Maillé family also owned a feudal castle on the site of the **Château de Champchevrier**, 10 km (6 miles) northwest of Luynes. The present Renaissance manor house, with various 18th-century additions, is set in a lush forest. Its elegant rooms are beautifully furnished, with particularly fine family portraits and Beauvais tapestries. A pack of hounds is kept at the château, and demonstrations of their skills are regularly staged.

♣ Château de Champchevrier

Cléré-les-Pins. **📞** 02 47 24 93 93. ◯ May–Jun: Sat, Sun & public hols; Jul–Sep: daily; Oct–Apr: groups by appt. 🏷 🎫 🔥 grd flr only.

The Chambre Royale in the Château de Champchevrier

LIFE IN A MEDIEVAL CHÂTEAU

During times of peace, life in a medieval château took on a pleasant routine. To fill the long winter days, nobles played board games, such as chess and draughts, or cards. Ladies, when they were not playing music or embroidering, had dwarves to entertain them, while the court jester kept banquet guests amused by making fun of everyone, even the king. Mystery plays (dramas based on the life of Christ) were very popular and cycles of these plays often lasted for several weeks. Outdoor pursuits enjoyed during the summer included bowling, archery and ball games, but it was the tournaments, with jousting and sword-play, that provoked the most excitement. Hunting was also favoured by kings and nobles and much practised in the woods and forests of the Loire Valley.

The illumination for August from *Les Très Riches Heures du Duc de Berry*

Château de Villandry **❹**

★ **Garden of Love**
Flower designs here symbolize four types of love: tragic, adulterous, tender and passionate.

Jeune Infante by Pantoja de la Cruz

T HE CHÂTEAU DE VILLANDRY, dating from the late Renaissance (1536), has an almost Classical elegance. But it is most famous for its superb gardens, which have been restored since the estate was bought in 1906 by the Spanish Carvallo family. Working from 16th-century designs, skilful gardeners mixed flowers and vegetables in strictly geometric patterns. The result is a fascinating insight into a typical Renaissance garden. The garden is on three levels: a water garden at the top, fringed by ancient lime trees; a flower garden level with the château; and, below it, the world's largest ornamental kitchen garden. There is also a play garden for children.

A collection of Spanish paintings is housed in the château.

Herb garden

Gardeners
Eight full-time gardeners raise and plant out some 60,000 vegetables and 45,000 bedding plants a year to fill both the kitchen garden and the ornamental flower garden.

CULTURE DE PRINTEMPS 1995

STAR FEATURES

★ **Garden of Love**

★ **Ornamental Kitchen Garden**

★ **Ornamental Kitchen Garden**
The current state of the garden can be studied in the plan pinned up near the moat. The plant and vegetable names for each square are listed and the colours shown.

RENAISSANCE KITCHEN AND HERB GARDENS

A 16th-century French treatise on diet reveals that the melons, artichokes, asparagus and cauliflower that fill Villandry's kitchen gardens today all also commonly appeared on Renaissance dinner tables. Herbs were widely used both for their medicinal and culinary applications. They formed the borders in the kitchen gardens of monasteries, such as that at Solesmes (see p162), which were the first to feature geometric planting. Villandry has a *jardin des simples* (herb garden) on its middle level.

Knautia dipsacifolia, from a 16th-century manual on plants

VISITORS' CHECKLIST

Road map D3. 02 47 50 02 09. Savonnières, then taxi.
Chateau & Gardens daily from 9am. Feb, mid-Oct–mid-Nov: to 5pm; Mar: to 5.30pm; Apr–Jun & Sep–mid-Oct: to 6pm; Jul–Aug: to 6.30pm.
W www.chateauvillandry.com

Shaped Pear Trees
In Villandry's gardens, nature is completely controlled. The pear trees are carefully pruned to form neat oval shapes.

The elegant stone balustrades above the kitchen garden have been restored.

The pool for irrigating the gardens is shaped like a gilt-framed mirror.

The flower gardens, including the garden of love, level with the south façade of the château

Decorative Cabbage
Ornamental Japanese cabbages were introduced by the wife of the present owner to provide year-round colour in the kitchen garden.

Château d'Azay-le-Rideau ❺

MEMORABLY DESCRIBED by Honoré de Balzac as a "faceted diamond set in the Indre", Azay-le-Rideau is one of the most popular châteaux in the Loire. Its graceful silhouette and richly decorated façades are mirrored in the peaceful waters of its lake, once a medieval moat. Azay was built from about 1518 by Gilles Berthelot, only to be confiscated by François I in 1527. The unknown architect, influenced by Italian design and innovative in his use of a straight staircase, took the defensive elements of an earlier, more warlike age and transformed them into charming ornamental features. Furnished in 16th–19th-century styles, the château has some notable Renaissance pieces and a famous portrait of Henri IV's mistress, Gabrielle d'Estrées.

Kitchen
The kitchen, situated in the west wing, has rib vaulting and a huge open fireplace.

Gabrielle d'Estrées
Henri IV's haughty mistress features in the château's finest painting, done in the style of François Clouet.

STAR FEATURES

★ Central Staircase

★ South Façade

AZAY'S CREATORS

Treasurer to François I and mayor of Tours, Gilles Berthelot acquired Azay-le-Rideau when his wife, Philippe Lesbahy, inherited the ruins of a medieval castle. He immediately began constructing a new pleasure palace, with his wife's guidance. The emblems of François I and Claude de France were engraved in stone above various doors in the château in an attempt to flatter the sovereigns. But flattery did not save Berthelot's career – about to be accused of embezzlement, he was forced to flee Azay before the building was completed.

François I's salamander emblem

The elegant turrets adorn the château's façade rather than protect it, as the sturdy towers of medieval fortresses had done in the past.

Entrance Façade
The entrance façade is dominated by the galleried stairwell topped by a tall gable. Its decoration, full of shells, medallions and candelabras, was influenced by Italian Renaissance artists.

Entrance

VISITORS' CHECKLIST

Road map D3. **☎** *02 47 45 42 04.* **🚌** **🕐** *Apr–Jun & Sep–Oct: 9:30am–6pm daily; Jul–Aug: 9:30am–7pm; Nov–Mar: 9:30am–12:30pm, 2–5:30pm (last adm: 30 mins before closing).* **●** *1 Jan, 1 May, 1 & 11 Nov, 25 Dec.* **🖼 📷 🎭** *Les Imaginaires d'Azay-le-Rideau (nightly, mid-May–Jul: 10:30pm–12:30am, Aug: 10pm–12:30am; Sep: 9:30pm–midnight).*

Red Room
This striking room is the antechamber to the Chambre de la Roi *(the King's Bedroom). The walls are hung with portraits of, among others, François I, Henri II and Henri III.*

★ Central Staircase
Azay's most significant design feature is its central staircase, consisting of three straight flights with landings, rather than the spiral staircase that was usual for the period.

Ballroom with Flemish tapestries

★ South Façade
Symmetry is the underlying motif of the exterior design, with its matching turrets and its stripe of decoration imitating machicolations.

Street-by-Street: Chinon ❻

THE CHATEAU DE CHINON stands on a golden-coloured cliff above the River Vienne. Below it, Chinon's old crooked streets resonate with history. The travel-weary Joan of Arc *(see p137)* arrived in the town on 6 March 1429, dismounting by a well in the Grand Carroi. It was here that she began her transformation from peasant girl to the warrior-saint shown sitting astride a charger in a statue in the marketplace. In the nearby Maison des Etats Généraux, now the Musée du Vieux-Chinon, Richard the Lionheart lay in state in 1199. His father, Henry Plantagenet, had died a few years earlier in the château, from which he had ruled England as well as much of the Loire Valley.

Tour de l'Horloge
This 14th-century clock-tower, which now houses a small exhibition on the life of Joan of Arc, is the entrance to the château.

★ Château
The long walls enclose three separate citadels, some entirely ruined, with magnificent views over the river. Here, in the Great Hall, Joan of Arc recognized the dauphin (see p52), a scene beautifully represented in a fine 17th-century tapestry.

0 metres		50
0 yards		50

RUE HAUTE ST-MAURICE

RUE BEAU

QUAI CHARLES VII

Eglise St-Maurice
Henry II rebuilt this church with Angevin vaults, retaining the Romanesque lower part of what is now the steeple.

Ramparts
The château's ramparts are an impressive sight from the opposite bank of the River Vienne.

★ **Musée du Vieux-Chinon**
Now a museum of local history, this building was once the scene of France's first attempt at a parliament, which met in an upper room to fund the war against the English in 1428.

VISITORS' CHECKLIST

Road map D3. 🏠 *9,000.* 🚊 *bd Gambetta.* 🚌 *bd Gambetta.* ℹ️ *pl Hofheim (02 47 93 17 85).* 🗓️ *Thu.* W *www.chinon.com*

Hôtel Torterue de Langardière's Classical façade is ornamented with wrought-iron balconies.

Musée Animé du Vin
Animated figures show 19th-century winemaking and coopering techniques.

Maison Rouge, a superbly restored medieval house, has sculpted beams across its red-brick façade.

Grand Carroi
This crossroads, at the heart of the old fortified town, is where Joan of Arc is said to have dismounted at a well.

François Rabelais
A bronze statue, made in 1882 by Emile Hébert, celebrates the famous satirist.

STAR SIGHTS

★ **Château**

★ **Musée du Vieux-Chinon**

KEY

– – – Suggested route

Exploring Chinon

A WALK THROUGH the narrow streets to the east of the château shows how much Chinon has to offer. High above the place Jeanne d'Arc is the remarkable Chapelle de Ste-Radegonde, carved into the limestone cliff. Behind this 12th-century frescoed chapel are ancient hermit caves (now displaying traditional crafts) and dizzying steps to an underground well. Lower down the hill, the important Romanesque monastery of St-Mexme is Chinon's oldest building. Rue Jean-Jacques Rousseau, leading to the 15th-century church of St-Etienne, has medieval houses.

♠ Château de Chinon

(02 47 93 13 45. **○** daily.
● 1 Jan, 25 Dec. **✏** **&** courtyard & grd flr only.

The château, much of it now in ruins, was built largely by Henry II, count of Anjou, who became Plantagenet king of England in 1154. It consists of three castles – Fort St-Georges, Château du Milieu and Fort du Coudray – separated by moats. Passing the ruins of Henry's Fort St-Georges, visitors enter the middle castle via the Tour de l'Horloge, in which there is a display on the life of Joan of Arc. Further on, at the Logis Royaux, the west wall is all that remains of the Great Hall where, in the light of 50 smoking flares, Joan picked out the dauphin from among his courtiers. Wax figures re-create the scene in the Logis' restored rooms. The views of Chinon, and from the westerly ruins of the Fort du Coudray, are delightful.

Statue of Joan of Arc by Jules Roulleau

🏛 Musée du Vieux-Chinon

44 rue Haute St-Maurice. **(** 02 47 93 18 12. **○** Apr–Oct: daily. **✏**

Amongst the treasures found in this intriguing museum of local history are a fine portrait of Rabelais by Eugène Delacroix (1798–1863), and the earliest large Arab tapestry brought to France, the "Cope of St. Mexme".

🏛 Maison de la Rivière

12 quai Pasteur. **(** 02 47 93 21 34.
○ Apr–Sep: Tue–Sun; Feb–Mar & Oct–19 Dec: Thu–Sun pm. **✏**

The past glory of the Loire's maritime trade is relived here on the banks of the Vienne, in a boat-builder's workshop.

Amongst a unique collection of scale-model boats are early Loire passenger steamboats (see p57), reassuringly called *Inexplosibles* as, unlike their predecessors, they were not in the habit of exploding on the river.

🏛 Musée Animé du Vin et de la Tonnellerie

12 rue Voltaire. **(** 02 47 93 25 63. **○** Apr–Sep: daily; Oct–Mar: groups by appt. **●** 1 Jan, 25 Dec. **✏**

Here you can taste sharp, dry, strawberry-like Chinon red wine, while watching automated models demonstrate the various stages in wine- and barrel-making (both are important Chinon industries) using some of the museum's 19th-century implements. Around the corner in the Caves Painctes, the Confrérie des Bons Entonneurs Rabelaisiens, a group of vine-growers, still hold banquets in a former inn (not open to visitors). These caves allegedly inspired Rabelais' description of the Temple of the Divine Bottle.

FRANÇOIS RABELAIS (1483–1553)

Priest, doctor, humanist and supreme *farceur* of French literature, François Rabelais is everywhere present in "Rabelaisie", as the area around La Devinière has become known. Rabelais enthusiasts will recognize in the old farmhouse the castle of Grandgousier, besieged by the hordes of King Picrochole, but saved by the arrival of giant Gargantua on his mare, who drowns most of them by creating a flood with her prodigious urination. Rabelais' thirst for knowledge imbued his *Gargantua* and *Pantagruel* (see p22) with a wealth of learning that sits surprisingly easily alongside a ribald *joie de vivre*.

The infant Gargantua

The Tour de l'Horloge, leading to the middle castle

View of the Château d'Ussé from the bridge crossing the River Indre

Musée de la Devinière **❼**

Road map D3. 🚌 *Chinon, then taxi.*
📞 *02 47 95 91 18.* 🔓 *daily.* 🔴 *1 Jan, 25 Dec.* ♿

THE RUMBUSTIOUS 16th-century writer François Rabelais was probably born in this pleasant, modest farmhouse, 2 km (1½ miles) southwest of Chinon. It now houses a small museum which is entirely devoted to the man, his work, and that of his contemporaries.

A dovecote, with its pigeonholes carved into the wall, and some troglodyte rooms add to the interest.

La Devinière farmhouse

Candes-St-Martin **❽**

Road map C3. 🚶 *250.* 🚌 *Chinon or Port Boulet, then taxi.* ℹ️ *Chinon (02 47 93 17 85).*

BEAUTIFULLY situated overlooking the shimmering waters where the Loire and Vienne rivers converge, picturesque Candes is famous as the place where St Martin died in 397. Stained glass in the 12th-century church depicts the saint's body being secretly rowed to Tours for burial. The porch of the church was fortified in the 15th century and is adorned with carved heads. Inside, the ceiling is a fine example of Angevin vaulting.

Château d'Ussé **❾**

Road map D3. 🚌 *Chinon, then taxi (15km/9 miles).* 📞 *02 47 95 54 05.* 🔓 *mid-Feb–mid-Nov: daily.* ♿ *park & grd flr only.*

WITH ITS COUNTLESS pointed turrets gleaming white against the sombre trees of the Forêt de Chinon, the Château d'Ussé is said to have inspired 17th-century French author Charles Perrault to write the fairy tale *The Sleeping Beauty*. The fortified château was begun in 1462 by Jean de Bueil on the foundations of a medieval castle. In 1485 it was sold to the Espinay family, chamberlains to both Louis XI and Charles VII, who softened the courtyard façades with Renaissance features that blend with its Gothic ancestry.

In the 17th century the north wing was demolished, opening up the main courtyard to views of the River Indre and the Loire Valley. Formal gardens were planted in terraces to the river and an orangery was added, completing the transformation from fortress to aristocratic country house *(see p17)*.

The château interior is also in a variety of styles. Some of the well-furnished rooms are populated with waxwork figures, including a tableau of *The Sleeping Beauty*.

On the edge of the forest is a lovely late-Gothic chapel, with some Renaissance decoration. Inside is a terracotta Virgin sculpted by Luca della Robbia (1400–82).

The late-Gothic exterior of Ussé's chapel

Mobile by Alexander Calder (1898–1976) in Saché

Saché ⑩

Road map D3. 👥 880. 🚉 Azay-le-Rideau, then taxi. 🛈 Azay-le-Rideau (02 47 45 44 40).

T HE PRETTY VILLAGE of Saché is notable for having been second home to both a writer and an artist of world fame: the 19th-century novelist Honoré de Balzac and the 20th-century American sculptor Alexander Calder, one of whose mobiles adorns the main square.

Admirers of the work of Balzac make pilgrimages to the **Château de Saché**. The plain but comfortable manor house, built in the 16th and 18th centuries, was a quiet place to work and a source of inspiration for many of the writer's best-known novels. The house has been well restored – one of the reception rooms has even been redecorated with a copy of the

bright green wallpaper with a Pompeiian frieze that was there in Balzac's day.

It is full of busts, sketches and memorabilia of the great man, including the coffee pot that kept him going during his long stints of writing. The top floor displays manuscripts and letters, as well as portraits of the women in Balzac's life: his pretty, but casual, mother; his first love, Madame de Berny; and his loyal friend, Madame Hanska, whom he finally married shortly before his death in 1850.

⛪ **Château de Saché**
📞 02 47 26 86 50. 🕐 daily. ⬤ 1 Jan, 25 Dec. 🚫 🖼 🚹 park only.

Villaines-les-Rochers ⑪

Road map D3. 👥 930. 🚉 Azay-le-Rideau, then taxi. 🛈 Azay-le-Rideau (02 47 45 44 40).

S INCE THE Middle Ages, willows from the local river valleys have been made into baskets in this peaceful town. Production has been on a more substantial scale since the mid-19th century, when the local priest organized the craftsmen into one of France's first cooperatives. Everything is still hand made by the many wickerworkers (*vanniers*) in the town. This explains the relatively high prices of the attractive furniture and baskets on sale in the **cooperative**'s shop. Craftsmen and women can be watched at work in

the adjoining studio. In the summer, you can also visit a small museum with displays on the subject of basket-making, the **Musée de l'Osier et de la Vannerie**.

🧺 **Coopérative de Vannerie de Villaines**
1 rue de la Cheneillère. 📞 02 47 45 43 03. 🕐 daily (Sat, Sun: no work in progress). ⬤ 1 Jan, 25 Dec. 🚹
🏛 **Musée de l'Osier et de la Vannerie**
22 rue des Caves-Fortes. 📞 02 47 45 23 19. 🕐 May–Sep: Tue–Sun, pm only; Oct–Apr: groups by appt. 🖼

A wickerworker in Villaines

Richelieu ⑫

Road map D4. 👥 2,300. 🚉 Chinon. 🛈 6 Grande Rue (02 47 58 13 62). 🛍 Mon, Fri.

I T WOULD BE DIFFICULT to find a better example of 17th-century urban planning than the town of Richelieu, on the border between Touraine and Poitou. Its rigid design was the brainchild of Armand Jean du Plessis who, as Cardinal Richelieu and chief minister, was the most powerful man in the kingdom, not excepting his monarch, Louis XIII.

The Cardinal was determined to build a huge palace near his modest family estate of Richelieu. In 1625 he commissioned the architect Jacques Lemercier to draw up the plans and, in 1631, he received permission from the king to proceed, not only with the palace, but also with the creation of a new walled town. Lemercier had already

The Château de Saché, often visited by Honoré de Balzac

designed the Palais Royal and the Church of the Sorbonne in Paris, and would later be appointed chief royal architect. His brothers, Pierre and Nicolas, were put in charge of the building work, which kept nearly 2,000 labourers busy for more than a decade.

The resulting town is a huge rectangle, surrounded by walls and moats (mostly taken up with gardens today) and entered through three monumental gates. The Grande Rue, running from north to south through the centre of the town and linking two large squares, is lined with identical Classical mansions. In the south square, place du Marché, the buildings include the Classical **Eglise Notre-Dame**, the market building with its superb timber framework, and the former law courts, in which the **Hôtel de Ville** (town hall) and a small **history museum** are now housed. In the north square, the place des Religieuses, stands a convent and the Royal Academy, founded by Richelieu in 1640.

An old-fashioned steam train runs between the town and Chinon during the summer months.

Richelieu clearly intended that his palace should be incomparably luxurious, and that vision was impressively realised. It was filled with priceless furniture and works

Richelieu's timber-framed market hall

of art, including paintings by Caravaggio and Andrea Mantegna. Michelangelo's *Dying Slaves*, statues that were originally designed for the tomb of Pope Julius II (now housed in the Louvre in Paris), adorned one of the courtyard façades.

Extremely fearful of competition, Richelieu ordered many of the châteaux in the area to be razed. While his town survived the ravages of the French Revolution intact, the palace, ironically, was confiscated, damaged and then dismantled. Today, only a few garden buildings remain intact, scattered around the 475-ha (1,174-acre) **Domaine du Parc de Richelieu**. In the Dôme, the only part of the château proper that is still

Cardinal Richelieu (1585–1642)

standing, there is an exhibition on the architectural history of what was once a magnificent building.

🏛 **Musée de l'Hôtel de Ville**
place du Marché. [02 47 58 10 13.
◯ Jul–Aug: Wed–Mon; Sep–Jun: Mon, Wed–Fri, pm only. ⓖ
🍀 **Domaine du Parc de Richelieu**
5 pl du Cardinal. [02 47 58 10 09.
◯ May–Sep: daily; Oct–Apr: Wed–Mon. ⓖ ♿ restricted.

ENVIRONS: Champigny-sur-Veude, 6 km (4 miles) to the north of Richelieu, was one of the châteaux demolished on Cardinal Richelieu's orders. All that can now be seen of this early 16th-century castle is the impressive Renaissance church of **Ste-Chapelle**, with its superb stained glass.

⛪ **Ste-Chapelle**
Champigny-sur-Veude. [La Mairie (02 47 95 73 48, 02 47 95 71 46).
◯ Easter–mid-Oct: Wed–Mon. ⓖ

BALZAC AT SACHÉ

Honoré de Balzac's (1799–1850) regular stays at the Château de Saché between 1829 and 1837 coincided with the most productive period in his highly industrious career as a writer. Here, hidden well away from his creditors, he would work at least 12 hours a day. Despite starting in the early hours of the morning, he remained able to entertain his hosts, Monsieur and Madame de Margonne, and their guests in the evenings by reading aloud the latest chunk of text from his novels, acting out all the characters as he did so.

Two of Balzac's major novels, *Le Père Goriot (Father Goriot)* and *Le Lys dans la Vallée (The Lily of the Valley)*, were written at Saché. The latter is set in the Indre valley, which can be seen from the house and does indeed have something of that "intangibly mysterious quality" to which Balzac refers with typical eloquence.

Balzac's bedroom at Saché

Le Grand-Pressigny 🔟

Road map D4. 👥 1,100
🚌 Châtellerault, then taxi. 🚏 Tours.
ℹ️ pl de Savoir Villars (02 47 94 96 82) 🔲 Thu.

Perched high above the hilly streets of the town, the **Château du Grand-Pressigny** has lovely views over the peaceful Claise and Aigronne valleys.

The château is part medieval ruins, part 15th-century castle and part Renaissance residence. The rectangular, 12th-century ruined keep contrasts dramatically with the elegant 16th-century Italianate wing. Some rooms have been adapted for the blind and partially sighted. The large gardens can also be visited.

Important prehistoric finds have been made in the area, and various excavations have revealed that the site was a key centre for the large-scale production of flint implements, such as blades, which were then exported as far afield as Switzerland and even Great Britain.

The château houses the **Musée de la Préhistoire**, whose collections, which were reorganized in 1992, are clearly displayed. Examples of tools and other objects from all the prehistoric eras are exhibited, along with rock flints, large blocks of obsidian and multi-coloured jasper. Particularly impressive are the yellowish flint blocks known familiarly as "pounds of butter". Interesting miniature

reconstructions of villages show how prehistoric peoples lived, and a separate wing houses a collection of fossils, some of which date back 60 million years.

On summer afternoons you can visit the **Archéolab**, 6 km (4 miles) northwest at Abilly-sur-Claise, where a transparent dome covers a site inhabited by stone cutters between 2800 and 2400 BC.

♣ **Château du Grand-Pressigny**
📞 02 47 94 90 20 🕐 Feb–Nov: daily. 🎫 ✅ ♿ park and grd flr only.
⛪ **Archéolab**
Abilly-sur-Claise. 📞 02 47 59 80 82 or 02 47 91 07 48. 🕐 mid-Jun–mid-Sep: daily, pm only. 🎫 ♿

Neolithic tool from the Musée de la Préhistoire

Loches 🔢

Road map D3. 👥 7,500. 🚗 🚌
ℹ️ pl de la Marne (02 47 91 82 82).
🔲 Wed, Sat.
🌐 www.lochesentouraine.com

Its medieval streets lined with picturesque houses, the peaceful town of Loches lies beside the River Indre on the edge of the Forêt de Loches. Thanks to its strategic location, it became an impor-

Agnès Sorel as the Virgin, painted by Jehan Fouquet

tant citadel in the Middle Ages, with an 11th-century keep begun by Foulques Nerra (see p50). The **château** remained in the hands of the counts of Anjou until 1194, when John Lackland gave it to King Philippe Augustus. John's brother, Richard the Lionheart, recaptured Loches in a surprise attack in 1195. It took Philippe Augustus nearly ten years to retake the castle by force, and eventually it became a French royal residence. It was in the 15th-century **Logis Royal** that Joan of Arc, fresh from her Orléans triumph, persuaded the dauphin to travel to Rheims and be crowned king of France as Charles VII. This key event is commemorated in the tapestry-hung Salle Jeanne d'Arc.

Another woman of influence in Charles VII's life was his mistress, Agnès Sorel, whose Gothic marble tomb is in the château. The famous beauty is shown with lambs resting at her feet. In an adjacent room is the tiny, late Gothic private chapel of twice-queen Anne of Brittany, whose ermine tail emblem recurs in the decoration. Also on show in the château are a fine *Crucifixion* triptych by Tours painter Jehan Fouquet (c.1420–80) or one of his pupils, and a copy of his colourful *Virgin with Child*, which was modelled on Agnès Sorel.

The massive keep with its surrounding towers is famous for its torture chambers. Prisoners are said to have been locked for years into small wood-and-iron cages.

Renaissance façade of the Gallery, Château de Grand-Pressigny

One of the most famous was
Lodovico Sforza, the duke of
Milan, who died as a prisoner
in the **Tour Martelet**, where
the tempera wall paintings he
made can still be seen.

Beside the château is the
Collégiale St-Ours, a church
with four pyramid-like spires
and a Romanesque portal.
Near the Porte Royale lies the
Maison Lansyer, the birthplace of the 19th-century
painter Emmanuel Lansyer.
Some of his canvases are on
display, along with his
collection of Japanese armour
and prints. It also houses a
folklore museum, exhibiting
typical 19th-century interiors.

♣ **Château de Loches**
🎫 Logis Royal *02 47 59 01 32;*
Donjon *02 47 59 07 86.* ⬜ *daily.*
🔴 *1 Jan, 25 Dec.* 🎭 🎫 *Spectacle
d'été (Jul–Aug, Fri & Sat), phone 02
47 59 07 98 to make a reservation.*
🏛 **Maison Lansyer**
1 rue Lansyer. 🎫 *02 47 59 05 45.*
⬜ *Jun–Sep: daily.* 🎭 🎫

Montrésor ⑮

Road map E3. 🏠 *360.* 🚉 *Loches,
then taxi.* ℹ️ *Grande Rue (02 47 91
43 07), La Mairie (02 47 91 43 00).*
🎪 *Sat.*

THE TURRETED **Château de
Montrésor**, largely built
in the 15th and 16th centuries,
stands on the site of medieval
fortifications built by Count
Foulques Nerra *(see p50)*. It
was bought in the mid-19th
century by Count Branicki, an
émigré Polish financier closely
linked to the future Napoleon
III. Still owned by Branicki's
descendants, the château's
Second Empire decor remains
virtually unaltered.

As well as a fine collection
of early Italian paintings and
some elegant portraits, there
are many gold and silver
pieces. The rooms, with their
mounted stags' and wolves'
heads and dark panelling,
retain a somewhat Central
European feel. The château
terrace and informal gardens
offer fine views of the river.

An estate building, which
used to house the château's
wine press, has been
converted into the Maison du

Pays, an information centre
and showcase for the Indrois
Valley and its products.

The village's small Gothic
and Renaissance church was
built by Imbert de Bastarnay,
lord of Montrésor, adviser to
François I and grandfather of
Diane de Poitiers *(see p108)*.
On the beautiful marble
Bastarnay tomb lie *gisants*
(effigies) of the lord, his lady
and their son, guarded by
angels and with their feet
resting on greyhounds. The
tomb, believed to be the
work of the Renaissance
sculptor Jean Goujon (c.1510–
68), is decorated with statues
of the apostles. There are also
some wonderful Flemish and
Italian paintings in the
church, and a 17th-century
Annunciation by Philippe de
Champaigne (1602–74), the
Baroque painter who worked
on the Luxembourg palace in
Paris with Nicolas Poussin.

In a lovely forest setting,
4 km (2½ miles) west of the
village of Montrésor, are the
ruins of the **Chartreuse du
Liget**, a Carthusian monastery
founded by the Plantagenet
king Henry II of England in

**Farm buildings and poppy fields
near the village of Montrésor**

expiation for the murder of
Archbishop Thomas à Becket.
The nearby Chapel of **St-Jean-
du-Liget** is decorated with
12th-century frescoes.

♣ **Château de Montrésor**
🎫 *02 47 92 60 04.* ⬜ *Apr–Oct: daily.*
🎭 🎫 ♿ *park and grd flr only.*
🔔 **Chartreuse du Liget &
Chapelle St-Jean-du-Liget**
🎫 *02 47 92 60 02.* ⬜ *phone first.*
🎭 ♿

Château de Montrésor, built on medieval fortifications

Château de Chenonceau ⑯

CHENONCEAU, STRETCHING ROMANTICALLY across the River Cher, is considered by many the loveliest of the Loire châteaux. Surrounded by elegant formal gardens and wooded grounds, this pure Renaissance building was transformed over the centuries from a modest manor and water mill into a palace designed solely for pleasure. Visitors are allowed to wander freely through the beautifully furnished rooms. A small waxworks museum illustrates the château's history, and the site also includes a restaurant in the old stables and a miniature train ride down the lovely tree-lined drive. Wines from Chenonceau's own vineyards are on sale.

★ Cabinet Vert
The walls of Catherine de Médicis' study were originally covered with green velvet.

Chapelle
The chapel has a vaulted ceiling and pilasters sculpted with acanthus leaves and cockle shells. The stained glass, ruined by a bomb in 1944, was replaced in 1953.

Louise de Lorraine's room
was painted black and decorated with monograms, tears and knots in white after the death of her husband.

The Tour des Marques
survives from the 15th-century castle of the Marques family.

The Three Graces
Painted by Charles-André Van Loo (1705–65), The Three Graces depicts the pretty Mailly-Nesle sisters, all royal mistresses.

STAR FEATURES

★ Cabinet Vert

★ Grande Galerie

★ Formal Gardens

Tapestries

As was the practice in the 16th century, Chenonceau is hung with Flemish tapestries that both warm and decorate its well-furnished rooms.

VISITORS' CHECKLIST

Road map D3. ☎ 02 47 23 90 07. 🚌 Chenonceaux. ☐ 1 Feb–15 Feb & 1 Nov–15 Nov: 9am–5pm daily; 16 Feb–28 Feb & 16 Oct–31 Oct: 9am–5:30pm; 1 Mar – 15 Mar & 1 Oct–15 Oct: 9am–6pm; 16 Mar–15 Sep: 9am–7pm; 16 Sep–30 Sep: 9am–6:30pm; 16 Nov–31 Jan: 9am–4:30pm. 🎧 📷 🍴 🛍 Au Temps des Dames de Chenonceau (Jul–Aug: 10:15pm daily). W www.chenonceau.com

CHÂTEAU GUIDE

Ground floor

First floor

1 Vestibule
2 Salle des Gardes
3 Chapelle
4 Terrasse
5 Librairie de Catherine de' Médicis
6 Cabinet Vert
7 Chambre de Diane de Poitiers
8 Grande Galerie
9 Chambre de François I
10 Salon Louis XIV
11 Chambre des Cinq Reines
12 Cabinet des Estampes
13 Chambre de Catherine de Médicis
14 Chambre de Vendôme
15 Chambre de Gabrielle d'Estrées

★ Grande Galerie

Catherine de Médicis added this elegant gallery to the bridge designed by Philibert de l'Orme in 1556–9 for Diane de Poitiers.

Chenonceau's Florentine-style gallery, which stretches across the River Cher for 60 m (197 ft)

The Creation of Chenonceau

CHENONCEAU REFLECTS the combined influence of five women, who brought a feminine touch to this graceful building. First came Catherine Briçonnet, wife of the royal chamberlain, who supervised the construction of the château. Later, Diane de Poitiers, Henri II's mistress, created a formal garden and built a bridge over the Cher. After Henri's death, his widow, Catherine de Médicis, reclaimed the château and topped the bridge with a gallery. Chenonceau survived the 1789 Revolution – because of local respect for Louise Dupin, wife of a tax collector – to be restored by Madame Pelouze in the 19th century.

Sphinxes
Inscrutable stone sphinxes guarding the entrance to the gardens came from the Château de Chanteloup, which was destroyed in the 19th century (see p111).

Diane de Poitiers
Henri II's mistress, here painted by François Clouet, created a large, formal garden, as well as the bridge across the Cher.

★ **Formal Gardens**
The current designs of the formal gardens of Diane de Poitiers and Catherine de Médicis date from the 19th century.

TIMELINE

1512 Thomas Bohier acquires the medieval Chenonceau. His wife, Catherine Briçonnet, rebuilds it

1559 On Henri's death, Catherine forces Diane to leave

Henri II

1575 Louise de Lorraine (1554–1601) marries Henri III, Catherine's son

1547 Henri II gives Chenonceau to Diane de Poitiers, his lifelong mistress

1533 Marriage of Catherine de Médicis (1519–89) to Henri II (1519–59). Chenonceau becomes a Loire royal palace

1913 The château is bought by the Menier family, the *chocolatiers* who still own it today

1789 Chenonceau is spared in the French Revolution, thanks to Louise Dupin

1730–99 Louise Dupin creates a salon for intellectuals at Chenonceau

1863 Madame Pelouze restores the château to its original state

1944 Chenonceau chapel is damaged in a bombing raid

1500	1600	1700	1800	1900

Catherine de Médicis
After ousting Diane de Poitiers, Catherine de Médicis made her own mark on Chenonceau's design. She built the Grande Galerie over the Cher and added a formal garden to rival Diane's.

Louise Dupin

A well-read beauty with huge brown eyes, Louise Dupin entertained all the literary lions of her day, including Montesquieu and Voltaire. One guest, Jean-Jacques Rousseau, stayed on to tutor her children and famously praised Chenonceau's cuisine, claiming he had become "as plump as a monk".

Catherine de Médicis' emblem

Madame Pelouze bought Chenonceau in 1863 and restored it to Catherine Briçonnet's original design. Fortunately, she stopped short of taking down the Grande Galerie.

Court Festivities

Catherine de Médicis staged lavish balls and festivities at Chenonceau, some featuring plaster triumphal arches and statues designed by Francesco Primaticcio, others with living "nymphs" leaping out of the bushes chased by "satyrs".

Louise de Lorraine

Catherine de Médicis left Chenonceau to her daughter-in-law, Louise de Lorraine. Louise had her room redecorated in black upon the death of her husband, Henri III.

Catherine Briçonnet supervised the creation of an innovative château design, with rooms leading off a central vestibule on each floor.

The Château d'Amboise, high above the town and the River Loire

Amboise ⑰

Road map D3. 🏰 *12,000.* 🚉
🛈 *quai du Général de Gaulle*
(02 47 57 01 37). 🚌 *Fri, Sun.*
🌐 *www.amboise-valdeloire.com*

THE BUSTLING little town of Amboise is mostly visited for its château, but this is not the town's only attraction.

♣ Château d'Amboise
📞 *02 47 57 00 98.* ⭕ *daily.* ⬤ *1 Jan, 25 Dec.* 🎫 🎭 *A la Cour du Roy François (Jul & Aug, Wed & Sat).*
The château belongs to the Comte de Paris, a direct descendant of France's last royal line. Much of it has been destroyed, but it is still possible to see the splendour that prevailed when first Charles VIII and then François I brought the Italian love of luxury and elegance to the French court.

Amboise has also played a tragic part in history. In 1560 a Protestant plot to gain religious concessions from the young King François II was uncovered, and 1,200 conspirators were slaughtered, their bodies strung up from the castle and town walls, from trees, and even from the balcony on the Logis du Roi.

This horrifying episode was to spell the end of Amboise's glory, and over the years that followed, the château was gradually dismantled. The enchanting, late-Gothic **Chapelle St-Hubert**, where Leonardo da Vinci is said to be buried, has fortunately survived, perched on the ramparts of the château. Carvings on the exterior lintel of

Sculpted detail from the Logis du Roi

the chapel depict St Hubert and St Christopher. Some of the guard rooms and state rooms in the part-Gothic, part-Renaissance **Logis du Roi** are open to visitors, along with fascinating 19th-century apartments once occupied by King Louis-Philippe. Flanking the Logis du Roi is the **Tour des Minimes**, the original entrance to the château, with its impressive spiral inner ramp, up which horsemen could ride.

♣ Château du Clos-Lucé
2 rue du Clos-Lucé. 📞 *02 47 57 62 88.* ⭕ *daily.* ⬤ *25 Dec, 1 Jan.* 🎫 ♿ *restricted.*
This graceful Renaissance manor house on the outskirts of Amboise was the last home of Leonardo da Vinci. In 1516 François I enticed Leonardo to the royal court at Amboise and the following year settled him at Le Clos-Lucé (called Cloux at the time), where he lived until his death in 1519.

While here, Leonardo almost certainly conceived the plans for the Château de Chambord (*see pp132–5*). He is known to have made various drawings of double staircases, similar to the one that was built there. His bedroom, reception room, study, kitchen and a small chapel built for Anne of Brittany by Charles VIII are open to visitors. There are

The late-Gothic Chapelle St-Hubert, with its highly ornate roof and spire models made from Leonardo's astonishing technical drawings in the basement.

🐟 Aquarium de Touraine

Lussault-sur-Loire. 🚇 📞 *02 47 23 44 44*. ◯ *daily.* ⬤ *25 Dec, 1 Jan.* 🖼️ ♿
With more than 10,000 freshwater fish on display in its 35 tanks, it is the largest such collection in Europe.

ENVIRONS:
♣ Château et Jardins de la Bourdaisière

Montlouis-sur-Loire. 📞 *02 47 45 16 31*. ◯ *Apr–mid-Nov: daily.* 🖼️ 🎫
Ⓦ www.chateaulabourdaisiere.com
Behind the Renaissance château, now also a smart hotel *(see p203)*, hides no ordinary *potager*, including 500 varieties of tomato, 150 kinds of lettuce and over 200 different herbs. Sample its produce in the excellent restaurant from June to September, or at the Tomato Festival in mid-September.

Leonardo da Vinci's bedroom at the Château du Clos-Lucé

Pagode de Chanteloup ⓲

Forêt d'Amboise. 📞 *02 47 57 20 97*. ◯ *mid-Feb–mid-Nov: daily.* 🖼️ ♿ *park only.*

I N THE FOREST of Amboise, southwest of Amboise itself, stands this curious Chinese-style pagoda, more than 44 m (140 ft) high and built in seven stories, linked by steep spiral staircases. Each layer is smaller than the preceding one and contains an airy, octagonal room with a domed ceiling. Seven avenues lead

LEONARDO DA VINCI (1452–1519)

François I, who developed a love of Italian Renaissance art during his military campaigns there, persuaded Leonardo to join his court at Amboise, offering him an annual allowance and free use of the manor house at Clos-Lucé. The great Italian painter arrived in Amboise in 1516 with some precious items in his luggage – three major paintings, in leather bags tied to a mule. One of them was the *Mona Lisa*, which François was to buy and place in the royal collection (hence its presence today in the Louvre in Paris).

Leonardo spent the last three years of his life at Le Clos-Lucé as the *Premier Peintre, Architecte, et Mécanicien du Roi* (first painter,

Engraving of Leonardo da Vinci

architect and engineer to the king), mainly writing and drawing. As he was left-handed, the paralysis that affected his right hand was not a major handicap. Fascinated by hydrology, he produced plans to link the royal residences of the Loire Valley via waterways and even proposed rerouting the river. He also organized a series of elaborate court festivities, planning them down to the last detail with the same meticulous care he lavished on his scientific designs.

A model of Leonardo's prototype for a "car"

into the forest from the pagoda, which is reflected in a large, semicircular lake.

This is all that is left of a splendid château built by Louis XV's minister, the Duc de Choiseul (1719–85). In the 1770s, Choiseul fell out with the king's mistress, Madame du Barry – he had been a protégé of her predecessor Madame de Pompadour – and was exiled from Versailles. He retreated to the château he had bought at Chanteloup in 1761 and rebuilt it. He spent his time entertaining on a large scale and dabbling in farming. After his death, the château was abandoned and then pulled down in 1823.

An exhibition in the pavilion explains the history of the once magnificent château and, for those brave enough to climb, there are impressive views of the Loire Valley from the top of the tower.

The Pagode de Chanteloup, in the heart of the forest of Amboise

Street-by-Street: Tours ⑲

THE MEDIEVAL OLD TOWN, Le Vieux Tours, is full of narrow streets lined with beautiful half-timbered houses. Now sensitively restored, it is a lively area crammed with little cafés, bars and restaurants that attract locals as well as tourists. There are also numerous chic fashion boutiques and small shops devoted particularly to craft work and to stylish kitchen equipment. At its heart is the attractive place Plumereau, which in fine weather is filled with parasol-shaded café tables.

0 metres   50

0 yards   50

★ Maison de Tristan
The brick-and-stone 15th-century Maison de Tristan is renowned for its vaulted spiral staircase.

Musée du Gemmail
Inside the vine-covered Hôtel Raimbault, a museum displays jewel-like works of art made from stained glass.

Place Pierre-le-Puellier
A Gallo-Roman and medieval cemetery has been excavated in this square, which once formed part of a Renaissance cloister.

STAR SIGHTS

★ Place Plumereau

★ Maison de Tristan

The Eglise St-Saturnin is a Carmelite church built in the 15th century.

★ Place Plumereau
The lively square is surrounded by tall, half-timbered buildings dating from the 15th century.

Hôtel de la Monnaie
This 18th-century mansion, at No. 5 rue de la Monnaie, stands in a street of mainly 17th-century houses.

Carved Posts
The wooden posts on the twin-gabled house at the corner of the rue du Change are adorned with carved figures and scenes.

Tour Charlemagne
A terracotta relief depicting St Martin can be seen on the Tour Charlemagne, one of two towers that have survived from the medieval Old Basilica of St-Martin.

KEY

– – – Suggested route

Exploring Tours

THE PLEASANT CATHEDRAL CITY of Tours, popular with foreign students eager to learn the country's purest French, is a perfect base for exploring Touraine's impressive châteaux. But Tours itself, its medieval heart imaginatively restored, repays exploration, too. Once a major Gallo-Roman centre and later filled with pilgrims flocking to St Martin's tomb, it has remained prosperous over the centuries. Yet despite the recent rapid expansion beyond the Loire and Cher rivers, it has kept its unhurried, provincial charm.

Tours's Pont Wilson, recently rebuilt, spanning the Loire

Tours Town Center

The area of the town close to the magnificent **Cathédrale St-Gatien** *(see pp116–17)* was part of the original Roman settlement. In the 3rd century AD, it was enclosed by a wall, the shape of which can still be seen in the rue des Ursulines, circling, the cathedral and the Musée des Beaux Arts. The rue du Général-Meunier, a curving cobbled street of elegant houses once occupied by the clergy, follows the line of a Roman amphitheater.

On the west side of Tours, a religious community grew up around the sepulchre of St Martin *(see p49).* The saint's tomb now lies in the crypt of the late 19th-century New Basilica, which was built on the site of the considerably larger, medieval Old Basilica. Two stone towers – the **Tour Charlemagne** and the **Tour de l'Horloge** – on either side of the rue des Halles, survive from the earlier building. Not far from the towers, the **place Plumereau**, with its charming medieval houses and tempting cafés, attracts locals, foreign students and tourists in large numbers.

The half-timbered house at No. 39 rue Colbert bears a wrought-iron sign dedicated to the *Pucelle Armée* (the armed maid), recalling that Joan of Arc *(see p137)* bought her suit of armour from a workshop here, before setting out to liberate Orléans in 1429. Nearby is the **place Foire-le-Roi**, a square where, thanks to a permit granted by the king in 1545, regular fairs were once held. The main merchandise was the silk that had been a key factor in the town's economy since the middle of the previous century. Of the gabled houses that line the square, the finest is the Renaissance Hôtel Babou de la Bourdaisière, named after the

finance minister to François I, who lived there. Slightly to the west, the 13th-century **Eglise St-Julien** stands on the site of an abbey founded in the 6th century.

The central bridge crossing the Loire, the **Pont Wilson**, is known locally as the *pont de pierre* (stone bridge). It is an exact replica of the town's original 18th-century bridge, which collapsed suddenly in 1978, making national headlines. It was rebuilt following the original design after a referendum of local residents backed the idea.

🏛 Musée des Beaux-Arts

18 pl François-Sicard. ☎ 02 47 05 68 73. ⬚ Wed–Mon. ⬤ 14 Jul, 1 & 11 Nov, 25 Dec & public hols. 🖼

The Museum of Fine Arts, conveniently situated next to the Cathédrale St-Gatien, is shaded by a cedar of Lebanon nearly two centuries old and fronted by attractive formal gardens. Once the Archbishop's Palace, the building dates mainly from the 17th and 18th centuries.

Its collections of paintings range from the Middle Ages to contemporary artists and include two celebrated altarpiece panels by Andrea Mantegna, *The Resurrection* and *Christ in the Olive Grove*, which were painted between 1456 and 1460 for the church of San Zeno in Verona.

To the right of the entrance courtyard is an outbuilding housing a huge stuffed circus elephant that died in Tours in the early 20th century.

Christ in the Olive Grove (1456–1460) by Andrea Mantegna

The Hôtel Goüin's elaborate Renaissance façade

🏛 Hôtel Goüin & Musée Archéologique

25 rue du Commerce. **02 47 66 22 32.** ◯ Feb–mid-Mar, Oct–Nov: Sat–Thu; mid-Mar–Sep: daily. 🖼

This fine example of early Renaissance architecture, its highly ornamented façade beautifully re-created following World War II destruction, now houses the city's archaeological museum. The collection, which commences with the prehistoric era and continues to the 18th century, includes an interesting group of Celtic coins from the Chartres area,

whose different values are denoted not by numerals but by pictures of animals. The most famous exhibit in the museum, however, is a set of scientific instruments collected in 1743 by the owner of Chenonceau château.

🏛 Musée des Vins de Touraine

16 rue Nationale. **02 47 61 07 93** ◯ Wed–Mon. ● public hols. 🖼

The vaulted cellars and parts of the cloisters of the 13th-century **Eglise St-Julien** now form a wine museum, with a huge Renaissance winepress, displays on early viticultural

VISITORS' CHECKLIST

Road map D3. 🚶 130,000
🚉 pl du Maréchal Leclerc.
🚌 pl du Maréchal Leclerc.
🛈 78 rue Bernard Palissy
(02 47 70 37 37). 🛒 daily.
🎉 Foire au Basilic et à l'Ail
(26 Jul, see p117); Semaines
Musicales de Tours (Jul).

history, and collections of wine making tools dating from the Middle Ages to the 19th century. In an adjacent courtyard there is an original Gallo-Roman winepress, which was discovered near Azay-le-Rideau in 1946.

Exhibits in the Musée des Vins de Touraine

TOURS TOWN CENTRE

Cathédrale St-Gatien ⑤
Château Royal ④
Eglise St-Julien ③
Hôtel Goüin ②
Musée des Beaux-Arts ⑥
Tour Charlemagne ①

KEY

▩ See pp112–113
🅿 Parking
✝ Church

0 metres 100
0 yards 100

Tours: Cathédrale St-Gatien

T HE FOUNDATION STONE of Tours' Gothic cathedral, named
after St Gatien, a 3rd-century bishop, was laid in the
early 13th century. Because building work continued until
the mid-16th century, the cathedral provides an illustration
of how the Gothic style developed over the centuries. The
Early Gothic chancel was the first area to be completed,
while the nave and transept represent the Middle or High
Gothic period and the highly decorated west façade is
Flamboyant (or Late) Gothic.

Cloître de la Psalette
*The cloisters, which lead off
the north aisle, are made up
of three galleries dating
from the mid-15th and
early 16th centuries.*

Inside the North Tower is
the elegant 16th-century
"royal staircase".

★ **West Façade**
*The richly carved
Flamboyant west façade has
three portals surmounted by
a fine rose
window.*

Colombe tomb

★ **Colombe Tomb** *(1499)*
*The marble tomb of Charles
VIII's and Anne of Brittany's
infant sons features lifelike
effigies by Michel Colombe
or one of his pupils.*

The narrow nave has a
vaulted ceiling, dating from
the late 15th century.

Fresco
*This 14th-century fresco,
restored in 1993, shows
St Martin giving half his
cloak to a beggar.*

VISITORS' CHECKLIST

Pl de la Cathédrale. **[** 02 47 70 37
36. **[** 7pm Mon–Fri; 7pm Sat
(May–Oct); 10am & 6:30pm Sun.

Colombe Statue

*This statue of
Tours' famous
sculptor, Michel
Colombe, stands
in a square near
the cathedral.*

In the chancel, the stained-
glass windows, depicting
Christ's Passion and the legends
of St Martin and other saints,
date from around 1265.

★ Stained-Glass Windows

*The stained glass is notable
for its rich, strong colours
and for the paler stained
panels, or grisailles, which
let in more light than
ordinary stained glass.*

STAR FEATURES

★ **Colombe Tomb**

★ **Stained-Glass
Windows**

★ **West Façade**

⚓ Château Royal de Tours

25 ave André Malraux. **Historial de
Touraine** **[** 02 47 61 02 95.
☐ mid-Mar–Oct: daily; mid-Nov–mid-
Mar: daily pm. 📷 **Atelier Histoire de
Tours** (entry from church square) **[**
02 47 64 90 52. ☐ mid-Mar–mid-Dec:
Wed & Sat (pm only); mid-Dec–mid-
Mar by appt only. ● public hols.

Parts of the château, which
served as a royal residence in
the 13th and 15th centuries,
have recently been restored.
The Tour de Guise is named
after the Duc de Guise, who
made a daring escape while
being held as a prisoner here
following the assassination of
his father at the Château de
Blois in 1588 *(see pp126–7)*.

The tower now houses the
Historial de Touraine, a
museum illustrating the
region's history in waxworks.
In the 18th-century Logis de
Mars, the waxworks continue.
One scene depicts the marriage in 1491 of Charles VIII
and Anne of Brittany, while
another shows Joan of Arc
(see p137) trying on her suit
of armour in a workshop in
Tours. The Logis also has a
tropical aquarium.

In the Renaissance Logis
des Gouverneurs, the exhibitions of the **Atelier Histoire
de Tours** explain the city's
long urban history using
models and plans.

🏛 Musée du Compagnonnage

1 rue Nationale. **[** 02 47 61 07 93.
☐ mid-Sep–mid-Jun: Wed–Mon;
mid-Jun–mid-Sep: daily. ● public
hols. 📷 📷

Housed in part of the abbey
once attached to the medieval
Eglise St-Julien, this unusual
museum is devoted to craftsmanship. It has a fascinating
collection of "master pieces"
made by members of a guild
of itinerant *compagnons*
(journeymen) who applied to
be awarded the prestigious
title of Master Craftsman.
Displays cover many trades,
ranging from the work of
stonemasons to that of clog
makers, and even include
some extraordinary spun-
sugar creations.

A barrel on display in the Musée
du Compagnonnage

GARLIC AND BASIL FAIR

On 26 July, the Feast of St Anne, the place du Grand-
Marché in the Old Town, near the colourful covered
market *(Les Halles)*, is the scene of the traditional Garlic
and Basil Fair *(Foire à l'Ail et au Basilic)*. Pots of basil form
a green carpet, and stalls are garlanded with strings of
garlic heads, purple onions and grey or golden shallots.

Stalls laden with basil and garlic in the place du Grand-Marché

BLÉSOIS AND ORLÉANAIS

THESE TWO CLOSELY-LINKED *regions are excellent starting points for an exploration of the central Loire Valley. The area's forests and marshlands have attracted nature lovers for centuries. During the Renaissance, magnificent hunting lodges were built by kings and nobles throughout the area, including the great Chambord, the sumptuously furnished Cheverny and the charming Beauregard.*

Blésois and Orléanais remain richly forested, with abundant game, including rabbits and hares, deer and wild boar. The great forest of Orléans, still magnificent, contrasts with the heaths and marshy lakes of the Sologne, a secretive region of small, quiet villages and low, half-timbered brick farmhouses. Although a paradise for hunters and fishermen, other visitors rarely venture into the depths of this area.

The northern stretch of the Loire flows through towns whose names resound throughout the history of France. Bridges and castles at Gien, Orléans, Beaugency and Blois all assumed strategic significance during wars from the Middle Ages to the 20th century.

It was at Orléans in 1429 that Joan of Arc, lifting the English siege of the town, galvanized the spirit of the French army engaged in the Hundred Years' War. The modern city's proximity to Paris has led to its growth as a commercial centre, but careful reconstruction after the devastation of World War II has meant that a sense of the past survives in the old *quartier*.

During the Wars of Religion, the château at Blois was sunk in political intrigue. Now restored, its walls still echo with the events of 1588, when the Duc de Guise was assassinated on the orders of the king, Henri III.

To the west of the region, the River Loir, smaller than its majestic sound-alike, flows through the countryside of the Vendômois and also through Vendôme itself, one of the most attractive towns in the region. Vendôme's cathedral, La Trinité, is only one of the memorable churches in Blésois and Orléanais, many of them decorated with early frescoes and mosaics.

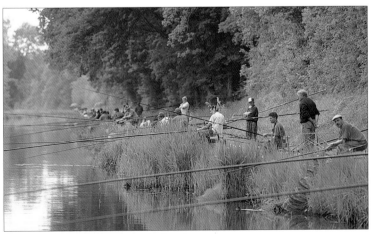

Anglers taking part in a competition on a local canal

◁ The nave of the Cathédrale Ste-Croix in Orléans

Exploring Blésois and Orléanais

O RLEANS, THE LARGEST CITY in Blésois and Orléanais, lies at the northernmost point of the River Loire. To the west is the Petite Beauce, fertile, wheat-growing land, while to the east is the great forest of Orléans, dense and teeming with wildlife. Blois, downstream from Orléans, is also surrounded by forests. To the south, the Sologne is a land of woods and marshes, scattered with small lakes, or *étangs*. The River Cher marks its southern border, as it flows through charming villages.

One of the region's stone farmhouses

0 kilometres   15

0 miles   15

GETTING AROUND

The fastest route by car from Paris is *L'Aquitaine* autoroute (A10), which passes through Orléans and Blois. Some Paris-to-Tours TGVs stop at Vendôme, only a 45-minute journey. The Corail express train from Paris takes one hour to Les Aubrais (a suburb of Orléans with a connecting train to the city centre) and 40 minutes to Blois via Beaugency and Meung-sur-Loire. Another Corail express (Tours to Nevers) follows the Cher, stopping at Montrichard, Thésée and St-Aignan. Bus services between towns are extremely limited, especially during the school holidays. The drive along the N76, which parallels the River Cher, is very scenic, and the roads through the cool, forested areas of the region are tranquil and pleasant.

The town of Blois with its distinctive bridge spanning the Loire

KEY

Motorway
Major road
Minor road
Scenic route
River
Viewpoint

Trôo's "speaking well"

Trôo ●

Road map D3. ♦ 320. ◻ *Vendôme, then taxi.* ◻ ◻ *Montoire-sur-le-Loir (02 54 85 23 30).*

O N A CLIFF above the Loir, this village should be entered from the top through its ruined medieval gate. To the left of the gate is a covered "speaking well"; at 45 m (150 ft) deep, it produces a very clear echo.

During the Middle Ages, a massive fortress stood here. It was fought over at the end of the 12th century by Richard the Lionheart, who lost it to the French king, Philippe Augustus. In 1590, the uncrowned Henri IV ordered the fortress to be dismantled. All that remains today is a mound, or *motte*, from the top of which there is a good view of the valley below.

Parts of the **Eglise St-Martin**, nearby, date from the 11th century, including the nave walls. The windows in the square Angevin tower are decorated with ornamental columns.

Steep paths wind down the hill towards the attractive **Château de la Voûte**, passing on the way the pretty flower gardens of a group of troglodyte dwellings, some of which are open to visitors. At the bottom of the hill is the

Grotte Pétrifiante, a cave full of stalactites that have been developing for more than 4,000 years.

Across the river, the little church at **St-Jacques-des-Guérets**, built in the 12th century, is justly famous for its 13 murals, painted in a distinctive Byzantine style. They were rediscovered in 1890 during restoration work. The *Christ in Majesty* in the apse is particularly beautiful.

St-Gilles chapel in nearby Montoire-sur-le-Loir is also worth a visit. It has some even finer 12th-century murals, remarkable for the range of colours used.

Lavardin ●

Road map D3. ♦ 250. ◻ *Vendôme, then taxi.* ◻ ◻ *Montoire-sur-le-Loir (02 54 85 23 30).*

T HE REMAINING fortifications of Lavardin's ruined **château**, towering above the reconstructed medieval bridge leading to the village, are an impressive sight. Situated on the boundary between the Capetian and Angevin kingdoms, the fortress was for centuries a key stronghold in battles between the French crown and the Plantagenet

Delicate murals in Lavardin's Eglise St-Genest

dynasty. In 1590, like the castle at Trôo, it was partly destroyed on the orders of Henri IV.

Memorable buildings in the town include the 11th-century town hall and the stone houses in the route de Villavard. Lavardin's treasure is the Romanesque **Eglise St-Genest** with its fragile and charmingly naïve murals dating from the 12th–16th centuries. Scenes from the life of Christ are alongside astrological symbols. Among the oldest of the frescoes is the *Baptism of Christ*, which is found at the entrance to the left chapel, together with the *Passion* and *Christ in Majesty*.

♠ **Château de Lavardin**
◻ *02 54 85 07 74 (Mairie).* ◻ *Easter–mid-Sep: Tue–Sun.* ◻ ◻

Vendôme ●

Road map D3. ♦ 18,000. ◻ ◻ ◻ *47–49 rue Poterie. (02 54 77 05 07).* ◻ *Fri & Sun.*

O NE OF FRANCE's most scenic towns, Vendôme is built over a group of islands in the Loir, its bridges, water gates and old stone buildings forming a delightful tableau. Now that it is just 45 minutes from Paris by rail, it has become a popular weekend retreat for many Parisians.

Situated on the border between the French and English feudal territories, the town changed hands many times. During the Hundred Years' War, it passed to the Bourbons in 1371, eventually becoming a duchy in 1515.

Later, held by the Holy League during the Wars of Religion, it was recaptured by Henri IV in 1589; the skulls of his leading Catholic opponents are by far the most grisly exhibit in the **Musée de Vendôme**. Set in an old abbey's cloisters, the museum also has a harp said to have been played by the ill-fated

Ornate façade of Abbaye de la Trinité in Vendôme

Marie-Antoinette, and some frescoes in the adjoining chapter house.

Vendôme's jewel is the abbey church of **La Trinité**, founded in 1034 by Geoffroy Martel, son of Foulques Nerra. It stands beside a 12th-century Romanesque bell-tower, with a spire reaching more than 80 m (260 ft). The church's bold, ornate façade was created by Jean de Beauce, who also designed the Old Bell-tower of Notre-Dame de Chartres. Its flame-like tracery is a typically virtuoso statement of the Flamboyant Gothic style.

Wooden carving from La Trinité

Inside, beyond the transept, which dates from the 11th century, are choir stalls carved with amusing figures. To the

left of the altar, a pretty latticework base with teardrop motifs once held a cabinet displaying a famous relic, which was said to be the tear supposedly shed by Jesus on the grave of Lazarus.

Shopping is centred around the place St-Martin, with its 15th-century clock-tower and carillon, and a statue of the count of Rochambeau, who commanded the French forces during the American Revolution. There is also a graceful, *fin-de-siècle* covered market just off rue Saulnerie.

The best views of the town's old fortifications are from the square Belot. Also visible from here is the Porte d'Eau, a water gate built during the 13th and 14th centuries, which once controlled the water for the town's mills and tanneries.

In the centre of town is the Parc Ronsard, with its 15th-century wash house, the Lavoir des Cordeliers, and the Old Oratorians College, which dates from the 17th and 18th centuries. Vendôme's ruined château stands on a bluff above the town, with the 12th-century Tour de Poitiers at one corner. The garden offers some delightful panoramic views of the town.

🏛 **Musée de Vendôme**
Cloître de la Trinité. **(** 02 54 77 26 13. ◯ Wed–Mon. ⬤ Nov–Mar, 1 May & Sun. 🎫

The Lavoir des Cordeliers in Vendôme's Parc Ronsard

Talcy's 300-year-old wine press, still in working order

Château de Talcy ❹

Road map E3. 🚊 *Mer, then taxi.*
(02 54 81 03 01. ◯ *Wed–Mon.*
⬤ *1 Jan, 1 May, 1 & 11 Nov, 25 Dec.*
🎫 🗹 *also night tours Jul–Aug.*
🎭 *Literature (May); Music (Jul–Aug).*

AFTER THE grander châteaux of the Loire Valley, Talcy comes as a delightful surprise: a fascinating, human-scale home, hiding behind a stern façade. The original building, a donjon, dates from the 15th century. It was transformed by Bernardo Salviati, a Florentine banker and cousin of Catherine de Médicis, who bought it in 1517 and added to the building significantly.

In 1545, the poet Pierre de Ronsard *(see p22)* fell in love with Salviati's 15-year-old daughter, Cassandre. Over the following decade, his love for her inspired the sonnets of his famous collection, known as *Amours de Cassandre*.

Bernardo Salviati gave Talcy its feudal look, adding the crenellated sentry walk and fake machicolations to the gatehouse. In the first courtyard, with its arcaded gallery, is an elegant domed well. A 3,000-bird dovecote in the second courtyard, dating from the 16th century, is the best-preserved in the Loire.

A huge, 300-year-old wooden wine press, still in working order, is worth a look. The château's vineyards are no longer productive, so the press is not in use. The grounds also contain old flower gardens.

Inside the château, the charming rooms have retained their original 17th- and 18th-century furnishings and decorative touches.

Street-by-Street: Blois ❺

A POWERFUL FEUDAL stronghold in the 12th century, Blois rose to glory under Louis XII, who established his court here in 1498. The town remained at the centre of French royal and political life for much of the next century. Now an important commercial centre for the agricultural districts of the Beauce and Sologne, Blois, with its harmonious combination of white walls, slate roofs, and redbrick chimneys, is the quintessential Loire town. The hilly, partly pedestrianized old quarter, bordered by the river, the château, and the cathedral, is full of architectural interest.

Hôtel d'Alluye
Blois' outstanding Renaissance mansion was built in 1508 by Florimond Robertet, treasurer to three kings.

| 0 metres | 10 |
| 0 yards | 100 |

Façade des Loges, the château's most theatrical side, has Renaissance window bays rising in tiers to a gallery.

★ Château de Blois
The rich history of the Château de Blois is reflected in its varied architectural styles.

Blois as seen from the Loire, with the three spires of the Eglise St-Nicolas in the centre

★ Eglise St-Nicolas
This striking, three-spired church once belonged to a 12th-century Benedictine abbey. Its high, narrow Gothic nave leads to an apse of magical beauty, sheltered by elegant Corinthian columns and lit through lovely blue glass.

KEY

— — — Suggested route

Escalier Denis-Papin
Named after the native son (1647–1714) who invented the pressure cooker, these stairs provide a remarkable view over the town and the river.

VISITORS' CHECKLIST

Road map E3. 🏘 50,000.
🚊 🚌 pl de la Gare. 🛈 3 av Jean-Laigret (02 54 90 41 41).
🛒 Tue & Sat.
🎭 Le Soleil à Rendez-vous avec la Lune (Jul–Aug).
Musée d'Histoire Naturelle
Couvent des Jacobins. 📞 02 54 90 21 00. ◯ Tue–Sun pm (Mon–Fri for groups). ● 1 Jan, 1 May, 1 Nov & 25 Dec. 🎫 ♿
Musée Diocésain des Arts Religieux Couvent des Jacobins.
📞 02 54 78 17 14. ◯ Tue–Sat.
● public hols. ♿

Maison des Acrobates, in the place St-Louis, has carvings of medieval characters on its posts.

Couvent des Jacobins now houses museums of religious art and natural history.

Cathédrale St-Louis
Most of the original building was destroyed by a hurricane in 1678. The present cathedral was erected during the reign of Louis XIV.

★ Quartier Vieux Blois
This well-preserved area of Blois has some marvellous 16th-century buildings. This galleried town house is at the top of rue Pierre de Blois.

STAR SIGHTS

★ Château de Blois

★ Eglise St-Nicolas

★ Quartier Vieux Blois

Château de Blois ❺

Porcupine emblem of the House of Orléans

HOME TO KINGS Louis XII, François I and Henri III, no other Loire château has such a sensational history of skulduggery at court. It culminated with the stabbing, on the order of Henri III, of the ambitious Duc de Guise, leader of the Catholic Holy League *(see pp54–5)*. This macabre event, which took place in the king's own bedroom, marked the end of the château's political importance. The building itself juxtaposes four distinct architectural styles dating from the 13th century, through the Gothic and Renaissance periods, to the Classical. The château is now emerging from major restorations begun in 1989.

Gaston d'Orléans Wing
The simplicity of the Classical design of this wing, as shown in the ceiling of the entrance hall, marked a departure from the rich decor of the Renaissance.

The Tour du Foix remains from the ramparts that surrounded the 13th-century feudal fortress.

King Louis XII
A statue of Louis XII (1462–1515) is the centrepiece of the entrance archway. Known as "Father of the People", he was popular for his benevolent domestic policies.

STAR FEATURES

★ **François I's Staircase**

★ **Cabinet de Catherine de Médicis**

★ **Salle des Etats Généraux**

TIMELINE

1200 Counts of Blois rebuild feudal fortress dating from 9th century

1391 Fortress passes to Louis d'Orléans, brother of Charles VI

1498 Louis XII adds three new wings and rebuilds the St-Calais chapel

1515 François I rebuilds north wing

1576 Etats Généraux meets in feudal hall

1635 Gaston d'Orléans replaces west wing with Classical building

1576 Etats Généraux meets in feudal hall

1588 Etats Généraux meets again. Henri III has Duc de Guise assassinated

1788 The decaying château is turned into barracks

1810 Napoléon makes city of Blois responsible for the château

1843 Félix Duban begins restoration of the château

1989 Major restoration programme begins

Architect Félix Duban

1200	1300	1400	1500	1600	1700	1800	1900

★ Cabinet de Catherine de Médicis
The queen's room has 237 carved panels, four with secret cupboards for her state papers, jewels or, some believed, poisons.

VISITORS' CHECKLIST

Pl du Château. 🚹 02 54 90 33 32.
🕐 Jan–Apr, mid-Nov–Dec:
9am–12:30pm, 2–5:30pm;
May–Jun & Oct: 9am–6pm;
Jul–Aug: 9am–7pm (last adm: 45
mins before closing). ⬤ 25 Dec,
1 Jan. 🈺 🗑 📷 🎥 Ainsi Blois
vous est conté (see p42).

The nave of the St-Calais chapel was pulled down during the 17th century to make way for Gaston d'Orléans' wing, leaving only the chancel standing today.

The Salle d'Honneur, previously partitioned, has a sumptuous west fireplace bearing the salamander and ermine emblems of François I and his mother, Louise.

Statue of Louis XII

The Gothic Louis XII wing has intricate, decorative brickwork.

★ François I's Staircase
Enclosed in an octagonal well, the staircase, with its highly ornate carving, is a Renaissance tour de force. From its open balconies, the royal family could watch events in the courtyard.

★ Salle des Etats Généraux
Used for royal receptions and Etats Généraux meetings (see pp54–5), the 13th-century room survives from the original fortress.

Château de Chaumont, towering above the town

Château de Chaumont **6**

Chaumont-sur-Loire. **Road map** D3.
🚉 Onzain, then taxi. 📞 02 54 51 26
26. ⭕ daily. ⬤ 1 Jan, 1 May, 1 &
11 Nov, 25 Dec. 🎫 🎪 Festival
International des Jardins.

SEEN FROM ACROSS the Loire,
Chaumont, set on a
wooded hill above the river,
appears like a fantasy of a
feudal castle. Its tall, white
donjon and round towers,
built between 1466 and 1510,
were never tested in battle
and have thus remained in
immaculate condition.

The main entrance, with its
double drawbridge and elaborate machicolated parapets,
is beautiful. Emblems carved
on the towers include the
crossed Cs of Charles II
d'Amboise, whose family had
owned a previous 12th-
century fortress on the site.

When Charles inherited
Chaumont in 1481, he
undertook several major
alterations. These were early
examples of the Renaissance
architectural style in France
and included the east wing,
with its elaborate frieze, and
the south wing, with its
entrance towers.

At one end of the south
wing, the projecting octagonal
tower, enclosing the main
spiral staircase, predates those
at Blois and Chambord (see
pp126–7 and pp132–5).

Catherine de Médicis, wife
of Henri II, acquired the

château in 1560. Legend has it
that Catherine's astrologer,
Ruggieri, used the tower
connected to her room as an
observatory. Here he is said
to have shown the queen the
fate of her three royal sons in
a magic mirror. Catherine's
chamber also has a balcony
adjoining the attractive
chapel, which
was restored
towards the end
of the 19th
century. In 1562
Catherine gave
Chaumont to
Diane de Poitiers,
mistress of the
late Henri II, after
forcing her out of
Chenonceau (see
pp108–9). Diane's
entwined Ds and
hunting motifs
are carved on the
machicolations of the entrance
and on the east wing.

Subsequent owners either
neglected the château or
altered it, sometimes radically,
to their own purposes. One
18th-century owner, aban-
doning the fortress design,
demolished the north wing so
that the whole courtyard was
opened up to the river views.

Sweeping improvements
began in 1875 when Prince
Amédée de Broglie came to

**Stained glass from the
dining room at Chaumont**

live in the château with his
wife Marie, a sugar heiress.
Their lavish lifestyle can be
sensed in the handsome
stables, which once housed
an elephant, given to them on
a visit to the Maharajah of
Kapurtala in India.

The council room has
tapestries by Reymbouts and
majolica floor
tiles, brought
from a 17th-
century Palermo
palace, while the
library has
medallions made
in the château by
JB Nini in the
18th century. The
château's park
was landscaped
in 1884 by
Achille Duchêne
and closely
follows the lines of an English
country garden.

Montrichard **7**

Road map D3. 🏘 3,800. 🚉 🚌
🛈 1 rue du Pont (02 54 32 05 10).
🗓 Mon pm, Fri am.
🔲 www.montrichard.fr

THIS SMALL VILLAGE built of
tufa rock is dominated by
the ruins of its **château**. The
11th-century drawbridge,

Montrichard, seen from across the River Cher

archers' tower and the remains of its Renaissance apartments remain, and the keep houses the small **Musée du Donjon** on local life.

Adjoining the chateau is the **Eglise Ste-Croix**. Here, in 1476, the future Louis XII reluctantly wed Jeanne, the tragically deformed daughter of Louis XI. The marriage was later annulled so Louis could marry Anne of Brittany.

On summer afternoons, the château's eagles take part in breathtaking falconry displays above Montrichard.

⚜ **Château de Montrichard & Musée du Donjon**
🕿 02 54 32 57 15. 🕘 mid-Apr–Sep: daily. 🦅 Eagle flights: mid-Mar–Jun & Sep–mid-Oct: daily pm; Jul & Aug: daily. ⬤ mid-Oct–Mar.

White tiger from Beauval Zoological Park

St-Aignan-sur-Cher ❽

Road map E3. 🏠 3,700. 🚉 St-Aignan-Noyers-sur-Cher. 🚌 ℹ 02 54 75 22 85. ⬤ Sat.

ONCE A RIVER PORT, St-Aignan is now an engaging summer resort for boating, swimming and fishing. The town is dominated by the Renaissance château of the dukes of Beauvillier and the collegiate church of St-Aignan, an underrated marvel of Romanesque art.

The château interior is not open to the public, but visitors can climb 19th-century stairs to look at its two elegant wings and enjoy the views from its courtyard terrace as a reward for their exertions. Ruined towers and

walls remain from a feudal fortress built by the counts of Blois. In rue Constant-Ragot, leading to the château and church, there is a fine half-timbered Renaissance house at No. 27.

The **Eglise de St-Aignan**, with its two impressive bell-towers, was begun around 1080. Its majestic chancel and sanctuary are built over an earlier Romanesque church, which now forms the crypt. Once used as a cowshed, the crypt still retains its Romanesque feel. Among the important frescoes to survive here are a portrayal of the miracles of St Gilles in the southern chapel and a rare 11th-century *Christ in Majesty* on the chancel vault.

Some of the 250 sculpted capitals in the main church are carved with scenes from the Old and New Testaments as well as allegories of sin and punishment. Others are worked with decorative motifs. In the Chapel of Our Lady of Miracles, the 15th-century ceiling paintings are equally fascinating.

The **Beauval Zoological Park**, 2 km (1¼ miles) south of the village, is among France's best. It contains over

St-Aignan's Chapel of Our Lady of Miracles

300 species of bird, a superb jungle house and otter pool, and impressive landscaped enclosures for big cats, including several magnificent prowling white tigers.

🐾 **Beauval Zoological Park**
🕿 02 54 75 50 00. 🕘 daily. 🦅 ♿

Thésée ❾

Road map E3. 🏠 1,100. 🚉 ℹ Jun–Sep: pl de la Gare (02 54 71 45 45). ⬤ Thu.

JUST OUTSIDE the charming little wine village of Thésée is the most important Gallo-Roman site in the Loire-et-Cher *département*, Les Maselles.

Impressive ruined walls with brick courses testify to the skills of stonemasons who, in the 2nd century AD, built Tasciaca. This settlement was a major staging post and ceramic-making centre on the road between Bourges and Tours. The **Musée Archéologique** within the town hall displays a quite dazzling and instructive array of jewels, coins, pottery and other interesting artifacts from this little-known site.

🏛 **Musée Archéologique**
Hôtel de Ville. 🕿 02 54 71 00 88. 🕘 Jul–Aug: Wed–Mon; Easter–Jun: Sat, Sun; public hols pms only: groups by appt. 🦅

Fresco of *Christ in Majesty*, from the Eglise de St-Aignan

Classical façade of the Château de Cheverny

Château de Cheverny ⑩

Road map E3. 🚐 ☎ 02 54 79 96 29.
⭘ daily. 📷 ♿ grd floor & park only.
ⓦ www.chateau-cheverny.fr

THE ELEGANCE of Cheverny's white tufa façade, with its pure Louis XIII lines, was achieved in a single phase of construction between 1620 and 1634, with all the finishing touches completed by 1648 (see pp16–17). Initiating a new architectural style for the châteaux and stately homes of the Loire Valley, Cheverny has no defensive elements, such as large turreted towers or formidable entrances. Instead, its Classical façade is

Arms and armour on display in Cheverny's Salle des Armes

striking in its simplicity. The château stands on the site of a previous castle, owned by the Hurault family. Henri Hurault, with his wife, Marguerite (who is thought to have influenced the elegance of the château), led its reconstruction, and the family has retained ownership of the château.

Jean Mosnier worked on the interior for ten years, using gilded beams, panels and ceilings. His finest work is in the dining room, with its scenes from Don Quixote's travels, and in the king's bedroom, where the combined effect of wall-hangings, painted ceilings and a bed canopied in Persian silk is stunning. The largest room in the château, the huge Salle des Armes, displays a collection of arms and armour and is adorned with Mosnier's paintings and a large Gobelins tapestry, the *Abduction of Helen*.

Paintings in the château include a portrait of Cosimo de' Médici by Titian and Pierre Mignard's striking portrait of the Countess of Cheverny above the fireplace in the Grand Salon. There is a collection of fine portraits by Jean Clouet and Hyacinthe Rigaud in the adjoining gallery. The Tapestry Room, with pieces of work designed by David Teniers, also features a lacquered

commode and a fascinating balance-wheel clock showing phases of the moon, both of which are in the distinctive Louis XV style. The château inspired Hergé to create the Château de Moulinsart for his *Tintin* stories.

The Cheverny hunt, which rides twice a week in winter to the call of ornate spiral horns, is famous throughout the Sologne. A visit to the kennels is a highlight of the château, especially at 5pm when 70 hounds politely wait their turn to eat. The Trophy Room is an eerie sight, with 2,000 pairs of antlers mounted on the walls and ceiling.

The Trophy Room at Cheverny

Château de Beauregard ⑪

Cellettes. Road map E3. 🚊 Blois, then taxi. ☎ 02 54 70 40 05. ⭘ Feb–Mar & Oct–Nov: Thu–Tue; Apr–Sep: daily. ● Dec–mid-Feb. 📷 ♿ ⓦ www.beauregard-loire.com

BEAUREGARD STANDS in a well-tended park on the edge of the Russy forest. Originally built at the beginning of the 16th century as a hunting lodge for François I, it was transformed into a graceful private manor house more than a century later by Jean du Thier, scholarly secretary of state to Henri II. It was du Thier who commissioned the king's Italian cabinet-maker, Scibec de Carpi, to make him an exquisite study panelled in gilded oak, the Cabinet des Grelots. This little room is

Detail from Beauregard's portrait gallery

Château de Villesavin ⓬

Villesavin. **Road map** E3. 🚉 *Blois, then taxi.* 📞 *02 54 46 42 88.* ⭘ *Feb–Dec: daily.* ● *25 Dec.* 🅿 ♿ *grd flr only.*

VILLESAVIN, built between 1527 and 1537 by Jean Breton, was his home while he supervised works at Chambord *(see pp132–5)* nearby. Stone carvers from the royal château ornamented Villesavin and presented Breton with the beautiful Florentine basin made of Carrara marble that stands proudly in the entrance courtyard.

Now in need of restoration, this is one of the least altered of the many late-Renaissance châteaux in the Loire Valley. Villesavin, with its low walls and unusually high roofs, was built around three very spacious courtyards. The elegant southern façade ends with a large dovecote, which has 1,500 pigeonholes and a revolving ladder.

One of Villesavin's antique carriages

The château's essentially domestic spirit is also evident in the service court, overlooked by a spacious kitchen with a working spit. The interesting collection of old carriages on display here includes an 18-m (59-ft) long *voiture de chasse* with four rows of seats, from which ladies could watch the hunt.

ENVIRONS: Situated on the southern banks of the Beuvron river, Bracieux is worth a visit for its grand covered market, which was built during the reign of the Renaissance king François I (1515–47). At that time, the town acted as an important staging post on the routes between the towns of Tours, Chartres and Bourges.

The market is built of brick, stone and wood, with an upper tithe barn. Its original oak posts were strengthened during the 19th century. There are also attractive 17th- and 18th-century houses.

decorated with the bells, or *grelots*, found on du Thier's crest, and has some charming paintings from the studio of Niccolo dell'Abate.

The portrait gallery, the château's most spectacular feature, was added in the 17th century by Henry IV's former treasurer, Paul Ardier. A complete catalogue of famous European faces from 1328 to 1643 – kings, queens, saints, explorers – is arranged in three rows around the gallery. Adding to the impact of these 327 portraits are beautiful beams and panels painted by Jean Mosnier and the largest delft-tiled floor in Europe, which depicts an army on the move in Louis XIII costume.

Other delights include the southern gallery, with its rich Brussels tapestry and carved furniture, and the kitchen, with its flagstone floors and a table built around the central column. Above the ratchet-operated spit, a motto on the chimney breast advises that those who keep promises have no enemies.

Garden façade of the Château de Villesavin

Château de Chambord ⑬

Henry James once said: "Chambord is truly royal – royal in its great scale, its grand air, and its indifference to common considerations." The brainchild of the extravagant François I, the château began as a hunting lodge in the Forêt de Boulogne. In 1519 the original building was razed and Chambord begun, to a design probably initiated by Leonardo da Vinci. By 1537 the keep, with its towers and terraces, had been completed by 1,800 men and two master masons. The following year, François I began building a private royal pavilion on the northeast corner, with a connecting two-storey gallery. His son Henri II continued the west wing with the chapel, and Louis XIV completed the 440-roomed edifice in 1685.

Statue of Diana in the Salle de Diane

The Château de Chambord with the Closson, a tributary of the Loire, in the foreground

The roof terraces include miniature spires, stair turrets, sculpted gables and cupolas.

★ **Skyline**
Chambord's skyline is its most astonishing feature – a bizarre jumble of different forms, likened to an overcrowded chess board.

The central keep, with its four circular towers, forms the nucleus of the château.

Salamander
François I's emblem appears more than 700 times in the château. It symbolizes patronage of the good and destruction of the bad.

Chapel
Begun by François I shortly before his death in 1547, the chapel was given a second storey by Henri II. Later, Louis XIV embellished the roof.

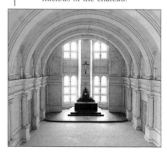

STAR FEATURES

★ **Skyline**

★ **Grand Staircase**

François I Staircase
The external spiral staircase located in the northeastern courtyard was added at the same time as the galleries, starting in 1538.

VISITORS' CHECKLIST

Road map E3. 🚆 *Blois, then taxi.* 📞 *02 54 50 40 00.* 🕐 *Oct–Mar: 9am–5:15pm daily; Apr–Sep: 9am–6:15pm daily.* 🕐 *1 Jan, 1 May & 25 Dec.* 🎫 ♿ 🚻 🏛 *Spectacle d'Art Equestre* 📞 *02 54 20 31 01 for reservations (May–Sep daily).* 🅦 *www.chambord.org*

The lantern tower, 32 m (105 ft) high, is supported by flying buttresses.

The guardrooms, which were once the setting for royal balls and plays, have ornate, vaulted ceilings.

François I's bedchamber in the east wing, as it was at his death in 1547.

Cabinet de François I
The king's barrel-vaulted study (cabinet) in the outer north tower was turned into an oratory in the 18th century by Queen Catherine Opalinska, wife of Stanislas Leszczynski (Louis XV's father-in-law and the deposed king of Poland).

★ Grand Staircase
Seen here from the guardrooms, this innovative double staircase was supposedly designed by Leonardo da Vinci. Two flights of stairs spiral around each other.

Louis XIV's Bedchamber
The Sun King's state apartments are the grandest in the château.

The History of Chambord

CHAMBORD, the largest château in the Loire, was a *folie de grandeur* of the young François I, whose ruling passions were hunting and flirting. "He is forever chasing, now stags, now women," the Venetian ambassador once said of him. The king personally supervised the enclosure of the game park surrounding Chambord with the most extensive wall in France – nearly 32 km (20 miles) long and 2.5 m (8 ft) high. At one point, he even suggested diverting the Loire to flow in front of his château, but instead settled for redirecting the nearer Closson to fill his moat.

Louis XIV portrayed as Jupiter, conquering La Fronde

François I as a young man, with various symbols of his kingship

After François I

On his father's death, Henri II took charge of François I's ambitious project. Subsequent owners – Louis XIII, who had no great love of hunting, and his brother Gaston d'Orléans – continued to modify the château. By the 17th century, Chambord comprised 440 rooms and had 365 chimneys, 14 main staircases and 70 smaller stairways.

Louis XIV, whose chief youthful amusement was hunting, took Chambord very seriously. His full court retinue visited the château numerous times. With balls, plays by Molière and operatic ballets, he re-created the glittering lifestyle of François I.

Louis XV also hawked at Chambord, but by 1725 he was ready to relinquish the château to his father-in-law, Stanislas Leszczynski. The exiled King of Poland is reported to have disliked the winter draughts. Certainly, he filled in the moats to prevent malarial fevers.

The last owner to enjoy Chambord's theatricality was the Maréchal de Saxe, victor over the English troops at the Battle of Fontenoy in 1745.

As well as lodging his actress mistress here, Saxe also kept two cavalry regiments whose mock battles he watched from the roof terraces.

During the second half of the 18th century, Chambord fell into neglect. Stripped during the French Revolution, the château was hardly used by the Bourbon pretender, Henri, Duc de Bordeaux, to whom it was given by public subscription in 1821. It was sequestered by the state in 1915, which bought it in 1930. A restoration programme was begun in the 1970s.

A view of Chambord (detail) by PD Martin (1663–1742)

TIMELINE

Maréchal de Saxe

1547–59 Henri II adds the west wing and second storey of the chapel

1560–74 Charles IX continues tradition of royal hunting at Chambord and writes *Traité de la Chasse Royale*

1840 Chambord declared a *Monument Historique*

1500	1600	1700	1800	1900

1670 Molière's *Le Bourgeois Gentilhomme* staged at Chambord

1519–47 The Count of Blois' hunting lodge is demolished by François I and the château created

1748 Acquired by the Maréchal de Saxe. On his death the château falls into decline

1725–33 Inhabited by exiled king of Poland

1685 Louis XIV completes the building

1970s Under Giscard d'Estaing, Chambord is restored and refurnished and the moats redug

Royal Hunting at Chambord

UNDER THE INFLUENCE of François I and his heirs, hunting and hawking were the foremost pastimes of the court during the 16th century. A Tuscan nobleman complained that the king only stayed in a place "as long as the herons last". They were quick prey for the 500 falcons that travelled with the rest of the royal retinue.

Within his vast oak forests, the king rode out at dawn to a prepared picnicking spot, there to feast and await the selection of a red deer tracked by his beaters. The quarry flushed, he would ride at full tilt in pursuit, sometimes for hours. For ladies of the court, Chambord's

St Hubert, patron saint of hunting

roof terraces offered matchless views of these exertions. François' son Henri II and grandson Charles IX were also keen and practised hunters, sometimes pursuing quarry on foot. Louis XIV favoured the English sport of following packs of hounds, but falconry was preferred by Louis XV.

Hunting was regarded as an art by the court, and its tools – weapons, horns and costumes – were carefully designed and crafted. For centuries, it was also a favourite subject for painters and tapestry designers, whose works were used to decorate palaces and hunting lodges.

Matchlock

Engraved barrel

Arquebus, an early form of musket, dating from the 16th century

Wild boar was a favourite beast of the chase because of its strength and ferocity. Its head was considered a delicacy.

The crossbow was a popular hunting weapon thanks to its versatility and rapid rate of fire.

Greyhounds, prized for their speed and keen eyesight, were used as hunting dogs.

The Boar Hunt *comes from the* Traités de Fauconnerie et de Vénerie *(1459), one of many treatises on falconry and hunting to hounds. In the foreground, beaters and dogs chase their quarry. Behind them, animals and men witness the end of the hunt.*

Beaugency

Road map E3. 🏠 *7,200.* 🚗 🚌
ℹ️ *3 pl de Docteur Hyvernaud (02 38 44 54 42).* 🗓️ *Sat.* 🎪 *Festival de Beaugency (first & second weekend Jul).*

WITH THE LOIRE racing beneath its famous 23-arch bridge, the medieval town of Beaugency makes a delightful base for exploring the Orléanais area. The town is surprisingly well preserved, although its bridge, the best on the Loire between Orléans and Blois, has attracted the attentions of a number of armies over the centuries. Restored in the 16th century, the bridge was damaged again in 1940 when the Allied army blew up its southern end to prevent the Nazis from crossing the river.

On the place Dunois at the top of rue de l'Abbaye stands a massive 11th-century keep. Opposite is the Romanesque abbey church of **Notre-Dame**, where Eleanor of Aquitaine's marriage to Louis VII was annulled in 1152, leaving her free to marry the future Henry II of England.

Higher up is the 16th-century Tour St-Firmin, near an equestrian statue of Joan of Arc. Next to the keep, her companion-in-arms, Jean Dunois, Bastard of Orléans and Lord of Beaugency, built the **Château Dunois**, now a folk museum. Nearby, in rue des Trois Marchands, is a

Beaugency's 11th-century clock-tower, once gateway to the town

medieval clock-tower and the Renaissance façade of the Hôtel de Ville. A flower-lined stream runs through the old mill district.

⚜️ Château Dunois (Musée Régional de l'Orléanais)
Pl Dunois. 📞 *02 38 44 55 23.*
🕐 *Wed–Mon.* ⬤ *1 Jan, 1 May, 24, 25 & 31 Dec.* 📷

Meung-sur-Loire ⑮

Road map E3. 🏠 *6,300.* 🚗 🚌
ℹ️ *42 rue Jehan-de-Meung (02 38 44 32 28).* 🗓️ *Sun am, Thu pm.*

THIS PRETTY little village, sloping down to the Loire, was the birthplace of Jean de Meung (*see p22*), one of the

authors of the 13th-century masterpiece *Le Roman de la Rose*. There has been a town on this site since Gallo-Roman times, when it was known as Magdunum.

Beside the impressive Romanesque church of **St-Liphard**, built from the 11th to the 13th century, rise the feudal towers of the **Château de Meung**. Frequently altered from the 12th century to the 18th century, the château was built in a variety of styles. The 18th-century wing has an interesting collection of furniture, paintings and tapestries put together by the current owner.

More intriguing are the underground passages and dungeons of the older castle, dating from the 12th to 13th centuries and used for 500 years by the bishops of Orléans as a prison. In 1461, the poet François Villon (*see p22*), renowned for his life of disrepute as well as his fine writing, spent five months fighting with the other condemned criminals on a ledge above a cesspool in the château's claustrophobic oubliette. Thanks to a royal pardon from Louis XI, he was the only prisoner ever to emerge alive from there.

⚜️ Château de Meung
📞 *02 38 44 36 47.* 🕐 *mid-Feb–mid-Nov: daily; mid-Nov–mid-Feb: Sat, Sun pm. (groups by appt).* ⬤ *25 Dec, 1 Jan.* 📷 🎥 ♿ *grd flr only.*

Beaugency's medieval bridge, the Tour St-Firmin and the keep rising above the trees

The entrance to the Château de Chamerolles

Château de Chamerolles ⑯

Chilleurs-aux-Bois. **Road map** E2.
🚌 Orléans. 🎫 02 38 39 84 66.
⏰ Feb–Jun & Sep–Dec: Wed–Mon;
Jul–Aug: daily. ● 25 Dec. ♿

O N THE EDGE of the huge
forest of Orléans, this
Renaissance château was built
between 1500 and 1530 by
Lancelot du Lac, Governor of
Orléans (who was named
after the legendary
Arthurian knight).
Although it was
constructed in
the form of a
fortress, with a
drawbridge
crossing a moat
and a courtyard
enclosed by
turreted wings,
Chamerolles
was designed as
a pleasant per-
sonal residence.

**Baccarat
perfume bottle
in Chamerolles'
museum**

Pretty Renaissance gardens,
accurately reconstructed with
trellised walks, extend to a
gazebo offering views back to
the château across a "mirror"
lake. There is an area of rare
aromatic plants, many of
which were used during the
16th century for making
medicines and perfumes.

A museum in the château
traces the development of per-
fumery through the centuries,
covering the variety of uses
for perfumes as well as the re-
finement of the science of
making them. This includes
the laboratories of perfumers
and naturalists and glittering
displays of bottles, as well as
a charming gift shop.

JOAN OF ARC

Joan of Arc is the supreme national
heroine, a virgin-warrior, patriot and
martyr whose shining self-belief
turned the tide of the Hundred
Years' War against the English.
Nowhere is she more honoured
than in the Loire Valley, scene
of her greatest triumphs.

Responding to heavenly
voices telling her to "drive the
English out of France", Joan
left her home soon after her
17th birthday in 1429 and
travelled via Gien to Chinon
to see the dauphin, the as yet
uncrowned Charles VII. He

**Joan of Arc, pictured in a
medieval tapestry**

faced an Anglo-Burgundian alliance on the verge of
capturing Orléans. Joan convinced him she could save the
city, armed herself in Tours, had her standard

blessed in Blois and entered Orléans with
a small force on 29 April. Galvanized
by her leadership, the French drove
the English off on 7 May. The
people of Orléans have celebrated
8 May as a day of thanksgiving
almost ever since. Joan returned to
Gien to urge Charles forward to
Reims for his coronation in July. In
1430 she was captured and accused
of witchcraft. Handed over to the

**Stained-glass portrait of
Charles VII from Loches**

English, she was burned at the stake at the age of 19. Joan's
piety, patriotism and tragic martyrdom led to her canonization almost 500 years later, in 1920.

***Joan of Arc Entering Orléans** by Jean-Jacques Sherrer (1855–1916)*

Orléans ⑰

ORLEANS WAS THE CAPITAL of medieval France and a royal duchy until the 18th-century French Revolution, when it became staunchly Republican. Its historical fame might, at first glance, seem submerged by its 20th-century role as a rail junction, food processing and business centre, especially as the old quarter of the city was badly damaged during World War II. However, an area of the old town near the river, now reconstructed, is full of interest for the visitor, and there are many beautiful gardens in this "city of roses".

Heroic Joan of Arc

Exploring Orléans

A sense of grandeur lingers in Vieil Orléans, the old quarter bounded by the cathedral, the River Loire and the **place du Martroi**. Dominating this square is Denis Foyatier's statue of the city's heroine, Joan of Arc, whose festival on 8 May is a highlight of the year. The plinth of the statue, which was erected in 1855, is beautifully sculpted with the events of her life. Two splendid Classical buildings, the Chancellery and the Chamber of Commerce, are also found in the square.

A few medieval buildings have survived in the narrower streets around rue de Bourgogne, a partly pedestrianized shopping street with an astonishing range of ethnic restaurants. Other delightful and often inexpensive restaurants can also be found close to the **Nouvelles Halles**, the city's covered market. The most sophisticated shopping street is the rue Royale, which leads to the 18th-century bridge, the Pont George V.

🏛 Maison de Jeanne d'Arc

3 pl de Gaulle. 📞 02 38 52 99 89.
🕐 May–Oct: Tue–Sun; Nov–Apr: Tue–Sun pm only. 🌑 1 Jan, 1 May, 8 May, 25 Dec. 🎫

A reconstruction of the half-timbered house that lodged the warrior-saint for ten days in 1429, the Maison de Jeanne d'Arc presents scenes from her life as well as mementos, costumes and banners.

The evocative audiovisual dioramas include one that shows Joan's assault on the English-held Tourelles fort.

Orléans' Renaissance Hôtel Groslot, once a private residence

🏠 Hôtel Groslot

Pl de l'Etape. 📞 02 38 79 22 30.
🕐 Mon–Fri. 🌑 public hols.

The most handsome of the many Renaissance buildings in the city, the Hôtel Groslot, built between 1549 and 1555, served until recently as the town hall.

Built out of red brick crossed with black, this was a grand residence, with scrolled staircase pillars, caryatids and an ornately tooled interior. It was once considered fine enough to lodge the kings of France. Here, in 1560, the sickly, young François II died after attending a meeting of the Etats Généraux with his child bride, Mary, later Queen of Scots. The beautiful statue

of Joan of Arc guarding the steps was sculpted by Princess Marie d'Orléans in 1840. Walk through the building to visit a charming little park, backed by the re-erected façade of the 15th-century Flamboyant Gothic chapel of St-Jacques.

🔒 Cathédrale Ste-Croix

Pl Ste-Croix. 📞 02 38 24 05 05 (tourist office). 🕐 daily. 🎫

The cathedral, set on a spacious esplanade, was begun in the 13th century. The original building was completely destroyed by Huguenots in the 16th century and then restored in a supposedly Gothic style between the 17th and 19th centuries. Behind the ornate façade, the towering nave is lit by the radiating spokes of the rose window dedicated to the "Sun King", Louis XIV. The chapel of Joan of Arc, whose martyrdom is portrayed in stained glass, features a kneeling sculpture of Cardinal Touchet, who fought for her canonization. In the crypt, ecclesiastical treasures in gold and enamel are on display, as well as the masterly painting *Christ Bearing the Cross*, by the Spanish religious painter, Francisco de Zurbarán (1598–1664).

The nave of the Cathédrale Ste-Croix

The peaceful Parc Floral in Orléans-la-Source

ENVIRONS: The suburbs of
Orléans can be pleasant
places to relax after a day
spent sightseeing in the city
centre. In Olivet, for example,
it is possible to go boating on
the River Loiret. This river
also provides opportunities
for pretty walks. A tributary
of the Loire, the Loiret flows
underground from near the
town of St-Benoît-sur-Loire
(see p140) and rises in the
grand **Parc Floral** of Orléans-
la-Source. A 100-ha (245-acre)
nature reserve, the park is a
mass of blooms from April.
Adjoining the park is the 17th-
century Château de la Source
and the buildings of the University of Orléans.

🏛 Musée des Beaux-Arts

1 Rue Fernand Rabier. 📞 *02 38 79
21 55.* 🗓 *Tue–Sun.* 🔴 *1 Jan, 1 & 8
May, 11 Nov, 25 Dec.* 🎫 ♿
The high standard of the
collection, which includes a
self-portrait by Jean-Baptiste-
Siméon Chardin (1699–1779)
and *St Thomas* by the young
Diego Velázquez (1599–1660),
represents the strength of
European painting from the
14th to the early 20th century.
There is a charming collection
of miniature enamelled
statuettes on the second floor,
a contrast to the richness of
the 19th-century paintings.

🏛 Musée Historique et Archéologique

Square de l'Abbé Desnoyers. 📞 *02
38 79 25 60.* 🗓 *May–Jun & Sep:
Tue–Sun pm only; Jul–Aug: Tue–Sun;
Oct–Apr: Wed, Sat & Sun pm.* 🔴 *1
Jan, 1 May, 1 Nov, 25 Dec.* 🎫
The chief treasures of this
museum are the Celtic statues
discovered at Neuvy-en-
Sullias in 1861, which include
a fine horse from the 2nd
century AD *(see p49)*. The
museum also has a beautiful
painted stone head of Joan
of Arc and a pleasing variety
of arts and crafts from the
Middle Ages onwards.

🍁 Parc Floral

Orléans-la-Source. 📞 *02 38 49 30
00.* 🗓 *Apr–mid-Nov: daily; mid-Nov–
Mar: daily pm only.* 🔴 *1 Jan, 25 Dec.*
🎫 ♿

ORLÉANS TOWN CENTRE

Cathédrale Ste-Croix ④
Hôtel Groslot ②
Maison de
    Jeanne d'Arc ①
Musée des
    Beaux-Arts ③

KEY

🅿️ Parking

✝️ Church

0 metres   250

0 yards   250

The Romanesque façade of the abbey church of St-Benoît

St-Benoît-sur-Loire ⑱

Road map F3. 🏛 2,000. 🚌
ℹ 44 rue Orléanaise (02 38 35 79 00).
ⓦ www.saint-benoit-sur-loire.fr

T̲HIS QUIET TOWN has one of the finest Romanesque abbey churches in France, constructed between 1067 and 1108. The most appealing feature of the façade is the belfry porch, probably built early in the 11th century by Abbot Gauzlin, son of the first Capetian king, Hugh. On the capitals of its 50 golden pillars are carved figures, including beasts and goblins.

Inside, thickset columns separate the side aisles from the rib-vaulted Gothic nave. The chancel, dating from the earlier Romanesque period, has blind arcades and a mosaic floor brought from Rome. The bas-relief head of a Norman raider is carved on the wall of the north transept. Its cheeks are pierced to expel its pagan spirit.

In the crypt, a lamplit casket contains the relics of St Benedict, the 6th-century father of Western monasticism. They were spirited here in 672 from Benedict's own monastery of Monte Cassino in Italy. By the 11th century, when the present building was begun, the Benedictine order was rich and St-Benoît-sur-Loire was renowned for its scholarship as well as its purloined relics. St-Benoît is a living monastery, and one of the best ways to experience the spirit of the place is to attend evening vespers or recitals of Gregorian chant.

The 9th-century church of **St Germigny-des-Prés** lies 5 km (3 miles) along the D60 from St-Benoît-sur-Loire. The small cupola of the east apse has an enchanting mosaic of angels bending over the Ark of the Covenant – a composition made up of 130,000 coloured-glass cubes probably assembled during the 6th century.

Gien ⑲

Road map F3. 🏛 16,500. 🚊 🚌
ℹ pl Jean-Jaurès (02 38 67 25 28).
🗓 Wed, Sat. ⓦ www.gien.fr

S̲ENSITIVELY RESTORED after being devastated during World War II, Gien is considered one of the Loire's prettiest towns. From its handsome quays and 16th-century bridge, houses of brick, slate and pale stone rise steeply to a château. It was built for Anne de Beaujeu, who acted as regent for her brother Charles XIII at the end of the 15th century.

Only the steeple tower of the **Eglise Ste-Jeanne d'Arc**, next to the château, survived the

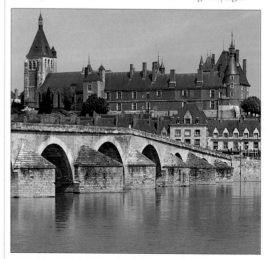

Max Ingrand's stained glass

destruction of the war, but a remarkable church replaced it in the 1950s. Warm facings, composed of bricks made in Gien's famous pottery kilns, blend with the patterned red and black brickwork of the château. The interior glows with stained glass by Max Ingrand and the faïence that is a speciality of the area. A museum of fine china and earthenware is open daily at the factory, which was founded in 1821 (see p221).

The **château** of Anne de Beaujeu, built between 1484 and 1500 on the site of one of the Loire's oldest castles, sheltered the young Louis XIV and the Queen Mother during the Fronde civil war (1648–53). Its grand beamed halls and galleries now house a superb museum of hunting, tracing the sport's development since prehistoric times. The collection covers the weaponry, costumery, techniques and related artistry of almost every associated activity, from falconry to the royal chase. The memorable entrance hall of the château features a 17th-century painting of St Hubert, the patron saint of hunting, depicting his conversion by the vision of a resurrected stag carrying a

Gien's château and its 16th-century bridge across the Loire

crucifix between its horns. An Italian crossbow and a powder horn decorated with images of the mythical and tragic encounter between Diana and Actaeon are beautiful examples of 17th-century carving. Other prominent artists on display here include the 20th-century sculptor Florentin Brigaud, the Flemish etcher, Stradanus, and François Desportes, whose fine paintings dominate the spectacular trophy hall.

♣ Château et Musée International de la Chasse
📞 02 38 67 69 69. ⏰ daily. ● 1 Jan & 25 Dec. 🌐

A pleasure boat crossing Briare's elegant bridge-canal

Briare-le-Canal ❷⓪

Road map F3. 🏠 6,000. 🚉 🚌
🛈 pl Charles-de-Gaulle (02 38 31 24 51). 🛒 Fri.

THIS SMALL TOWN, with its attractive marina, is the setting for a sophisticated engineering masterpiece – the longest bridge-canal in Europe (see pp56–7). With stonework and wrought-iron flourishes designed by Gustave Eiffel (1832–1923), the structure crosses the Loire, linking the Briare-Loing canal with the Canal Latéral. These waterways in turn join the Seine and the Rhône rivers respectively. Visitors can stroll its length, lined in the style of a Parisian boulevard with elegant lampposts, or sail across the 662-m (2,170-ft) bridge in a bateau-mouche.

Fishing on one of the peaceful étangs of the Sologne

The Sologne ❷①

Road map E3. 🚉 🚌 Romorantin-Lanthenay. 🛈 (02 54 76 43 89).

B ETWEEN GIEN and Blois, the Loire forms the northern boundary of the Sologne, a vast area of flat heathland, marshes and forests covering nearly 500,000 ha (1,235,000 acres). The area is dotted with étangs, broad lakes teeming with fish, which are magnets for migratory birds and waterfowl. The forests are just as attractive to hunters and nature lovers now as they were during the Renaissance, when members of royalty chose to build their grand hunting lodges here. Much of the land is privately owned, although there are some public paths.

Romorantin-Lanthenay is the "capital" of the Sologne. With its 17th- to 19th-century buildings and its medieval quarter, it is pleasant to visit. The town is also home to the **Musée de Sologne**, whose

exhibits explain the economy and wildlife of the area.

St-Viâtre, just north of Romorantin-Lanthenay, is a centre for bird-watching on the étangs of Brosses, Grande Corbois, Favelle, Marcilly and Marguilliärs. The **Maison des Etangs** at St-Viâtre gives guidance on ornithology.

For game, there are four observation hides in the park of Chambord (see pp134–5), where deer can often be seen – and heard in the autumn rutting season. Another large, public nature reserve is the **Domaine du Ciran**, 25 km (15 miles) south of Orléans, near Ménestreau-en-Villette.

🏛 Musée de Sologne
📞 02 54 95 33 66. ⏰ Wed–Sat, Sun pm–Mon. ● 1 Jan, 1 May, 25 Dec. 🌐 ♿

🦌 Maison des Etangs
📞 02 54 88 23 00. ⏰ mid-Sep–mid-Jun: by appt; mid-Jun–15 Sep: daily. 🌐

🦌 Domaine du Ciran
Ménestreau-en-Villette. 🚉 La Ferté-St-Aubin, then taxi. 🛈 Ménestreau-en-Villette (02 38 76 90 93).

A typical, half-timbered building of La Sologne

BERRY

BERRY LIES IN THE VERY CENTRE OF FRANCE, *south of the Paris Basin and just north of the Massif Central. It is a varied land of wheat fields, pastures and vineyards, ancient forests, rolling hills and lakes, peaceful villages and elegant manor houses. Mainly off the beaten tourist track, the region gives visitors an opportunity to experience the rural heart of France.*

Bourges, the principal town of Berry, was one of the capitals of Aquitaine in the Gallo-Roman period. It then enjoyed another moment of glory in the 14th century, with the administration of Jean, Duc de Berry. This warmongering patron of the arts built a splendid palace in the city (now destroyed) and collected paintings, tapestries, jewellery and illuminated manuscripts.

In the 1420s, when Charles VII was fighting for the French crown *(see pp52–3)*, Bourges was his campaign base. Afterwards, his treasurer Jacques Cœur did much to make the kingdom financially secure. The Palais Jacques-Cœur in Bourges competes with the city's magnificent cathedral in drawing crowds of admiring visitors.

Berry is ideal for those who love the outdoors, whether walking in the many well-tended forests, fishing or bird-watching in La Brenne, or sailing and canoeing on its rivers and lakes. Among the region's literary associations are George Sand's novels *(see p22)* and Alain-Fournier's evocative tale *Le Grand Meaulnes* (1913), which combines his childhood memories of the Sologne in the north and the rolling country of the south.

The culinary highlights of Berry include dishes made from local game and wild mushrooms. To the northeast, the renowned Sancerre wine district *(see p155)* is also known for its excellent goats' cheeses, such as the famous Crottin de Chavignol.

A river view by the village of Argenton-sur-Creuse

◁ **The vineyards of Sancerre**

Exploring Berry

BOURGES IS THE NATURAL starting point for exploring the heart of France. From here it is only a short drive to the edge of the Sologne *(see p141)* in the north or La Brenne in the southeast, both havens for wildlife. Below Bourges is the Champagne Berrichonne, a vast agricultural region producing wheat, barley and oil-rich crops such as rape and sunflowers. The River Loire forms the ancient border between Berry and Burgundy to the east as it flows through the vineyards of the Sancerrois hills.

The Palais Jacques-Cœur in Bourges

0 kilometres 15

0 miles 15

Orléans

VIERZON

VALENÇAY **1**

D960

D960

A20 (E09)

D956

D926

D918

Tours

N143

Indre

VILLEGONGIS **2**

D956

D925

D926

D925

N143

N151

D918

D925

CHÂTEAUROUX

ISSOUD

LA BRENNE **3**

D975

D43

D943

4 FONTGOMBAULT

N151

A20 (E09)

Indre

LE BLANC

N151

Creuse

N151

ARGENTON-SUR-CREUSE

6 NOH

Poitiers

N151

D975

5

D48

D927

D943

CHATEAUMEI

D40

D940

A20 (E09)

Fresselines

Limoges

GETTING AROUND

The A71 autoroute from Paris passes through Vierzon, Bourges and St-Amand-Montrond and is an excellent way of travelling from north to south. The TGV does not stop in the region, but Corail trains from Gare d'Austerlitz in Paris take just over two hours to either Bourges (not direct) or Châteauroux. There are also frequent trains between Bourges and Tours. Public transport to the more isolated sights is limited and a car is a great advantage, especially when touring the Sancerre wine estates or La Brenne nature reserves.

A riverside scene, typical of the Berri region's gentle landscape

D948

de Sauldre

D8

AUBIGNY-SUR-NÈRE 15

D751

LA LOGNE

14 **LA VERRERIE**

D923

SANCERRE

13

D944

D940

WINE AND CHEESE TOUR 16

Loire

D955

N151

BOURGES

(11)

12

Yèvre

** NE BERRICHONNE**

D976

Cher

A71 (E11)

N144

Auron

N76

Allier

Nevers

Moulins

11 **MEILLANT**

NOIRLAC 10

D951

AINAY-LE-VIEIL 9

A71 (E11)

8 **CULAN**

Montluçon

KEY

Motorway

Major road

Minor road

Scenic route

River

Viewpoint

The hilltop town of Sancerre, surrounded by vineyards

A resident peacock in front of the Château de Valençay

Château de Valençay **①**

Road map E4. *Valençay.*
 02 54 00 10 66. **Château & Park**
 Mar: Mon–Fri pms, Sat & Sun;
Apr–Oct: daily; Nov–Feb: Sat, Sun and
school hols pms. *restricted.*
 A Day with Prince Talleyrand
(Easter–Nov: weekends; Jul–Aug: daily).
Musée de l'Automobile *02 54*
00 07 74 (phone for information).
 www.chateau-valencay.com

FROM ITS TREE-LINED approach, the Château de Valençay is a fine sight. Started in 1510, it took more than 300 years to complete, but its Renaissance and Classical elements are convincingly blended. In 1803, it was bought by Bonaparte's foreign minister, Charles-Maurice de Talleyrand Périgord. Until his death in 1838, the famous statesman entertained many of Europe's dignitaries here. His descendants still lived in the château until 1980.

Valençay's rooms are richly furnished, mostly in the Empire style, and they display many *objets d'art* connected with Talleyrand. Indeed, in summer, visitors can spend the day in the great man's company, with members of his entourage, including his famous chef, Carême.

Formerly within the park, the **Musée de l'Automobile**, a collection of motoring memorabilia and vintage cars (all in working order), is reopening nearby. Peacocks, deer, swans, and less usual creatures such as llamas and kangaroos are, however, still seen in the grounds.

Château de Villegongis **②**

Road map E4. *Châteauroux, then*
taxi. *02 54 36 60 51.* *closed*
to public until further notice.

ELEGANT AND MOATED, the Château de Villegongis was probably built by Pierre Nepveu, one of the master masons for Chambord *(see pp132–5).* Since the 15th century, ownership has stayed in the same family. Barely touched since that time, it is one of the purest examples of the French Renaissance style.

The château's most striking features are its richly decorated chimneys, which suggest the link with Chambord, and its cylindrical towers at either end of the main building.

The interior is exceptionally well furnished, with some fine 17th- and 18th-century pieces. There is also a remarkable carved stone staircase.

La Brenne **③**

Road map E4. *Mézières-en-Brenne, Le Blanc.* *Maison du Parc, Rosnay (02 54 28 12 13); Mézieres-en-Brenne (02 54 38 12 24).*
 www.parc-naturel-brenne.fr

THE PARC NATUREL Régional de la Brenne, covering 165,000 ha (407,700 acres), is better known as the *Pays des Mille Etangs* (The Land of a Thousand Meres). A beautiful region of lakes and wooded hills, La Brenne is a paradise for nature lovers. It has been estimated that 250 of the 450 bird species known in Europe can be observed here.

Several specialist reserves are open to visitors, such as the **Réserve Naturelle de Chérine**, good for spotting European pond tortoises, and the **Parc Animalier de la Haute-Touche**, home to endangered species of deer. The town of Mézières-en-Brenne houses the **Maison de la Pisciculture**, whose aquaria display local fish species.

 Réserve Naturelle de Chérine
St-Michel-en-Brenne. *02 54 38 12 24.* **Observatory** *daily.*
 1 Jan, 25 Dec. *Bird-watching tours: Apr–Oct: daily am.*
 Parc Animalier de la Haute-Touche
Obterre. *02 54 02 20 40.*
 Easter–Oct: daily.
 Maison de la Pisciculture
Mézières-en-Brenne. *02 54 38 12 99.* *Wed–Mon, pm only.*
 1 Jan, 1 May, 25 Dec.
 grd flr only.

One of the many idyllic lakes in La Brenne

Abbaye de Notre-Dame de Fontgombault ❹

Road map E4. **(** 02 54 37 12 03, 02 54 37 30 98. ☐ daily. 🕆 Mass: 10am daily; Vespers: 6pm Mon–Sat, 5pm Sun. ♿

THE BEAUTIFUL Benedictine **Abbaye de Notre-Dame de Fontgombault**, famous for its Gregorian chant, was founded in 1091 but, by 1741, when the number of monks had dwindled to just five, it was abandoned. Restored by a local priest in the 19th century, it now houses monks from Solesmes *(see p162)*.

The church, with its five radiating chapels, has a richly decorated doorway, carved capitals and a much-venerated 12th-century statue known as Notre-Dame du Bien-Mourir, believed to comfort the dying. Gregorian chant is still sung during services and is more prominent in the morning service. The monks run a pottery, whose products can be bought from the exhibition centre beside the church.

The radiating chapels of the Abbaye de Notre-Dame de Fontgombault

Old houses overhanging the river in Argenton-sur-Creuse

Argenton-sur-Creuse ❺

Road map E4. 🚶 5,420. 🚉 🚌 ℹ pl de la République (02 54 24 05 30). ☖ Thu & Sat. 🎭 Murcuria International Folklore Festival, biennial (Jul).

ARGENTON-SUR-CREUSE is one of the prettiest towns along the river, which winds from Fresselines to Argenton, passing through deep gorges. Streets of picturesque houses climb the hillside to Argenton's chapel of Notre-Dame-des-Bancs, dominated by its 6-m (20-ft) gilded statue of the Virgin Mary. There are fine views from here and from the Vieux Pont, a medieval bridge.

In the 19th century, the town became an important centre for the clothing industry. This feature of the town's heritage is honoured by the informative collections of the **Musée de la Chemiserie et de l'Elégance Masculine**.

🏛 **Musée de la Chemiserie et de l'Elégance Masculine**
Argenton-sur-Creuse. **(** 02 54 24 34 69. ☐ mid-Feb–Dec: Tue–Sun. 🎥 ♿

Château de Nohant ❻

Road map E4. **(** 02 54 31 06 04. 🚉 🚌 Châteauroux. ☐ daily. ● 1 Jan, 1 May, 1 & 11 Nov & 25 Dec. 🎥 🎭 Fêtes Romantiques de Nohant (Jun); Chopin chez George Sand (Jul). 🕆 02 54 31 07 37.

GEORGE SAND, the *nom de plume* of the celebrated novelist, Baroness Aurore Dudevant (1804–76), was largely brought up in this charming manor house beside a tiny Romanesque church. She frequently returned here during her eventful and unconventional life, to enjoy the calm and beauty of her beloved Berry countryside.

Many of George Sand's novels, including *La Mare au Diable (The Devil's Pool)* and *La Petite Fadette (The Little Fairy)*, are set here *(see p22)*. Sand's admirers can view the boudoir where she first wrote, at a desk inside a cupboard; the stage on which she and her guests acted out her plays; the puppets made by her son, Maurice; the bedroom used by her lover, Frédéric Chopin; and the room in which she died in 1876.

MONET AT FRESSELINES

In 1889 the Impressionist painter Claude Monet travelled to the village of Fresselines, perched high above the Creuse. He visited a local beauty spot, with views plunging down into the river gorge, was captivated, and painted a series of canvases showing the scene in different lights. In February, bad weather forced him to stop painting and wait for spring. He then found that new growth had changed the view and had to pay the owner of an oak featured in five of his paintings to strip the tree of its new leaves.

Valley of the Petite Creuse by Claude Monet

Châteaumeillant ⑦

Road map F4. 👥 *2,110.* 🚉 *St Amand-Montrond.* 🚌 ℹ️ *rue de la Libération (02 48 61 39 89).* 🛒 *Fri.*

T HE CHIEF GLORY of this town is the Romanesque **Eglise St-Genès**, built between 1125 and 1150, with its elegant pink and grey west façade. The interior is exceptionally airy, due not only to its great height, but also to its very wide chancel with six apsidal chapels and side passages that are separated by graceful double bays to create a cloisters effect.

Châteaumeillant was once an important Gallo-Roman centre. The **Musée Emile-Chenon**, based in a 15th-century manor house, contains Roman artifacts and local medieval finds.

🏛 **Musée Emile-Chenon**
ℹ️ *rue la Victoire (02 48 61 39 89).* ⭕ *Jun–Sep: daily; Oct–May: by appt only.* 📷 ✅

Château de Culan ⑧

Road map F4. 📞 *02 48 56 66 66.* ⭕ *Apr–Oct: daily.* 📷 Ⓦ *www.chateau-de-culan.com*

S TRATEGICALLY positioned on an escarpment above the River Arnon, this medieval fortress dates from the 13th and 14th centuries. Its three conical towers are topped by wooden siege hoardings. A series of furnished rooms relate the castle's long history,

The interior courtyard of the Château d'Ainay-le-Vieil

recalling famous visitors who have stayed there, including the Admiral of Culan, who was a comrade-in-arms of Joan of Arc (who also stayed there in 1430), and the writers George Sand *(see p22)* and Madame de Sévigné, and telling of an attack during the 17th-century Fronde uprising.

Lovely views over Culan's newly replanted gardens and the pastoral Arnon Valley can be enjoyed from the terrace of the château.

Château d'Ainay-le-Vieil ⑨

Road map F4. 🚉 *St-Amand-Montrond, then taxi.* 📞 *02 48 63 50 03.* ⭕ *Feb: Wed–Mon pms; Mar, Oct & Nov: Wed– Mon; Apr–Sep: daily.* 📷 ✅

F ROM THE OUTSIDE, Ainay-le-Vieil has the appearance of a fortress, with formidable walls and its nine massive towers, lit only by thin arrow slits. The octagonal enclosure, surrounded by a moat, is entered through a huge, 13th-century postern gate. The exterior belies the fact that hidden inside is a graceful Renaissance château designed for an elegant lifestyle, with its richly decorated façade enlivened by sunny loggias.

The castle changed hands many times during its early history. In the 15th century, it belonged briefly to Charles VII's treasurer Jacques Cœur *(see p151)*, but in 1467 it was bought by the Seigneurs de Bigny whose descendants still live here today.

The Grand Salon was decorated in honour of a visit by Louis XII and Anne of Brittany around 1500. It has a painted ceiling and a monumental fireplace, which is said to be one of the most attractive in the Loire Valley. On display is a portrait of Louis XIV's chief minister Jean-Baptiste Colbert and portraits of other family members, as well as an amber pendant that belonged to Queen Marie-Antoinette and several *objets de vertu*, friendship gifts given by Napoleon to General Auguste Colbert.

The tiny Renaissance chapel has some beautiful, late 16th-century wall paintings, which were discovered under 19th-century decoration. Its stained-glass windows were made by an artist who also worked on the Cathédrale St-Etienne in Bourges *(see pp152–3)*.

In the park is a delightful and sweet-smelling rose garden. Some of the varieties of roses which are grown here date back to the 15th century.

The Château de Culan, set high above the River Arnon

Abbaye de Noirlac ⑩

Road map F4. St-Amand-Montrond, then taxi. *02 48 62 01 01.* ○ *daily.* ● *1 Jan & 25 Dec.* *L'Eté de Noirlac (Jul–Aug).*

THE CISTERCIAN Abbaye de Noirlac, founded in 1136, is a fine example of medieval monastic architecture. The Cistercian Order's austerity is reflected in the pure lines of the partly 12th-century church and visually echoed in its sober, modern stained glass.

The chapter house, where the monks' daily assemblies were held, and the *cellier*, where the lay brothers were in charge of the food, wine and grain stores, were also built in this plain but elegant style. The cloisters, with their graceful arches and decorated capitals, date from the 13th and 14th centuries, which was a less severe period.

At **Bruère-Allichamps**, 4 km (2½ miles) northwest of the abbey, a Gallo-Roman milestone marks the alleged exact central point of France.

Château de Meillant ⑪

Road map F4. St-Amand-Montrond, then taxi. *02 48 63 32 05.* ○ *Feb–Nov: daily.* *grd flr only.*

SUMPTUOUSLY furnished rooms and the elaborate carved ceilings of this well-preserved Berry château complement its

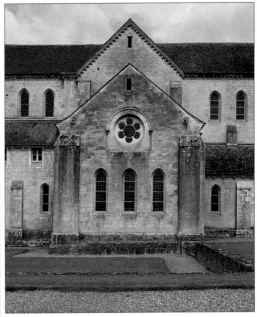

The austere lines of the Abbaye de Noirlac

rather exuberantly decorated courtyard façade. Built for Charles d'Amboise in 1510 by skilful Italian craftsmen, the château represents a fine combination of late Gothic and early Renaissance architecture. It is dominated by the *Tour de Lion* (Lion's Tower), an octagonal three-storey staircase tower. The plainer west façade, mirrored in a moat, dates from the early 14th century.

A small grotesque carving in Meillant

Other highlights of a visit include the château's graceful chapel and its surrounding grounds in which peacocks strut. The grounds also feature **La Mini'stoire**, an interesting miniature park, where models of buildings depict the ways in which architectural styles have varied over the centuries.

🏛 **La Mini'stoire**
○ *Feb–Nov: daily.*

LIFE IN A CISTERCIAN ABBEY

The Rules of the Cistercian Order were based on the principles of austerity and simplicity. Abbeys were divided into two communities, which did not mix. Lay brothers, not bound by holy vows, ensured the self-sufficiency of the abbey by managing the barns, tilling the fields, milling corn and welcoming guests. The full, or choir, monks were the only ones allowed into the cloister, at the heart of the

A Cistercian monk labouring in the fields

complex, and could not leave the abbey without the permission of the abbot.

The monks' days started at 2am and ended at 7pm and were regularly punctuated by religious devotions, which included prayers, confession, meditation and mass. The strict rule of silence was broken only to read from the Bible or from the Rules of the Order. Many monks were literate, and monasteries played a leading role in copying manuscripts.

Bourges ⑫

THE HEART OF MODERN BOURGES, once the Roman city of Avaricum, is the network of ancient streets around its magnificent cathedral. Despite a dramatic fire in 1487, the city was an important religious and arts centre in the Middle Ages and, by the late 19th century, it was a prosperous industrial town. Today Bourges has a quiet atmosphere that complements its excellent museums, housed in superb old buildings. It comes to life in the spring during the *Printemps de Bourges*, a rock festival attracting a large, predominantly young audience.

The 16th-century *Concert Champêtre*, displayed in the Hôtel Lallement

🏛 Hôtel des Echevins & Musée Estève

13 rue Edouard Branly. (02 48 24 75 38. ○ Mon, Wed–Sat; Sun pm only. ● 1 Jan, 1 May, 1 & 11 Nov & 25 Dec. ♿

The Hôtel des Echevins (the house of the aldermen), which is remarkable for its intricately carved octagonal tower, was built in 1489 and served as the seat of the city council that governed Bourges for more than three centuries.

The building was classified an historic monument in 1886. In 1985 work to renovate the building began, and in 1987 it became the Musée Estève, displaying paintings by the self-taught artist Maurice Estève, who was born in Culan in the south of Berry (*see p148*). The collection is mainly made up of Estève's powerful, brightly coloured canvases. However, this permanent display is augmented by temporary exhibitions of his watercolours, collages and line drawings. The collection is arranged in chronological order on three levels, connected by elegant stone spiral staircases. This modern work seems surprisingly at home in the spacious Gothic rooms.

Samsâra by Maurice Estève (1977)

🏛 Hôtel Lallemant & Musée des Arts Décoratifs

6 rue Bourbonnoux. (02 48 57 81 17. ○ Tue–Sat; Sun pm only. ● 1 Jan, 1 May, 1 & 11 Nov & 25 Dec.

This Renaissance mansion, built for a rich merchant family originally from Germany, houses the city's decorative arts museum. It still has the little chapel used by the Lallemant family, its coffered ceiling carved with alchemical symbols, and an elegant, restored courtyard. On display is a fine collection of tapestries, clocks, ceramics, glass, paintings and furniture, including a beautiful 17th-century ebony inlaid cabinet. In another part of the mansion, there is a collection of toys dating from the 17th century to the present.

🏛 Musée du Berry

4–6 rue des Arènes. (02 48 70 41 92. ○ Mon, Wed–Sat; Sun pm only. ● 1 Jan, 1 May, 1 & 11 Nov & 25 Dec. ♿ grd flr only.

The Musée du Berry, housed in the Renaissance Hôtel Cujas, concentrates on local history. The collections include a large display of Gallo-Roman artifacts, many of which were unearthed in the area. There is some wonderful Gothic sculpture, especially Jean de Cambrai's weeping figures from the base of the tomb of Jean, Duc de Berry, the upper section of which can be seen in the crypt of the Cathédrale St-Etienne (*see pp152-3*).

On the upper floor of the museum is a permanent exhibition of Berry's rural arts, crafts, and everyday objects, including the distinctive stoneware made in La Borne near Sancerre.

Jehan Fouquet's Angel Ceiling in the Palais Jaques-Cœur

JACQUES CŒUR

The son of a Bourges furrier, Jacques Cœur (c.1400–56) became one of the richest and most powerful men in medieval France. With his merchant fleet he sailed to the eastern Mediterranean and Far East, bringing back luxury goods such as silks, spices and precious metals, until Charles VII appointed him head of the Paris Mint, then treasurer of the Royal Household. In 1451 he was accused of fraud and falsely implicated in the death of the king's mistress, Agnès Sorel. He was arrested, tortured and imprisoned, but escaped to Rome. There he took part in the pope's naval expedition against the Turks and died on the Greek island of Chios.

The merchant Jacques Cœur

VISITORS' CHECKLIST

Road map F4. 🏠 76,000. 🚉 pl Général Leclerc. 🚌 rue Doulet. 🛈 21 rue Victor Hugo (02 48 23 02 60). 🛒 Thu, Sat–Sun. 🎭 Printemps de Bourges (Apr); Eté à Bourges (street festival, mid-Jun–Sep).

The fireplace in the south gallery of the Palais Jacques-Cœur

🏛 Palais Jacques-Cœur

Rue Jacques-Cœur. 📞 02 48 24 06 87. ◯ daily. ⬤ 1 Jan, 1 May, 1 & 11 Nov, 25 Dec. 🎟 ✓

This splend palace, built on the remains of the city's Gallo-Roman walls, is among the finest secular Gothic buildings in Europe. It was constructed at great expense between 1443 and 1451 for Jacques Cœur, one of the most fascinating men in medieval France.

The palace has a number of innovations remarkable for their period. Rooms open off corridors instead of leading into each other, as they did in most buildings at the time, and a stone lavatory shows that sanitation was a consideration. Appealingly, each room is "labelled" over the doorway with carved scenes that illustrate its function.

From *trompe l'oeil* figures peeping out from the turreted entrance façade to the mysterious, possibly alchemical, symbols carved everywhere, the palace offers a feast of interesting details. Hearts are a common motif – the newly ennobled Jacques Cœur naturally had hearts, *cœurs* in French, on his coat of arms.

Other notable features are a large courtyard, superb wooden vaulting in the galleries, and the beautiful ceiling in the chapel, painted by Tours artist Jehan Fouquet *(see p23)*.

BOURGES TOWN CENTRE

Cathédrale St-Etienne ⑤
Hôtel des Echevins (Musée Estève) ③
Hôtel Lallemant (Musée des Arts Décoratifs) ④
Musée du Berry ①
Palais Jacques-Cœur ②

KEY

🅿	Parking
🛈	Tourist information
✝	Church, cathedral

0 metres   350
0 yards   350

Bourges: Cathédrale St-Etienne

Stained-glass window detail

St-Etienne, one of France's finest Gothic cathedrals, was built mainly between 1195 and 1260. The unknown architect designed St-Etienne without transepts, which, combined with the interior's unusual height and width, makes it seem much lighter than most Gothic cathedrals. This effect is beautifully enhanced by the brilliant hues of the medieval stained glass. Also unusual are the asymmetrical west front; the double row of flying buttresses rising in pyramid-shaped tiers; and a "crypt", a lower, window-lit church, created because the ground is 6 m (20 ft) lower at the east end.

Vast Interior
The interior is 124 m (400 ft) long and 37 m (120 ft) high.

The Tour Sourde (Deaf Tower) is so called because it has no bell.

★ Astrological Clock
Dating from the 1420s, this fascinating clock was designed by Canon Jean Fusoris, a mathematician.

Entrance

THE LAST JUDGMENT

The tympanum on the central portal of the west façade depicts Archangel Michael weighing souls. Those found wanting are hustled by devils into the mouth of Hell, while the elect are gathered into the bosom of Abraham. The youthful, naked dead lift up their tombstones in a dramatic Resurrection scene.

The Last Judgement portal of the Cathédrale St-Etienne

The Grand Housteau is a striking rose window, donated by the renowned patron of the arts Jean, Duc de Berry.

The five portals of the west front are surrounded by carved scenes. The doorways vary in size and shape, adding to the asymmetry of the façade.

★ Stained-Glass Windows
The medieval stained glass in the choir was sponsored by local guilds, whose members are depicted practising their crafts at the bottom of each window.

The Chapelle Jacques-Cœur has a glorious Annunciation window.

VISITORS' CHECKLIST

Pl Etienne Dolet. 📞 02 48 65 72 89. ⏰ 8am–7:30pm daily. 📷 Apr–Oct. ✝ Mon–Sat: 6:30 pm; Sun: 9am (summer), 11am. **Crypt** ⏰ Mon–Sat: 9am–noon 2–6pm daily (5pm winter). 🎫 📷

Praying Figures
In the crypt are statues of the Duc and Duchesse de Berry. During the Revolution the statues were decapitated and the existing heads are copies.

The crypt, or lower church, was built in the earlier Gallo-Roman moat.

The Romanesque portal on the cathedral's south side is decorated with a *Christ in Majesty* and the 12 apostles.

★ St Sépulcre
This dramatic sculpture of the Entombment of Christ *was placed at the far end of the lower church in 1540.*

STAR FEATURES

★ **Astrological Clock**

★ **Stained-Glass Windows**

★ **St Sépulcre**

Jean, Duc de Berry
The recumbent marble effigy of Jean, Duc de Berry, his feet resting on a bear, was originally part of his tomb.

A Sancerre vineyard

Sancerre ⑬

Road map F3. 🏘 2,100. 🚌
🛈 02 48 54 08 21. 🚌 Sat.
🎪 Foire aux Crottins (goat's cheese fair, early May); Foire aux Vins (wine fair, Whitsun); Foire aux Vins de France (French wine fair, late Aug).
ⓦ www.sancerre.net

THE ANCIENT Berry town of Sancerre is perched on a domed hill, a rare sight in the flat landscape of the Loire Valley. Its narrow streets boast interesting 15th- and 16th-century houses. All that remains of the medieval castle that once dominated the town is the **Tour des Fiefs**, which gives a superb view of the River Loire. The town and surrounding area are famous for their dry white wines.

Located in a lovely pastoral setting, 10 km (6 miles) to the west of Sancerre, the **Château de Boucard** is part medieval in origin, but has an elegant Renaissance courtyard.

🏰 **Tour des Fiefs**
🔲 Mar–Oct: Sun & public hols pm only (Jul–Aug: Sat pm too).
🏯 **Château de Boucard**
Le Noyer. 📞 02 48 58 72 81.
🔲 Easter–Nov: Fri–Wed. 🎫

Château de la Verrerie ⑭

Road map F3. 🚉 Gien, then taxi.
📞 02 48 81 51 60. 🔲 Easter–Nov: daily. 🎫 🦽 See **Where to Stay**, p205.

THIS FINE, early Renaissance château is on the edge of the Forêt d'Ivoy. The land was given to the Scot Sir John Stewart of Darnley by Charles VII, in thanks for defeating the English at the battle of Baugé in 1421. John's son, Béraud Stewart, began to build the château several decades later. It was completed by Béraud's nephew, Robert.

La Verrerie reverted to the French crown in 1670. Three years later Louis XIV gave the château to Louise de Kéroualle. She lived here until her death in 1734 at the age of 85.

La Verrerie has a lovely Renaissance gallery with 16th-century frescoes. The chapel also has fine frescoes, which date from the same period. In the 19th-century wing are four beautiful alabaster statuettes from the tomb of the Duc de Berry (see pp152–3).

The grounds have a good restaurant and some of the château's rooms are available for visitors to stay overnight.

Alabaster statuettes in the Château de la Verrerie's 19th-century wing

Aubigny-sur-Nère ⑮

Road map F3. 🏘 6,000. 🚌 🛈 rue de l'Eglise (02 48 58 40 20). 🚌 Sat.
🎪 Fête Franco-Ecossaise (mid-Jul).
ⓦ www.aubigny-sur-nere.fr

ATTRACTIVE AUBIGNY, is proud of its association with the Scottish Stewart clan. In 1423 the town was given by Charles VII to Sir John Stewart of Darnley, along with nearby La Verrerie. After a major fire in 1512, the Stewarts rebuilt Aubigny in the Renaissance style and also constructed a new château.

In 1673 Louis XIV gave the duchy of Aubigny to Louise de Kéroualle. Although she spent most of her time at La Verrerie, Louise had a large garden created at the Château d'Aubigny. The Aubusson tapestries presented to her by the king are displayed in the château, which now serves as the town hall and also houses two museums. The unusual **Musée de la Vieille Alliance Franco-Ecossaise** is devoted to the Auld Alliance, the town's long ties with Scotland: Jacobite refugees settled here during the 18th century.

The 13th-century **Eglise St-Martin**, in transitional Gothic style, was largely rebuilt by the Stewarts. It has a beautiful wooden Pietà and a moving 16th-century Entombment.

Berry has a reputation for sorcery, a tradition well illustrated in Concressault's lively **Musée de la Sorcellerie**, 10 km (6 miles) east of Aubigny. Here waxworks bring to life the history of herbalism, healing and magic, and portray the gruesome fate of those accused of witchcraft during the Inquisition.

🏛 **Musée de la Vieille Alliance Franco-Ecossaise & Musée Marguerite-Audoux**
Château d'Aubigny. 📞 02 48 81 50 07. 🔲 Easter–Jun & mid-Sep–Oct: Sat, Sun & public hols pms only; Jul–mid-Sep: daily; Nov–Easter: Sun & public hols. 🎫 🦽 Musée de la Vieille Alliance only.
🏛 **Musée de la Sorcellerie**
La Jonchère, Concressault. 📞 02 48 73 86 11. 🔲 Easter–Oct: daily. 🎫 🦽

The Maison de François I, one of the many old houses in Aubigny-sur-Nère

Wine and Cheese Tour ⑯

The Sancerrois in eastern Berry is renowned for its wines and goats' cheese. Gourmets can visit the top-class Sancerre caves and taste the fresh and fragrant white wines made from the Sauvignon grape, or charming light reds and rosés made from the Pinot Noir. The flavours combine beautifully with the sharp little goats' cheeses called Crottins de Chavignol, which are also produced locally. This rural route passes by gently hilly vineyards and fields of grazing red goats. It takes in the locales of many of the major producers, as well as a few local museums that explain the long history of both wine and cheese.

Sancerre wine

Verdigny ⑤
The Musée de la Vigne et du Vin, located here, charts the history of winemaking in the Sancerrois. Exhibits include an ancient wooden wine press.

Goats' cheese label

Chavignol ④
This picturesque town gives its name to the little cheeses. The Musée de la Cure exhibits traditional cheesemaking techniques and peasant costumes.

Amigny

Sancerre ①
In the vast cellars of the Caves de la Mignonne, visitors can taste the different varieties of Sancerre and get information about local producers.

Vinon ②
At the Elevage Caprin des Garennes, Crottins de Chavignol can be tasted and the cheesemaking process watched.

Bué ③
Many vintners are based in and around this important *commune viticole*, including Cordier, Reverdy and Roger.

BOURGES

Bannon

Tips for Drivers

Tour length: 30 km (19 miles).
Stopping-off points: Motorists should have little trouble in spotting places to stop and sample wine and cheese. La Tour and La Tasse d'Argent in Sancerre are recommended (see p218).

Key

▬▬ Tour route

══ Other roads

0 kilometres ────── 1

0 miles ────── 1

NORTH OF THE LOIRE

THE PEACEFUL MAYENNE *and Sarthe regions seem worlds away from the tourist-frequented château country of the central Loire Valley. A grouping of districts with little common history, the area north of the Loire has very different attractions from the former royal domains to the south. The rivers, hills, forests and plains abound with opportunities for fishing, boating and country walks.*

River boats cruise along the quiet Sarthe, through pretty wooded scenery and meadowlands, to Sablé-sur-Sarthe, near the Abbaye de Solesmes, famous for its tradition of superb Gregorian chant.

The more dramatic scenery of the Mayenne valley, from Laval southwards, with steep cliffs and villages perched on wooded hills, makes a pleasant spot for a restful break from château-visiting. The river, studded with locks, runs into the Maine and then into the Loire, a pattern also followed by the Loir (Le Loir, which is not to be confused with La Loire).

The valley of the Loir is also very pretty, the slow-moving river flowing through peaceful villages. It is a perfect place for relaxing and enjoying the countryside. The valley also offers a few spectacular sights of its own, including the château at Le Lude, with its four imposing corner towers and the stern-faced château of Châteaudun further upstream, which was once a stronghold of the counts of Blois. Le Mans, world famous for its 24-hour car race, also has an attractive old town, Le Vieux Mans. East of the town, gentle scenery gives way first to the wooded hills of the Perche and then to the vast wheat-fields on the plain of the Beauce, which is dominated by the magnificent cathedral at Chartres. Two lovely châteaux, Anet and Maintenon, were homes to royal mistresses: Diane de Poitiers *(see p55)*, mistress of Henri II, retreated to Anet, and Madame de Maintenon was the mistress of Louis XIV. Like Chartres Cathedral, these great houses stand on the edge of the Ile de France, the region around Paris, so they attract many day visitors from the country's capital.

Clog-making at the woodwork centre in Jupilles in the Forêt de Bercé

◁ **The River Sarthe near the village of St-Céneri-le-Gérei**

Exploring the North of the Loire

CONSISTING OF THE *départements* of Mayenne, Sarthe and Eure-et-Loire, the region north of the Loire borders Brittany, Normandy and the Ile de France. It combines characteristics of all these regions with those of the central Loire Valley. In the north, the hills of the Alpes Mancelles have more in common with the landscapes of Normandy than they do with the rolling fields further south. The rivers traversing the region – the Loir, Sarthe and Mayenne – are smaller and gentler than the mighty Loire but still very scenic. The largest towns in the region are Chartres, Le Mans and Laval, all of them worth a visit.

One of Chartres' winding cobbled streets

Cruising on the River Sarthe, upstream from Sablé

GETTING AROUND

Chartres and Le Mans are both reached from Paris by the A11 autoroute *(L'Océane)*, which continues to Angers. The A81 crosses the region from Le Mans to Laval, and the new section of the A28 from Alençon to Ecommoy. Trains from Paris are frequent: the TGV takes 55 minutes to Le Mans and Corail Express trains take 60 minutes to Chartres. From Chartres to Le Mans is also an hour. Bus services link most of the main towns in the region but are less regular during school holidays. Boating is one of the best ways of seeing the countryside.

Key

Motorway	
Major road	
Minor road	
Scenic route	
River	
Viewpoint	

The waterfront at
Malicorne-sur-Sarthe

D16

Avre

ANET ⑰

DREUX ●

Eure

D939

D983

A11 (E50)

Paris

Eure

CHARTRES
⑱

N23

**ILLIERS-
COMBRAY**
⑯

A11 (E50)

N10

N154

Huisne

D13

Loir

D921

D927

A11 (E50)

D927

⑮ **CHATEAUDUN**

Orléans →

D302

Tours →

N157

D303

OURTANVAUX ⑭

D305

0 kilometres   15

0 miles   15

View of the Old Town in Le Mans from the river

Musée Robert Tatin ❶

Road map B2. La Frénouse. 🚗
Laval. 🚌 Cossé-le-Vivien. 📞 02 43
98 80 89. ⬜ Apr–mid-Oct: Tue
pm–Mon; mid-Oct–Mar: Wed–Fri, Sat
& Sun pm only. ⬤ Jan. 🖼 ♿
courtyard & grd flr only.

THE MULTI-TALENTED artist, Robert Tatin (1902–83), devised an extra-ordinary museum, in the little village of La Frénouse, near Cossé-le-Vivien. The building is approached via the Allée des Géants (Giants' Avenue): lining the path are huge, strange concrete figures, depicting people who impressed Tatin, including Pablo Picasso, Toulouse-Lautrec, Joan of Arc and the Gallic warrior, Vercingetorix. Beyond them, a statue of a huge dragon with enormous jaws stands guard.

Tatin's statue of Picasso at the Musée Robert Tatin

In the museum are some 400 examples of Tatin's work: paintings, sculpture, frescoes, mosaics and ceramics. Tatin was also a cabinet-maker and much else besides. He was influenced by the megalithic monuments in Brittany and the traditional costumes worn by Breton men and women, as well as by Aztec art – he lived and travelled in South America for five years.

Laval ❷

Road map C2. 🏛 54,000. 🚗 🚌
🛈 1 allée du Vieux St-Louis (02 43
49 46 46). 🛒 Tue, Sat.
🖥 www.laval-tourisme.com

LAVAL STRADDLES the River Mayenne, which can be crossed via the humpbacked Gothic Vieux Pont (Old Bridge). Beside it on the west bank is the **Vieux Château**. This castle dates from the early 11th century, when the region was under the sway of Foulques Nerra, Count of Anjou – it formed one link in his chain of fortresses designed to keep out the invading Bretons and

Normans. Although it has been heavily rebuilt and added to over the centuries, the original medieval round keep has survived. The flower-filled courtyard, with a terrace offering good river views, has an attractive Renaissance façade.

The château has a collection of the equipment used by Laval native, Ambroise Paré (1510–c.1592), known as "the father of modern surgery". It is best known, however, for its **Musée d'Art Naïf** (Museum of Naïve Art) which was inspired in part by Henri Rousseau (see p23). He was known as Le Douanier, his nickname deriving from the period when he worked as a customs officer. His Paris studio, complete with piano, has been well reconstructed here. Although

the museum has only two of Rousseau's paintings, there are many gems in its 450-strong collection, including a painting of the ocean liner Normandie by Jules Lefranc (1887–1972).

Laval's old town has attractive houses as well as the **Cathédrale de la Ste-Trinité**, with its Aubusson tapestries. Laval also has one of France's few surviving bateaux-lavoirs, **Bateau-Lavoir St-Julien**, now a museum. Such floating laundries first appeared in the mid-19th century on the banks of rivers in the western Loire Valley.

🏛 **Château & Musée du Vieux Château**
Pl de la Trémoille. 📞 02 43 53 39 89.
⬜ mid-Aug–mid-Jul: Tue–Sun; mid-Jul–mid-Aug: daily. ⬤ 1 Jan, 1 May,
1 & 11 Nov, 25 Dec. 🖼 📷 ♿ grd
flr only.
🏛 **Bateau-Lavoir St-Julien**
Quai Paul-Boudet. 📞 02 43 53 39
89. ⬜ Jul–Aug: Tue–Sun; Sep–Jun:
groups by appt.

Le Lancement du Normandie by Jules Lefranc, at the Musée d'Art Naïf

Ste-Suzanne ❸

Road map C2. 🚶 *1,020.* 🚌 *Evron, then taxi.* ℹ️ *13 rue de la Cité (02 43 01 43 60).* 🌐 www.sainte-suzanne.com

THIS VILLAGE, high on a hill, is still partly surrounded by the fortifications designed as a defence against marauding Normans in the 10th century – it was sturdy enough to withstand an attack by William the Conqueror, whose former encampment site can be seen just 3 km (2 miles) outside the town. Although much of the original castle was pulled down by the English in the early 15th century, a 10th-century keep has withstood the ravages of time. The present castle, the **Château des Fouquet de la Varenne**, constructed of white tufa and grey slate, dates from the early 17th century.

The village has a museum, the **Musée de l'Auditoire**, which covers local history, with reconstructions of events and vignettes of daily life.

Church doorway, St-Léonard-des-Bois

🏛 Château des Fouquet de la Varenne
Promenade de la Poterne. 📞 *02 43 01 40 77.* ⏰ *mid-Apr–mid-Jun & mid-Sep–early Nov: daily, pm only; mid-Jun–mid-Sep: daily; mid-Nov–mid-Apr: groups by appt.* 💶

🏛 Musée de l'Auditoire
7 Grande Rue. 📞 *02 43 01 42 65, 02 43 01 42 16.* ⏰ *Apr–Oct: daily pm only; Nov–Mar: Sun pm.* 💶

Les Alpes Mancelles ❹

Road map C2. 🚌 *Alençon.* 🚌 *Fresnay-sur-Sarthe.* ℹ️ *19 av du Dr Riant, Fresnay-sur-Sarthe (02 43 33 28 04).*

THE NAME of this region of wooded hills and green meadows, between Fresnay-sur-Sarthe and Alençon, means "Alps of Le Mans". Although certainly an exaggeration, there is something faintly alpine in the landscape, with its streams winding through

St-Céneri-le-Gérei's Romanesque church, perched on a hill

gorges, sheep, fruit trees and heather-clad hillsides.

The prettiest villages are **St-Céneri-le-Gérei**, which has a Romanesque church containing 12th- and 14th-century frescoes, and **St-Léonard-des-Bois**, also with a Romanesque church. There are walks through the countryside, along the River Sarthe, and the area is popular for all sorts of sports *(see pp224–7).*

Fresnay-sur-Sarthe ❺

Road map C2. 🚶 *2,500.* 🚌 *Alençon, Sillé-le-Guillaume, La Hutte.* 🚌 ℹ️ *19 av du Dr Riant (02 43 33 28 04).* 🛒 *Sat.*

ALTHOUGH INDUSTRIAL on its outskirts, the rest of Fresnay still retains a somewhat medieval feel. There were

originally three rings of walls surrounding the town and fragments of them are still visible from the river.

The castle, which is strategically located on a rocky spur above the Sarthe, was besieged by William the Conqueror in 1073. During the Hundred Years' War *(see pp52–3)*, this was the last fortress in the region to be surrendered by the English. The remains of the castle now stand as a reminder of more turbulent times amid acres of pleasant parkland.

From the 16th to the 19th century, Fresnay-sur-Sarthe was an important centre for cloth-weaving, and its involvement in the clothing industry is documented in the interesting **Musée des Coiffes** (Headdress Museum) which is now housed in the remains of the castle.

The town also has a long tradition of encouraging local craftspeople, some of whose work is displayed in the **Maison du Tourisme et de l'Artisanat**.

Situated at the end of the avenue du Dr Riant, the **Eglise Notre-Dame**, with both Romanesque and Gothic elements, has an unusual tower with an octagonal base and a beautiful, intricately carved, old oak door.

🏛 Musée des Coiffes
Pl de Bassum. 📞 *02 43 97 22 20.* ⏰ *Easter–Jun & Sep: Sun & public hols; Jul–Aug: daily.* ⏰

🏛 Maison du Tourisme et de l'Artisanat
Pl de Bassum. 📞 *02 43 33 75 98.* ⏰ *Jan, Mar–May, Sep–Nov: Fri pm–Sun; Jun–Aug & Dec: daily.* ⬤ *Feb.*

The River Sarthe from the town of Fresnay-sur-Sarthe

Sablé-sur-Sarthe ❻

Road map C2. 🏠 *12,700.* 🚉
🚌 ℹ *pl Raphaël-Elizé (02 43 95 00 60).* 🍽 *Mon, Fri–Sat.* 🎭 *Festival et Académie de Danses et Musiques Anciennes (Aug).*
🌐 www.sable-sur-sarthe.com

A GOOD BASE from which to take river cruises along the Sarthe, Sablé is pleasant, although fairly industrial. There is some surprising modern sculpture in this traditional setting: in the cobbled place Raphaël Elizé in the town centre stands a contemporary sculpture entitled *Hymne à l'Amour*, by local sculptor Louis Derbré, and around the square are several piles of "cannon balls", a rather curious modern installation that was inspired by an 18th-century fashion.

Sablé has some attractive shops in the pedestrian rue de l'Ile and in the square, where the Maison du Sablé sells the famous shortbread-like biscuits to which the town has given its name.

The town's château, which was built in the early 18th century by a nephew of Louis XIV's chief minister, Jean-Baptiste Colbert, now houses workshops for restorers of old books and manuscripts of the Bibliothèque Nationale, the national library of France. Although the château cannot be visited, the pleasant park that surrounds it is open.

On the route de Solesmes, opposite the summer swimming pool, is the Jardin Public, from which there are views of the Abbaye de Solesmes.

The Tomb of Our Lord, part of the "saints of Solesmes" group of stone carvings in the church of the Abbaye de Solesmes

Abbaye de Solesmes ❼

Road map C2. 🚉 *Sablé-sur-Sarthe, then taxi.* ℹ *02 43 95 03 08.*
Abbey Church 🕐 *daily.* ✝ *10am daily; vespers: 5pm daily.* ♿
🌐 www.solesmes.com

S ERVICES AT THE Benedictine Abbaye de St-Pierre, part of the Abbaye de Solesmes, attract visitors who come from far and wide to listen to the monks' Gregorian chant. For over a century, the abbey has been working to preserve and promote this ancient form of prayer. Books and recordings produced by the monks are sold, outside church service times, in the shop near the entrance to the abbey.

Originally founded in 1010 as a priory, the abbey was substantially rebuilt in the late 19th century in a somewhat forbidding, fortress-like style.

The interior of the **abbey church** has an austere beauty. Its nave and transept are both Romanesque, while the 19th-century choir imitates the medieval style. Both arms of the transept are adorned by groups of stone carvings made in the 15th and 16th centuries and known collectively as the "saints of Solesmes". The chapel to the left of the high altar contains *The Tomb of Our Lord*, with the haunting figure of Mary Magdalene kneeling at Christ's feet, deep in prayer. In *The Dormition of the Virgin*, which can be seen in the chapel on the right, the lower scenes illustrate the Virgin Mary's death and burial, while the scenes above depict her Assumption and heavenly Coronation.

The little **parish church**, which is located beside the entrance to the abbey, is worth visiting for its interesting modern stained-glass windows.

The imposing Abbaye de Solesmes, reflected in the River Sarthe

Asnières-sur-Vègre 8

Road map C2. 🚶 340. � *Sablé-sur-Sarthe, then taxi.* ℹ️ *Sablé-sur-Sarthe (02 43 95 00 60).*

T HIS PRETTY VILLAGE of old houses and water mills, with a 12th-century hump-backed bridge, is largely built in pinkish-yellow stone. Its tiny church has lively wall paintings, dating from the 12th and 15th centuries. In warm ochre and terracotta tones, they depict scenes from medieval life and moral warnings in the shape of the damned being herded into hell by huge, slavering hounds. The 13th-century **Cour d'Asnières** is an impressive Gothic building, built as a meeting place for the canons of the Cathédrale St-Julien in Le Mans.

Nearby **Juigné** is situated on the old road from Le Mans to Sablé-sur-Sarthe. Its château was rebuilt in the early 17th century. Although private, its park and terraces, with their panoramic views of the river, are open to the public. It is possible to hire boats from Juigné's tiny harbour, from which there are good views of the church perched on the cliff above.

Detail from the frescoes in Asnières' church

The 12th-century humpbacked bridge in Asnières-sur-Vègre

🏛 **Cour d'Asnières**
Manoir de la Cour. 📞 *02 43 92 40 47.* 🕐 *for restoration until 2006.* 📷 ✔

Malicorne-sur-Sarthe 9

Road map C3. 🚶 1,700. 🚉 *Noyen-sur-Sarthe, La Suze-sur-Sarthe.* 🚌 ℹ️ *pl Bertrand Duguesclin (02 43 94 74 45).* 🅿 *Fri.* 🎭 *Fête de la Pôterie (late Sep).* 🌐 *www.ville-malicorne.fr*

T HE CHIEF CLAIM to fame of this little town on the Sarthe is its faïence (tin-glazed earthenware). Jean Loiseau, a potter, first set up here in 1747. At the **Faïenceries Artistiques du Bourg-Joly** visitors can buy the open-work ware known as *Faïence de Malicorne*. The **Faïenceries d'Art de Malicorne**, (pottery) just outside the village, also has a factory shop and a small museum. A more extensive pottery museum is the **Malicorne Espace Faïence**, in the centre of town.

Malicorne's small harbour is a popular spot for boaters, and both cruises and the hire of small motorboats are possible. The village also boasts the pretty **Château de Malicorne**, dating from the 18th century, as well as a charming Romanesque church.

🏛 **Faïenceries Artistiques du Bourg-Joly**
16 rue Carnot. 📞 *02 43 94 80 10.* **Workshop** 🕐 *Mon–Fri by appt.* **Shop** 🕐 *Mon–Sat & Sun pm.*

🏛 **Faïenceries d'Art de Malicorne**
18 rue Bernard Palissy. 📞 *02 43 94 81 18.* **Workshop** 🕐 *Apr–Sep: Tue–Sat.* **Shop** 🕐 *Mon–Sat.* 📷 ♿ ✔

🏛 **Malicorne Espace Faïence**
Rue Victor Hugo. 📞 *02 43 48 07 17.* 🕐 *Apr–Oct: daily; Nov–Mar: Wed–Sun.* 📷 ♿

🏰 **Château de Malicorne**
📞 *02 43 94 84 65.* 🕐 *Jul–Aug: Wed–Sun pm only.* 📷 ♿ ✔

The harbour at Malicorne, surrounded by former water mills

Street-by-Street: Le Mans ⑩

Carving on
house in rue
des Chanoines

THE HILLY, PICTURESQUE Old Town (Le Vieux Mans) can only be explored on foot. Its narrow, cobbled streets are lined by 15th- and 16th-century half-timbered houses interspersed with Renaissance mansions. Several of the finest buildings served as temporary residences for France's kings and queens, although the one named after Richard the Lionheart's queen Bérengère, or Berengaria, was built two and a half centuries after her death. The quarter is bounded to the northwest by the old Roman walls, which run beside the River Sarthe.

Maison d'Adam et Eve
The carvings on this doctor's house illustrate the importance of astrology in 16th-century medicine.

Hôtel d'Argouges
Louis XI is said to have stayed in this 15th-century turreted mansion in 1467.

The Roman walls are among the best-preserved in Europe.

| 0 metres | 50 |
| 0 yards | 50 |

Hôtel Aubert de Clairaulnay
The sundial on the side of this late 16th-century mansion was placed there in 1789 by Claude Chappe, the inventor of semaphore.

RUE DE VAUX

RUE DE LA VERRERIE

GRANDE RUE

RUE ST-FLACEAU

RUE DES FOSSES

RUE ST-BENOIT

RUE DE LA VIEILLE PORTE

KEY

– – – Suggested route

Le Grabatoire is a 16th-century mansion, built on the site of an infirmary for sick canons.

Menhir
Tradition has it that visitors should make a wish while placing their fingers in one of the little cavities in the menhir, a prehistoric standing stone, resting against the west front of the cathedral.

The Maison de la Reine Bérengère houses a museum of local history.

★ **Cathédrale St-Julien**
This magnificent cathedral, renowned for its intricate flying buttresses, combines Romanesque and Gothic elements.

★ **Rue des Chanoines**
Among the historic buildings in this attractive street is the 12th-century St Martin's Priory at No. 11.

STAR SIGHTS

★ **Rue des Chanoines**

★ **Maison des Deux Amis**

★ **Cathédrale St-Julien**

★ **Maison des Deux Amis**
This building is named for its carving of two friends holding a coat of arms.

Exploring Le Mans

Although best known for its gruelling 24-hour motor race, Le Mans has many other attractions, not least of which is the magnificent Cathédrale St-Julien. The city's history stretches back to Roman times. The walls surrounding the Old Town, once the Roman city of Vindunum, date from the late 3rd and early 4th centuries. They originally stretched for some 1,300 m (1,400 yards). Eleven towers are still standing, all but one on the river side, and their massive walls are decorated with geometric patterns created by using courses of brick alternating with undressed stone in various colours. Outside the city walls, Le Mans has developed into a bustling, modern city with several memorable museums and a number of attractive churches.

⛪ Cathédrale St-Julien

Pl St Michel. **C** 02 43 28 28 98. ◯ daily. &

The best view of Cathédrale St-Julien's highly dramatic flying buttresses, unlike those of any other cathedral in their complex arrangement, is from the place des Jacobins. The cathedral is something of a hybrid: the 12th-century nave is essentially Romanesque, and the transepts were built a century later than the pure Gothic choir, one of the tallest in France, which dates from the 13th century. From the entrance via the Romanesque south portal, the view of the detailed 16th-century tapestries that hang against the pillars in the choir and are suspended over the choir stalls is striking. The splash of colour they provide is echoed in the beautiful medieval stained glass.

🏛 Musée de la Reine Bérengère

Rue de la Reine Bérengère. **C** 02 43 47 38 51. ◯ Easter–Oct: Tue–Sun. ● public hols. 🖼 & grd flr only.

This museum is set in three attractive half-timbered houses in the Old Town, their wooden façades lively with carved figures. Its collections of art and local history include faïence and pottery from many periods, with some examples of Malicorne ware (see p163). The museum also shows furniture made in the region. On the second floor, the 19th-century paintings by local artists show how relatively little the town of Le Mans has changed over the years. Also of note is Jean Sorieul's wonderfully dramatic canvas, *The Battle of Le Mans of 13 December, 1793.*

The Curate's Meal (1786), from the Musée de la Reine Bérengère

The Plantagenet Enamel (1150) displayed in the Musée de Tessé

🏛 Musée de Tessé

2 av de Paderborn. **C** 02 43 47 38 51. ◯ Tue–Sat. ● public hols. 🖼 except Sun & public hols. &

The bishop's palace, with its pretty, well-kept garden, was converted in 1927 into Le Mans' art museum, devoted to the fine and decorative arts, as well as archaeology. The permanent collection of paintings on the ground floor ranges from the late Middle Ages to the 19th century, and the archaeology section is mainly Egyptian and Greco-Roman. The Tessé's most famous exhibit is the vivid Plantagenet Enamel, a medieval enamelled panel depicting Geoffroy V, known as Le Bel (The Handsome). Geoffroy's son, King Henry II of England, was born in Le Mans in 1133.

🏛 Musée de l'Automobile de la Sarthe

Circuit des 24-Heures. **C** 02 43 72 72 24. ◯ daily. 🖼 &

Near Le Mans' famous race track is this museum, which displays a dazzling range of vintage, classic and modern racing cars and motorbikes. It includes some of the early designs of Amédée Bollée, an industrialist whose first pioneering car design dated from 1873. Bollée's family made the city famous for car design decades before the first 24-hour race (see p57).

16th-century tapestry hanging in the Cathédrale St-Julien

La Flèche ⓫

Road map C3. 16,500.
blvd de Montréal (02 43 94 02 53). Wed, Sat & Sun.
Festival des Affranchis (2nd weekend Jul).
www.ville-lafleche.fr

La Flèche's chief glory is the Prytanée Militaire, the French military academy. Founded as a Jesuit college in 1604 by Henri IV, it was assigned its present function by Napoléon in 1808.

The entrance to the academy is through a large Baroque doorway, the Porte d'Honneur, which leads into the Cour d'Austerlitz. The Chapelle St-Louis is in the central courtyard. Its interior is richly decorated, and urns containing the ashes of the hearts of Henri IV and Marie de Médicis are displayed.

The château's gardens, with spectacular views over the river, are open to the public. On the opposite bank of the river is Port Luneau from where Jérôme le Royer de la Dauversière and his companions set off for the New World. Nearby, the bustling place Henri IV, with a statue of the king, is lined with cafés.

At the heart of the town, the 15th-century Château des Carmes, the former town hall (now an art gallery), is reflected in the River Loir.

⊞ Prytanée Militaire
Rue du Collège. 02 43 48 67 99.
Jul–Aug: daily; Sep–Jun: groups by appt.

Place Henri IV in La Flèche, with the statue of the king in the centre

Le Lude ⓬

Road map C3. 4,500. pl F-de-Nicolay (02 43 94 62 20).
Thu. Foire du Raillon (Apr); Foire du Printemps (Sep).
www.lelude.com

The oldest section of this market town is the area surrounding the Château du Lude, where houses dating from the 15th to 17th centuries line the narrow streets. Although the site has been fortified for more than 1,000 years, the present château dates from the 15th century. Over the next 300 years the building's originally square layout and four corner towers were transformed as its function changed to that of a country house.

The interior is beautifully furnished, largely in the 19th-century style, although there are some pieces from the 17th and 18th centuries, including both French and Flemish tapestries. The Oratory is decorated with 16th-century frescoes, which depict Old Testament scenes. The formal gardens, on two levels, lead down to the River Loir.

♣ Château du Lude
02 43 94 60 09. Château mid-Jun–Aug: daily; Apr–mid-Jun & Sep: Thu, Tue. Park Apr–Sep: daily. Oct–Mar: groups by reservation.
ground floor.

The imposing towers of the Château du Lude

Les 24 Heures du Mans

The name of Le Mans is known throughout the world, thanks to its famous 24-hour car race. Since it began on 26 May 1923, the event has attracted huge crowds every June, both from France and abroad – these days, more than 250,000 spectators and 1,800 journalists watch the race. The circuit is to the south of the city and is 13.6-km (8½-miles) long, including some stretches on ordinary roads. Nowadays, drivers can cover some 5,000 km (3,100 miles) within the time limit. Within the course is the Hunaudières track where, in 1908, Wilbur Wright staged the first aeroplane flight in France.

One of the early races in Le Mans

Tour of the Loir Valley ⑬

B ETWEEN PONCÉ-SUR-LE-LOIR and La Flèche, the River
Loir passes through peaceful, unspoiled countryside and picturesque villages. An unhurried tour of
the valley takes two days and allows time to try some
of the numerous riverside and forest walks. Families
may enjoy the sailing, riding, angling and cycling
facilities available in the area, while art lovers can
seek out little-known churches adorned with delicately
coloured Romanesque frescoes. Wine buffs will be
interested in trying some of the area's wines, which
can be sipped from locally blown glass – the Loir
Valley also has an excellent reputation for its crafts.

**The banks of the tranquil Loir,
ideal for fishing and walking**

La Flèche ①
The home of the Prytanée
Militaire (military academy,
see p167), La Flèche is a
charming town with
wonderful views across
the River Loir.

**Entrance to the
Prytanée Militaire**

Vaas ④
The Moulin de Rotrou, on the edge of
this pretty village, is a working flour mill
and museum of breadmaking. In Vaas,
the Eglise St-Georges has fine
17th-century paintings.

Zoo de la Flèche ②
Just outside the town, this zoo
is one of the largest in France,
with nearly 900 inhabitants.

TIPS FOR DRIVERS

Tour length: 103 km (64 miles).
Stopping-off points: The forests
and riverbanks along the Loir are
ideal for picnicking, and shops in
the region sell delicacies to make
a cold meal very special. This will
be a doubly satisfying experience
if you buy local produce from a
market, such as that in Le Lude,
first. If you prefer to eat in a
restaurant, La Fesse d'Ange in La
Flèche has local dishes on the
menu (see p218). For those
wishing to stay overnight, Le
Relais Cicéro in La Flèche is
recommended (see p206).

Le Lude ③
This market town is known mainly for its
spectacular château *(see p167)*.

The entrance to the Château du Lude

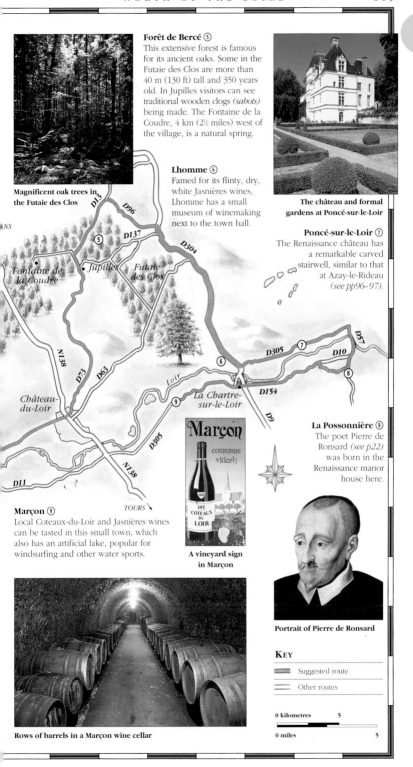

Forêt de Bercé ⑤
This extensive forest is famous for its ancient oaks. Some in the Futaie des Clos are more than 40 m (130 ft) tall and 350 years old. In Jupilles visitors can see traditional wooden clogs (*sabots*) being made. The Fontaine de la Coudre, 4 km (2½ miles) west of the village, is a natural spring.

Magnificent oak trees in the Futaie des Clos

Lhomme ⑥
Famed for its flinty, dry, white Jasnières wines, Lhomme has a small museum of winemaking next to the town hall.

The château and formal gardens at Poncé-sur-le-Loir

Poncé-sur-le-Loir ⑦
The Renaissance château has a remarkable carved stairwell, similar to that at Azay-le-Rideau (*see pp96–97*).

La Possonnière ⑧
The poet Pierre de Ronsard (*see p22*) was born in the Renaissance manor house here.

Marçon ⑨
Local Coteaux-du-Loir and Jasnières wines can be tasted in this small town, which also has an artificial lake, popular for windsurfing and other water sports.

A vineyard sign in Marçon

Portrait of Pierre de Ronsard

Rows of barrels in a Marçon wine cellar

KEY

Suggested route

Other routes

0 kilometres   5

0 miles   5

The Château de Courtanvaux with its towering walls

Château de Courtanvaux **⓮**

Road map D3. **☎** 02 43 35 34 43. ◯ Easter–Oct: Wed–Mon. 🈲 🎫

ALTHOUGH DIFFICULT to find and rather unpromisingly approached through an ugly industrial estate, this large Gothic and Renaissance private château, restored in 1815, is a romantic sight as it looms up at the end of a tree-lined drive. Turrets surmount the towering walls and the impressive gateway, and willows weep gracefully over the moat.

From the 15th century until 1978, when its Renaissance gateway was officially classed as an historical monument, the château was never sold – its ownership was transferred either through inheritance or through marriage. Although unfurnished, its formal gardens are home to a tiny Gothic chapel, and visitors are free to explore the woods and pools of its 63 ha (156 acres) of pleasant parkland.

Châteaudun **⓯**

Road map E2. 🏘 15,300. 🚉
ℹ 1 rue de Luynes (02 37 45 22 46). 🔄 Thu. 🎏 Fête de la Rosière (crowning of the rose queen, Jul). 🆆 www.ville-chateaudun.com

DOMINATED BY ITS fierce-looking **château**, the town of Châteaudun is situated above the River Loir

where the Beauce plain meets the Perche district. Châteaudun was owned at one time by the aristocratic poet Charles d'Orléans (see p22), who then handed it on to his half-brother Jean Dunois, known as the bastard of Orléans and one of Joan of Arc's loyal companions-in-arms (see p137). It was Jean who began the château's south wing in 1460, and built the beautiful late Gothic chapel, adorned with murals and life-size statues. The other wing was built half a century later.

Both wings are hung with wonderful tapestries, which date from the 16th and 17th centuries. Visitors can tour the château's living rooms, kitchens and prison, and walk around its sentry path.

Châteaudun's Old Town has a number of picturesque buildings, as well as several interesting churches: the Romanesque **Eglise de la Madeleine**, built in stages and now restored after damage sustained in 1940, and **St-Valérien**, with its tall square belfry. Situated on the far bank of the River Loir, the **Eglise St-Jean-de-la-Chaine** is also Romanesque.

♦ Château
☎ 02 37 94 02 90. ◯ daily. ● 1 Jan, 1 May, 1 & 11 Nov, 25 Dec. 🈲 🚻 restricted.

Illiers-Combray **⓰**

Road map E2. 🏘 3,400. 🚉
ℹ 5 rue Henri Germond (02 37 24 24 00). 🔄 Fri. 🎏 Journée des Aubé-pines (Proustian May Day, May).

THE LITTLE MARKET TOWN of Illiers has added the word "Combray" to its name in honour of Marcel Proust's magnificent novel, *Remembrance of Things Past*, in which it is depicted as Combray (see p23). As a child, Proust spent many happy summer holidays in the town, walking by the banks of the River Loir, which he later portrayed in his work, as the "Vivonne". With its quiet church square, it seems surprisingly unspoilt to the author's admirers, who make pilgrimages to the places described in the novel. They can also visit the house once owned by Proust's uncle Jules Amiot, **La Maison de Tante Léonie**. The house is now a small and touching museum, with displays about the famous writer's life, complete with the kitchen where the "Françoise" of the novel (who was actually Ernestine, the family cook) reigned supreme.

Remembrance of Things Past by Proust

🏛 La Maison de Tante Léonie
4 rue du Dr Proust. **☎** 02 37 24 30 97. ◯ Tue–Sun. ● mid-Dec–mid-Jan. 🈲 🎫

A view of Châteaudun's castle from across the River Loir

Carved hounds and stag on the gateway of the Château d'Anet

Château d'Anet ⑰

Road map E1. 🚉 Dreux, then taxi. 📞 02 37 41 90 07. ⏰ Feb–Mar & Nov: Sat–Sun pm; Apr–Oct: Wed–Mon pm. ● Dec–Jan. ♿ restricted ▣

WHEN THE MISTRESS of Henri II, Diane de Poitiers, was banished from Chenonceau after the king's accidental death in 1559, she retired to Anet, which she had inherited from her husband, and remained here until her death in 1566. It had been rebuilt for her by Philibert de l'Orme, who also designed the bridge over the Cher at Chenonceau (see pp106–7). The château was superbly decorated and furnished, as befitted the woman who reigned over a king's heart for nearly 30 years.

The château was sold after the Revolution and, in 1804, the new owner pulled down the central apartments and the right wing. However, you can still admire the magnificent entrance gate (the bronze relief of Diane by Benvenuto

Cellini is a copy), the chapel, decorated with bas-reliefs by the Renaissance sculptor Jean Goujon (c.1510–68), and the richly furnished west wing. Just beside the château stands the mausoleum where Diane de Poitiers is buried.

Chartres ⑱

Road map E2. 🚶 42,000. 🚉 🚌 ℹ pl de la Cathédrale (02 37 18 26 26). 🛍 Sat. 🎵 Festival d'Orgue (organ music; Jul–Aug). 🌐 www.ville-chartres.fr

SURROUNDED BY the wheat fields of the Beauce plain, Chartres was for many years a major market town. Visitors who come to see the Gothic cathedral (see pp172–3) should explore the town's old streets, particularly the rue Chantault, the rue des Ecuyers, the rue aux Herbes and, over the Eure, the rue de la Tannerie (which took its name from the tanneries that once lined the river).

The **Musée des Beaux-Arts**, occupying the elegant 18th-century building that was once the bishop's palace, is to the north of the cathedral. It has some fine Renaissance enamel plaques, a portrait of Erasmus in old age by Holbein, and many 17th- and 18th-century paintings, by French and Flemish artists. There is also a collection of 17th- and 18th-century harpsichords and spinets.

Beautiful stained glass is not restricted to the cathedral: the Gothic **Eglise St-Pierre** beside the river has lovely windows dating from the 14th century,

Half-timbered houses in the rue Chantault in Chartres

those in **St-Aignan** date from the 17th century.

The **Centre International du Vitrail**, a stained glass centre, is housed in the converted attics of the Cellier de Loëns, which was part of the cathedral's chapter house. Visitors can enjoy temporary exhibitions of old and new stained glass, as well as two informative permanent exhibitions that explain the techniques used in making stained glass and describe the glass in the cathedral's windows.

🏛 Musée des Beaux-Arts
29 cloître Notre-Dame. 📞 02 37 36 41 39. ⏰ Wed–Mon. ● Sun ams & public hols. ♿

🏛 Centre International du Vitrail
5 rue du Cardinal Pie. 📞 02 37 21 65 72. ⏰ daily. ● 1 Jan, 25 Dec (and between exhibitions). ♿ ▣

🏛 Conservatoire de l'Agriculture
Le Compa, pont de Mainvilliers. 📞 02 37 84 15 00. ⏰ Tue–Sun. ● 1 Jan, 1 May, 1 Nov & 25 Dec. ♿ ▣

IN THE FOOTSTEPS OF PROUST

No visit to Illiers-Combray is complete without retracing the hallowed walks of Marcel Proust's childhood holidays. When he stayed with his Aunt and Uncle Amiot, he would join in the family walks that became, in *Remembrance of Things Past*, "Swann's Way" and "Guermantes Way".

The first takes the walkers towards the village of Méréglise, crossing the Loire and passing through a park that was once Uncle Jules' Pré Catelan and appears in the novel as "Tansonville Park". The "Guermantes" walk covers a few kilometres towards St-Eman, following the river to its source, now trapped unromantically in a wash house in the village. The walks are signposted and guides are available at the local tourist office.

Illiers-Combray's "Tansonville Park"

Chartres: Cathédrale Notre-Dame

Elongated Statues
These statues on the Royal Portal represent Old Testament figures.

ACCORDING TO ART HISTORIAN Emile Male, "Chartres is the mind of the Middle Ages manifest". The Romanesque cathedral, begun in 1020, was destroyed by fire in 1194; only the south tower, west front and crypt remained. Inside, the sacred Veil of the Virgin relic was the sole treasure to survive. In a wave of enthusiasm, peasant and lord alike helped to rebuild the church in just 25 years. There were few alterations after 1250 and, unlike other cathedrals, Chartres was unscathed by the Wars of Religion and the French Revolution. The result is a Gothic cathedral with a true "Bible in stone" reputation.

Part of the Vendôme Window

STAR FEATURES

★ **Royal Portal**

★ **South Porch**

★ **Stained-Glass Windows**

The taller of the two spires dates from the start of the 16th century. Flamboyant Gothic in style, it contrasts sharply with the solemnity of its Romanesque counterpart.

Gothic Nave
As wide as the Romanesque crypt below it, the nave reaches a record height of 37 m (121 ft).

★ **Royal Portal**
The central tympanum of the Royal Portal (1145–55) shows Christ in Majesty.

The lower half of the west front is a survivor of the earlier Romanesque church, dating from the 11th century.

Labyrinth

The Labyrinth

The 13th-century labyrinth, inlaid in the floor of the nave, was a feature of most medieval cathedrals. As a penance, pilgrims used to follow the tortuous route on their knees, echoing the Way of the Cross. The journey of 262 m (860 ft), around 11 bands of broken concentric circles, took at least an hour to complete.

Visitors' Checklist

Pl de la Cathédrale. 02 37 21 56 33. 8:30am–6:45pm daily. Mon, Wed, Thu, Sat: 11:45am; Tue, Fri: 9am, 11:45am; Sun: 9:30am, 11am (6pm daily). English: noon, 2:45pm; French: 10:30am 3pm.

St-Piat Chapel
Built between 1324 and 1353, the chapel houses the cathedral treasures, including the Veil of the Virgin relic and fragments of the fragile 13th-century rood screen dismantled in 1763.

Vaulted Ceiling
A network of ribs supports the vaulted ceiling.

★ Stained-Glass Windows
The windows cover a surface area of over 3,000 sq m (32,300 sq ft).

★ South Porch
Sculpture on the South Porch (1197–1209) reflects New Testament teaching.

Crypt
This is the largest crypt in France, most of it dating from the early 11th century. It comprises two parallel galleries, a series of chapels and the 9th-century St Lubin's vault.

The Stained Glass of Chartres

DONATED BY THE GUILDS between 1210 and 1240, this glorious collection of stained glass is world-renowned. Over 150 windows illustrate biblical stories and daily life in the 13th century (bring binoculars if you can). During both World Wars the windows were dismantled piece by piece and removed for safety. Some windows were restored and releaded in the 1970s, but much more remains to be done.

Stained glass above the apse

Redemption Window
Six scenes illustrate Christ's Passion *and death on the Cross (c.1210).*

★ Tree of Jesse
This 12th-century stained glass shows Christ's genealogy. The tree rises up from Jesse, father of David, at the bottom, to Christ enthroned at the top.

★ West Rose Window
This window (1215), with Christ seated in the centre, shows the Last Judgment.

KEY

1 Tree of Jesse	**12** Noah	**22** St Anthony and St Paul	**33** St Theodore and St Vincent
2 Incarnation	**13** St John the Evangelist	**23** Blue Virgin	**34** St Stephen
3 Passion and Resurrection	**14** Mary Magdalene	**24** Life of the Virgin	**35** St Cheron
4 North Rose Window	**15** Good Samaritan and Adam and Eve	**25** Zodiac Window	**36** St Thomas
5 West Rose Window	**16** Assumption	**26** St Martin	**37** Peace Window
6 South Rose Window	**17** Vendôme Chapel Windows	**27** St Thomas à Becket	**38** Modern Window
7 Redemption Window	**18** Miracles of Mary	**28** St Margaret and St Catherine	**39** Prodigal Son
8 St Nicholas	**19** St Apollinaris	**29** St Nicholas	**40** Ezekiel and David
9 Joseph	**20** Modern Window	**30** St Remy	**41** Aaron
10 St Eustache	**21** St Fulbert	**31** St James the Greater	**42** Virgin and Child
11 St Lubin		**32** Charlemagne	**43** Isaiah and Moses
			44 Daniel and Jeremiah

North Rose Window
This depicts the Glorification
of the Virgin, *surrounded by
the kings
of Judah
and the
prophets
(c.1230).*

GUIDE TO READING THE WINDOWS

Each window is divided into panels, which are usually read
from left to right, bottom to top (earth to heaven). The
number of figures or abstract shapes used is symbolic: three
stands for the Church; squares and the number four symbolize
the material world or the four elements; circles eternal life.

Mary and Child in the
sacred mandorla (c.1150)

Two angels doing
homage before the
celestial throne

Christ's triumphal
entry into Jerusalem

Upper panels of the Incarnation Window

South Rose Window
This illustrates the
Apocalypse, *with*
Christ in Majesty
(c.1225).

STAR WINDOWS

★ West Rose Window

★ Tree of Jesse

★ Blue Virgin Window

★ Blue Virgin Window
Scenes of The Marriage at
Cana *show Christ changing
water into wine at the
request of the Virgin Mary.*

LOIRE-ATLANTIQUE AND THE VENDÉE

THE REGION STRETCHING *from Guérande in the north to the Marais Poitevin in the south turns away from the Vallée des Rois, the land of châteaux, to face the sea. Pale limestone gives way to darker granite and, beyond the hilly, wooded areas to the east, plains stretch into marshlands and estuaries inhabited by clouds of birds.*

Here, people have for centuries won their living either from the land or from the sea. Local communities were until quite recently isolated, conservative, religious and fiercely independent. Their loyalties were the basis of the Vendée Uprising *(see p187)* which, at the end of the 18th century, threatened the new French Republic and ended in the devastation of an entire region south of the Loire. Until the 1790s, Nantes, the capital of the Loire-Atlantique, and its environs were part of Brittany, one of the last French duchies to be brought under the crown.

Nantes itself grew prosperous on the wealth generated by its maritime trade to become the seventh largest city of France in the 18th and 19th centuries. With its fine museums and elegant 18th-century *quartiers*, it remains a fascinating and likeable city.

The coast and islands of the Loire-Atlantique to the north, and the Vendée – as the region to the south is known – now draw thousands of summer visitors. Part of their charm is that most of the holiday-makers are French, since the rest of the world has barely begun to discover the beauty of the rocky headlands of Le Croisic or the beaches of golden sand that stretch from La Baule to Les Sables d'Olonne. In the south, dry summers and warm winters on the Ile de Noirmoutier have given it an almost Mediterranean look, with its whitewashed houses and Roman tiles.

In contrast, the Marais Poitevin, at the southern tip of the Vendée, is one of France's most fascinating natural environments. This land has been won back from rivers and the sea through the construction of dykes, canals and dams over hundreds of years.

An oyster gatherer in the Bay of Aiguillon

◁ Romanesque capitals in the nave of the Collégiale St-Aubin in Guérande

Exploring Loire-Atlantique and the Vendée

T HE MIGHTY RIVER LOIRE finally reaches the sea at St-Nazaire, in the west of the Loire-Atlantique *département*. To the northwest lies the Guérandaise Peninsula, where long expanses of sandy, south-facing beaches give way to the dramatic, rocky Atlantic coastlines. The best Atlantic beaches stretch along the Vendée coastline, from the Ile de Noirmoutier to the Marais Poitevin in the south. The Marais Poitevin, 80,000 hectares (198,000 acres) of marshland, is networked with canals. To the east lie the Vendée Hills, where the roads wind gently through towns and along the hillsides, giving lovely views of the surrounding area.

A rocky inlet at L'Aubraie on the Atlantic coast

A canal in La Grande Brière

GUERANDE ●
LE CROISIC ●
● LA BAULE
① GUERANDAISE PENINSULA
② ILE DE NOIRMOUTIER
③ ILE D'YEU
④ LES SABLES D'OLONNE

Vannes
LA GRANDE BRIERE
Loire
BEAUVOIR-SUR-MER
● CHALLAN
BRETIGNE SUR-MER
Jaunay
Vie
Ligneron

0 kilometres   15
0 miles   15

GETTING AROUND

Nantes, with its international airport and major train station, is the transportation hub for the region. The TGV takes only two hours to reach Nantes from Paris, and some trains continue to Le Croisic, only one hour further on. The fastest route by car to Nantes is *L'Océane* autoroute (A11) via Le Mans and Angers. While the N137 is the most direct route south to the Marais Poitevin, the coastal route, stopping off at the beautiful beaches along the way, is far more scenic. Inland towards the Vendée Hills, the D960, D752 and D755 around Pouzages are scenic drives.

SIGHTS AT A GLANCE

Clisson **12**
Fontenay-le-Comte **8**
Goulaine **13**
Guérandaise Peninsula **1**
Ile de Noirmoutier **2**
Ile d'Yeu **3**
Luçon **7**
Marais Poitevin *(pp182–5)* **5**
Nantes *(pp190–93)* **14**
Pouzauges **10**
Puy-du-Fou **11**
La Roche-sur-Yon **6**
Les Sables d'Olonne **4**
Vouvant **9**

Harvesting salt the traditional way near Guérande

KEY

▬	Motorway
▬	Major road
▬	Minor road
▬	Scenic route
~	River
☀	Viewpoint

Guérandaise Peninsula ❶

Road map A3. 🚉 Le Croisic, La
Baule. 🚌 Le Croisic, La Baule, Brière,
Guérande. 🛈 Le Croisic (02 40 23
00 70), La Baule (02 40 24 34 44),
Guérande (02 40 24 96 71).

L^A BAULE, ONE OF the grandest
seaside resorts of the late
19th century, has a superb 8-
km (5-mile) sweep of golden
sand, now dominated by
apartment blocks built since
the 1930s. However, in the
pines behind the modern
buildings, there is a fascinating
assortment of eccentric turn-of-
the-century villas. The resort of
Pornichet, which adjoins La
Baule, also retains some older
villas beyond a modern
marina crammed with yachts.

Le Croisic, reaching into the
Atlantic on the west, has a
wilder charm. Beyond the
lively main port are miles of
salty headlands with small
beaches, pounding surf and
wind-sculpted pines. The
Océarium near the port is
one of France's largest,
privately-owned aquaria.

The medieval walled town
of Guérande grew rich on its
fleur de sel – gourmet Breton
salt "farmed" on extensive
marshlands between here and
Le Croisic. Exhibitions and a
video in the **Musée des
Marais Salants** at Batz-sur-
Mer give an excellent idea of
the painstaking techniques
used to maintain its quality.

Guérande is protected by its
ramparts, which are entered
through four fine, 15th-
century gateways. The main
gatehouse, St-Michel,
houses a regional
museum. In the centre
of the town is the
Collégiale St-Aubin, a
church first built in the
12th century and later
renovated. It has
stained glass from
the 14th and 16th
centuries and
Romanesque
capitals depicting
scenes from the
lives of martyrs,
mythology, arts
and entertainment.

Just 10 km (6
miles) to the east

A traditional thatched house in La Grande Brière

of Guérande is **La Grande
Brière**, a regional park of
40,000 hectares (100,000
acres) of marshlands. Guided
tours by flat-bottomed boat or
on foot, bicycle or horseback
are available from the tourist
office in what was once a clog-
maker's house in La Chapelle-
des-Marais. Kerhinet, a village
of 18 restored cottages, has
displays on regional life.

🐟 **Océarium**
Av de St-Goustan, Le Croisic. 📞 02 40
23 02 44. ⏰ daily. ● first 3 weeks
Jan. 🏷 &

🏛 **Musée des Marais Salants**
Batz-sur-Mer. 📞 02 40 23 82 79.
⏰ Jun–Sep & school hols: daily; Oct–
May: Sat & Sun. 🏷
& grd flr only.

🐟 **La Grande Brière**
Road map A3. 🚉 La Baule, Le Croisic,
Pontchâteau, St Nazaire. 🚌 🛈 La
Chapelle-des-Marais (02 40 66 85 01).

Porte St-Michel gatehouse, one of the entrances to Guérande

Ile de Noirmoutier ❷

Road map A4. 🚌 Noirmoutier-en-
l'Ile. 🛈 Noirmoutier-en-l'Ile (02 51 39
80 71). 🌐 www.ile-noirmoutier.com

W^HITEWASHED Midi-style
beach villas on a long,
low island of fertile polders
(land reclaimed from the sea)
give Noirmoutier a unique
character. The adventurous
visitor arrives along a bumpy
causeway nearly 5 km (3
miles) long, which is above
the sea for only three hours at
low tide. Cockle-collecting
locals park their cars in the
mud, but those who flirt with
the tides sometimes have to
climb to safety on platforms
(balises) along the causeway.
Crossing periods are posted
on the road at Beauvoir-sur-
Mer. There is also a tollbridge
from Fromentine.

The island's mild climate,
fishing industry and
salt marshes were the
basis of its wealth.
Now summer tourists
come to visit its long
dunes, pretty beaches
on the northeast and
the neat main
village of Noir-
moutier-en-l'Ile.
The dry-moated
**Château de
Noirmoutier**
dates from the
12th century. It
has displays on
aspects of local
history, including
the bullet-riddled

chair in which the Duc d'Elbée was executed during the Vendée Uprising (see p187). There is also an **aquarium** and the **Musée de la Construction Navale**, illustrating both boat-making and salt-panning techniques. **Parc Océanîle**, a water park that opened in 1994, includes water chutes and slides, pools with artificial waves, torrents and hot geysers.

♣ **Château de Noirmoutier**
Pl d'Armes. [02 51 39 10 42.
○ mid-Feb–mid-Jun & mid-Sep–mid-Nov: Wed–Mon; mid-Jun–mid-Sep: daily.

☆ **Aquarium-Sealand**
Rue de l'Ecluse. [02 51 39 08 11.
○ mid-Feb– mid-Nov: daily.
ground floor only.

🏛 **Musée de la Construction Navale**
Rue de l'Ecluse. [02 51 39 24 00.
○ Apr–mid-Jun & Sep: Tue–Sun; mid-Jun–Aug: daily.

🌊 **Parc Océanîle**
Site des Oudinières, route de Noir moutier. [02 51 35 91 35.
○ mid-Jun–mid-Sep: daily.

Polyprion americanas, one of the fish in Noirmoutier's aquarium

Ile d'Yeu ❸

Road map A4. 🚶 5,000. 🚢 from Fromentine to Port-Joinville. 🚉 Port-Joinville (02 51 58 32 58).
www.ile-yeu.fr

THE SANDY coves and rocky coastline of this island, only 10 by 4 km (6 by 2½ miles), attract summer visitors. Near the old fishing harbour of Port-de-la-Meule are a ruined 11th-century **castle** and the **Pierre Tremblante**, a giant Neolithic stone said to move when pressed at a critical spot.

The fishing village of La Chaume, near Les Sables d'Olonne

Les Sables d'Olonne ❹

Road map A4. 🚶 16,000. 🚉 🚌
🚉 1 promenade Marechal Joffre (02 51 96 85 85). 🚢 Tue–Sun.
www.ot-lessablesdolonne.fr

THE JUSTIFIABLE popularity of the fine, curving sands has helped to preserve the most elegant beach promenade in western France. Behind the 18th-century esplanade, hilly streets lead to a lively port on the sea channel. Opposite, the fishing village of La Chaume has a chic marina.

In Les Sables itself attractions include the morning market that takes place every day at Les Halles, near the church of Notre-Dame-de-Bon-Port. Running between Les Halles and the rue de la Patrie lies France's narrowest street, rue de l'Enfer, which is only 53 cm (21 in) wide at the entrance on rue de la Patrie.

Masterly views of Les Sables in the 1920s by Albert Marquet are in the **Musée de l'Abbaye Ste-Croix**. Built as a convent in the 17th century, this now houses mainly modern paintings, Surrealist multimedia works and maritime exhibits.

🏛 **Musée de l'Abbaye Ste-Croix**
Rue de Verdun. [02 51 32 01 16.
○ mid-Jun–Sep: Tue–Sun; Oct–mid-Jun: Tue–Sun pm only. ● public hols.
not Sunday.

THE BEST ATLANTIC COAST BEACHES

Les Sables d'Olonne hosted both the European surfing championship in 1987 and the world windsurfing championship in 1988. It also offers family bathing at the Grande Plage. Surfers enjoy the bigger waves at Le Tanchet (Le Château d'Olonne) and L'Aubraie (La Chaume). Other good surfing beaches are Sauveterre and Les Granges (Olonne-sur-Mer) and, further north, La Sauzaie at Brétignolles-sur-Mer. Apart from Les Sables, major esplanades and beaches with fine sands and good facilities include the Grande Plage at La Baule and Les Demoiselles at St-Jean-de-Monts.

The wide, sandy beach of L'Aubraie at La Chaume

Marais Poitevin **❺**

Kingfisher

The vast regional park of the Marais Poitevin stretches 80,000 ha (198,000 acres) across the south of the Vendée. In Roman times, most of it was under water. One thousand years of dyke building and drainage, first started by medieval monks, have produced the agricultural plains of the western Marais Desséché (dry marsh), which are protected from river floods inland by a complex network of canals. The enchanting aquatic mosaic of the Marais Mouillé (wet marsh), also known as the Venise Verte (Green Venice), lies to the east. Here, summer visitors punt or paddle along quiet, jade-coloured waterways under a canopy of willow, alder, ash, and poplar.

White Charolais Cattle
Prized for their meat, these cows are often transported by boat.

The Réserve Naturelle Michel Brosselin is a flourishing 200-ha (500-acre) nature reserve.

La Maison du Parc, at La Ronde, gives information on the complex hydraulic system of the entire Marais Poitevin.

Flat-bottomed Barque
This typical Marais Mouillé boat has a broad bow and a chisel-shaped stern. Skilled oarsmen row or pole the boat along the canals.

Mussel Farms
Mussels are farmed on the coast around L'Aiguillon-sur-Mer. The larvae are placed on ropes strung between posts embedded in the silt, exposed to the tide's ebb and flow.

STAR SIGHTS

★ **Eglise St-Nicolas, Maillezais**

★ **Coulon**

★ **Arçais**

KEY

	Mud flats
	Marais Desséché
	Marais Mouillé
※	Viewpoint
🧍	Hiking route
U	Horse riding
ℹ	Tourist information
⚓	Boating
🚲	Bicycles for rent

★ Eglise St-Nicolas, Maillezais

The 12th-century Eglise St-Nicolas is in the town of Maillezais, which is situated at the heart of the Marais Poitevin. The church has a Romanesque façade and an unusually spacious interior. To the left of the choir is a beautiful stone statue of the Virgin and Child, *dating from the 14th century. The town also has an attractive, ruined 10th-century abbey.*

Le Poiré-sur-Velluire is a small village where the annual opening of the common grazing rights is celebrated at the end of April.

★ Coulon

Coulon is the largest village in the Marais Poitevin. Its port is always crowded with the narrow, flat-bottomed boats that are traditional in this area.

★ Arçais

This village in the Venise Verte has a small, stylish port and a 19th-century château.

Exploring the Marais Poitevin

Sign advertising trips in a barque

EARLY DYKES, built to hold back the tide, did nothing to solve the problem of the rivers' annual flooding of the marshlands. So large canals were dug in the 12th and 13th centuries, under the supervision of monks who had acquired land rights to marshy areas. The Marais Mouillé (wet marsh) and the Marais Desséché (dry marsh) are still separated by one of these canals: the 13th-century Canal des Cinq Abbés, south of Chaillé-les-Marais, which was a joint effort by five abbeys. Peasants labouring for the monks were rewarded with common grazing rights, some of which are still in force. During the 17th century, Henri IV brought in Dutch engineers to improve the canals, hence the "Dutch Belt" (*La Ceinture des Hollandais*) southeast of Luçon. Current measures to control flooding on lands below high-tide level range from pressure-operated dam gates to bung holes that let water into the plains of the *marais* in summer.

Eastern Marais

The best way to see this area is by boat. Guided tours are available from a number of towns in the region, and braver souls can hire their own boats from Arçais, Coulon, Damvix, La Garette or Maillezais.

Coulon

Road map B5. 👥 2,170. 🚌 Niort.
🚺 31 rue Gabriel Auchier (05 49 35 99 29). 🛒 Fri & Sun.

With its narrow streets of old whitewashed houses and imposing 12th-century church, Coulon is the main entry point to the Marais Mouillé. The newly-restored quay on the Sèvre Niortaise river is lively in summer with punt tours and crews embarking on their day's negotiation of the maze of canals. The fish that try to hide under the duck weed can be seen at the **Aquarium de la Venise Verte**. Exhibits explaining local ways of life and the history of reclamation are displayed at the **Maison des Marais Mouillés**.

🐠 **Aquarium de la Venise Verte**
8 pl de l'Eglise. 📞 05 49 35 90 31.
🕐 Apr–Oct: daily; 🏷️ ♿
🏛️ **Maison des Marais Mouillés**
Pl de la Coutume. 📞 05 49 35 81 04.
🕐 Sep–Jun: Tue–Sun; Jul–Aug: daily.
🏷️

Maillezais

Road map B5. 👥 990. 🚌 Fontenay-le-Comte, then taxi. 🚺 rue du Dr-Daroux (02 51 87 23 01).

Maillezais was one of the most important inhabited islands in the former Gulf of Poitou. Whether from a canal boat or from a viewpoint within the

---

WILDLIFE OF THE MARAIS POITEVIN

An area of diverse natural habitats, including flood-plains, copses, reclaimed agricultural land and estuaries, the Marais Poitevin supports a rich array of wildlife. It is a paradise for bird-watchers, featuring 130 different species of nesting bird and more than 120 species of migrating and wintering birds. It also supports 44 species of mammal, 22 species of snake, 32 species of fish and hundreds of insect species.

The stands of elms, alders, willows and hawthorns supply herons with nest sites. Birds of prey such as the European kestrel and the common buzzard are present all year round, as well as breeding pairs of black kites, hobbys and, less commonly, honey buzzards in spring and summer. At night, long-eared and tawny owls scour the marshes for small rodents.

For bird-watchers, the real interest of the area lies in migratory waders and wildfowl. These can be seen on the huge, marshy plains of the Marais Mouillé, on the drier expanses of the Marais Desséché and on the wide mud flats of the Bay of Aiguillon where the Sèvre Niortaise river reaches the sea. Birds to be seen here in autumn and winter include the common redshank, black-tailed godwit and whimbrel, and rare species such as the spotted crake. The Marais Desséché is also an ideal winter refuge for frogs, toads and grass snakes, and its wide canals, bordered by thick vegetation, are home to two rare species of warbler: the great reed warbler and savi's warbler. Small numbers of another rare species, Montagu's harrier, hunt field voles in the area's reclaimed agricultural land.

Reed warbler

The kestrel, one of the Marais' birds of prey

The ruins of the 10th-century
Abbaye St-Pierre at Maillezais

town, the great ruined **Abbaye St-Pierre**, founded in the 10th century, is a dramatic sight. Much of the monastery was destroyed in 1587 by the Protestant armies. The church retains decorated capitals in the 11th-century narthex, the north wall of the nave and the Renaissance transept.

The abbey refectory is still standing, as is the kitchen, now a museum. Look out for the cell in which Rabelais sought refuge with the monks. To the right of the entrance is a small château, built in 1872 on the ruins of the bishop's palace.

Abbaye St-Pierre
02 51 00 70 11. ☐ daily. ☐ 3 weeks Jan. ☑ ☐ restricted.

Chaillé-les-Marais
Road map B5. ☒ 1,200. ☐ ☐ rue de l'An VI (02 51 56 71 17). ☐ Thu.
This village, beside cliffs once washed by the tide, was a centre for the reclamation works that established the fields of dark soil in the Marais Desséché. The techniques are explained at the **Maison du Petit Poitou**. This museum, covering different aspects of the Marais Poitevin, also has the shaggy donkey, a rare Poitou breed.

Maison du Petit Poitou
02 51 56 77 30. ☐ Apr–mid-Sep: daily; mid-Sep–Mar: groups by appt only. ☑ ☐

Western Marais
Much of the early drainage work in the *marais* was led by the monks of **St-Michel-en-l'Herm**. The Benedictine abbey on this former island was originally founded in 682, but has been destroyed and rebuilt several times since then. Its 17th-century chapter house and refectory are the most important remnants.

A short drive to the south, on the River Lay estuary, are the ancient fishing port of **L'Aiguillon-sur-Mer** and the Pointe d'Aiguillon, with its 19th-century Dutch-built dyke. From here, there are marvellous views across the bay to the Ile de Ré and La Rochelle.

Long-haired Poitou donkey

Shellfish farming, especially mussels and oysters, is a leading industry along this part of the coast as well as in the estuaries of the western *marais*. Mussels are grown on a forest of posts, which are visible at low tide, or on ropes hung from rafts in the Bay of Aiguillon.

HABITATS
The Marais Mouillé's extensive network of canals provides an ideal refuge for otters, while its many trees provide an ample choice of nest sites for the purple heron. Migrating birds, such as garganey ducks, and waders, such as the lapwing, thrive in the Marais Desséché.

Male garganey duck

Otter

A nesting purple heron

A lapwing wintering in the Marais Poitevin

Statue of Napoléon in the main square in La Roche-sur-Yon

La Roche-sur-Yon ❻

Road map B4. 👥 49,000. 🚉 🚌 ℹ rue Georges Clemenceau (02 51 36 00 85). 🛒 Tue, Thu & Sat. 🎭 Café de l'Eté (Jul–Aug). 🌐 www.ot-roche-sur-yon.fr

In 1804, La-Roche-sur-Yon was plucked from obscurity by Napoleon, who made it the administrative and military capital of the Vendée region.

The town's rectangular grid layout was centred on a very large parade ground, which is now called **place Napoléon**. In the middle of the square is a statue of the emperor seated astride his horse. As if to deflate these imperial pretensions, a fountain made of squashed oil cans stands playfully outside the Classical theatre building on the place du Théâtre. The 19th-century **Eglise St-Louis** is the largest church in the area.

Restored buildings of the old village are grouped around the place de la Vieille-Horloge. In one of these, **La Maison des Métiers**, there is a permanent exhibition of local products, including some lovely weaving, pottery and leather work.

🏛 **La Maison des Métiers**
Pl de la Vieille-Horloge. ☎ 02 51 62 51 33. ⏰ Tue–Sat. ⬤ Public hols.

Luçon ❼

Road map B4. 👥 10,000. 🚉 🚌 ℹ square Edouard Herriot (02 51 56 36 52). 🛒 Wed & Sat. 🎭 Les Nocturnes Océanes (mid-Jul–Aug).

Luçon, once a marshland port, was described by its most famous inhabitant, Cardinal Richelieu (see p56) as the muddiest bishopric in France. Sent there as a 23-year-old bishop in 1608, he went on to reorganize first the town and then the kingdom. Richelieu's statue stands in the square south of the **Cathédrale Notre-Dame**.

The cathedral has an impressive Gothic nave with Renaissance side chapels. One of these contains a pulpit and two canvases painted by Richelieu's gifted successor as bishop, Pierre Nivelle, a naturalist painter. The beautiful cloisters date from the 16th century.

Painted pulpit in Luçon cathedral

Fontenay-le-Comte ❽

Road map C4. 👥 15,400. 🚉 Niort. 🚌 ℹ pl de la Bascule (02 51 69 44 99). 🛒 Sat. 🎭 Les Histoires d'Eté (Jul–Aug).

Fontenay, sloping down to the River Vendée, was the proud capital of Bas-Poitou until the French Revolution. Napoléon downgraded it in favour of a more centrally-placed administrative centre, La Roche-sur-Yon, from which he could easily control the Royalist Vendée.

Although the city's castle and fortifications were destroyed in 1621, following repeated conflicts in the Wars of Religion, much of its Renaissance quarter survived, and a prosperous postwar town has sprung up around it.

The **Eglise Notre-Dame**, with its commanding spire, is a good place to begin threading through the old streets that lead down from the place Viète. The building with the corner turret at No. 9 rue du Pont-aux-Chèvres was once the palace of the bishops of Maillezais. Many Renaissance luminaries, including the poet Nicolas Rapin and François Rabelais (see p100), lived in rue Guillemet, rue des Jacobins and the arcaded place Belliard. Rabelais was later to satirize soirées he attended here during his five years as an unruly young priest in the Franciscan friary (1519–24).

Fontenay's motto "A fountainhead of fine spirits" is incised on the **Quatre-Tias** fountain in the rue de la Fontaine, which was built in the 16th century and embellished in 1899 by Octave de Rochebrune, a local artist and intellectual.

In the **Musée Vendéen**, displays range from Gallo-Roman archaeology to an excellent scale model of Fontenay during the Renaissance. Several 19th-century portraits convey the suffering of the Vendée in the wake of the 1793 insurrection. There are also displays on daily life in the *bocage*, the wooded region bordering the city.

Once a manor house, the **Château de Terre-Neuve** on the rue de Jarnigande, was converted into something

The high Gothic nave of the Cathédrale Notre-Dame in Luçon

The medieval walls surrounding Vouvant, reflected in the River Mère

more imposing for Nicolas Rapin, poet and grand provost, at the beginning of the 17th century. Two hundred years later, Octave de Rochebrune added decorative flourishes, including statues of the Muses.

The interior of the château has beautiful ceilings and two wonderful fireplaces together with a collection of fine art, furniture, panelling and a door brought from the royal study in the Château de Chambord.

🏛 Musée Vendéen
Pl du 137e Régiment d'Infanterie.
📞 02 51 69 31 31. 🕐 mid-Jun–mid-Sep: Tue–Fri, Sat & Sun pm; mid-Sep–mid-Jun: Wed–Sun, pm only. 🗓 ♿

⚓ Château de Terre-Neuve
Rue de Jarnigande. 📞 02 51 69 99 41, 51 69 17 75. 🕐 May–Sep: daily; Oct–Apr: groups by appt. 🗓

Vouvant ❾

Road map B4. 🏰 920.
🚌 Fontenay-le-Comte. 🚂 Luçon.
ℹ pl du Bail (02 51 00 86 80). 🛒 2nd Thu of month (except Jul–Aug). 🎭 Fête Folklorique (2nd Sun in Aug).

THE ROMANESQUE **Eglise Notre-Dame** in the medieval village of Vouvant has a fantastically carved twin-portal doorway, from which rows of sculptures look down on an arch decorated with a Romanesque bestiary. On the tympanum, Samson wrestles a lion as Delilah advances with her shears.

Vouvant is a starting point for tours of the popular Mervant-Vouvant forest with its signposted walks, boating lakes, grottoes and folklore surrounding the serpent-fairy Mélusine: she tried to lead a life as a woman, but once a week her lower half would turn into a serpent's tail. The **Tour Mélusine** has splendid views of the River Mère.

The twin portals of Vouvant's Eglise Notre-Dame

THE VENDÉE UPRISING

Although it may at times seem a footnote to the French Revolution, the Vendée Uprising has never been forgotten in this region. The Revolution outraged the conservative, Royalist people here. Rising taxes, the persecution of Catholic priests and the execution of Louis XVI in January 1793 were then followed by attempts to conscript locals for the Republican army. This triggered a massacre of Republican sympathizers in the village of Machecoul on 11 March by a peasant mob. As the riots flared, peasant leaders, such as the wagoner Cathelineau and the gamekeeper Stofflet, took charge. They were joined by nobles including Charette, Bonchamps and La Rochejaquelain under the emblem of the sacred heart.

Using guerilla tactics, the Grand Royal and Catholic Army (Whites) took nearly all the Vendée plus Saumur and Angers by June 1793. They won several battles against Republican armies (Blues) but lost at Cholet on 17 October. Nearly 90,000 Whites fled, vainly hoping for reinforcements to join them. The Blues laid waste to the Vendée in 1794, massacring the populace. More than 250,000 people from the Vendée died.

Portrait of Cathelineau (1824) by Anne-Louis Girodet-Trioson

Detail from the frieze in the church in Pouzauges

Pouzauges ⑩

Road map C4. 🏃 *5,500.* 🚉 *La Roche.* 🚌 🛈 *28 pl de l'Eglise (02 51 91 82 46).* ⏰ *Sat, 1st & 3rd Thu of month.*

THIS SMALL TOWN'S ruined 12th-century castle was one of several in the Vendée owned by Gilles de Rais in the 15th century. Once Marshal of France, de Rais' distinguished military career ended in charges of abduction and murder, and he later came to be associated with the story of Bluebeard.

The little **Eglise Notre-Dame du Vieux-Pouzauges**, with its 13th-century frescoes uncovered in 1948, is one of the treasures of the Vendée. The frescoes depict charming scenes from the life of the Virgin Mary and her family. A short audio-visual programme describes the paintings. On

the left, 4 m (12 ft) from the ground, a bestiary frieze, also discovered in 1948, illustrates the months of the year.

Château du Puy-du-Fou ⑪

Road map B4. 🚌 🛈 *Ecomusée, Les Epesses.* 📞 *02 51 57 60 60.* ⏰ *Feb–Dec: daily.* 🅿️

THE BRICK-AND-GRANITE Renaissance château of Puy-du-Fou is 2 km (1 mile) from the little village of Les Epesses. Partly restored after its destruction in the Vendée Uprising, it now houses a museum and an ambitious theme park, and is the backdrop to the **Cinéscénie**, a thrilling son et lumière spectacle *(see pp58–9).*

In the **Ecomusée de la Vendée**, the Vendée Uprising is explained by an illuminated model accompanied by slides, together with a display of paintings and portraits. Prehistoric, Gallo-Roman and medieval exhibits illustrate the history, character and architecture of the region.

The large theme park, **Le Grand Parc**, offers plenty of entertainment. It has two reconstructed villages, one medieval and one 18th-century, with costumed "villagers" and artisans. Other features include wooded walks, lakes, aquatic organ pipes, a wolf's lair and lively displays of juggling, jousting, stunt-riding and especially

falconry, during which falcons, eagles and vultures skim over the heads of seated spectators.

Cinéscénie
📞 *02 51 64 11 11/ 08 36 68 68 85.*
⏰ *late May–early-Sep: Fri & Sat. Spectacle begins: May–Jul: 10:30pm; Aug–early Sep: 10pm (arrive 1 hour earlier); reservations required.* 🅿️ ♿
🌐 *www.puydufou.tm.fr*
🏛 **Ecomusée de la Vendée**
⏰ *Feb–Dec: daily.* 🅿️ ♿
Le Grand Parc
⏰ *May: Sat, Sun, public hols; Jun–mid-Sep: daily.* ⚫ *mid-Sep–Apr.* 🅿️ ♿

Château de Clisson, a feudal fortress now in ruins

Clisson ⑫

Road map B4. 🏃 *6,000.* 🚉 🚌 🛈 *pl du Minage (02 40 54 02 95).* ⏰ *Tue, Wed, Fri.* 🎭 *Festival de Musique (Jul).*
🌐 *www.clisson.com*

CLISSON, PERCHED on two hills straddling the Sèvre Nantaise river, is notable for its Italianate beauty. After much of the town was destroyed in 1794 by punitive Republican forces following the collapse of the Vendée Uprising, Clisson was rebuilt by two brothers, Pierre and François Cacault, working with the sculptor Frédéric Lemot. Lemot's country home is now the **Parc de la Garenne Lemot**, which celebrates the style of ancient Rome with grottoes and tombs, including Lemot's own.

The evolution of defensive strategies can be followed in the massive, ruined **Château de Clisson**, dating from the 12th century and gradually

"Villagers" at work in Puy-du-Fou's Grand Parcours

strengthened in stages up to the 16th century. This was a key feudal fortress for the dukes of Brittany.

Visitors can peer into the dungeons, and into a well with a grisly story behind it: in the vengeful aftermath of the Vendée's defeat, Republican troops butchered and flung into it 18 people who were trying to make bread in the ruins. Next to the château is a fine Renaissance covered market, which survived the destruction because it was used as Republican barracks.

🌷 **Parc de la Garenne Lemot & Maison du Jardinier**
📞 *02 40 54 75 85.* 🕐 *Apr–Sep: Mon pm–Sun (Park: daily); Oct–Mar: Tue–Sun.* ♿ *restricted.*
⚜ **Château de Clisson**
Pl du Minage. 📞 *02 40 54 02 22.* 🕐 *Oct–Mar: Wed–Sun; Apr–Sep: Wed–Mon.* ⬤ *25 Dec.* 📷 ✓

Château de Goulaine ⑬

Road map B3. 🚆 *Nantes, then taxi (15km/8 miles).* 🚌 *Bas Goulaine.* 📞 *02 40 54 91 42.* 🕐 *Easter–mid-Jun: Sat, Sun & public hols pm; mid-Jun–mid-Sep: Wed–Mon; mid-Sep–Oct: Sat, Sun & public hols pms.* 📷 ♿ *grd fl. chât & butterfly park.*

The machicolated entrance tower at the Château de Goulaine

ONLY A SHORT distance southeast of Nantes, this is the most westerly of all the limestone-and-slate Loire châteaux. The same family has made wine here for 1,000 years; the building dates from the 15th century with 17th-century wings. One tower survives from the 14th century. Towers rise from the central building: on one, there is a sculpture of Yolande de Goulaine, who is said to have spurred on her soldiers to repulse the besieging English by threatening to stab herself.

The château survived the Revolution because the family sold it to a Dutchman, only to recover it 70 years later. The present marquis, Robert de Goulaine, has restored the château and also opened a butterfly park where exotic species flutter about a large glasshouse. Butterflies also embellish the label of one of his *sur lie* Muscadets. The multicoloured fireplace in the grand salon is typical of the château's rich decorations.

CINÉSCÉNIE

Puy-du-Fou's late-night show is on a grand scale, with 800 performers and 12,000 seated spectators. It was conceived as a theatre of Vendée history using the full resources of contemporary open-air multimedia techniques. Laser lighting, music, water-jets and fireworks are all carefully orchestrated by computer.

Against the backdrop of the ruined château and its lake, hundreds of locally-recruited actors form living tableaux to dance or grieve, joust or slaughter each other. Horses thunder about, fountains and fireworks soar, bells ring and the château bursts into "flames".

Although the spectacle can be enjoyed for itself, translations of the commentary are available in English, German, Italian or Japanese to 150 of the seats on the huge stand. Warm clothing and advanced booking are advised.

A fire-eater in the Cinéscénie at Puy-du-Fou

Nantes

THE ANCIENT PORT of Nantes was the ducal capital of Brittany for 600 years, but is now considered to be part of the Pays de la Loire. Many of its fine 18th- and 19th-century buildings and houses were built on profits from maritime trade, especially in slaves, sugar, cotton and ship's supplies. The port has been extended downstream towards St-Nazaire, where a modern bridge, the longest in France, crosses the estuary *(see p34)*. This has become an industrial zone attracting trade and breathing new life into the area. Nantes itself remains a vigorous modern city, with good museums, wide open spaces and chic restaurants, bars and shops.

The Neo-Classical theatre in the place Graslin

Exploring Nantes

The most fashionable area of town is the **quartier Graslin**. Constructed between 1780 and 1900, the district's centrepiece is the place Graslin, with its Neo-Classical theatre

The dining room of Nantes' Art Nouveau brasserie, La Cigale

approached by a steep flight of monumental steps. The architect, Mathurin Crucy, designed the place Graslin as a rectangle within a semicircle with eight streets radiating from it. The theatre is fronted by eight Corinthian columns, and statues of eight Muses look down on the square. The wall behind the columns is made of glass, allowing light to stream into the foyer during the day.

Crucy's elegant architecture is seen again in the nearby cours Cambronne, a pedestrianized avenue with fine matching houses built in the early 1800s, and in the place Royale with its splendid fountain celebrating ocean and river spirits.

On the **Ile Feydeau**, the former island where Jules Verne *(see p193)* was born, 18th-century town planning combined with middle-class trading wealth helped to produce

beautiful Neo-Classical façades along streets such as allée Turenne, allée Duguay-Trouin and especially rue Kervégan where 18th-century architect Pierre Rousseau occupied No. 30. Wrought-iron balconies rise in pyramidal sequence supported by luxuriant carvings.

Just north of the Ile Feydeau is the place du Commerce and the ancient Bourse, an elegant 18th-century building, now the tourist office.

🍽 La Cigale

4 pl Graslin. **☎** *02 51 84 94 94.* ⭘ *daily.* See **Restaurants** *p219.*
Facing the theatre, and in dazzling counterpoint to it, stands the famous brasserie-restaurant La Cigale, opened on 1 April 1895. This *fin-de-siècle* fantasy was conceived and largely executed by Emile Libaudière. The building is crammed with Art Nouveau motifs including the cicada from which it takes its name. The rich blues of its Italian tiling, its sinuous wrought-iron, bevelled windows and mirrors, sculptures and painted panels and ceilings have made this restaurant a favourite venue for aesthetes and food-lovers for a century.

🍽 Passage Pommeraye

⭘ *daily.*
To the east of place Graslin, rue Crébillon is the most elegant shopping street in Nantes. It is linked with the rue de la Fosse by a remarkable covered shopping arcade, the passage Pommeraye.

The interior of the elegant passage Pommeraye

Named after the lawyer who financed its construction, it opened in 1843 and must have astonished the bourgeoisie visiting its 66 shops.

The arcade's three galleries are on different levels, each linked by a handsome wooden staircase, lined with statues and lamps. The decoration is highly ornate. Charming sculpted children look down on the galleries, lined with shops and rich with busts, bas-reliefs and other details in stone and metal, all beneath the original glass roof.

🏛 Musée Dobrée

18 rue Voltaire. **[** 02 40 71 03 50.
◯ Tue–Fri, Sat & Sun pm. **●** public
hols. **▨** (except Sun).

Thomas Dobrée (1810–95), son of a rich shipowner and industrialist, spent most of his life building this collection of paintings, drawings, sculpture, tapestries, furniture, porcelain, armour, religious works of art, stamps, letters and manuscripts. The impressive and palatial museum he built for them is based on a plan by the Gothic Revival architect Eugène-Emmanuel Viollet-le-Duc.

Part of the carved alabaster altarpiece in the Musée Dobrée

One of the reliquaries stands out – it is a gold casket, surmounted by a crown, which contains the heart of Anne of Brittany, who asked for it to be buried in her parents' tomb

VISITORS' CHECKLIST

Road map B3. **⌖** 270,200.
✈ 12 km (8 miles) Nantes-
Atlantic. **◻** bd Stalingrad.
▭ allée Baco. **ℹ** pl du
Commerce (02 40 20 60 00).
◆ Tue–Sun. **◆** Les Folles
Journées (music, Jan). Printemps
des Arts (Baroque music,
May–Jun); Festival d'Eté (music,
Jun); Les Rendez-vous de l'Erdre
(jazz, early Sep); Festival des Trois
Continents (cinema, Nov).

in Nantes cathedral (see p55). A complete 15th-century altarpiece carved in alabaster statues from Nottingham, England, is another treasure.

In a second part of the complex, the Manoir de la Touche, there are exhibits dealing with the Vendée Uprising. These include the death mask of François de Charette, a charismatic Vendéen Royalist leader who was captured and shot in Nantes in March 1796. An adjoining modern museum houses an archaeological collection, with Egyptian, Greek and some locally found Gallo-Roman artifacts.

NANTES TOWN CENTRE

Cathédrale St-Pierre et St-Paul ④
Château des Ducs de Bretagne ⑤
Jardin des Plantes ⑦
Musée des Beaux-Arts ⑥
Musée Dobrée ①
Place Graslin ②
Tour de Bretagne ③

KEY

▣ Railway station

▥ Bus terminus

P Parking

ℹ Tourist information

✝ Church

0 metres 400
0 yards 400

Around the Château

THE TOUR DE BRETAGNE, the skyscraper built in 1976 that towers above Nantes, is a landmark dividing the city centre around place du Commerce and place Graslin to the west from the older district around the château and cathedral to the east. There are sensational views from the top. It can be entered (free of charge) from the cours des Cinquante Otages, which sweeps through the centre where the Erdre canal once flowed. This busy avenue has a memorial at the top, in place du Pont Morand, to the 50 hostages after which it is named. Their execution by the Nazis in reprisal for the assassination of the city's military commandant in 1941 turned many Nantais against the Vichy government.

The façade of the Cathédrale St-Pierre et St-Paul

⚜ Château des Ducs de Bretagne

4 pl Marc Elder. **(** *02 40 41 56 56.* ● *for renovation until 2006.* 📷 ✔ ♿

Under major renovation until 2006, only the château's exteriors can be admired from the main courtyard.

The château itself is now surrounded by a landscaped moat and has strong curtain walls and round bastions in the style of the Château d'Angers *(see pp74–5)*. This was the birthplace of Anne of Brittany, who became duchess at 11 and then was coerced into marrying Charles VIII of France in 1491 at the age of 14. Charles died at Amboise in 1498 and, the following year, Anne married his successor, Louis XII, in the château chapel.

Anne's influence can be seen in the dormer windows and loggias of the **Grand Logis** to the right of the entrance, a graceful blend of Flamboyant and Renaissance styles. It was begun by her father, Duc François II, who built most of the château. A smaller royal lodging lies to the west of it. It was here, in Brittany's Catholic bastion, that Henri IV signed the 1598 Edict of Nantes, granting all Protestants permission to worship.

⛪ Cathédrale St-Pierre et St-Paul

Place St-Pierre. ● *daily.*

Nantes has the most accident-prone cathedral on the Loire. The story of its construction and destruction over centuries is vividly told in the crypt. Most recently, on 28 January 1972, a workman's match caused an explosion that blew off the roof. Following the resulting fire, a major restoration programme was undertaken, now completed. The cathedral has been left with an unusual lightness and unity.

A notable feature of this spacious Flamboyant Gothic building is the splendid black-and-white marble tomb of François II, father of Anne of Brittany, and his two wives, sculpted by Michel Colombe *(see pp116–17)*. Situated in the southern transept, it was created between 1500 and 1507 and is among the earliest examples of the Renaissance style in France.

🏛 Musée des Beaux-Arts

10 rue Georges Clemenceau. **(** *02 40 41 65 65.* ● *Wed–Mon.* ● *public hols.* 📷 *except 1st Sun of month.* ♿

The grandeur of this museum and its collections is a good measure of Nantes' civic pride and wealth in the early 19th century. The galleries are on two levels and surround a huge, arched patio, whose clean lines are an appropriate setting for contemporary exhibitions. Although the museum has some sculptures, it is known mainly for its large collection of paintings,

Gustave Courbet's *The Corn Sifters* (1854) in the Musée des Beaux-Arts

Nantes' lovely botanical garden, the Jardin des Plantes

especially those representing key movements from the 15th to the 20th centuries.

Notable Italian works from the 14th century include a *Madonna and Saints* (c.1340) by Bernardo Daddi. This came from the collection of the Cacault brothers who restored Clisson (*see p189*). So did an elegant altarpiece section by Perugino, *Saints Sebastian and Anthony* (c.1475).

Tranquil Dutch and Flemish landscapes and still lifes are offset by a typically robust Rubens, *The Triumph of Judas Maccabaeus* (1635). The master of light, Georges de la Tour, dominates a section of fine, French 17th-century paintings with some of his best work – *The Hurdy-Gurdy Player, The Dream of St Joseph* and *The Denial of St Peter*, all dating from the 1620s.

Other highlights of the museum are in the 19th- and early 20th-century sections, beginning with a luxuriant portrait by Jean-Auguste-Dominique Ingres, *Madame de Senonnes* (1814). Talented local painters, including James Tissot of Nantes and Paul Baudry of La Roche-sur-Yon, are represented, as well as the great innovators Eugène Delacroix, Gustave Courbet, Claude Monet and Vasili Kandinsky. Perhaps the most famous picture in the museum is Courbet's memorable scene, *The Corn Sifters* (1854).

⏛ Musée Jules Verne

3 rue de l'Hermitage. 【 02 40 69 72 52. ☐ Wed–Sat & Sun pm–Mon. ◑ public hols. ◪ except Sun.

A remarkably comprehensive display representing the life, work and world of Jules Verne (1828–1905) starts with a room of furnishings from the house in Amiens in which he wrote most of his books. The museum is packed with mementos, splendidly bound books, cartoons, maps, magic lanterns and models.

♣ Jardin des Plantes

Bd Stalingrad. ☐ *daily.*

Covering 7 ha (17 acres), the plants that make up this extensive botanical garden began as an 18th-century collection of medicinal and exotic plants. The original specimens were brought to Nantes by homecoming ships when a royal decree obliged sea captains to bring exotic plants and seeds back from their travels.

In the mid-19th century, the director, Dr Ecorchard, made changes to the gardens after an inspirational visit to Kew Gardens in London. He introduced the English style of landscaping, with ponds and winding paths, transforming the entire area into a delightful park. Here visitors can see Europe's oldest magnolia tree as well as several outstanding displays of camellias.

THE WORLD OF JULES VERNE

Just past the Pont Anne de Bretagne is a disused section of cobbled quay which, in 1839, was lined with boats. It was here that the 11-year-old Jules Verne slipped aboard a ship to see the world. He got as far as Paimbœuf, a short trip down river, before his father caught up with him. Later, while studying law, Verne started to publish plays and librettos. His science-fiction novels, including *A Journey to the Centre of the Earth* (1864), *Twenty Thousand Leagues Under the Sea* (1870) and *Around the World in Eighty Days* (1873), have been hugely successful, and he is among the most widely read and translated authors in the world.

Bust of Jules Verne (1906) by Albert Roze

TRAVELLERS' NEEDS

WHERE TO STAY

Loire valley hotels are as charming as their surroundings. Family-style inns predominate, with dining rooms that are also popular among locals and comfortable, usually old-fashioned, bedrooms. The region also boasts some prestigious *Relais et Châteaux* establishments, often mansions or châteaux converted into luxury hotels with elegant rooms, superb cuisine – and prices to match. A fascinating alternative is staying in a private château or manor

A hotel doorman

house *(see pp200–201)*, which allows you access to privately-owned, often historic buildings as a (paying) guest of the owners. The hotel listings on pages 202–7 give details of establishments throughout the region, in every price category and style. *Gîtes*, the self-catering accommodation for which France is rightly famous, are also widely available in the Loire Valley, allowing you to take advantage of the marvellous range of fresh ingredients on offer in the local markets.

THE CITY HOTEL

The main towns and cities along the banks of the Loire have at least one long-established *grand hôtel* in the centre. These large hotels typically have spacious entrance halls and public rooms, but some of the once large bedrooms may well have been carved up to allow for en suite bathrooms. Rooms are liable to vary considerably in quality, so it is advisable to ask to see the room offered if you have not made a booking in advance. When you make a reservation, be sure to specify a room away from a main

road or busy square (most of these city hotels have some much quieter rooms, which overlook a courtyard). Bars are likely to be frequented by members of the local business community, who also entertain clients in the hotel restaurant, where you can expect classic French cuisine rather than regional dishes.

THE CHÂTEAU HOTEL

A number of châteaux and manor houses in the Loire Valley have been converted into expensive hotels. Often set in well-kept grounds and offering outstanding cuisine, they

range from Renaissance manor houses to huge, turreted 19th-century piles. The **Relais et Châteaux** association, of which many are members, publishes an annual brochure.

Rooms are usually spacious and elegant, with some suites available. Some château hotels also offer more modest accommodation, in outbuildings or even in bungalows in the grounds, enabling you to acquire a taste of *la vie de château* and enjoy the restaurant's cuisine without breaking the bank. If you prefer to be in the main building, specify this when booking – advance reservations are essential.

THE CLASSIC FAMILY HOTEL

These typically French small hotels, generally run by the same family for several generations, are to be found throughout the Loire Valley. The bar and dining room are likely to be widely used by locals, especially for Sunday lunch in country districts. The atmosphere is usually friendly, with helpful staff able to provide leaflets and other information about local sightseeing and shopping.

Most of these hotels have only a small number of rooms, often reasonably spacious and pleasantly furnished with well-worn antiques and flowery wallpaper. Plumbing may be erratic, although many hotels of this type have made efforts to spruce up their bathrooms. Few family hotels in the rural

The elegant Domaine des Hauts-de-Loire hotel in Onzain *(see p205)*

The grand staircase of the Hôtel de l'Univers in Tours *(see p203)*

areas have single rooms, but these are more common in the region's towns.

Many family hotels belong to the **Logis de France** association, which publishes an annual booklet listing more than 4,000 family-run hotels in France. *Logis* hotels are proud of their restaurants, which tend to specialize in regional cuisine. Most are basic roadside inns, with only a few listed in the main towns, but off the beaten track you can find charming farmhouses and inexpensive hotels.

Many family-run hotels are shut in the afternoon and do not like visitors to arrive then, although hotel guests have keys. Their restaurants are also shut at least one day a week (except possibly in the tourist season).

Logo of the Logis de France association

THE MODERN CHAIN HOTEL

FRANCE HAS an increasing number of modern chain hotels, on the edges of towns or close to motorways.

The cheapest are the one-star, very basic **Formule 1** motels. Two-star chains, which are widely used by French families on a low budget, include **Ibis**, **Campanile**, **Climat de France** and **Inter Hôtel**. More comfortable, but lacking in atmosphere or regional charm, are the **Novotel** and **Mercure** three-star chains. All the chain hotels offer some family rooms, and in some

children can sleep in their parents' room without charge. Most have restaurants where the food is adequate.

THE RESTAURANT-WITH-ROOMS

A FEW OF THE well-known and expensive restaurants in the Loire Valley region also have rooms available for over-night guests. The rooms may be as chic as the restaurant. However, they might be modest bedrooms left over from the days before the restaurant was a gourmet's magnet and will therefore allow you to spend an inexpensive night to make up for a budget-busting meal.

In rural areas, it may be practical to spend the night at the restaurant, rather than return to a remote hotel. Check in the listings on pages 214–19 for restaurants-with-rooms.

MEALS AND FACILITIES

BECAUSE MOST VISITORS to the Loire Valley choose to tour around, few hotels offer full-board rates to those who settle in for holidays. However, for more than three nights in one place, it may be possible to obtain *pension* (full-board) or *demi-pension* (half-board). But half-board may apply only to lunch, which makes sightseeing difficult, and the meals for full-board guests are likely to be less interesting than the fixed-price menus. Always

check whether the room rate includes breakfast. If not, you may prefer to have your breakfast in a nearby café.

Traditionally, family hotel rooms offer double beds, but twin beds are more likely to be found in city and chain hotels. Prices are usually fixed per room, but single travellers may be allowed a small reduction. Bathrooms with a shower rather than a bath make the room less expensive. Those with only a *cabinet de toilette* (an alcove containing basin and bidet) are the cheapest.

It is perfectly acceptable to ask to view the room before making a decision.

GRADINGS AND PRICES

FRENCH HOTELS are officially graded into one, two, three and four stars, plus four-star deluxe. These categories take account of facilities such as telephones, televisions and en suite bathrooms, but do not necessarily indicate the quality of the decor or service. A few very modest hotels do not rate a star ranking.

Prices rise as the number of stars increases. Rooms may vary in quality within an establishment, so it is not easy to classify hotels solely by price. Rates for a double room start at around 25€ per night without breakfast, although they may start at 150€ in château hotels. Check whether a local tax *(taxe de séjour)* will be added to your bill, but service will already be included. It is usual to leave a small tip for the chambermaid.

Typical Loire Valley manor house hotel

The Domaine des Hautes Roches at Rochecorbon *(see p203)*

BOOKING

RESERVE WELL IN ADVANCE for hotels in popular tourist areas during July and August. If booking by telephone it may be necessary to send a fax confirmation, giving a credit card number. You may need to speak French to make a telephone booking for some hotels, but letters in English are normally acceptable. Local tourist offices can supply listings of hotels and provide a reservation service (for up to a week in advance).

BED AND BREAKFAST

FRENCH bed-and-breakfast accommodation, called *chambres d'hôte*, can vary widely from modest rooms above a hayloft to an elegant room in a manor house. Local tourist offices keep lists of those families willing to take in guests. Some hosts will cook dinner if given advance warning. Many such rooms are registered and inspected by the **Gîtes de France** organization – look out for their green and yellow logo.

SELF-CATERING

GÎTES DE FRANCE is also the best-known organization monitoring and booking self-catering accommodation. Run by the French government, it offers predominantly rural accommodation, ranging from a cottage to an entire wing of a château. Booking is essential and can be done through **Brittany Ferries**, UK booking agents for *Gîtes de France*. Their brochure is a selection from the *Gîtes de France's* own much larger departmental brochures, obtained from the Paris head office, or from its departmental offices, or via Internet *(see Directory)*. Local tourist offices also have lists of properties for rent within the surrounding area, but try to book early. The lower-priced *gîtes* have only very basic facilities. For more luxury properties scour the major US and European newspapers, specialist magazines and the Internet or use a letting agency. Whatever the price, a holiday in a *gîte* is a great way to experience Loire Valley life.

DIRECTORY

HOTELS

Campanile
🛈 01 64 62 46 46.

Climat de France
🛈 01 64 62 48 88.

Inter Hôtel
🛈 01 42 06 46 46.

Formule 1
🛈 08 36 68 56 85.

Ibis, Novotel, Mercure, Sofitel
🛈 01 60 87 90 00.

Relais et Châteaux
🛈 (0870) 242 0052 UK.
🛈 (212) 856-0115 US.

Logis de France
83 av d'Italie, 75013 Paris.
🛈 01 45 84 70 00.
www.logis-de-france.fr

BED AND BREAKFAST

Maison des Gîtes de France
59 rue St. Nazaire

75009 Paris.
🛈 01 49 70 75 75
www.gites-de-france.fr

SELF-CATERING/ EFFICIENCIES

Brittany Ferries (UK booking agent for Gîtes de France)
🛈 (0990)143537 (for brochure);.(0990) 360360 (reservations).

Gîtes de France
ARART, B.P. 139,
38 rue A-Fresnel, 37171
Chambray-les-Tours.
🛈 02 47 48 37 12.
📠 02 47 48 13 39.

CAMPING

Castels et Camping Caravaning
PIBS CP26, 56038 Vannes.
🛈 02 97 42 55 83.

CAMPING CARNETS

GB Car Club (UK)
🛈 (01794) 515444.

National Campers and Hikers Association (US)
🛈 (716) 668-6242.

HOSTELS

CROUS
39 av. G-Bernanos,
75005 Paris.
🛈 01 40 51 36 00.

Fédération Unie des Auberges de Jeunesse
27 rue Pajol, 75018 Paris.
🛈 01 44 89 87 27.

YHA (UK)
🛈 (01727) 855215.

AYH (US)
🛈 (202) 783-6161.

DISABLED TRAVELLERS

Association des Paralysés de France
17 bd Auguste Blanqui
75013 Paris.
🛈 01 53 62 84 00.

CNRH
236 bis rue Tolbiac,
75013 Paris.
🛈 01 53 80 66 66.

Mobility International USA
PO Box 10767, Eugene,
OR 97440.
🛈 (541) 343-1284.

RADAR (Royal Association for Disability and Rehabilitation UK)
12 City Forum, 250 City
Rd, London EC1V 8AF.
🛈 (020) 7250 3222.

TOURIST OFFICES

French Govt Tourist Office (UK)
178 Piccadilly,
London W1V 0AL.
🛈 (020) 7399 3500.
📠 (020) 7493 6594.

French Govt Tourist Office (US)
444 Madison Ave,
New York, NY 10022.
🛈 (212) 838 7800.

CAMPING

CAMPING IS A CHEAP and fun way of seeing the Loire Valley. Information on camp sites can be obtained from departmental tourist offices. Some of these do not accept visitors without a special camping *carnet* (available from the AA and RAC and from the addresses listed in the Directory). French camp sites are graded into four starred categories, but even one-star sites have lavatories, public telephones and running water (although this may be only cold). The top-ranked sites are remarkably well equipped. Always book ahead where possible.

Gîtes de France logo

The **Gîtes de France** organization has a guide to unpretentious sites on farm land (ask for *camping à la ferme*), and *camping sauvage* (camping outside official sites) is occasionally possible if you come to an agreement with the landowner. **Castels et Camping Caravaning** is an up-market association of sites within the grounds of châteaux and manor houses.

HOSTELS

HOSTELS PROVIDE budget accommodation, but for two or more people sharing a room, an inexpensive hotel will probably cost the same. To stay in a youth hostel, you need to purchase a membership card from the **Youth Hostel Association** in your own country, or buy an "Ajiste" card from French hostels. See the Directory for the address of the *auberges de jeunesse* (youth hostel) organization. **CROUS**, the Centre Régional des Oeuvres Universitaires, can provide details of university rooms available during the summer vacation. **Gîtes de France** is once again a valuable source of information: ask for the *Gîtes d'étape* guide to dormitory accommodation in farmhouses for those on walking, riding or cycling holidays.

DISABLED TRAVELLERS

A GUIDE PUBLISHED by **RADAR** (Royal Association for Disability and Rehabilitation), *Holidays and Travel Abroad*, details wheelchair access to hotels, youth hostels and self-catering accommodation, and *Gîtes accessibles à tous* lists officially classified *gîtes* suitable for the disabled. Information on hotel access is also available from **CNRH** (Comité National pour la Réadaptation des Handicapés), and the **Association des Paralysés de France** also publishes a guide to accommodation accessible for wheelchairs.

SOURCES OF INFORMATION

THE INVALUABLE GUIDE *The Traveller in France*, listing hotel chains, booking agencies and tour operators specializing in travel to and in France, is published by the **French Government Tourist Office**. The tourist office is also able to supply brochures and booklets for **Logis de France** hotels, **Gîtes de France** and other types of accommodation. **Regional Tourist Committees** will send lists of hotels, hostels, camp sites and private self-catering accommodation. The regional **Loisirs Accueil** centre and Departmental Tourist Committ-ees (in the major city of each department) are also useful sources of information. When you are in the Loire Valley, contact local tourist offices *(see p231)* for hotel lists and details of local families taking in guests.

USING THE LISTINGS

The hotels on pages 202–7 are listed according to area and price category. The symbols summarize the facilities at each hotel.

🛏 all rooms with bath or shower
24 24-hour room service
TV TV in all rooms
🏞 rooms with good views
▤ all rooms with air-conditioning
🏊 hotel pool or beach
🧒 children's facilities
♿ wheelchair access
🛗 lift
P hotel parking available
❂ grounds or terrace
🍽 restaurant in hotel
★ highly recommended
● annual closure
💳 credit cards accepted
AE American Express
MC Mastercard
DC Diners Club
V Visa

Price categories for a standard double room (not per person) with bath or shower for one night, including tax and service, but not breakfast.

€ Under 30€
€€ 30–60€
€€€ 60–90€
€€€€ 90–150€
€€€€€ Over 150€.

Camping in a forest in the Loire Valley

Staying in a Château

THE ESTABLISHMENTS FEATURED HERE have been selected from our listings of recommended places to stay on pages 202–7. They offer a unique opportunity to experience the style of life in a private Loire Valley château, spending a night within walls steeped in history, but often with all the comforts of a modern hotel. You will be greeted like a house guest, and efforts are made to make you feel part of the owner's family, who may have lived in the château for many generations. They may also create the atmosphere of a private party at dinner, which can be booked and paid for in advance.

Château de Blanville
Close to Chartres and surrounded by beautiful gardens, the Château de Blanville has been owned by the same family for more than 250 years. After a period as a hotel, its future is now uncertain.

Château des Briottières
This 18th-century château, furnished in period and lived in by the same family for six gener-ations, has attractive grounds and a heated pool. (See p202.)

0 kilometres   50

0 miles   50

Château de la Millière
Close to Les Sables d'Olonne, this 19th-century château is set in extensive grounds, complete with an outdoor pool. (See p207.)

Château des Réaux
The owners of this pretty 15th-century château, with red and white brickwork, offer a warm welcome and attractive rooms. (See p202.)

The countryside surrounding the Château du Plessis-Beauregard in the region close to Orléans offers visitors a scene of pastoral tranquillity.

Château de la Verrerie
The "Stuarts' château" (see p154), magically reflected in a lake and surrounded by dense woodland, has spacious, comfortable rooms and an attractive cottage-style restaurant on the grounds. (See p205.)

Château du Plessis-Beauregard
This turreted château has a lived-in feel, with light, pretty bedrooms. (See p204.)

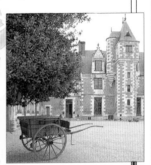

Château de Jallanges
An energetic couple have turned this brick-and-stone Renaissance dwelling, with a period garden and pretty chapel, into a charming home. (See p204.)

Château de la Bourdaisière
A princely greeting (from one of the Princes de Broglie) awaits you in this beautifully modernized château, the birthplace of Gabrielle d'Estrées. (See p203.)

Château de la Commanderie
Owned by the same family for four generations, this 12th-century manor house was once the Commandery of the Knights Templar. A château was added in the 19th century. (See p206.)

ANJOU

ANGERS

Hôtel Continental

Road map C3. 14 rue Louis de Romain, 49000. **(** 02 41 86 94 94. **FAX** 02 41 86 96 60. **Rooms:** 25. 📶 📺 ♿ ▦ 🅿 AE, MC, DC, V. €€
W www.hotellecontinental.com

Modernized in bright Kandinsky colours, this hotel is in a quiet side street only minutes from the best shopping areas. The rooms are all soundproofed, and the balconies are decorated with flowers.

Hôtel du Mail

Road map C3. 8 rue des Ursules, 49000. **(** 02 41 25 05 25. **FAX** 02 41 86 91 20. **Rooms:** 26. 📶 📺 🅿 ▦ AE, MC, DC, V. €€

This old-fashioned hotel was built in 1643 as part of a convent, and the first floor rooms have particularly high ceilings. Despite being centrally located, it is quiet. Self-service breakfasts are available.

BRIOLLAY

Château de Noirieux

Road map C3. 26 rte du Moulin, 49125. **(** 02 41 42 50 05. **FAX** 02 41 37 91 00. **Rooms:** 19. 📶 📺 ▦ ♨ 🅿 🅾 ❙❙ ▦ AE, MC, DC, V. €€€€€
W www.chateaudenoirieux.com

This hotel combines a 15th-century château, a manor house and a chapel. Each bedroom is decorated in a different style, ranging from the 17th to the 20th centuries. The restaurant offers new versions of classic dishes and a seven-course gastronomic menu.

CHÂTEAUNEUF-SUR-SARTHE

Château des Briottières

Road map C3. Champigné 49330. **(** 02 41 42 00 02. **FAX** 02 41 42 01 55. **Rooms:** 15. 📶 ▦ ♨ 🅿 🅾 ❙❙ ★ ▦ AE, MC, DC, V. €€€€€
W www.briottieres.com

This 18th-century château hotel, has extensive grounds with on-site cycling, fishing and swimming. A 6-room mansion within the grounds is also available. Visitors can join their hosts for a candlelit dinner. Booking is essential.

FONTEVRAUD-L'ABBAYE

Hôtellerie Prieuré St-Lazare

Road map C3. Abbaye de Fontevraud, 49590. **(** 02 41 51 73 16. **FAX** 02 41 51 75 50. **Rooms:** 52. 📶 📺 ▦ ♨ 🅿 🅾 ❙❙ ▦ ▦ AE, MC, V. €€€
W www.hotelfp-fontevraud.com

Located in the abbey complex (see pp86–7), this hotel is in the former St-Lazare priory. The bedrooms are in a 19th-century wing, and the restaurant in the salle capitulaire spreads out into the cloisters in the summer.

GENNES

Hôtel le Prieuré

Road map C3. Chênehutte-les-Tuffeaux, 49350. **(** 02 41 67 90 14. **FAX** 02 41 67 92 24. **Rooms:** 36. 📺 ▦ ♨ 🅿 🅾 ❙❙ ▦ AE, MC, DC, V. €€€€€
W www.prieure.com

This Renaissance manor house, has rooms decorated in the Louis XIII style, some with views of the Loire. It is set in a 15-ha (37-acre) park, with a swimming pool and tennis courts. The restaurant extends onto the terrace.

MONTREUIL-BELLAY

Splendid Hôtel

Road map C4. 139 rue Docteur-Gaudrez, 49260. **(** 02 41 53 10 00. **FAX** 02 41 52 45 17. **Rooms:** 60. 📺 📶 ♿ ▦ 🅿 🅾 ❙❙ ▦ MC, V. €€€
W www.splendid-hotel.fr

Part of this hotel is located in a renovated house in the centre of town. It also has a 17th-century annexe, Le Relais du Bellay. The restaurant serves regional food.

SAUMUR

Hôtel St-Pierre

Road map C3. 8 rue Haute St-Pierre, 49400. **(** 02 41 50 33 00. **FAX** 02 41 50 38 68. **Rooms:** 14 & 2 apartments. 📶 📺 ♿ ▦ 🅿 ▦ AE, DC, MC, V. €€€€

Located in a small street just off the place St-Pierre, this elegant hotel is generally quiet, apart from the occasional sound of organ music from the nearby church. There are two salons, one with a 17th-century open fireplace.

TOURAINE

AMBOISE

Le Lion d'Or

Road map D3. 17 quai Charles-Guinot, 37400. **(** 02 47 57 00 23. **FAX** 02 47 23 22 49. **Rooms:** 13. 📶 🅿 ❙❙ 🅾 Dec–Jan. ▦ MC, V. €€

This typically French, traditional hotel is welcoming and efficiently run, with comfortable rooms and a restaurant, beside the Loire.

AZAY-LE-RIDEAU

Hôtel de Biencourt

Road map D3. 7 rue Balzac, 37190. **(** 02 47 45 20 75. **FAX** 02 47 45 91 73. **Rooms:** 17. 📶 ▦ ♿ ▦ MC, V. €€

Not far from the entrance to one of the loveliest Loire Valley châteaux, this hotel is in an 18th-century town house. The rooms are quiet and pretty, some of them overlooking a garden, and there are several restaurants nearby.

Le Grand Monarque

Road map D3. 3 pl de la République, 37190. **(** 02 47 45 40 08. **FAX** 02 47 45 46 25. **Rooms:** 25. 📶 🅿 🅾 ❙❙ ▦ AE, MC, V. €€€
W www.legrandmonarque.com

Run by the same family for generations, this hotel offers comfortable well-furnished rooms and friendly service. In summer, the courtyard garden, shaded by tall trees, provides a delightful setting for the restaurant's regional cuisine.

BOURGUEIL

Château des Réaux

Road map C3. Le Port Boulet, 37140. **(** 02 47 95 14 40. **FAX** 02 47 95 18 34. **Rooms:** 10. 📶 ▦ ♿ 🅿 🅾 ★ ▦ AE, MC, V. €€€

This Renaissance château has been home to the Goupil de Bouillé family for more than a century. They welcome guests in their attractive rooms and suites, four of them actually in a cottage in the delightful gardens.

CHENONCEAUX

Hôtel du Bon Laboureur et du Château

Road map D3. 6 rue du Docteur-Bretonneau, 37150. (02 47 23 90 02. FAX 02 47 23 82 01. Rooms: 26. 🖭 🚃 🏊 🛎 👭 💶 mid-Nov–mid-Dec. 🍴 AE, MC, DC, V. €€€€

This family-run hotel looks like a cosy inn. However, its many delights include a heated outdoor pool with its own cocktail bar, and a restaurant with a good reputation.

CHINON

La Boule d'Or

Road map D3. 66 quai Jeanne-d'Arc, 37500. (02 47 93 03 13. FAX 02 47 93 24 25. Rooms: 13. 🖭 🔌 🍴 AE, MC, DC, V. €€

This friendly hotel, set in an ancient coaching inn beside the Vienne, has pretty rooms, some overlooking a courtyard. Its restaurant serves outdoor meals in fine weather.

Château de Marçay

Road map D3. Marçay, 37500. (02 47 93 03 47. FAX 02 47 93 45 33. Rooms: 34. 🖭 🔌 🚃 🏊 🛎 👭 ★ 🍴 AE, MC, DC, V. €€€€€

A turreted medieval château, 9 km (5 miles) south of Chinon, built of traditional white tufa. It has tennis courts, a swimming pool and even a heliport. The restaurant and its excellent wine cellar are renowned.

LANGEAIS

Hôtel l'Hosten

Road map D3. 2 rue Gambetta, 37130. (02 47 96 82 12. FAX 02 47 96 56 72. Rooms: 11. 🖭 📺 🔌 🍴 💶 mid-Feb–Mar. 🍴 AE, MC, DC, V. €€€ 🌐 www.errard.com

This traditional hotel close to the castle has been run by the same family for decades. Some of the rooms look onto a pretty terrace. It also has an excellent restaurant.

LOCHES

Le George Sand

Road map D4. 39 rue Quintefol, 37600. (02 47 59 39 74. FAX 02 47 91 55 75. Rooms: 20. 🖭 📺 🍴 💶 MC, V. €€€

This Logis de France is set in an old coaching inn below the château ramparts. Some of the rooms are reached by a stone staircase from a medieval watchtower. The restaurant serves regional dishes.

LUYNES

Domaine de Beauvois

Road map D3. Le Pont Clouet, Les Pins 37230. (02 47 55 50 11. FAX 02 47 55 59 62. Rooms: 36. 🖭 📺 🚃 🏊 👭 ★ 🍴 AE, MC, DC, V. €€€€€ 🌐 www.beauvois.com

A 15th- and 16th-century manor house, with an outdoor pool and tennis courts, this elegant Relais et Châteaux hotel is 4 km (2 miles) northwest of Luynes.

MONTBAZON

Château d'Artigny

Road map D3. Rte de Monts, 37250. (02 47 34 30 30. FAX 02 47 34 30 39. Rooms: 65. 🖭 📺 🚃 🏊 🔌 👭 🍴 ★ 🍴 AE, MC, DC, V. €€€€€

The parfumier François Coty built this château between 1912 and 1928 in 18th-century style. There are musical weekends in winter.

MONTLOUIS-SUR-LOIRE

Château de la Bourdaisière

Road map D3. 25 rue de la Bourdaisière, 37270. (02 47 45 16 31. FAX 02 47 45 09 11. Rooms: 15. 🖭 📺 🔌 🚃 🛎 🔌 👭 🍴 ★ 🍴 MC, V. €€€€ 🌐 www.chateaulabourdaisiere.com

In 1565, Gabrielle d'Estrées, Henri IV's mistress, was born here. It offers a pool, tennis courts and horse riding (see p111).

TOURS

Central Hôtel

Road map D3. 21 rue Berthelot, 37000. (02 47 05 46 44. FAX 02 47 66 10 26. Rooms: 41. 🖭 📺 🔌 👭 🍴 AE, MC, DC, V. €€

As central as the name suggests, this pleasant hotel has comfortable rooms and a little garden as well as parking, a real benefit in Tours.

Hôtel Colbert

Road map D3. 78 rue Colbert, 37000. (02 47 66 61 56. FAX 02 47 66 01 55. Rooms: 18. 🖭 📺 🔌 👭 🍴 AE, MC, DC, V. €€

This friendly hotel near the cathedral has been renovated, but retains its classic style. Many good-value restaurants are to be found nearby. In summer, breakfast is served outside.

Domaine des Hautes Roches

Road map D3. 86 quai de la Loire, Rochecorbon, 37210. (02 47 52 88 88. FAX 02 47 52 81 30. Rooms: 15. 🖭 📺 🔌 🚃 🛎 🔌 👭 🍴 ★ 🍴 AE, MC, DC, V. €€€€€ 🌐 www.leshautesroches.com

This unique hotel combines an 18th-century building with unusual but comfortable troglodyte bedrooms carved out of the tufa cliffside. Tours is only 5 km (3 miles) away.

Hôtel de l'Univers

Road map D3. 5 bd Heurteloup, 37000. (02 47 05 37 12. FAX 02 47 61 51 80. Rooms: 85. 🖭 📺 🔌 🚃 🛎 🔌 👭 🍴 AE, MC, DC, V. €€€€€

Tours' "grand hotel", is now a deluxe establishment, with elegant rooms. The trompe l'oeil paintings in the lobby depict well-known past guests, including Sarah Bernhardt and Winston Churchill.

VEIGNÉ

Le Moulin Fleuri

Road map D3. Rte de Ripault, 37250. (02 47 26 01 12. FAX 02 47 34 04 71. Rooms: 12. 🖭 🔌 🚃 🏊 👭 🍴 💶 Feb. 🍴 AE, MC, V. €€

An old watermill beside the Indre has been turned into this charming hotel. Its modest yet large bedrooms are above a riverside restaurant.

VILLANDRY

Le Cheval Rouge

Road map D3. 9 rue Principale, 37510. (02 47 50 02 07. FAX 02 47 50 08 77. Rooms: 20. 🖭 🔌 🚃 👭 🍴 MC, V. €€

Just a few minutes' walk from the gardens of Château de Villandry, this hotel offers good-value, modern bedrooms. It also makes a handy base for visiting Azay-le-Rideau, Langeais and Ussé.

For key to symbols see p199

VOUVRAY

Château de Jallanges

Road map D3. Vernou-sur-Brenne, 37210. 📞 02 47 52 06 66. **FAX** 02 47 52 11 18. **Rooms:** 6. 🚪 🛁 🕏 🅿 📧 ★ 🗠 AE, MC, V. €€€€ �W www.jallanges.com

An energetic family offer private accommodation in this 15th-century château. The rooms overlook the peaceful grounds, where guests can go horse riding, travel in carriages or hot-air balloons, or stroll in the Renaissance garden before dining with the owners.

YZEURES-SUR-CREUSE

Hôtel de la Promenade

Road map D4. 1 pl du 11 Novembre, 37290. 📞 02 47 91 49 00. **FAX** 02 47 94 46 12. **Rooms:** 15. 🚪 TV 🕏 🅿 🍴 🗠 MC, V. €€

This former coaching inn in Touraine is near the archaeological sites of Le Grand-Pressigny and Preuilly-sur-Claise and is also convenient for the nature reserve of La Brenne.

BLESOIS AND ORLEANAIS

BEAUGENCY

La Sologne

Road map E3. 6 pl St-Firmin, 45190. 📞 02 38 44 50 27. **FAX** 02 38 44 90 19. **Rooms:** 16. 🚪 TV 🗠 MC, V. €€ �W www.hoteldelasologne.com

This attractive little hotel, housed in a stone building in the old town, makes a pleasant stopover. Its small but pretty and well-equipped rooms overlook a garden, where breakfast is served. It is advisable to book ahead.

BLOIS

Hôtel Anne de Bretagne

Road map E3. 31 av Jean-Laigret, 41000. 📞 02 54 78 05 38. **FAX** 02 54 74 37 79. **Rooms:** 29. 🚪 TV 🕏 🅿 🍴 Jan. 🗠 MC, V. €€

This modest inn – a *Logis de France* but, unusually, with no restaurant – is popular with both French and foreign tourists for its good-value,

brightly decorated rooms and its friendly atmosphere. It is situated close to the château, but away from the summer crowds, on a small square.

Le Médicis

Road map E3. 2 allée François-1er, 41000. 📞 02 54 43 94 04. **FAX** 02 54 42 04 05. **Rooms:** 12. 🚪 TV 🗐 🕏 🅿 🔝 🗠 AE, MC, DC, V. €€€ �W www.le-medicis.com

This stylish 19th-century building is conveniently near the train station and only 15 minutes' walk from the château. Le Médicis has elegant, cool rooms, decorated in different styles. The restaurant is popular for its classic cuisine and range of fixed-price meals.

CHAMBORD

Le Grand St-Michel

Road map E3. Le Village, 41250. 📞 02 54 20 31 31. **FAX** 02 54 20 36 40. **Rooms:** 38. 🚪 TV 🕏 🅿 📧 🍴 🗠 mid-Nov–mid-Dec. 🗠 MC, V. €€

Opposite the magnificent château, this traditional hotel is a peaceful retreat at the end of a day. Some of the comfortable bedrooms have spectacular château views. The hotel's tennis courts are good for an early-evening workout, before adjourning to one of restaurant's terrace tables, which are, not suprisingly, in great demand.

CHÂTEAUNEUF-SUR-LOIRE

Château du Plessis-Beauregard

Road map E2. Vitry-aux-Loges, 45530. 📞 02 38 59 47 24. **FAX** 02 38 59 47 48. **Rooms:** 3. 🚪 🛁 🅿 📧 ★ 🗠 €€€

Set in the Forêt d'Orléans, 6 km (4 miles) from Châteauneuf-sur-Loire, this turreted, brick château has light, airy rooms and a swimming pool. A set dinner is available if ordered well in advance.

CHEVERNY

Château de Breuil

Road map E3. Rte de Fougère-sur-Brièvre, 41700. 📞 02 54 44 20 20. **FAX** 02 54 44 30 40. **Rooms:** 15. TV 🕏 🅿 🍴 🔝 mid-Nov–mid-Mar. 🗠 AE, MC, V. €€€€

This grand 18th-century château is set in extensive grounds, and all the bedrooms, suites and public rooms are luxuriously furnished with antiques. A surviving 15th-century tower has also been converted into a unique bedroom and sitting area.

COUR-CHEVERNY

Le St-Hubert

Road map E3. Rue Nationale, 41700. 📞 02 54 79 96 60. **FAX** 02 54 79 21 17. **Rooms:** 24. 🚪 🕏 🅿 📧 🍴 🔝 Jan. 🗠 MC, V. €€

Named after the patron saint of hunting, this family-style hotel is very popular during the shooting season. In the summer it offers angling. Each room is decorated in modern style. The restaurant has special meals for children.

GIEN

Le Rivage

Road map F3. 1 quai de Nice, 45500. 📞 02 38 37 79 00. **FAX** 02 38 38 10 21. **Rooms:** 19. 🚪 TV 🗐 📧 🕏 🅿 🍴 ★ 🗠 AE, MC, DC, V. €€

All the rooms in this elegant hotel are furnished with antiques, and some have views across the gardens to the river. The air-conditioned restaurant successfully blends classic and *nouvelle* cuisine.

MONTRICHARD

La Tête Noire

Road map D3. 24 rue de Tours. 📞 02 54 32 05 55. **FAX** 02 54 32 78 37. **Rooms:** 35. 🚪 🅿 📧 🍴 🔝 Jan. 🗠 MC, V. €€

This traditional, reliable hotel has pleasant rooms, some of them in an annexe. The buildings are set in a garden beside the River Cher.

NOUAN-LE-FUZELIER

Moulin de Villiers

Road map E3. Rte de Chaon, 41600. 📞 02 54 88 72 27. **FAX** 02 54 88 78 87. **Rooms:** 16. 🚪 TV 🗐 🕏 🅿 📧 🍴 🔝 Tue, Wed pm. 🗠 MC, V. €€

This converted mill gives a sense of the Sologne. Surrounded by woods, it has a lake for both anglers and bird-watchers. The rooms are basic but charming, and the restaurant is also good value.

OLIVET

Les Quatre-Saisons

Road map E2. 351 rue de la Reine-Blanche, 45160. **(** *02 38 66 14 30.* **FAX** *02 38 66 78 59.* **Rooms:** 7. 🛏 📺 ❄ 🏃 P ❚❚ 🏊 *AE, MC, V.* €€€
W www.les-quatre-saisons.com

The bedrooms of this comfortable hotel are bright and furnished with antiques. Many rooms have views of the River Loiret, as does the delightful dining room.

ONZAIN

Domaine des Hauts-de-Loire

Road map D3. Rte Mesland, 41150. **(** *02 54 20 72 57.* **FAX** *02 54 20 77 32.* **Rooms:** 35. 🛏 📺 ❄ 🏊 P 🏃 ♿ ❚❚ ★ ● *Dec–mid-Feb.* 🏊 *AE, MC, V.* €€€€€
W www.domainehautsdeloire.com

Once a hunting lodge, this *Relais et Châteaux* member is now an elegant hotel. Guests can swim, play tennis or even ride in a hot-air balloon or a helicopter.

ORLÉANS

Hôtel Jackotel

Road map E2. 18 Cloître St-Aignan, 45000. **(** *02 38 54 48 48.* **FAX** *02 38 77 17 59.* **Rooms:** 62. 🛏 📺 ❄ ♿ 🏊 P ❚❚ ● *Sun pm.* 🏊 *AE, MC, DC, V.* €€

This unpretentious hotel, near the rue de Bourgogne, is housed in a former cloister. Corner rooms have views of the slate roofs of the city and of the cathedral towers.

ROMORANTIN-LANTHENAY

Grand Hôtel du Lion d'Or

Road map E3. 69 rue Georges-Clemenceau, 41200. **(** *02 54 94 15 15.* **FAX** *02 54 88 24 87.* **Rooms:** 16. 🛏 📺 ❄ 🏊 ♿ P ❚❚ ★ 🏊 *AE, MC, DC, V.* €€€€
W www.hotel-liondor

This Renaissance mansion has been a hotel since 1774. A *Relais et Châteaux* member, it has attractive rooms, a courtyard modelled on a medieval herb garden and an excellent restaurant.

SALBRIS

Le Parc

Road map E3. 8 av d'Orléans, 41300. **(** *02 54 97 18 53.* **FAX** *02 54 97 24 34.* **Rooms:** 23. 🛏 📺 🏃 P 🏊 ❚❚ 🏊 *MC, V.* €€

This hotel in the heart of the Sologne is surrounded by parkland, and the rooms are always filled with flowers. The restaurant boasts a large stone fireplace.

VENDÔME

Hôtel Vendôme

Road map D3. 15 faubourg Chartran, 41100. **(** *02 54 77 02 88.* **FAX** *02 54 73 90 71.* **Rooms:** 35. 🛏 📺 ❄ P ❚❚ 🏊 *AE, MC, V.* €€€

This attractive hotel is typical of a French provincial establishment. Rooms are stylish, as is the restaurant. The hotel was built on the site of a medieval *auberge*, once a pilgrims' rest on the road to Santiago de Compostela.

BERRY

ARGENT-SUR-SAULDRE

Relais de la Poste

Road map F3. 3 rue Nationale, 18410. **(** *02 48 81 53 90.* **FAX** *02 48 73 30 62.* **Rooms:** 10. 🛏 📺 ❄ ♿ 🏊 P 🏃 ❚❚ ● *20 Feb–10 Mar.* 🏊 *AE, MC, V.* €€

Exposed beams and floral upholstery give a cottagey feel to this typical Sologne inn. The restaurant offers delicious game and wild mushrooms in season.

ARGENTON-SUR-CREUSE

Le Manoir de Boisvillers

Road map E4. 11 rue du Moulin-de-Bord, 36200. **(** *02 54 24 13 88.* **FAX** *02 54 24 27 83.* **Rooms:** 14. 🛏 📺 ❄ P 🏊 ● *20 Dec–mid-Jan.* 🏊 *AE, MC, V.* €€
W www.manoir-de-boisvilliers.com

A surprising find in the heart of the town, this is a peaceful 18th-century manor house. Its pretty garden centres on an open-air swimming pool. The rooms are spacious and comfortable.

AUBIGNY-SUR-NÈRE

Auberge de la Fontaine

Road map F3. 2 av du Général Leclerc, 18700. **(** *02 48 58 02 59.* **FAX** *02 48 58 36 80.* **Rooms:** 16. 🛏 📺 ❄ 🏊 P 🏃 ❚❚ 🏊 *AE, MC, DC, V.* €€

This friendly modern hotel is only a short walk from the château and its museums. The front bedrooms look onto a pleasant park, while the back bedrooms have views of the pretty terrace. The restaurant offers special children's meals.

Château de la Verrerie

Road map F3. Oizon, 18700. **(** *02 48 81 51 60.* **FAX** *02 48 58 21 25.* **Rooms:** 12. 🛏 ❄ 🏃 P 🏊 ❚❚ ★ ● *22 Dec–mid-Feb.* 🏊 *AE, MC, V.* €€€€€

Scots Stewart connections abound in this early Renaissance château. La Verrerie is owned by the Comte and Comtesse de Vogüé, who are unfailingly charming and helpful. They offer private dining for those staying in their spacious and beautifully furnished rooms and run a restaurant in the grounds.

LE BLANC

Domaine de l'Etape

Road map D4. Rte de Bélâbre, 36300. **(** *02 54 37 18 02.* **FAX** *02 54 37 75 59.* **Rooms:** 35. 🛏 📺 ❄ ♿ 🏊 P 🏊 ❚❚ 🏊 *AE, MC, DC, V.* €€
W www.domainedeletape.com

This peaceful hotel, set in extensive gardens, offers a good mixture of modern facilities and antique furnishings. It has its own lake for angling and canoeing, and stables from which it offers pony treks through the countryside.

BOURGES

Hôtel d'Angleterre

Road map F4. 1 pl des Quatre Piliers, 18000. **(** *02 48 24 68 51.* **FAX** *02 48 65 21 41.* **Rooms:** 31. 🛏 ❄ 📺 ❄ 🏃 🏊 P ❚❚ ● *24 Dec–1 Jan.* 🏊 *AE, MC, DC, V.* €€€

This established hotel is in the heart of Bourges, very close to the Palais Jacques-Cœur. Although it has recently been modernized in appearance, it has nonetheless managed to retain its traditional, courteous ambiance.

For key to symbols see p199

Hôtel de Bourbon

Road map F4. Bd de la République, 18000. **C** 02 48 70 70 00. **FAX** 02 48 70 21 22. **Rooms:** 59. 🛏 📺 ❖ 👫 🎿 🅿 🍽 🍸 AE, MC, DC, V. €€€€€ *See also* **Restaurants,** *p217.*

Set in a renovated Renaissance abbey, this hotel offers modern, soundproofed bedrooms and elegant public areas. Its restaurant is in the former chapel.

BRINON-SUR-SAULDRE

La Solognote

Road map F3. Le Village, 18410. **C** 02 48 58 50 29. **FAX** 02 48 58 56 00. **Rooms:** 13. 🛏 📺 🅿 🍸 🍽 ★ ● Tue, Wed, 5 weeks Feb & Mar. 🗐 MC, V. €€ *See also* **Restaurants,** *p217.*

This charming *Logis de France* is a typical Sologne inn, furnished with antiques. The rooms overlook a quiet courtyard garden. Popular in the shooting season, the hotel also has an excellent restaurant.

BUZANÇAIS

L'Hermitage

Road map E4. Rte d'Argy, 36500. **C** 02 54 84 03 90. **FAX** 02 54 02 13 19. **Rooms:** 14. 🕹 🖥 📺 🅿 🍸 🍽 ● 1-15 Jan, 3rd wk Sep. 🗐 MC, V. €€

If you seek a little fishing, peace and quiet, head for this lovingly run Logis de France hotel, 25kms NW of Chateauroux. Most rooms overlook the garden, through which meanders the River Indre.

LA CHÂTRE

Château de la Vallée Bleue

Road map E4. Rte de Verneuil, 36400. **C** 02 54 31 01 91. **FAX** 02 54 31 04 48. **Rooms:** 15. 🛏 📺 🖥 🍸 👫 🅿 🍸 🍽 ● mid-Nov–early Mar. 🗐 MC, V. €€€ 🌐 www.chateauvalleebleue.com

This elegant 19th-century château was once the home of George Sand's doctor, who used to walk over to Nohant to visit his illustrious patient. It is now a hotel set in large grounds with a swimming pool and a practice course for golfers. There are two excellent golf courses nearby, at Pouligny-Notre-Dame and Issoudun.

ST-AMAND-MONTROND

Hôtel de la Poste

Road map F4. 9 rue du Docteur-Vallet, 18200. **C** 02 48 96 27 14. **FAX** 02 48 96 97 74. **Rooms:** 18. 🛏 👫 🅿 🍸 🍽 ● 2 weeks Jan. 🗐 AE, MC, V. €€

This friendly hotel, built around an inner courtyard, started life in 1584 as a pilgrims' inn. Rooms on the second floor have sloping ceilings. It is a cosy base for visiting Abbaye de Noirlac and the châteaux of Ainay-le-Vieil, Culan and Meillant. There is also a popular restaurant.

Château de la Commanderie

Road map F4. Farges-Allichamps, 18200. **C** 02 48 61 04 19. **FAX** 02 48 61 01 84. **Rooms:** 7. 🛏 🖥 🅿 🍸 ★ 🗐 AE, MC, V. €€€€€

This charming 12th-century manor house has been owned by the same family since the 17th century. The Comte and Comtesse de Jouffroy-Gonsans offer elegant accommodation both here and in a 19th-century château, as well as candle-lit dinners.

SANCERRE

Hôtel Panoramic

Road map F3. Rempart des Augustins, 18300. **C** 02 48 54 22 44. **FAX** 02 48 54 39 55. **Rooms:** 57. 🛏 📺 🖥 ❖ 👫 🖥 🗓 🅿 🍸 🍽 🗐 AE, MC, V. €€

Many of the rooms in this modern hotel have views over the Sancerre vineyards. The hotel has its own car park, which is useful in this town of narrow, winding streets, as well as a garden, an outdoor pool and a pleasant restaurant.

VALENÇAY

Hôtel d'Espagne

Road map: E4. 9 rue du Château, 36600. **C** 02 54 00 00 02. **FAX** 02 54 00 12 63. **Rooms:** 16. 🛏 📺 🖥 👫 🖥 🅿 🍸 ★ 🗐 AE, MC, DC, V. €€€

Quiet and elegant, this *Relais et Châteaux* member has been run by the same family since 1875. It is known for courteous service, comfortable bedrooms and classic cuisine, served in a delightful courtyard in the summer.

NORTH OF THE LOIRE

CHARTRES

Hôtel de la Poste

Road map E2. 3 rue Général Koëneg, 28000. **C** 02 37 21 04 27. **FAX** 02 37 36 42 17. **Rooms:** 57. 🛏 📺 🖥 🗓 🅿 🍽 🗐 AE, MC, DC, V. €€ 🌐 www.hotelposte-chartres.com

This attractive hotel is close to the cathedral. One room is furnished with Breton antiques, while the others are in a contemporary style.

Le Grand Monarque

Road map E2. 22 pl des Epars, 28000. **C** 02 37 21 00 72. **FAX** 02 37 36 34 18. **Rooms:** 55. 🛏 📺 👫 🖥 🅿 🍸 🍽 🗐 AE, MC, DC, V. €€€€€ 🌐 www.bw-grand-monarque.com

Established as a coaching inn in the 18th century, this hotel has long been popular with visitors to Chartres. It is now modernized and has an elegant restaurant.

LA FLÈCHE

Le Relais Cicéro

Road map C3. 18 bd d'Alger, 72200. **C** 02 43 94 14 14. **FAX** 02 43 45 98 96. **Rooms:** 21. 🛏 📺 ❖ 🅿 🍸 🗐 AE, MC, V. €€€ 🌐 www.cicero.fr

This quiet hotel, located near the Prytanée Militaire, is housed in a rather grand 17th-century mansion. The rooms are stylishly furnished with antiques.

FRESNAY-SUR-SARTHE

Hôtel Ronsin

Road map C2. 5 av Charles-de-Gaulle, 72130. **C** 02 43 97 20 10. **FAX** 02 43 33 50 47. **Rooms:** 12. 🛏 📺 🅿 🍽 🗐 AE, MC, DC, V. €€

This is a traditional French hotel, with plain, but well-planned rooms. Its restaurant offers a wide range of fixed-priced meals.

LAVAL

Gerbe de Blé

Road map B2. 83 rue Victor-Boissel, 53000. **C** 02 43 53 14 10. **FAX** 02 43 49 02 84. **Rooms:** 8. 🛏 📺 🍽 🗐 AE, MC, V. €€

This friendly inn is situated on the old corn market square, not far from the River Mayenne. It has an excellent restaurant with cheerful, cottagey decor.

LE MANS

Hôtel Chantecler

Road map C2. 50 rue de la Pelouse, 72000. **C** 02 43 14 40 00.
FAX 02 43 77 16 28. **Rooms:** 35.
🛏 24 TV 🏊 🐕 🅿 🗷 AE, MC, V.
€€ w www.hotelchantecler.com

This modern hotel, within walking distance of the Old Town, has comfortable bedrooms and attractive bar and lounge areas.

MONHOUDOU

Château de Monhoudou

Road map C2. Monhoudou, 72260.
C 02 43 97 40 05. **FAX** 02 43 33 11 58. **Rooms:** 8. 🛏 🏊 🐕 🅿 🗑
€€€€ w www.monhoudou.com

The de Monhoudou family still owns and runs this delightful 18th-century château, which stands in 20 ha (50 acres) of its own parkland. Guests can stroll in these landscaped gardens among horses, sheep, swans and peacocks.

ST-LÉONARD-DES-BOIS

Touring Hôtel

Road map C2. Le Village, 72590.
C 02 43 31 44 44. **FAX** 02 43 31 44 49. **Rooms:** 35. 🛏 TV 🏊 🌊
♿ 🐕 🗑 🅿 🗑 🍴 mid-Dec–mid-Jan. 🗷 AE, MC, DC, V.
€€€

This modern hotel makes a pleasant base for exploring the Alpes Mancelles. The rooms have either hill or garden views. The hotel also has an indoor pool and a good restaurant.

SOLESMES

Grand Hôtel de Solesmes

Road map C2. 16 pl Dom-Guéranger, 72300. **C** 02 43 95 45 10.
FAX 02 43 95 22 26. **Rooms:** 34.
🛏 TV 🏊 🌊 🅿 🗑 🍴
🗷 AE, MC, DC, V. €€€€

Opposite the abbey, this hotel has large rooms, a fitness centre, an art gallery and an excellent restaurant.

LOIRE-ATLANTIQUE AND THE VENDEE

ILE D'YEU

Flux Hôtel

Road map A4. 27 rue Pierre-Henry, Port-Joinville, 85350. **C** 02 51 58 36 25. **FAX** 02 51 59 44 57. **Rooms:** 16.
🛏 TV 🌊 🐕 🅿 🗑 🍴
🍴 mid-Nov–mid-Jan. 🗷 MC, V.
€€€

Ask for a room in the annexe of this modern hotel if you would like a balcony. If you bring your freshly caught fish or shellfish back in the afternoon, the chef will serve them to you for dinner.

NANTES

Hôtel de la Duchesse Anne

Road map B3. 3–4 pl de la Duchesse Anne, 44000. **C** 02 51 86 78 78.
FAX 02 40 74 60 20. **Rooms:** 68.
🛏 TV 🌊 🌊 🅿 🍴 🗷 AE, MC, V. €€€

Located in a 19th-century building, the hotel offers renovated rooms, or less modern ones for a reduced price. Some of the older rooms are charming, and many of both types have cathedral and château views.

Hôtel La Pérouse

Road map B3. 3 allée Duquesne, 44000. **C** 02 40 89 75 00. **FAX** 02 40 89 76 00. **Rooms:** 47. 🛏 TV 🌊
🗒 🌊 🅿 🗷 AE, MC, DC, V.
€€€
w www.hotel-laperouse.com

Built in a radically minimalist style, this hotel has won several architectural awards. Centrally placed at the cours des Cinquantes Otages, it is still quiet for a city hotel. There is free parking nearby at the Tour de Bretagne.

NOIRMOUTIER-EN-L'ISLE

Hôtel du Général d'Elbée

Road map A4. pl du Château, 85330. **C** 02 51 39 10 29.
FAX 02 51 39 08 23. ● Oct–Easter.
Rooms: 30. 🛏 🌊 ♿ 🐕 🗑
🗷 AE, MC, DC, V. €€€€
w www.generaldelbee

Named after the Vendéen general who died in the square, the hotel occupies an historic building beside a canal. It also has a walled garden with swimming pool.

LA ROCHE-SUR-YON

Logis de la Couperie

Road map B4. D80, La Roche-sur-Yon, 85000. **C** 02 51 37 21 19. **FAX** 02 51 47 71 08. **Rooms:** 7. 🛏 TV 🌊
🐕 🅿 🗑 🗷 AE, MC, V. €€€

A ducal residence from the 14th century until 1789, La Couperie is still surrounded by parkland with a lake. Five minutes' drive from the town centre, its rooms are furnished with antiques, and the main *salon* has a log fire.

LES SABLES D'OLONNE

Les Roches Noires

Road map A4. 12 promenade Georges-Clemenceau, 85100. **C** 02 51 32 01 71. **FAX** 02 51 21 61 00. **Rooms:** 37,
🛏 TV 🌊 ♿ 🐕 🗷 AE, MC, DC, V.
€€
w www.bw-lesrochesnoires.com

This hotel is reasonably inexpensive considering its beachfront location, but it is a bracing walk to the town centre. Some of the rooms have sea views.

Château de la Millière

Road map A4. St-Mathurin, 85100.
C 02 51 23 85 75. **FAX** 02 51 22 73 29. **Rooms:** 5. 🌊 🌊 🌊 🅿 🗑 ★
🗷 MC, V. €€€

Situated 8 km (5 miles) from the town, this 19th-century château has 18 ha (44 acres) of parkland. Visitors can enjoy some lovely walks or take advantage of the on-site fishing or swimming pool. Dinner in the château must be ordered before midday.

ST-LYPHARD

Auberge de Kerhinet

Road map A3. Kerhinet, 44410.
C 02 40 61 91 46. **FAX** 02 40 61 97 57. **Rooms:** 7. 🅿 🗑 🍴 🗷 AE, MC, DC, V. mid-Dec–mid-Jan. €€

A pretty cottage in creamy local stone with a thatched roof, the *auberge* is in the salt marshes of La Grande Brière. It is simply decorated, with a collection of old photographs on the walls. Its restaurant specializes in fish dishes.

For key to symbols *see p199*

WHERE TO EAT

I N THIS GENERALLY prosperous region, with its excellent local produce, eating out is popular, and interest in cuisine is high even by the standards of this food-loving country. Lunch remains the main meal of the day: even in larger towns such as Tours, Orléans or Nantes, most office workers return home during their two-hour lunch break. Restaurants serve lunch from about noon, and it can be hard to find one willing to serve

A café sign in Berry

a meal if you arrive after 1pm, although cafés and brasseries in the towns are more flexible. Dinner is served from about 8pm onwards (sometimes earlier in the main tourist areas). Beware of last orders, which may be as early as 9pm, especially in country districts. The restaurants on pages 214–19 have been carefully selected for their excellence of food, decor and ambience, and cover all price ranges.

An outdoor café in the historic heart of Richelieu

TYPES OF RESTAURANT

I N COUNTRY DISTRICTS and small towns, the most pleasant restaurants are often to be found in hotels, especially if they belong to the **Logis de France** association, which puts particular emphasis on good (and good value for money) regional cooking. Larger towns offer a broad range of places to eat, from basic pizzerias and crêperies to chic, gourmet establishments via cafés and brasseries. Cafés are handy for a snack, coffee or aperitif, or as places from which to watch the world go by, and brasseries are good for quick meals. Unlike restaurants, brasseries and cafés generally serve a limited range of dishes outside regular mealtimes.

The Loire also has an ever-widening choice of restaurants specializing in foreign cuisines (most commonly Vietnamese and North African).

VEGETARIAN FOOD

T RUE VEGETARIANS do not fare well in France. It can be more convenient to head for a Vietnamese restaurant or a pizzeria, although in some of the university towns, the occasional vegetarian restaurant may be found. A few large cafés or brasseries in the tourist districts of major towns sometimes offer a small number of vegetarian dishes, and omelettes and other egg-based dishes are usually available. Alternatively, ask the chef for the meat or fish to be left out of a salad. In full-scale restaurants, it is essential to enquire in advance whether it is possible to have a vegetarian dish specially prepared. Non-meat-eaters need have no fears: Loire Valley restaurants serve excellent fish dishes, and cafés and brasseries usually offer at least one fish dish on the menu.

READING THE MENU

T HE VAST MAJORITY of Loire Valley restaurants offer at least one *menu*, or fixed-price menu. You will often find a range of *menus*, culminating in an expensive *menu gastronomique* (gourmet meal), which may be available only if all members of your party choose it. Look out for a *menu régional* or *menu du terroir*, which will feature a selection of regional specialities.

The less expensive menus often feature starters such as local *charcuterie* (pork specialities), a salad or *crudités* (raw vegetables), whereas gourmet menus offer more complex dishes. Vegetables are often served separately.

Cheese is considered a separate course, served between the main course and dessert – local goats' cheeses are likely to predominate.

A typical Loire Valley restaurant terrace

Many restaurants, especially in country districts, do not have a *carte* from which individual dishes may be selected. If they do, eating *à la carte* almost always works out to be more expensive than choosing from a fixed-price menu, since it is not considered acceptable to skip the starter and order only a main dish (skipping dessert is more acceptable).

Cafés and brasseries offer a *plat du jour* (dish of the day), often with a regional flavour, along with standard French fare such as steak or fish with fried potatoes, complemented by a range of salads or vegetables.

The rustic Auberge de la Petite Fadette in Nohant *(see p217)*

Auberge du Moulin de Chaméron at Bannegon in Berry *(see p217)*

MAKING RESERVATIONS

IT IS ALWAYS advisable to book tables in advance at restaurants near the well-known châteaux, especially during the main tourist season (Easter to late September). If you enjoy eating alongside the residents at local restaurants in towns, which rarely take reservations over the telephone, make sure you arrive early. Restaurants in country districts are often closed on Sunday evenings as well as for at least one whole day during the week.

DRESS CODE

MOST FRENCH people take considerable trouble with their appearance but, with the exception of a few very chic and expensive places, formal dress is not required, and ties are rarely a necessity even in the top restaurants, providing you are neatly turned out.

HOW MUCH TO PAY

IT IS DIFFICULT to classify restaurants by price, as most offer a range of fixed-price meals. Prices can be as low as 10€ or as high as 75€, but good, copious meals can be had everywhere for between 25€ and 30€.

A service charge of 12.5–15 per cent is usually included in the prices on menus, which in all but the most expensive places are posted up outside for you to study before venturing in. It is usual to leave a few extra francs as an additional tip. In more expensive restaurants, cloakroom attendants are given about 1€ and lavatory attendants about 30 cents.

Visa credit cards are widely accepted. Check first with the restaurant to find out whether Eurocheques and American Express, MasterCard or Diners Club cards can be used.

CHILDREN AND PETS

CHILDREN ARE well received everywhere in the region, but they should be discouraged from leaving their seats and wandering about during the meal. High chairs are rarely available. Some restaurants offer special low-priced children's menus, called *repas d'enfant*. Well-behaved dogs are usually accepted in restaurants (but are often banned from food shops).

WHEELCHAIR ACCESS

BECAUSE FEW restaurants make special provision for wheelchairs, it is wise when booking to mention that you or one of your party need

space for a *fauteuil roulant*. A list on page 198 gives names and addresses of various organizations that offer advice to disabled travellers to the Loire Valley region.

SMOKING

FRENCH LEGISLATION requires restaurateurs to offer the choice of smoking or non-smoking areas, but the latter is often no more than a table or two in an alcove with a "No Smoking" sign pinned to the wall. Bars and cafés are likely to be smoke-filled.

USING THE LISTINGS

Key to the symbols in the listings on pages 214–19.

◘ opening times
● annual closure
¶◉¶ fixed-price menu(s)
Ħ children's portions
Ⅴ vegetarian or vegetarian options
⊞ outdoor eating
占 wheelchair access
Ⅱ jacket and tie required
Ⓩ non-smoking section
Ⓠ excellent wine list
★ highly recommended
Ⓒ credit cards accepted
AE American Express
MC Mastercard
DC Diners Club
V. Visa

Price categories for a three-course evening meal for one, including a half-bottle of house wine, cover charge, tax and service:
€ Under 25€
€€ 25€–40€
€€€ 40€–55€
€€€€ 55€–75€
€€€€€ Over 75€.

What to Eat in the Loire Valley

Fresh seasonal strawberries

LOIRE VALLEY CUISINE is made up of straightforward dishes carefully cooked from wonderfully fresh ingredients. Shad, pike-perch, pike and salmon, all straight from the rivers, are served with a subtle *beurre blanc* or sorrel sauce while, at the mouth of the Loire, fresh prawns and oysters glisten on seafood platters. The mild climate and fertile soil produce succulent early fruit and vegetables. The sandy soil beside the Loire is perfect for growing asparagus, and in autumn the trees are laden with apples and pears. Berry's forests offer plump game, served with wild mushrooms or the button variety *(champignons de Paris)* grown in the tufa caves near Saumur.

Rillons de Tours, *largish chunks of pork cooked slowly in their own fat until crisp, are found in every charcuterie in the Touraine region.*

Noisettes de porc au pruneaux, *a speciality of Tours, is pork loin gently stewed in Vouvray wine, served with prunes steeped in Vouvray and a smooth sauce made with redcurrant jelly and cream.*

Caneton de Nantes aux navets *is roast duckling from Nantes, traditionally served with young turnips.*

Rillettes du Mans, *a tasty, traditional first course, is made from shredded and potted pork, or sometimes goose or rabbit.*

Poulet en barbouille, *a speciality of the Berry region, is made with a plump chicken, braised with carrots and onions in brandy and wine, and served with a sauce that is traditionally made from the chicken's own blood.*

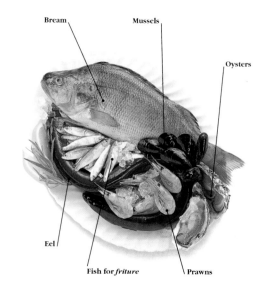

Bream

Mussels

Oysters

Eel

Fish for *friture*

Prawns

FISH AND SEAFOOD

Local fish and seafood is served throughout the region. Fish is usually simply prepared, served with a complementary sauce that allows its fresh flavour to come through.

Alose à l'oseille *is grilled shad, a round fish not unlike herring, served with a creamy sorrel sauce.*

Chapon du Mans à la broche, *generally spit-roasted, is a fine capon from the Le Mans region.*

Matelote d'anguilles *is chunks of eel stewed in Chinon red wine with button mushrooms and tiny onions.*

Friture de la Loire, *a dish often found in restaurants near rivers, offers a mound of tiny, freshwater fish, quickly fried and served with a lemon wedge.*

Sandre au beurre blanc *is pike-perch (also known as zander) accompanied by the Loire speciality of a melted butter sauce flavoured with shallots and wine vinegar.*

Pithiviers *is a puff-pastry almond cake, named after a town near Orléans.*

Crémets d'Anjou *is a delicious dessert made from whipped double cream and egg whites.*

Tarte Tatin, *perhaps the most famous dessert of the Loire, is a caramelized upside-down apple tart invented by the Tatin sisters in their Sologne inn.*

Valençay

Crottins de Chavignol

Sainte-Maure de Touraine

Selles-sur-Cher

CHEESES

The Loire Valley's finest cheeses are made with goats' milk: the round Crottins de Chavignol from Sancerre; Sainte-Maure de Touraine with a straw through the middle and often coated with ashes (*cendré*); and Valençay, like a truncated pyramid. But Olivet is a cows' milk cheese not unlike Camembert.

Poirat, *a Berry speciality, is a pear pie flavoured with pure fruit spirit and often served with a glass of rosé wine.*

What to Drink in the Loire

THE LOIRE VALLEY is a wine region *(see pp30–31)*, so naturally the traditional tipple in cafés and bars is *un petit coup de rouge* or *un petit coup de blanc* (a small glass of red or white wine). The light rosés, such as Rosé d'Anjou or Rosé de Touraine, are drunk chilled, either in the afternoon with a slice of cake or as an apéritif. In November, bars and cafés serve *bernache*, the greenish, fermented juice left after the grapes have been pressed for winemaking. There is also a wide variety of other alcoholic drinks, including *eaux de vie* made with local fruits and light, lager-style beers, as well as non-alcoholic drinks such as coffees, teas and juices.

A waiter in a Loire Valley bar

White Sancerre

Red Bourgueil

Sparkling wine

WINE

WINE USUALLY accompanies meals in the Loire, as it does throughout France. Local wine is often served in carafes. Ordering a *demi* (50 cl, approximately ½ pint) or *quart* (25 cl) is an inexpensive way to try out a wide variety of the wines of the region before buying any to take home *(see pp30–31)*.

French law divides domestic wines into four classes, in ascending order of quality: *Vin de Table*, *Vin de Pays*, *Vin Délimité de Qualité Supérieure* (VDQS) and finally *Appellation d'Origine Contrôlée* (AOC). *Vin de Table* wines are rarely found in good restaurants. If in doubt, order the house wine *(la réserve)*. Very few restaurants will risk their reputation on an inferior house wine, and they often provide good value for money.

APÉRITIFS AND DIGESTIFS

A GLASS of locally-produced sparkling wine can be an excellent apéritif or a pleasant accompaniment to the dessert course. Slightly sparkling Vouvray *pétillant* is popular, and further west in Anjou you will find Saumur *champenoise*, made by the *méthode champenoise*. Keep an eye open, too, for Crémant de Loire, another local sparkling wine.

A *kir* – white wine with a touch of *crème de cassis*, a blackcurrant liqueur – is a

---

HOW TO READ A WINE LABEL

Even the simplest label will provide a key to the wine's flavour and quality. It will bear the name of the wine and its producer, its vintage if there is one, and whether it comes from a strictly defined area (*appellation contrôlée* or VDQS) or is a more general *vin de pays* or *vin de table*. It may also have a regional grading. The shape and colour of the bottle is also a guide. Most good-quality wine is bottled in green glass, which helps to protect it from light. The label's design may be appealing, but does not indicate quality.

The property or producer

Estate-bottled, rather than a blend from a merchant or growers' co-operative

Pictures may be accurate or fanciful

Capacity of the bottle

The address of the vineyard

The wine's *appellation contrôlée*

popular Burgundian apéritif, and an appealing variation, often served as the house apéritif, combines sparkling wine with raspberry or peach liqueur. Bars, cafés and restaurants also stock the usual range of French apéritifs as well as international gins, sherries, ports and whiskies.

After dinner, a little glass of clear fruit brandy made from local raspberries, pears or plums (*eaux de vie de framboise, de poire, de prune*) is a delicious aid to digestion. Other traditional French *digestifs*, such as cognac or calvados, are also drunk after meals in the region.

BEER

THE LOCALS DRINK mostly lager-style draught beer in cafés – ask for *un demi*. A range of bottled beers can also be found, both French (which is considerably cheaper) and imported.

Café crème, often served at breakfast with a fresh croissant

COFFEE AND TEA

CAFES, STILL THE MAIN focus of community life, serve good strong *exprès* (a tiny cup of black coffee). White coffees are prepared with hot milk and come in two sizes: small (*petit crème*) and large (*grand crème*). Together with fresh croissants, they make a good breakfast.

Tea served in cafés is often of the teabag variety (with a slice of lemon, it is *un thé citron*). Tearooms in towns, however, are more likely to use tea leaves. Many cafés also offer a range of exotic fruit and herb teas, which are caffeine-free. In restaurants an infusion of limeflower leaves (*tilleul*), mint (*menthe*) or camomile (*camomille*) is often drunk after dinner as an aid to digestion.

OTHER DRINKS

CHILDREN ENJOY the colourful drinks served in tall glasses known as *menthe à l'eau* (green, minty syrup with tap water) and *grenadine* (a red fruit syrup), but these may be too sweet for adult tastes. Served with Vittel mineral water, for example, they become *Vittel menthe*, *Vittel grenadine*, and so on. *Vittel citron amer* (with bottled, still bitter lemon) is more refreshing than *Vittel citron* (with lemon syrup). Best of all for quenching the thirst – but also more expensive – is a *citron pressé* : freshly-squeezed lemon juice served with a carafe of water and packets of sugar to mix to taste. *Orange pressée* is orange juice served in the same way. Bottled fruit juices (*jus de fruits*) are also available everywhere.

Tap water is safe to drink, but many people prefer mineral water (*eau minérale*), either sparkling (*gazeuse*) or still (*non-gazeuse*).

WHERE TO DRINK

CAFES ARE THE traditional place to pop in for a coffee or beer, to meet a friend or watch the world go by. City centres have bustling cafés on every corner, and many squares are crowded with outdoor tables when the weather is fine. However, the traditional café, with its long bar counter lined by regulars, is gradually being superseded, at least in towns, by more elaborate places.

Bars and *bars à vin* (old-style wine bars) are often the haunts of more hardened drinkers and of late-night revellers, although hotel bars can attract a more eclectic clientele. In larger towns,

A wood-panelled hotel bar in Touraine

Locally-made apple juice

many new-style wine bars, often with high-tech decor, serve wine by the glass, with light meals, plates of *charcuterie* or cheeses with crusty bread. Traditional *salons de thé* (tea-rooms), which serve coffee, tea and hot chocolate, are mainly frequented by women. They also serve *pâtisseries* and chocolates, which can be bought to take away. The newer version offers light lunches and less sophisticated sweets, cakes and tarts to a younger, mixed clientele.

People enjoying a break in a stylish café in Orléans

ANJOU

ANGERS

La Salamandre

Road map C3. 1 bd Maréchal-Foch.
📞 *02 41 88 99 55.* ⏱ *noon–1:30pm,
7:30–9:30pm daily.* 🍽 🎅 Ⅴ 🏠
AE, MC, DC, V. €€€

The restaurant in the Hôtel d'Anjou is decorated in the Renaissance style. But the reasonably-priced cuisine is far from over-elaborate, and the wine list is excellent. Try the ravioli stuffed with lobster.

CHAMPTOCEAUX

Le Champalud

Road map B3. Promenade Champalud. 📞 *02 40 83 50 09.* ⏱ *noon–2 pm, 7–9pm.* ⬤ *2 weeks Oct, 25 Dec–2 Jan.* 🍽 🎅 🐧 Ⅴ 🏠 🌠 🍷 ★ 🏠 *AE, MC, V.* €€€

This pretty restaurant in an old converted house is the perfect spot for enjoying local specialities, especially of the fish variety.

CHOLET

La Touchetière

Road map B4. 41 bd du Docteur-Roux.
📞 *02 41 62 55 03.* ⏱ *noon–2:15pm, 7:15–10:30pm Sun–Fri, 7:15–10:30pm Mon–Sat.* ⬤ *3 wks in Aug.* 🍽 🎅 🐧 🌠 🏠 *AE, MC, V.* €€

An old farmhouse has been converted into a restaurant serving a menu that emphasizes fish dishes, supported by an excellent wine list. Everything is beautifully fresh. Book ahead for Sunday lunch.

FONTEVRAUD L'ABBAYE

La Licorne

Road map C3. Allée Ste-Catherine.
📞 *02 41 51 72 49.* ⏱ *12:15–1:45pm Tue–Sun, 7:15–9pm Tue–Sat (summer: daily).* ⬤ *mid-Dec–mid-Jan.* 🍽 🎅 Ⅴ 🏠 🏠 *AE, MC, DC, V.* €€

This delightful restaurant is near St-Michel, the church built by Henry II of England. The cuisine in the 18th-century building, is refined, and the lowest-priced lunch menu is great value.

GENNES

L'Aubergade

Road map C3. 7 av des Cadets.
📞 *02 41 51 81 07.* ⏱ *noon–1:30pm Thu–Tue, 7:30–9pm* 🍽 🎅 🐧 Ⅴ 🏠 🏠 *MC, V.* €€

A traditional Anjou building houses this reliable restaurant with a menu strong on dishes from the regional repertoire. Wines from Touraine and Anjou make the perfect accompaniments to meals here.

LE LION-D'ANGERS

La Table du Meunier

Road map C3. Le Moulin, Chenillé-Changé. 📞 *02 41 92 10 98 or 02 41 95 10 83.* ⏱ *noon–2pm Thu–Sun, 7–9:30pm Thu–Sat (summer: daily).* ⬤ *Feb.* 🍽 🎅 🐧 🐧 🏠 *MC, V.* €€

This old mill, 10 km (6 miles) from Le Lion-d'Angers, once produced the walnut oil that gives French country cooking its special flavour. The menu has some sophisticated touches but is largely traditional. Among the specialities are *terrine d'anguilles maison* (an eel terrine) and *crème d'oignons gratinée* (a type of onion soufflé).

MONTSOREAU

Diane de Méridor

Road map C3. 12 quai Philippe de Commynes. 📞 *02 41 51 71 76.*
⏱ *noon–3pm, 7–9:30pm Thu–Mon (Jul–Aug: daily).* ⬤ *Jan.* 🍽 🎅 🏠 *MC, V.* €€

From the rustic dining room there are fine views of the Loire and of Montsoreau château. The menu offers many freshwater fish dishes, including *sandre* (freshwater pike-perch) and *brochet* (pike).

LES ROSIERS-SUR-LOIRE

Auberge Jeanne de Laval

Road map C3. 54 rue Nationale. 📞 *02 41 51 80 17.* ⏱ *noon–2pm Tue–Sun, 7:30–9:30pm Tue–Sun (summer: daily).* ⬤ *25 Dec–1 Jan.* 🍽 🎅 🐧 Ⅴ 🏠 🐧 🏠 *MC, V.* €€€€

This family-run restaurant serves mainly classic cuisine, but also some interesting new dishes, including home-made terrines. It is wise to book ahead.

ST-GEORGES-SUR-LOIRE

Relais d'Anjou

Road map B3. 29 rue Nationale.
📞 *02 41 39 13 38.* ⏱ *noon–2pm Tue–Sun, 7:30–9pm Tue–Sat.* 🍽 🎅 🐧 Ⅴ 🍷 🏠 *AE, MC, V.* €€

This inn is close to the Château de Serrant. The cuisine is satisfying and good value, drawn from the classic French repertoire. Many of the dishes are served with sauces prepared using Anjou wines.

SAUMUR

L'Auberge Saint Pierre

Road map C3. 6 place Saint Pierre.
📞 *02 41 51 26 25.* ⏱ *noon–3pm, 7–10pm.* ⬤ *Sun D; Oct–Mar: Mon.* 🍽 🎅 🐧 Ⅴ 🏠 🍷 ★ 🏠 *AE, MC.* €€

The tranquil atmosphere of this converted inn belies the level of skill that produces an array of local dishes, such as zander in wine and *boeuf bourguignon*.

Les Caves de Marson

Road map C3. Rou-Marson. 📞 *02 41 50 50 05.* ⏱ *mid-Apr–mid-Sep: 12:30pm & 8:30pm Tue–Sun; mid-Sep–mid-Apr: 12:30pm Sun, 8pm Fri–Sat.* ⬤ *2 weeks Jan.* 🍽 🎅 🐧 🏠 *MC, V.* €€

Booking is a must at this troglodyte restaurant. Set sittings of the three-course menu include fresh bread rolls filled with goats' cheese and *rillettes (see p210)*, and home-made fruit tarts for dessert.

Les Ménestrels

Road map C3. 11 rue Raspail. 📞 *02 41 67 71 10.* ⏱ *12:15–2pm daily, 7:30–9:30pm Mon–Sat (summer: daily).* 🍽 🎅 🐧 Ⅴ 🍷 🏠 *AE, MC, DC, V.* €€€

This oak-beamed extension to the Hôtel Anne d'Anjou, serves classic cuisine with a regional touch.

TOURAINE

AMBOISE

Le Choiseul

Road map D3. 36 quai Charles-Guinot.
📞 *02 47 30 45 45.* ⏱ *noon–2pm, 7–9.30pm daily.* 🍽 🎅 🐧 Ⅴ 🐧 ★ 🏠 *AE, MC, DC, V.* €€€€

The River Loire flows past this elegant restaurant, whose menu centres on fish with sauces based on regional wines. A stroll up to the nearby "Caesar's grainstores", caves hollowed out of the tufa cliff, rounds off the evening.

Le Manoir St Thomas

Road map D3. Pl Richelieu. (02 47 57 22 52.) noon–2pm Wed–Sun, 7– 9:30pm Tue–Sat. |@| 🎽 ▮ 🍽 AE, MC, DC, V. ◼ 2 weeks Feb. €€€

The Baroque decor, the fine chef, and a sensational wine cellar, make this place irresistible. The *canard laqué médiéval* (honey-glazed roast duck with cinnamon and ginger) is typical – traditional cuisine with a modern touch.

AZAY-LE-RIDEAU

L'Aigle d'Or

Road map C3. 10 rue Adelaïde-Riché. (02 47 45 24 58.) noon–2pm, 7:30–9pm Tue, Thu–Fri (Sat in summer). ◼ Mon D; Dec–Mar. |@| 🎽 ▮ 🔥 ★ 🍽 MC, V. €€

This excellent restaurant near the château offers local produce such as freshwater pike-perch (*sandre*) or rabbit with a sauce based on Chinon wine.

BLÉRÉ

Le Cheval Blanc

Road map D3. 5 pl C Bidault. (02 47 30 30 14.) Jul & Aug: noon–2pm, 7:30–9:15pm Tue–Sun (Sep–Jun: Tue–Sat). ◼ Jan–mid-Feb. |@| 🎽 ▮ ★ 🍽 AE, MC, DC, V. €€€

This is one of Touraine's top restaurants. The delicious *escalope de sandre* (pike-perch escalope) served with a crab and *beurre blanc* sauce is typical of his style. The prices are very reasonable for the quality, and the atmosphere is friendly. One can also stay here.

CHENONCEAUX

Au Gâteau Breton

Road map D3. 16 rue du Docteur-Bretonneau. (02 47 23 90 14.) noon–2:30pm daily, 7–10pm Thu–Tue. |@| 🎽 ▮ 🔥 📅 🍽 MC, V. €

A short walk from the château, this is no tourist trap. Its traditional French, good-value meals are served in the garden in the summer.

CHINON

Hostellerie Gargantua

Road map D3. 73 rue Voltaire. (02 47 93 04 71.) noon–2pm daily, 7:30–10pm daily. |@| 🎽 ▮ 🍽 MC, V. €€

Chinon's visitors have long flocked to this medieval-style restaurant in a 15th-century mansion in the heart of the Old Town. At weekends, waiting staff dress in period costume. The portions are every bit as generous as Gargantua, Rabelais' giant hero, would have expected.

Au Plaisir Gourmand

Road map C3. 2 rue Parmentier. (02 47 93 20 48.) noon–1:30pm Tue–Sun, 7:30–9:15pm Tue–Sat. |@| 🎽 ▮ ★ 🍽 AE, MC, V. €€€

Chinon's top restaurant is housed in a 16th- and 17th-century building of local white tufa stone. The food is superb, with a special menu of regional dishes that will give you a taste for Touraine's gastronomic delights. The wine list, featuring local wines, is top class.

CORMERY

L'Auberge du Mail

Road map D3. 2 pl du Mail. (02 47 43 40 32.) noon–1:45pm Sun–Thu (summer: daily), 7:30–9:15pm Sat–Wed (summer: daily). |@| 🎽 ▮ 🍽 AE, MC, V. €€

This delightful restaurant is situated in a quiet village in the Indre Valley, famous for its biscuits (*see p222*). The wholesome cooking and friendly atmosphere never fail to please. The fixed-price menus are all named after composers. The restaurant is halfway between Tours and Loches.

LE PETIT-PRESSIGNY

La Promenade

Road map D4. 11 rue de Savoreaux. (02 47 94 93 52.) 12:30–2pm Wed–Sun, 7:30–9:30pm Tue–Sat. ◼ 3 weeks Jan, 2 weeks Sep–Oct. |@| ▮ 🔥 ★ 🍽 MC, V. €€

This restaurant is owned by Jacques Dallais, a former pupil of top Paris chef Joël Robuchon. If you have a sweet tooth, sample the *feuilleté de cacao au chocolat épicé* (fine-layered pastry with spicy chocolate), served with a topping of vanilla ice cream.

SACHÉ

Auberge du XIIe Siècle

Road map D3. Rue du Chateau. (02 47 26 88 77.) 12–2pm Wed–Sun, 7:30–9pm Tue–Sat. ◼ Jan, 1 week May. |@| 🎽 ▮ 🔥 🍽 MC, V. €€€

This picturesque, half-timbered inn is situated opposite the manor house where Balzac wrote some of his best-loved novels (*see p103*). It has a large dining room with old beams and a superb fireplace, and a smaller one that is more cosy. A range of fixed-price meals include some local specialities, such as the flavoursome breed of chicken known as *géline*.

ST-OUEN

L'Aubignière

Road map D3. 29 rue Jules Gautier. (02 47 30 15 29.) 12:30–1:30pm, 7:30–9pm daily. ◼ Feb. |@| 🔥 ▮ 🍽 ★ 🍽 AE, MC, V. €€

The beauty of this restaurant's garden (it backs onto a river) is equalled by exquisite food that focuses on a variety of fresh produce from the market.

TOURS

Le Bistro des Halles

Road map D3. 31 place Gaston-Pailhou. (02 47 61 54 93.) noon–2:30pm, 7:30–11:30pm daily. ◼ late Dec. |@| 🔥 🍴 🎽 ★ 🍽 MC, V. €

It is difficult to miss the red-and-green facade of this centrally-located venue in a quiet street; but then one would not want to miss the delights of its classic regional cuisine, least of all a highly reputed *tarte tatin*.

La Roche Le Roy

Road map D3. 55 route de St-Avertin. (02 47 27 22 00.) 11:30am–2:30pm, 7–11pm Tue–Sat. ◼ 2 weeks Nov & Christmas. |@| 🔥 ▮ ★ 🍽 MC, V. €€€

The type of dish served in this 16th-century building towards the southern end of town depends entirely on the season. The chef conjures fish and meat specialities (venison is always a particular treat here) that seem to embody the natural beauty of the area. The atmosphere is sophisticated.

Jean Bardet

Road map D3. 57 rue Groison. 📞
02 47 41 41 11. 🕐 noon–2pm daily
(Oct–Mar: Tue–Sun), 7–10pm daily
(Oct–Mar: Tue–Sat). 🍴 👟 Ⓥ ♿
🛏 🌿 ★ 📇 AE, MC, DC, V.
€€€€€

One of France's top chefs, Jean
Bardet has converted a 19th-
century mansion into a spacious
restaurant and an elegant hotel.
After enjoying dishes prepared
from the finest ingredients, you
can admire the herb and vegetable
gardens whose produce adds a
distinctive flavour to your meal.

VILLANDRY

Domaine de la Giraudière

Road map D3. Rte de Druye. 📞
02 47 50 08 60. 🕐 mid-Mar–
mid-Nov: noon–3pm, 7:30–9:30pm
daily. 🔴 11 Nov–15 Mar. 🍴 👟 Ⓥ
🌿 📇 MC, V. €€

A working farm, which visitors are
welcome to explore, is ideal for a
rustic lunch, including quiches
and omelettes. Many ingredients
are produced on the farm.

BLESOIS AND ORLEANAIS

LES BÉZARDS

Auberge des Templiers

Road map F3. Boismorand. 📞 02
31 80 01. 🕐 noon–1:45pm, 7:30–
9:45pm daily. 🍴 👟 Ⓥ 🛏 ♿ 🌿
★ 📇 AE, MC, DC, V. €€€€€

Once a country inn, this creeper-
covered building is now a hotel-
restaurant. The oak-beamed
dining room looks onto a garden
where meals are served. The
cuisine blends classic and modern.

BLOIS

Au Rendez-Vous des Pêcheurs

Road map E3. 27 rue du Foix. 📞
02 54 74 67 48. 🕐 noon–2pm
Tue–Sat, 7:30–10pm Mon–Sat. 🔴
Sun–Mon L; 2 weeks Aug & 2 weeks
Jan. 🍴 👟 Ⓥ ★ 📇 MC, V.
€€

This lively bistro, in what was
once a café-cum-grocer's, offers
some of the best cuisine in town.

L'Orangerie du Château

Road map E3. 1 ave Jean Laigret.
📞 02 54 78 05 36. 🕐 11:30am–
3pm, 7:30–11:30pm Thu–Tue. 🔴
mid-Feb– mid-Mar. 🍴 ♿ 🛏
🌿 🛏 ★ 📇 MC, V. €€€

Fortuitously situated in the
château's winter garden, this
restaurant produces classic French
fare to a standard that is much
higher than the provincial norm.
The roasts are astonishing.

BRACIEUX

Bernard Robin

Road map E3. 1 av de Chambord.
📞 02 54 46 41 22. 🕐 noon–2pm,
7:30–9pm Thu–Mon (Jul–Aug: daily).
🔴 20 Dec–end Jan. 🍴 Ⓥ ♿ 🛏
★ 📇 AE, MC, DC, V. €€€€

In a half-timbered inn between
Chambord and Cheverny, Bernard
Robin, one of France's finest chefs,
produces superb regional cuisine.
Game features highly on the menu:
look out for the *lièvre à la Royale*
(hare served with a *foie gras* sauce).
Booking is essential.

CHAUMONT-SUR-THARONNE

La Croix Blanche

Road map E3. Pl de l'Eglise.
📞 02 54 88 55 12. 🕐 noon–2pm,
7:30–9:30pm daily. 🔴 Tue L, Thu L.
🍴 👟 Ⓥ ♿ 🛏 🌿 📇 MC, V.
€€

This former abbey has been an
inn since the 15th century. Since
1779 its chef-owner has been a
woman, with an all-female staff.
You pass through her kitchen on
the way to the panelled dining
room. The cuisine is a mixture of
Sologne and southwestern dishes.

COMBREUX

L'Auberge de Combreux

Road map F2. 35 rue du Gâtinais. 📞
02 38 46 89 89. 🕐 12:15–2pm
Tue–Sun, 7:15–9:30pm daily. 🔴 mid-
Dec–Jan. 🍴 👟 Ⓥ 🛏 🌿 📇
MC, V. €€

This creeper-covered inn in the
Forêt d'Orléans is charming. Food
is traditional, with emphasis on
cuisine bourgeoise. In the summer,
meals are served outside.

MONTOIRE-SUR-LE-LOIR

Le Cheval Rouge

Road map D3. Pl Foch. 📞 02 54 85
07 05. 🕐 noon–2pm Thu–Mon
(Jul–Aug: Wed–Mon), 7:30–9pm
Thu–Mon (Jul–Aug: daily). 🔴 mid-
Nov–Dec, mid-Jan-Feb. 🍴 👟 Ⓥ
♿ 🌿 📇 AE, MC, V. €€

Close to Trôo and Lavardin, this
restaurant serves classic cuisine in
a lighter, contemporary style, so it
is never too rich. The inn also has
15 modest rooms.

OLIVET

Le Rivage

Road map E2. 635 rue de la Reine-
Blanche. 📞 02 38 66 02 93.
🕐 noon–2pm Sun–Fri, 7:15–9:30pm
daily (winter: Mon–Sat). 🔴 15 Apr,
11 Nov, 25 Dec–20 Jan. 🍴 👟 Ⓥ
🛏 🛏 🌿 📇 AE, MC, DC, V. €€€

In summer try to get a table on
the terrace beside the River Loiret.
But in winter, the airy dining room
will still make you feel like you're
on the river as you enjoy some of
the finest cuisine in the area.

ONZAIN

Domaine des Hauts-de-Loire

Road map D3. Route Mesland.
📞 02 54 20 72 57. 🕐 noon–2pm
Tue–Sun, 7:30–9pm Wed–Sun (Jul-
Aug: daily). 🔴 Dec–mid-Feb. 🍴
👟 ♿ 🌿 📇 AE, MC, DC, V.
€€€€

The restaurant of this *Relais et
Châteaux* hotel has two Michelin
stars. The menu includes delights
such as *filet de boeuf poché au vin
de Montlouis* (poached fillet of beef
cooked in white Montlouis wine).

ORLÉANS

Les Antiquaires

Road map E2. 2 rue au Lin. 📞 02
38 53 52 35. 🕐 noon–1:30pm,
7:30–10pm Tue–Sat. 🍴 👟 Ⓥ
📇 AE, MC, V. €€€

This restaurant is very popular
with locals. Game is served in
season, including wild duck, boar,
hare and the house speciality of
noisettes de biche sauce poivrade
(marinaded venison fillet in a
peppery garlic and herb sauce).

La Chancellerie

Road map E2. 27 pl Martroi.
C 02 38 53 57 54. **◯** noon–3pm,
7:30pm–1am Mon–Sat. **†⊚‖ ♨ ♿**
V ♿ ↗ *AE, MC, V.* €€

In an 18th-century building on a busy square near the cathedral, this lively brasserie and wine bar offers adventurous dishes to complement their excellent wines. In season, *faisan aux champignons* (pheasant with wild mushrooms) and *lièvre aux airelles* (hare with bilberries) are popular.

ST-DYÉ-SUR-LOIRE

La Bouriche aux Appetits

Road map E3. 65 route Nationale.
C 02 54 81 65 25. **◯** 11am–
2:30pm, 7–11pm Tue–Sun. **●** 2
weeks Christmas. **†⊚‖ ♨ ★ ↗** *AE,*
MC, DC, V. €€

Fish dishes are the speciality in this centrally-located restaurant that was once a wine-grower's store house. There is also an impressive variety of fresh *pâtés*, and high-quality food is even available to take away.

SOUVIGNY-EN-SOLOGNE

La Perdrix Rouge

Road map E3. 22 rue du Gâtinais.
C 02 54 88 41 05. **FAX** 02 54 88 05
56. **◯** noon–2pm, 7:30–9:30pm
Wed–Sun. **†⊚‖ ♨ ♿ ↗**
↗ *AE, MC, V.* €€

This typical Sologne inn is popular in the shooting season when it serves excellent game, including the partridge that gives its name. Other local produce is made good use of during the rest of the year.

BERRY

ARGENTON-SUR-CREUSE

Moulin des Eaux-Vives

Road map E4. Tendu. **C** 02 54 24
12 25. **FAX** 02 54 24 34 62. **◯** noon–
1:30pm Wed–Mon, 7:30–9:30pm
Wed–Sun (mid-Apr–mid-Oct: daily).
†⊚‖ ♨ V ↗ ↗ *AE, MC, V.* €€

Once an 18th-century water mill, this restaurant is 8 km (5 miles) north of Argenton-sur-Creuse. The

menu changes seasonally and may have *côtes de sanglier au vinaigre de framboises* (boar in raspberry vinegar sauce) and grape sorbets.

AUBIGNY-SUR-NÈRE

Le Bien-Aller

Road map F3. 3 rue des Dames.
C 02 48 58 03 92. **◯** noon–2pm,
7–9:30pm daily. **†⊚‖ ♨ V ↗ ↗**
↗ *AE, MC, V.* €€

This inn lies only 1 km (just over half a mile) from the Château de la Verrerie. The menu includes many original recipes, such as the crème caramel with fresh thyme.

BANNEGON

Auberge du Moulin de Chaméron

Road map F4. Le Village. **C** 02 48
61 84 48. **◯** 12:15–1:45pm, 7:30–
9pm Tue–Sun (Jun–Sep: daily). **●**
mid-Nov–Feb. **†⊚‖ ♨ ♿ ↗** *AE,*
MC, V. €€

A welcoming hotel-restaurant has been created from a picturesque 18th-century water mill. The cuisine is good, with many regional touches.

BOURGES

Le d'Antan Sancerrois

Road map F4. 50 rue Bourbonnoux.
C 02 48 65 96 26. **◯** noon–2pm
Tue–Sat, 7–10:30pm Mon–Sat. **●**
1st 3 weeks Aug, 25 Dec–1 Jan. **♨**
V ↗ ↗ ↗ *AE, MC, V.* €€

The locals flock to this restaurant set in a medieval building with exposed beams. The hearty cuisine is prepared with finesse, and the wine list is excellent.

Abbaye St-Ambroix

Road map F4. Bd de la République.
C 02 48 70 80 00. **◯** noon–2pm,
7:30–10pm daily. **†⊚‖ ♿ ♀ ↗**
AE, MC, DC, V. €€€

The Hôtel de Bourbon's restaurant is set in the abbey's former chapel. The sophisticated cuisine uses the best of French produce. All desserts are made to order.

Le Jacques Coeur

Road map F4. 3 place Jacques Coeur.
C 02 48 70 12 72. **◯** noon–
1:30pm, 7:30–10pm daily. **●** mid-
Dec–mid-Jan. **†⊚‖ ♨ ★ ↗** *AE,*
MC, V. €€€€

The chef in this clean and friendly restaurant sees himself as an artist. The fish dishes, such as monkfish in stewed tomatoes, add definite creedence to his self-appraisal.

BRUÈRE-ALLICHAMPS

Auberge de l'Abbaye de Noirlac

Road map F4. Le Village. **C** 02 48
96 22 58. **◯** noon–2:30pm, 7–9:30pm
Thu–Tue. **●** mid-Nov–mid-Mar. **†⊚‖**
♨ V ↗ ↗ ↗ *MC, V.* €€

This inn, surrounded by meadows, is just a few minutes' walk from the beautiful Abbaye de Noirlac. The decor is rustic and the cuisine satisfying. Light meals are also available for those in a hurry.

CHÂTEAUMEILLANT

Le Piet-à-Terre

Road map F4. Rue du Château. **C** 02
48 61 41 74. **◯** noon–1:30pm Tue–
Sun, 7:30–9pm Tue–Sat (summer: daily).
†⊚‖ ♨ V ↗ ↗ ↗ *MC, V.* €€

This is a serious restaurant offering interesting cooking. Its specialities include *poulette braisée farcie*, a braised young chicken stuffed with *foie gras*. The weekday lunch menu is particularly good value.

NOHANT

Auberge de la Petite Fadette

Road map E4. Le Village. **C** 02 54 31
01 48. **◯** noon–2:30pm, 7–9:30pm
daily. **†⊚‖ ♨ V ↗ ↗ ↗** *AE,*
MC, V. €€

Named after one of George Sand's novels, this inn is cosy in winter yet delightfully airy in the heat of summer. Try the Berry dish, *poulet en barbouille (see p210).*

ST-AMAND-MONTROND

La Croix d'Or

Road map F4. 28 rue du 14 juillet.
C 02 48 96 09 41. **◯** noon–2:30pm,
7–9:30pm daily. **†⊚‖**
♨ V ↗ ↗ *AE, MC, V.* €€€

Charolais beef, best accompanied by a good Sancerre, is a speciality of this restaurant. The dining room, with its curved ceiling and forest of plants, is spacious.

For key to symbols *see p209*

SANCERRE

La Tour

Road map F3. 31 pl de la Halle.
【 *02 48 54 00 81.* ◯ *12:30–2pm,
6–10pm daily.* ● *23 Dec–15 Jan.*
¶●¶ 🏃 Ⓥ 🖥 🚳 🗷 *AE, MC, V.*
€€€

This restaurant has two dining
rooms: downstairs has an open
fire; upstairs is more modern. In
both, the food is excellent. *Sandre*
(pike-perch) with a red Sancerre
sauce is one of many local dishes.

VIERZON

La Maison de Celestin

Road map E3. 20 ave Pierre-Sémard.
【 *02 48 83 01 63.* ◯ *11am–3pm,
7–11pm Tue–Sun.* ¶●¶ 🚳 🖥 ★
🗷 *AE.* €

This establishment, which faces a
lovely garden, provides excellent,
good-value food in modern
surroundings. There are two
floors: if possible, go for a table
on the balcony. Lobster and duck
are particular specialities.

NORTH OF THE LOIRE

ARNAGE

Auberge des Matfeux

Road map C2. 289 av Nationale.
【 *02 43 21 10 71.* ◯ *noon–2pm
Tue–Sun, 7:30–9pm Tue–Sat.* ● *23
Dec–15 Jan.* ● *2-20 Jan; 27 Jul-27
Aug.* ¶●¶ Ⓥ 🚳 🗷 🗷 *AE. MC,
DC, V.* €€€

This old inn, 9 km (6 miles) south
of Le Mans, serves light cuisine
making full use of the vegetables
and herbs that are grown in the
garden. The dining room has a
very pretty conservatory.

CHARTRES

Le Buisson Ardent

Road map E2. 10 rue au Lait. 【 *02
37 34 04 66.* ◯ *12–2pm Wed–Mon,
7:30–9:30pm daily.* ¶●¶ 🏃 Ⓥ 🗷
MC, V. €€

The classic cuisine of this popular
restaurant, close to the cathedral,
is equally good value and equally
enjoyable either for a speedy
lunch or a more leisurely dinner.

Le Grand Monarque

Road map E2. 22 pl des Epars.
【 *02 37 21 00 72.* ◯ *noon–
2:30pm, 7:30–10pm daily.* ¶●¶ 🚳
🗷 *AE, MC, DC, V.* €€€
See also **Where to Stay,** p206.

The restaurant of this hotel serves
both traditional French food and
local delicacies, including *pâté de
Chartres* (foie gras inside duck
liver pâté). The wine cellar offers
a wide selection of Loire wines.

CHÂTEAUDUN

L'Arnaudière

Road map E2. 4 rue St-Lubin.
【 *02 37 45 98 98.* ◯ *noon–
2:30pm Tue–Sun, 6:30–10pm
Tue–Thu, Fri-Sat.* ¶●¶ 🏃 Ⓥ 🖥 🗷
🗷 *AE, MC, V.* €

This restaurant has a courtyard
garden for summer meals. The
cuisine is tasty, and the fixed-price
menus are good value.

LA FLÈCHE

La Fesse d'Ange

Road map C3. Pl du 8 mai 1945.
【 *02 43 94 73 60.* ◯ *noon–1:30pm
Tue–Sun, 7:15–9:30pm Wed–Sat
(closed 1-22 Aug).* ¶●¶ 🏃 Ⓥ 🚳
🗷 🗷 *MC, V.* €€

Based on seasonal produce, the
cooking is much appreciated by
the locals. Chickens and ducks
from Loué are often on the menu.

LAVAL

Bistro de Paris

Road map B2. 67 rue du Val-de-
Mayenne. 【 *02 43 56 98 29.*
◯ *noon–1:45pm, 7:15–9:30pm
Tue–Sat.* ● *Sun, Mon.* ¶●¶ 🏃 Ⓥ
🚳 🗷 ★ 🗷 *MC, V.* €€

Beside the River Mayenne and close
to the château, this bistro serves
meals that are remarkable value.

MALICORNE-SUR-SARTHE

La Petite Auberge

Road map C3. 5 pl des Geusclins.
【 *02 43 94 80 52.* ◯ *Jun–Aug:
noon–2pm, 7–9pm daily; Sep–May:
noon–2pm Tue–Sun, 7–9pm Tue–Sat.*
¶●¶ 🏃 Ⓥ 🗷 🗷 *MC, V.* €€€

This small restaurant, beside the
town's marina and close to the
famous faïence workshops, is a
good spot for lunch during a tour
of the Sarthe valley.

LE MANS

Le Grenier à Sel

Road map C2. 26 place de L'Eperon.
【 *02 43 23 26 30.* ◯ *11:30am–
3pm, 7:15–10:30pm Tue–Sun.* ● *3
weeks Feb, 2 weeks Aug.* ¶●¶ 🏃
🚳 ★ 🗷 *AE, MC, DC, V.* €

It is a challenge to select the jewel
in this restaurant's crown, so good
are the décor, service and food.
Ultimately, however, delicacies
such as wild fowl in chives with
stewed apple and baked figs
make the biggest impression.

La Rascasse

Road map C2. 6 rue de la Mission.
【 *02 43 84 45 91.* ◯ *11:30am–
3pm, 7:30–11pm Tue–Sun L.* ¶●¶
🏃 🚳 ★ 🗷 *AE, V.* €€

La Rascasse is a real treat: the
décor is the typically French
combination of stunning and
tasteful. So is the food. Try the
langoustines in a purslane salad
and the mullet in puréed olives.

ST-DENIS-D'ANJOU

Auberge du Roi-René

Road map C3. 4 Grande-Rue.
【 *02 43 70 52 30.* ◯ *noon–2:30pm,
8–10pm daily.* ¶●¶ 🏃 Ⓥ 🖥 🚳
🗷 🗷 *AE, MC, DC, V.* €€

The dining room is set in a medieval building. The cuisine is light,
with some dishes, like the *nougat
de foie de canard aux figues* (duck
liver terrine with figs), combining
sweet and savoury flavours.

SOLESMES

Grand Hôtel de Solesmes

Road map C2. 16 pl Dom-
Guéranger. 【 *02 43 95 45 10.* ◯
noon–2pm, 7:30–9:30pm daily. ●
28 Dec–1 Jan. ¶●¶ 🏃 Ⓥ 🚳 🗷 🗷
AE, MC, DC, V. €€ See also
Where to Stay, p207.

This hotel has an excellent restaurant overlooking a garden. The
traditional cuisine features local
fish specialities, including *sandre
à la mousse d'oseille* (pike-perch
with sorrel mousse).

LOIRE-ATLANTIQUE AND THE VENDEE

ARÇAIS

L'Auberge de la Venise Verte

Road map B4. Route de Damvix.
(05 49 35 37 15. **◯** 7:30–10pm
daily (winter: Sat & Sun only).
● mid-Nov–Feb. **†●†** **♿** **V** **&**
⊘ MC, V. **€**

This restaurant is a cheap and cheerful place for supper, especially if you are mooring your boat for the night at Arçais' port. The menu emphasizes local fish and eels.

LA BAULLE

Le Petit Bouchon Gourmand

Road map A3. 275 ave du Maréchal de Lattre de Tassigny. **(** 02 40 60 95 58. **◯** 7:30pm–1am daily. **●** Christmas. **†●†** **▦** **&** **★** **⊘** MC, DC, V. **€**

This extremely fashionable, Paris-style restaurant has a friendly and fun-loving atmosphere. The cuisine, which covers all the French classics, is excellent.

CLISSON

Bonne Auberge

Road map B4. 1 rue Olivier de Clisson.
(02 40 54 01 90. **◯** noon–1:30pm Wed–Sun, 8–10pm Tue–Sat. **†●†** **▦** **V** **&** **⊁** **★** **⊘** AE, MC, V. **€€**

Local produce is used for the inventive dishes served in this restaurant. Try the Vendéen duck with figs or the poached with spices, and leave space for their delectable desserts.

FONTENAY-LE-COMTE

Auberge de la Rivière

Road map B4. Velluire. **(** 02 51 52 32 15. **◯** noon–2pm Tue–Sun, 8–9:30pm Tue–Sat. **●** Jan–Feb. **†●†** **♿** **&** **⊁** **⊘** MC, V. **€€**

Sited near the northern end of the Marais Poitevin, southwest of Fontenay-le-Comte, this *auberge* offers country comfort and delicious cooking. The fish dishes and langoustines are especially good.

HAUTE-GOULAINE

Le Manoir de la Boulaie

Road map B3. 33 rue Chapelle St-Martin. **(** 02 40 06 15 91. **◯** 11:30am–3pm, 7–11pm Thu–Tue. **●** Jan. **†●†** **▦** **♿** **★** **⊘** MC, V. **€€€**

Star chef Laurent Saudeau has brought a touch of modern class and a taste of the exotic flavours of the Mediterranean to customers of this beautiful restaurant, which has the added benefit of being located in the middle of some of the area's prettiest vineyards.

ILE D'YEU

La Marée

Road map A4. 27 rue Pierre-Henry, Port-Joinville. **(** 02 51 58 36 25. **◯** noon–2pm daily, 7–9pm Mon–Sat. **●** mid-Nov–mid-Jan. **†●†** **♿** **⊘** MC, V. **€€** See also **Where to Stay**, p207.

La Marée, the restaurant of the Flux Hôtel, specializes in fish and seafood dishes. For a health-giving dessert, try a *tartilaise*, the legendary Ile d'Yeu prune tart.

MAILLEZAIS

Le Collibert

Road map B5. Rue Principale.
(02 51 87 25 07. **◯** noon–2:30pm, 7:30–9:30pm Tue–Sun (mid-Jun–mid-Sep daily). **†●†** **♿** **V** **&** **⊘** MC, V. **€€**

Situated in the Marais Poitevin at the entrance to La Venise Verte, this restaurant is highly regarded for its regional buffet and versions of local specialities.

MORTAGNE-SUR-SÈVRE

Hôtel de France

Road map B4. Pl du Docteur Pichat.
(02 51 65 03 37. **◯** 12:15–2pm Mon–Fri & Sun, 7:30–9pm Mon–Sat (Apr–Oct: daily). **†●†** **♿** **V** **&** **⊁** **⊘** AE, MC, V. **€€**

A cheerful atmosphere and hearty, robust food awaits diners at this 400-year-old coaching inn. There are in fact two restaurants here: La Taverne, and the slightly cheaper La Petite Auberge (which provides lunch only). Both are definitely well worth a visit. Rooms are also available.

NANTES

La Cigale

Road map B3. 4 pl Graslin. **(** 02 51 84 94 94. **◯** 7:30am–1am daily. **†●†** **♿** **&** **⊁** **⊘** MC, V. **€€**

The interior of this Belle Epoque brasserie (*see p190*) is decorated with glazed tiles and gilding. The quality of the cuisine is also exceptional, featuring a wide choice of fresh seafood and fish.

Manoir de la Comète

Road map D3. 21 rue de la Libération, St Sébastien-sur-Loire. **(** 02 40 34 15 93. **◯** noon–2:30pm Mon–Fri, 7:30–10pm Mon–Sat. **●** 24 Dec–4 Jan. **†●†** **⊘** AE, MC, V. **€€€**

Just outside Nantes city centre, this stylish restaurant offers refined French cuisine in a friendly atmosphere. The chef creates imaginative dishes, such as duck and baby spinach with a Chinon sauce, from regional ingredients.

Les Temps Changent

Road map B3. 1 place Aristide-Briand. **(** 02 51 72 18 01. **◯** noon–2pm, 7:30–11pm Mon–Sat. **●** Christmas. **†●†** **▦** **★** **⊘** V. **€€€**

This is a most welcoming venue, with a growing reputation for the quality of its cuisine. The shredded crab and fried *foie gras* excel.

LES SABLES D'OLONNE

Beau Rivage

Road map A4. 1 blvd de Lattre de Tassigny. **(** 02 51 32 03 01. **◯** 12:30–2:30pm Tue–Sun, 7:30–9pm Mon–Sat (Jun–Sep: daily). **●** Jan. **†●†** **♿** **V** **&** **⊘** AE, MC, DC, V. **€€€** and cheaper bistro: **€**

Although no longer in its enviable beachfront location, it is still worth seeking out this restaurant for the quality of its locally-caught fish.

ST-LYPHARD

Auberge de Kerhinet

Road map A3. Kerhinet. **(** 02 40 61 91 46. **◯** noon–3pm Thu–Tue, 7:30–11pm Thu–Mon (Jul–Aug: daily). **†●†** **♿** **V** **&** **⊁** **⊘** AE, MC, DC, V. **€€** See also **Where to Stay**, p207.

This hotel restaurant is decorated with old photographs and farm tools. Typical local fish specialities include *anguilles au rocquefort* (eel with Rocquefort).

For key to symbols *see p209*

SHOPS AND MARKETS

SHOPPING FOR SPECIALITIES of the Loire Valley is always a pleasure, and the region's towns and cities also offer many opportunities to purchase the goods that France is famous for – fashion accessories and clothes, kitchenware, porcelain and crystal, and particularly food. Specialist shops are everywhere, and

Bourges shop sign

visiting the region's open-air and indoor food markets gives the visitor a wonderful opportunity to buy a vast range of local produce and culinary specialities. This section provides guidelines on shopping in the Loire Valley, and pages 222–3 show some of the best regional foods, wines and other specialist goods available.

Chocolates on display in La Livre Tournois, a *confiserie* in Tours

OPENING HOURS

SMALL FOOD SHOPS in the Loire region open early – around 7:30 or 8am and close at around 12:30 for lunch, then reopen at about 3:30 or 4pm until 7 or 8pm. Other small shops are open from roughly 2 to 6:30 or 7pm on Mondays (many remain closed all day), 9am to noon and 2 to 6:30 or 7pm, Tuesday to Saturday. Small supermarkets generally take a long lunch break, but department stores and large supermarkets do not close for lunch. Sales are usually held in late-June and January.

Open-air food markets take place one, two or three mornings a week, often including Sundays, while the large indoor food markets *(les halles)* are usually open from Tuesday to Saturday for the same hours as small food shops. This guide lists the market days for each town featured.

SPECIALIST SHOPS

DESPITE THE mushrooming of supermarkets and large superstores, small specialist shops have continued to

thrive in France, and they add enormously to the pleasure of shopping trips. Food shops in particular often specialize in a single theme. *Boulangeries* sell fresh bread, but they may be *boulangeries-pâtisseries*, which means that tempting cakes and pastries will also be on offer. *Traiteurs* sell prepared dishes, while *épiceries* are small grocers. *Crèmeries* specialize in dairy products, *fromageries* sell only cheese and *charcuteries* specialize in cooked and cured meats with a few prepared, cold dishes. An *épicerie fine* focuses on high-class groceries and is a good source of gifts to take home, such as local mustards or vinegars in attractive jars or bottles.

An *alimentation générale* (general food store) may have a self-service system. In small villages, this is sometimes the only shop, although fresh bread will always be available either there or from the local café. A travelling van also supplies fresh bread in some regions.

Cleaning products are bought in a *droguerie*, hardware from a *quincaillerie*, books from a *librairie* and stationery (much of which is particularly stylish in France) from a *papeterie*.

The area has some specialist shops that focus on a single product, such as umbrellas or walking sticks, chess sets or stamps, or in a single field such as militaria or natural history books. Their owners are usually extremely knowledgeable about their particular subject, and they enjoy sharing it if you show an interest. Antique shops *(magasins d'antiquités)* tend to be very pricey. Head instead for a *brocante* (bric-à-brac shop), or try hunting for bargains in local flea markets.

TASTING AND BUYING WINE

Sign for a charcuterie

THE LOIRE VALLEY is famous for its wines and the region is scattered with producers. Signs beside the road saying *"dégustation"* mean that a "tasting" is held in the vineyard. It is important to remember that the local *vigneron* will expect a modest purchase of a few bottles after you have drunk several experimental glasses. However, in Saumur it is possible to tour the *chais* (the wine growers' own cellars) with the minimum of sales pressure. Best of all, visit the *Maisons du Vin* in most major towns, where the literature, information and often free tastings are very helpful and interesting.

HYPERMARKETS AND CHAIN STORES

SUPERSTORES and the larger hypermarkets (*hypermarchés*) are usually situated on the outskirts of towns, often as part of a *centre commercial* (shopping complex) that may also include small boutiques, a DIY outlet and a petrol station. Many of these big stores belong to the Auchan, Carrefour or Continent chains.

The old-style *grand magasin,* or department store, found in the region's towns has generally either been converted into a series of boutiques or taken over and modernized by the up-market Nouvelles Galeries or Printemps national chains. These chic stores are good for clothes, accessories and perfumes. The popular Monoprix and Prisunic stores are worth visiting if you are looking for inexpensive stationery, lingerie and cosmetics. Many of them also have a reasonably priced food department.

A flower-seller and customer at the village market in Luynes

MARKETS

OPEN-AIR FOOD markets are one of the delights of the Loire Valley. Their offerings are mouth-watering: mounds of succulent vegetables, *charcuterie* specialities, goats' cheeses and plump poultry and game. Of this excellent fare, most is produced locally, often in small-scale market gardens owned and worked by the stall-holder. Produce that has

Fresh local produce on sale in the market in Saumur's place St-Pierre

been grown locally is labelled *pays.* Look out for unusual specialities, such as the strangely-shaped squashes and pumpkins that appear in autumn, wild mushrooms and flavoured honeys. Honey stalls often sell honey-flavoured confectionery and honey soap, too. Spice and herb stalls are also interesting, providing a wealth of gift ideas. Some markets have stalls selling clothes or shoes and leather goods. Look out also for local craft work.

Flea markets (*marchés aux puces*) are regular events in many towns and are often held in small towns and villages in countryside districts during the summer holiday season.

VAT REBATES

SINCE THE ADVENT of the Single European Market, rebates of value-added tax (*taxe à la valeur ajoutée* or *TVA*) are only available to those not resident in a European Union country. They apply only to purchases totalling at least 200€ in a single shop, on the same day, and taken out of the EU within three months. The export sales form you receive on purchase must be handed to the customs officer as you leave the EU. Reimbursements usually go directly to your bank. Not all articles qualify for rebates. In stores frequented by foreign tourists, staff are familiar with the process.

Local goats' cheese for sale in Amboise market

REGIONAL SPECIALITIES

Angers
Pâtisserie La Petite Marquise
22 rue des Lices.
📞 02 41 87 43 01.
Quernons d'Ardoise and sweets.

Bourges
Epicerie du Berry
Ilot Victor Hugo,
41 rue Moyenne.
📞 02 48 70 02 38.
Berry honey and Forestines.

Guérande
La Maison du Sel
Pradel.
📞 02 40 62 08 80.
Salicornes and Guérande salt.

Nantes
La Friande
12 rue Paul Bellamy.
📞 02 40 20 14 68.
Nantaise biscuits.

Orléans
La Chocolaterie Royale
53 rue Royale.
📞 02 38 53 93 43.

Tours
La Livre Tournois
6 rue Nationale.
📞 02 47 05 42 00.
Pruneaux Fourrés and chocolates.

ARTS AND CRAFTS

Gien
Faïencerie de Gien
78 Pl de la Victoire.
📞 02 38 67 00 05.
Porcelain.

Malicorne
Faïenceries Artistiques du Bourg-Joly
16 rue Carnot.
📞 02 43 94 80 10.

Poncé-sur-le-Loir
Centre d'Artisanat d'Art
📞 02 43 44 45 31.
Craft workshops and shop.

Villaines-les-Rochers
Coopérative de Vannerie de Villaines
1 rue de la Cheneillère.
📞 02 47 45 43 03.
Wickerwork studio and shop.

What to Buy in the Loire Valley

THE BEST BUYS IN THE LOIRE tempt the eye as well as the stomach. A gourmet's paradise, the food shops and open-air markets of the region attract visitors with their delicious scents and sights. Local producers are justifiably proud of their goods and pack them with respect, in attractive crates or pottery jars. But gourmet treats are not the only local goods worth looking for. The region has long been famous for its china from Gien and for the fabric and lace of the Touraine, evocative of the remarkable history of the Loire.

A beautifully wrapped package of sweets

CONFECTIONERY

Local confectionery specialities make good gifts to take home, especially when they are so prettily packaged. The region is well-known for its wide range of sweets, which are available from tearooms and specialist confectioners, and many towns also have their own mouth-watering treats.

COULEON Olivier
SUCCESSEUR DAUNAY
FABRICANT · 37 CORMERY · 18 47 43 40 20
AUX VÉRITABLES
MACARONS
DE L'ABBAYE
DE CORMERY

MAISON POCHET FONDÉE EN 1892

Forestines from Bourges

Macaroon biscuits from Cormery

Pruneaux fourrés, prunes stuffed with marzipan

QUERNONS D'ARDOISE

Chocolates resembling traditional slate tiles

Fruit-flavoured sweets

SOUVENIRS

The châteaux and museums of the Loire Valley have well-stocked shops that sell an array of appealing souvenirs. In addition to the usual booklets and posters, many sell gifts with an historical theme, such as replica playing cards or tapestries. Wine bought direct from a local vineyard is another special souvenir (see pp30–31).

VDR VDR
JEU HENRI IV

Playing cards with historical figures

1992
CHATEAU DE
CHENONCEAU

Wine made at Chenonceau

THE FLAVOURS OF THE LOIRE

It is impossible to visit the Loire without being amazed by the abundance of delicious food. Much comes perfectly packaged for travelling. Near the game-filled forests of the Berry, you can buy jars and tins of pâtés and terrines. Goats' cheeses are moulded into a variety of shapes, and the firmer varieties travel successfully. Heather honey from Berry's heathland and wine vinegars from Orléans are also specialities of the region.

Confiture de vin, jelly made from wine

Poulain chocolate made in Blois

Pickled samphire

Goats' cheese

Cotignac, quince
jelly from Orléans

**Sea salt from
Guérande**

**Crémant de Loire,
sparkling wine**

LOCAL CRAFTS

Traditional crafts survive throughout the Loire Valley, and you can often visit craftsmen and women at work in their studios. Many towns in the region have long been renowned for their craft specialities, such as Malicorne for its lattice-work faïence, Villaines-les-Rochers for its baskets or Gien for its china.

**Pottery from La
Borne in Berry**

Gien china side plate

Wicker basket from Villaines

Dinner plate from Gien

ACTIVITIES IN THE LOIRE VALLEY

A HOLIDAY IN THE Loire Valley can combine the cultural highlights of visits to the spectacular châteaux with enjoyment of the region's wealth of natural environments. The gentle terrain and beautiful forests are perfect for exploration on foot, horseback or mountain bike, and the clear waters of the lakes and rivers – not to mention the spectacular Atlantic coastline – are enticing spots for swimming or boating. Here is a selection of just a few of the activities on offer in the region. For more information contact the departmental *Loisirs-Accueil* offices (*see p227*), which focus on leisure activities, or the local tourist offices in towns and villages.

WALKING

THE LOIRE VALLEY is renowned for its many accessible and scenic walks, which are called *Randonnées* (*see pp26–7*). Although these routes are clearly signposted, it is a good idea to carry a Topo-Guide, which are only available in French but do contain maps, a description of the itinerary, details of sites of architectural or natural interest to be found along the route, an estimate of the time it will take you to complete the walk and the addresses of local hotels, restaurants, hostels and camp sites. Most Topo-Guides cost around F100. There is also a one-volume Topo-Guide describing the GR3 between Orléans and Guérande. A complete list of walks in the Loire Valley is available from the **Fédération Française de la Randonnée Pédestre**.

You will never be more than a day's walk away from a town or village where you will be able to find food and accommodation, so it is not necessary to carry a large amount of equipment, but, as always, you should wear good, strong walking shoes. Remember that some paths can be damp and muddy during the spring and autumn.

CYCLING

THE GENERALLY flat landscape of the Loire Valley makes it perfect for cyclists. Because many of the châteaux are so near to each other, it is easy to visit several by bicycle in only a few days. Mountain bike enthusiasts will enjoy riding the clearly signposted paths through the region's forests and nature reserves.

Motorways and a few other major roads are forbidden to cyclists, and these are clearly marked: the sign has a white background with a red border and a cyclist in the middle. Cycle lanes, when they exist, are compulsory. Bicycles must have two working brakes, a bell, a red rear reflector and yellow reflectors on the pedals, as well as a white front light and a red rear light after dark. It is also advisable to wear a helmet and to carry a few essential spare parts in case of breakdown. While bicycle shops are common in the region, foreign spare parts may not be available.

It is possible to hire touring bicycles and mountain bikes throughout the region. Local tourist offices will be able to provide you with a list of cycle hire centres. The SNCF (*see p242*) also runs a *Train et Vélo* service, which offers cycles for hire at some train stations in the region.

Transporting your bicycle on local trains is free in most cases, although on major train routes the SNCF requires you to register your bicycle and will levy a small charge. The booklet *Guide du Train et du Vélo*, available at train stations and from the SNCF, gives more information on transporting bicycles by train.

A number of local tourist offices have organized itineraries for cyclists and will provide comprehensive route maps. In the central Loire Valley, a group of hoteliers and camp sites are members of *Vélotel-Vélocamp*. This means that they are particularly friendly to cyclists and can arrange bicycle hire, organize local itineraries and provide you with a picnic lunch on request.

The **Fédération Française de Cyclisme** is the umbrella organization for more than 2,800 cycling clubs in France. They are able to provide advice, local contacts and a number of cycling itineraries in the region if you write to them well in advance.

Cycling, one of the most pleasant ways to see the Loire Valley

A riverside pony trek in the beautiful Vendée region

HORSE RIDING AND PONY TREKKING

H ORSE LOVERS will enjoy a visit to the National Riding School in the important equestrian town of Saumur, where the world-famous Cadre Noir riding team perform in regular displays *(see p83)*.

The forests of the Loire Valley, with their well-maintained networks of trails and well-marked bridle paths, are ideal for riding. Topo-Guides are as useful for riders as they are for walkers.

Experienced riders can hire horses by the hour, half-day or day from numerous stables in the region. A sign reading *Loueur d'Equidés* means that horses are for hire without an instructor. If you prefer to be accompanied when riding, you should search out an *Ecole d'Equitation* or a *Centre Equestre* (riding school).

Many stables also offer longer treks on horseback, called *randonnées*, which last between a weekend and a week. Small groups are accompanied on the trek by an experienced guide, and accommodation is usually in quite basic hotels or hostels, although some luxury tours are also available.

The rental of old-fashioned horse-drawn caravans is becoming increasingly popular in the Loire Valley. Travellers sleep in the carriage overnight and journey at a slow, leisurely pace during the day. Generally caravans come in two sizes: the smaller one carries four adults or two adults and three children; the other carries six to eight people. There are also larger, open wagons, driven by a guide, that are used for group excursions of up to 15.

FISHING

T HE RIVERS of the Loire Valley are teeming with freshwater fish, including bream, bullhead, carp, grey mullet, perch, pike, roach, shad and zander. There are also trout in some of the faster-running tributaries of the Loire.

Freshwater fish

To fish in private waters, you must make arrangements with the owner. To fish in state-controlled waters, you must buy a permit, which is available from many tackle shops and tourist offices. Applicants must provide proof that they are a member of an angling association at home and pay a fishing tax.

There are two kinds of fishing tax: the basic tax covers fishing with worms in rivers that do not have trout runs; the special tax covers spinning, fly-fishing, and fish-bait fishing in all rivers, including those with trout. You cannot fish more than half an hour before sunrise or after sunset. There are set seasons for certain fish and limits on their size.

The **Conseil Supérieur de la Pêche**, which supervises all fishing in France, uses the tax money to promote and improve fishing conditions. It also publishes a helpful, free booklet, *Fishing in France*, which explains the regulations and includes a map giving useful information about all the French rivers. Ocean fishing is free from any tax as long as you do not use nets, although there are restrictions on the equipment a boat can carry. *Fishing in France* also has information on fishing from boats and underwater fishing.

Fly-fishing on the tranquil River Loir

GOLF

Evidence of the growing popularity of golf in France can be seen throughout the Loire Valley, which has many beautiful and challenging courses. Some of the region's golf courses, such as the Golf du Val de l'Indre, located near Châteauroux in Berry, and La Bretesche in Missillac in the Loire-Atlantique, are set in the grounds of châteaux.

In the Loiret, seven courses around Orléans have joined up to provide a golf pass that combines greens fees for the different courses and the added option of accommodation in nearby two- or three-star hotels. For more information, contact the Loiret *Loisirs-Accueil* office in Orléans, or the respective golf courses.

A booklet on the golf courses of the Western Loire, available from the tourist office in Nantes *(see p231)*, includes a Golf Passport – play on five courses in the western Loire and the greens fee on the sixth is free. The comprehensive brochure also suggests top-class accommodation within easy reach of the courses.

BOATING AND WATER SPORTS

Because the Loire Valley is criss-crossed with beautiful rivers, most visitors cannot resist the temptation to take at least one boat trip. A wide variety of short excursions is available from riverside *ports de plaisance* (marinas) throughout the Loire region, and in general they do not require advance reservations.

The marshes of the Marais Poitevin *(see pp182–5)* are best viewed from its canal network in a *barque* (the traditional, flat-bottomed boat).

One option is to base your entire visit on the water by renting a house-boat or a cruiser for a period of a few days or for one or two weeks. Boats of different sizes and styles are available, from old-fashioned canal boats to sophisticated modern cruisers. Most prices are for round trips and include bedding, kitchen equipment and full training, and it may also be possible to rent bicycles or canoes, or to make a one-way *(simple)* trip. Further information is available from the main tourist offices.

If you are looking for a more adventurous way of enjoying the region's rivers, try canoe-ing or kayaking. It is best to take a guided tour from one of the clubs based along the river. Although the river may look calm, there can be dangerous undercurrents and obstacles.

Kayaking on the River Mayenne

There are good activity centres beside many of the rivers and lakes in the Loire Valley, and there may also be facilities for renting pedaloes, canoes and yachts – some centres even offer water-skiing. A good number of the Atlantic coastal resorts also have facilities for renting windsurfers – Les Sables d'Olonne *(see p181)* was host to the world wind-surfing championships in 1988.

Swimmers should stay in the approved areas. While the sand banks may look inviting, there are risks from strong currents and shifting sands. Further information on water safety is given on pages 234–5.

Windsurfing at La Tranche-sur-Mer on the Atlantic Coast

THE LOIRE FROM THE AIR

ONE OF THE most luxurious ways to see the Loire Valley is from a hot-air balloon (*montgolfière* in French). There are daily flights in the summer, weather permitting, from Tours, Nantes and Amboise. **France Montgolfière** will put together custom-made excursions.

You can also take a tour in a helicopter or light aircraft. In addition to major airports at Tours and Nantes, there are many other airfields throughout the region. The tourist offices provide complete information. Flying lessons are also available at some of these centres. Learning to fly in France can be much cheaper than elsewhere. Details can be obtained from the **Fédération Nationale Aéronautique**. Visitors interested in gliding or hang-gliding should contact the **Fédération Française de Vol Libre**.

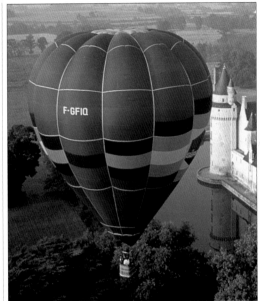

Ballooning over Le Plessis-Bourré in Anjou

DIRECTORY

SERVICES LOISIRS-ACCUEIL

Cher
5 rue de Séracourt,
18014 Bourges.
📞 02 48 67 00 18.

Eure-et-Loir
10 rue Docteur Maunoury,
28002 Chartres.
📞 02 37 84 01 00.

Indre
1 rue St-Martin,
36003 Châteauroux.
📞 02 54 07 36 36.

Indre-et-Loire
38 rue Augustin-Fresnel,
37171 Chambray-lès-Tours.
📞 02 47 48 37 27.

Loire-Atlantique
Comité Régionale du
Tourisme (CRT)
2 rue Loire,
44204 Nantes.
📞 02 40 48 24 20.

Loiret
8 rue d'Escures,
45041 Orléans.
📞 02 38 62 04 88.

Maine-et-Loire
Pl Kennedy,
49051 Angers.
📞 02 41 23 51 11.

Mayenne
84 av Robert Buron,
53000 Laval.
📞 02 43 53 18 18.

Sarthe
40 rue Joinville,
72000 Le Mans.
📞 02 43 40 22 50.

Vendée
BP233.8 pl Napoléon,
85006 La Roche-sur-Yon.
📞 02 51 47 88 20.

WALKING

Fédération Française de la Randonnée Pédestre
14 rue Riquet,
75019 Paris.
📞 01 44 89 93 93.

CYCLING

Fédération Française de Cyclisme
Bâtiment Jean Monnet,
5 rue de Rome, 93110
Rosny-sous-bois Cedex.
📞 01 49 35 69 00.
FAX 01 48 94 09 97.

FISHING

Conseil Supérieur de la Pêche
134 av de Malakoff,
75016 Paris.
📞 01 45 02 20 20.

GOLF

Fédération Française de Golf
68 rue Anatole France,
92309 Levallois Perret.
📞 01 41 49 77 00.

HORSE RIDING

Fédération Française d'Equitation
81-82 av Edouard Vaillant,
92100 Boulogne
Billancourt
📞 01 58 17 58 17.

SAILING/SURFING

Fédération Française de Voile
55 av Kléber,
75016 Paris.
📞 01 44 05 81 00.

CANOEING AND KAYAKING

Ligue Pays de la Loire de Canoë-Kayak (LPLCK)
75 av du Lac de Maine,
49000 Angers.
📞 02 41 72 07 04.

THE LOIRE FROM THE AIR

Fédération Française de Vol Libre
4 rue de Suisse,
06100 Nice.
📞 04 97 03 82 82

Fédération Nationale Aéronautique (FNA)
155 av Wagram,
75017 Paris.
📞 01 44 29 92 00.

France Montgolfière
La Riboulière,
41400 Monthou-sur-Cher.
📞 02 54 71 75 40.

SURVIVAL GUIDE

PRACTICAL INFORMATION

IN THE LOIRE VALLEY, as elsewhere in France, the peak holiday period is from mid-June to the end of August. The area is very well prepared to meet the practical needs of its many visitors, however, providing accommodation ranging from top hotels and private châteaux to small camp sites, as well as a selection of excellent restaurants.

Because of the profusion of places of great historical, aesthetic or natural interest, ranging from stunning châteaux and cathedrals to windswept Atlantic beaches and wild marshlands, it is a

National logo for tourist information

good idea to draw up a list of priority visits before you travel. You should also check that the places you plan to visit are not closed for seasonal breaks or for restoration work. Before you leave home, the French Government Tourist Offices are invaluable sources of information. The local tourist information offices in most towns in the region offer advice on the spot.

With a wide variety of activities available, the Loire Valley has something to offer all its visitors. The following tips will help you make the most of your visit.

Tourist information office in Fontenay-le-Comte

TOURIST INFORMATION

MOST LARGE TOWNS have a tourist information office, known either as the *Syndicat d'Initiative* or the *Office de Tourisme*. This guide provides the address and telephone number of the tourist office in each town featured in its pages. In smaller towns the town hall (*hôtel de ville*) will offer information. Tourist offices supply free maps, advice on accommodation (which can include booking hotels) and information on regional recreational and cultural activities, such as festivals. The main branches are listed opposite. You can also obtain details in advance from French Government Tourist Offices before leaving your own country.

OPENING TIMES

GENERALLY, most shops and banks open from 8 or 9am until noon, and from 2 or 3pm until 6pm, Tuesday to Saturday (*see pp220–21 and pp236–7*). Opening hours vary with the size of town. Many shops and banks are closed on Mondays and also close for lunch daily, although big department stores, supermarkets, tourist offices and some sights may remain open all day. Restaurants may close for one day a week, so it is best to check before setting off (*see pp208–19*). Off season, some seaside resorts,

Brochures for sights in the Loire Valley

as well as many châteaux and smaller museums, close down. Telephone to check, as some hotels and restaurants shut for several months of the year.

SIGHTSEEING

IN FRANCE, MANY museums close for lunch – normal opening hours are between 9am and noon and from 2pm until 5:30pm. They usually also close for one day each week: national museums close on Tuesdays and municipal museums on Mondays. Several museums also close throughout the month of November. Opening hours tend to vary according

Tables outside a café in Les Sables d'Olonne

Entertainment at a festival in Luçon

to season. Generally, most museums are open for longer hours between May and September.

Museum admission charges range from 1.5 to 6.5€. Passes for more than one museum or monument are rare. Normally, you will need to buy separate tickets for each sight within a town.

There are usually some discounts available for students who have valid International Student Identity Cards (ISIC) *(see p233)* or the French *carte jeunes*. Anyone aged under 18 or over 65 can also be eligible for a price reduction. National museums are free the first Sunday of each month in winter (Oct–May); most others offer reductions on all Sundays.

Churches and cathedrals open every day but may shut during lunch. There is sometimes a small charge to visit cloisters, bell-towers and crypts.

**CHATEAU
DE
CHENONCEAU**
Propriété Privée

**Entrée pour
1 personne**

369230

**Entrance ticket to
Chenonceau**

**National logo for
the disabled**

DISABLED ACCESS

A LTHOUGH IN SOME of the Loire Valley's medieval villages, narrow streets can make it difficult for disabled travellers to get around, wheelchair access in the area is generally good. Many châteaux and museums offer special services and facilities for disabled visitors, which staff are happy to explain;

however, it is advisable to telephone and check about access before your visit.

Access to hotels and restaurants has been improved in many cases to accommodate disabled customers. Information specific to the area is available from town halls or from regional tourist offices. Parking spaces reserved for vehicles that have disabled permits are marked with a special sign. For more information about special facilities for disabled before departure, contact the International Relations Department of the **Association des Paralysés de France (APF)**.

ENTERTAINMENT INFORMATION

T HERE ARE SEVERAL sources of entertainment information in the Loire Valley. Magazines and brochures listing forthcoming events are available at tourist information offices as well as in many hotels and camp sites. Both newsagents (*maisons de la presse*) and tobacconists' shops (*tabacs*) sell newspapers and magazines. Local papers can also provide details of festivals and sporting events as well as the weather forecast.

**Sign for a
tobacconist**

DIRECTORY

**FRENCH GOVERNMENT
TOURIST OFFICES
ABROAD**

Australia
Level 22
25 Bligh St, Sydney,
NSW 2000.
((2) 9231 5244.

Canada
1918 Ave McGill College,
Suite 490, Montréal,
Quebec H3A 2W9.
((514) 288 4264.

United Kingdom
179 Piccadilly,
London W1V 0BA.
((020) 7399 3500.

United States
444 Madison Ave,
New York, NY 10022.
((212) 838-7800.

**TOURIST OFFICES IN
THE LOIRE VALLEY**

Angers
Pl Kennedy.
(02 41 23 51 11.

Blois
3 ave Jean-Laigret.
(02 54 90 41 41.

Bourges
21 rue Victor-Hugo.
(02 48 23 02 60.

Chartres
Pl de la Cathédrale.
(02 37 18 26 26.

Le Mans
Rue de l'Etoile.
(02 43 28 17 22.

Nantes
Pl du Commerce.
(02 40 20 60 00.

Orléans
Pl Albert 1er.
(02 38 24 05 05.

Tours
78–82 rue Bernard Palissy.
(02 47 70 37 37.

DISABLED TRAVELLERS

**Association des
Paralysés de France
(APF)**
17 bvd Auguste Blanqui
Paris 75013.
(01 40 78 69 00.
FAX 01 45 89 40 57.
W www.apf.asso.fr

VISAS

There are no French visa requirements for citizens of the European Union. Tourists from the United States or New Zealand who are staying in France for less than three months need not apply for a visa. After three months, a *visa de long séjour* is required. Visitors from Australia, Canada and other countries should request visa information from the French authorities in their own country before departure.

French perfumes, available tax-free

TAX-FREE GOODS

If you are resident outside the European Union you can reclaim the TVA (VAT or sales tax) on French goods if you spend more than 200€ in the same shop in one day obtain *un bordereau de vente à l'exportation* (an export sales form) and take the goods out of the EU within three months. Ask for this form when making your purchases. It consists of three sheets which must be signed by the retailer and yourself. Hand it in at customs when leaving the EU and the refund will be sent on to you, usually via your bank. In all instances, the sheets certified by customs must be received by the retailer within six months of sale.

The main exceptions for *détaxe* rebate are food and drink, medicines, tobacco, cars and motorbikes.

DUTY-FREE LIMITS

For travel within the EU duty free was abolished in June 1999. For non-EU nationals arriving in the EU, the following may be imported: up to 2 litres of wine, and a litre of spirits or 2 litres of drink less than 22° proof ; 50g of perfume; 500g of coffee; 100g of tea; and up to 200 cigarettes. Visitors under 17 may not import or export duty-free tobacco or alcohol, even as gifts.

DUTY-PAID LIMITS

There are no longer any restrictions on the quantities of duty-paid and VAT-paid goods you are allowed to take from one European Union country to another, as long as the goods are for your own use and are not intended for resale. Customs officers may ask you to prove that the goods are for your personal use if they exceed the suggested amounts: 10 litres of spirits, 90 litres of wine, 110 litres of beer and 800 cigarettes.

IMPORTING OTHER GOODS

In general, personal goods (such as a car or a bicycle) may be imported to France duty-free and without any paperwork as long as they are obviously for personal use and not for resale. *Voyagez en toute liberté,* a brochure

available from the **Centre des Renseignements des Douanes**, clarifies this. At the border, customs officers are also able to give advice and information, although this is likely to be in French.

Special rules apply, both within and without the EU, for the import and export of endangered plant and animal species, works of art and national treasures, human medicines, weapons and ammunition. Consult your own, or French, customs.

An ISIC international student card

STUDENT INFORMATION

Students who hold a valid International Student Identification Card (ISIC card) can benefit from discounts of between 25 and 50 per cent when they produce the card at museums, theatres, cinemas and also at many public monuments. The region's principal universities are in Nantes and Tours. Other large universities are located in the towns of Le Mans, Angers, Laval, Orléans and La Roche-sur-Yon.

In Orléans, the offices of the **Centre Information de Jeunesse** offer a great deal of useful information about student life in the area and can also provide a list of inexpensive accommodation for young people.

ETIQUETTE

It is important to respect the French rituals of politeness, which apply in the Loire Valley just as much as they do everywhere else in the country.

Friends greeting each other with two or three kisses

When you are introduced to someone, it is correct to shake hands with them. In shops, you should be prepared to say *bonjour* to the assistant before asking for what you want, and then *merci* when you receive your change and finally *au revoir, bonne journée* (goodbye, have a nice day) when you depart. The usual greeting among friends of either sex is generally two or three kisses on the cheek.

Throughout the Loire Valley region, and particularly in the smaller communities, all efforts by English speakers to make enthusiastic use of their French, however limited, and to show a real interest in the area will be met with encouragement by the local people.

LOIRE VALLEY TIME

THE LOIRE VALLEY is one hour ahead of Greenwich Mean Time (GMT). France is in the same time zone as Germany, Italy, Spain and other western European countries.

Standard time differences between the Loire Valley and some major cities of the world are as follows: London: minus 1 hour; New York: minus 6 hours; Dallas: minus 7 hours;

Los Angeles: minus 9 hours; Perth: plus 7 hours; Sydney: plus 9 hours; Auckland: plus 11 hours; and Tokyo: plus 8 hours. These can vary according to local summer alterations to the time.

The French use the 24-hour clock (they do not use the am and pm system): after midday, just continue counting 13, 14 and so on to provide the 24-hour clock time. For example, 1pm = 13:00.

CONVERSION CHART

Imperial to metric

To convert	Multiply by
Inches to centimetres	2.54
Feet to metres	0.3
Yards to metres	0.91
Miles to kilometres	1.6
Ounces to grams	28
Pounds to kilograms	0.45
Pints to litres	0.6
Gallons to litres	4.5

Metric to imperial

To convert	Multiply by
Centimetres to inches	0.4
Metres to feet	3.3
Metres to yards	1.09
Kilometres to miles	0.6
Grams to ounces	0.04
Kilograms to pounds	2.2
Litres to pints	1.8
Litres to gallons	0.22

French two-pin electrical plug

ELECTRICAL ADAPTORS

THE VOLTAGE in France is 220 volts. The plugs on French electrical appliances have two small round pins; the heavier-duty appliances have two large round pins. Some up-market hotels offer built-in adaptors for shavers only.

Multi-adaptors, which are useful because they have both large and small pins, can be bought at most airports before departure. Standard adaptors can be purchased from most department stores.

RELIGIOUS SERVICES

ALTHOUGH THE MAJOR religion in the region is Catholicism, the Loire Valley also has many Protestant churches, and some Jewish synagogues and Islamic mosques, particularly in the larger towns. These reflect the religious diversity of modern French society.

DIRECTORY

CUSTOMS INFORMATION

Paris
Centre des Renseignements des Douanes, 84 rue d'Hauteville, Paris 75010.
☎ 08 25 30 82 63.
W www.douane.gouv.fr

STUDENT INFORMATION

Orléans
Centre Info de Jeunesse, 5 blvd de Verdun.
☎ 02 38 78 91 78.
W www.cij-centre.org

YOUTH HOSTELS

Angers
Centre d'Accueil du Lac de Maine, 49 av du Lac de Maine.
☎ 02 41 22 32 10.

Bourges
Auberge de Jeunesse, 22 rue Henri Sellier.
☎ 02 48 24 58 09.

Le Mans
Auberge de Jeunesse, 23 rue Maupertuis.
☎ 02 43 81 27 55.

Nantes
Résidence Sonacotra Julienne David, 85 rue Félix Ménétrier.
☎ 02 40 93 28 30.

Orléans
Auberge de Jeunesse, 14 fbg Madeleine.
☎ 02 38 62 45 75.

Tours
Auberge de Jeunesse, 5 rue Bretonneau.
☎ 02 47 37 81 58.

PLACES OF WORSHIP

Catholic
La Cathédrale St-Etienne, Pl de la Cathédrale, Bourges.
☎ 02 48 65 72 89.

La Cathédrale Notre-Dame, Pl de la Cathédrale, Chartres.
☎ 02 37 21 56 33.

La Cathédrale St-Gatien, Pl de la Cathédrale, Tours.
☎ 02 47 70 37 36.

La Cathédrale St-Pierre-et-St-Paul, Pl St-Pierre, Nantes.
☎ 02 40 20 33 92.

Protestant
Temple Protestant, 8 pl Victor Bernier, Angers.
☎ 02 41 48 06 07.

Eglise Protestante, 21 rue de Cheverus, Laval.
☎ 02 43 53 74 90.

Jewish
Synagogue, 4–6 bd Paixhans, Le Mans.

Synagogue, 14 rue Robert de Courtenay, Orléans.
☎ 02 38 62 16 62.

Islamic
Mosquée, Av Rembrandt, Le Mans.

Grande Mosquée de Tours, 18 rue Lobin, Tours.
☎ 02 47 66 38 03.

Personal Security and Health

O N THE WHOLE, the Loire Valley is a safe place for visitors: take normal precautions, such as keeping an eye on your possessions at all times, and avoid isolated and unlit urban areas at night. If you fall ill during your stay, pharmacies are an excellent source of advice. Consular offices can offer help and advice in an emergency. In the case of a serious medical problem, call the emergency services.

Policeman   Fireman

PERSONAL PROPERTY

I N BIG CITIES, try not to carry conspicuous valuables with you and only take as much cash as you think you will need. Traveller's cheques are the safest method of carrying large sums of money. You should always make sure you are covered by an adequate insurance policy.

In major towns, the multi-storey car parks are kept under surveillance by video cameras. Parking there will reduce the threat of car crime and avoid the greater risk of parking in an illegal space and being towed away to a police pound.

In the event of a theft, go to the nearest police station, or *gendarmerie*, with your passport or other identity papers (and vehicle registration and insurance documents, if relevant). The report process (a *PV* or *procès-verbal*) may take time, but you will need a full police statement for any insurance claim. If your passport is stolen, contact the police and your nearest consulate.

Ambulance

Fire engine

Police car

PERSONAL SAFETY

V IOLENT CRIME is rare in the Loire Valley, although random incidents are sometimes reported. If travelling late at night, it is a good idea, especially for women, to remain within busy, well-lit areas and to be careful about talking to, or accompanying, strangers. If you are involved in a dispute or car accident, avoid confrontation. In potentially difficult situations, try to stay calm and speak French if you can, as your efforts may diffuse the situation.

LEGAL ASSISTANCE

I F YOUR INSURANCE policy is comprehensive, including a service in France such as Europ Assistance or Mondial Assistance, they will be able to help with legal advice on claims, such as accident procedure. If not, you should call your nearest consulate office and ask their advice.

INTERPRETERS

I F YOU REQUIRE an interpreter, telephone the Société Française des Traducteurs Professionnels or contact them via Minitel (*see p239*).

BEACH AND RIVER SAFETY

M OST OF THE BEACHES on the Atlantic coast are guarded in the summer by lifeguards (*sauveteurs*). There are a number of good family beaches, where bathing is not generally dangerous. However, a system of coloured flags tells bathers whether it is safe to swim. Green flags mean that bathing is permitted and is safe. Orange flags warn that bathing may be dangerous and usually only part of the beach is guarded. The guarded area is marked out by flags, beyond which you should not swim. Very dangerous conditions (high waves, shifting sands and strong undercurrents) are denoted by red flags, which mean that any bathing is strictly forbidden. Many of the region's beaches also display the blue flags, which are used throughout the European Union as a sign of cleanliness.

The River Loire and its tributaries also tempt summer bathers, but beware of the treacherous currents and shifting sands. It is safest to stick to established bathing areas.

A green flag shows the sea is safe for bathers

MEDICAL TREATMENT

ALL EUROPEAN UNION nationals are entitled to French social security coverage, but treatment must be paid for at the time, and hospital rates vary. Reimbursements may be claimed if you have obtained an E111 form from a post office in the UK before leaving. The claims process can be lengthy, so it is best to purchase your own insurance. The law obliges non-EU nationals to carry medical insurance, taken out in the visitor's home country before departure. In case of medical emergencies, call the SAMU (ambulance) or the *Sapeurs Pompiers* (fire service), who offer a first aid and ambulance service.

French pharmacists are able to diagnose minor health problems and to suggest appropriate treatments. Pharmacies can be recognized by the green cross sign outside their shops.

PUBLIC TOILETS IN THE LOIRE VALLEY

Modern automatic toilets are now found in many towns in the Loire Valley. Do not let children under ten use these alone as the automatic cleaning function can be dangerous.

Even when using the toilets in cafés or restaurants where you are a customer, you should take some change with you, as there is often a small charge or you may be expected to leave a tip for the cleaner. Traditional *pissoirs* and keyhole toilets, still found in more rural areas, are not always very clean. Toilet facilities are provided on the *autoroute* at drive-in rest areas every 20 km (12 miles).

1 Put the amount indicated in the slot.

2 Press the button to open the sliding door.

3 The light shows vacant or engaged.

Banking and Local Currency

IN THE LOIRE VALLEY, as elsewhere in France, the banks usually offer the best rates of exchange. Privately-owned *bureaux de change* are common in tourist areas, especially around the châteaux, but tend to have more variable rates. Take care to check the commission and minimum charges before you complete a transaction. Traveller's cheques are still the safest form of money, but using credit cards and some ATM (automatic teller machine) cards to withdraw cash beats bank queues any day, although you will undoubtedly be charged by the card issuer for this service.

BANKING HOURS

BANKS IN BIG TOWNS are usually open from 9am to noon and from 2 to 6pm, Tuesday to Saturday. They often close on Mondays. Over public holiday weekends, they may be shut from noon Friday until Tuesday morning. Opening hours can be more limited in smaller towns.

USING BANKS

THERE IS NO LIMIT to the amount of money you may bring into France, but if you want to take more than 7,500€ back to the UK, you should declare it on arrival. Most banks have a *bureau de change*, offering the best exchange rates but also charging commission. Most banks now have ATMs that take major crdit cards as well as some cashpoint cards. To take out money, you need to tap in a PIN (Personal Identification Number). ATM instructions are usually in French, English and German.

It is also possible to withdraw up to 300€ each day on Visa or MasterCard at the foreign counter of any bank where their logos are displayed. You will need your passport or ID to make any transaction over a bank counter in France.

Since the arrival of the Euro, old-style Eurocheques have been phased out by most banks, and very few places in France continue to accept them.

Keypad to check your PIN

TRAVELLER'S CHEQUES AND CREDIT CARDS

TRAVELLER'S CHEQUES can be obtained from American Express, Thomas Cook or your bank, building society or some post offices. American Express cheques are widely accepted in France, and Amex offices exchange them without charging commission.

In France, Visa/Carte Bleue and Eurocard/MasterCard are the most common credit cards, while American Express cards are not always accepted.

French credit and debit cards are now smart cards (*cartes à puce*). Retailers are equipped with machines that read smart cards and older magnetic strips. If your card cannot be read in the smart card slot, you will be told you have a *puce morte*. Ask the cashier to put the card through the *bande magnétique* (magnetic reader). You may also have to tap in your PIN and press the green key (*validez*) on a small keypad.

CONVERSION CHART

THE FOLLOWING is a rough guide to equivalent currency values, rounded up or down for ease of use.

EUROS	FRANCS
1	6.5
5	33
10	65
20	130
25	165
50	330
75	495
100	650
150	980

DIRECTORY

BUREAUX DE CHANGE

Angers
Office de Tourisme,
11 pl Président
Kennedy.
█ 02 41 23 51 11.

Bourges
La Poste Principale,
rue Moyenne.
█ 02 48 68 82 82.

Chartres
Place de la Cathédrale
█ 02 37 36 42 33.

Crédit Agricole
1 rue Daniel Boutet
█ 02 37 27 31 31.

Le Mans
Crédit Lyonnais,
33 pl de la République.
█ 02 43 47 33 33.

Société Générale,
43 pl de la République.
█ 02 43 21 57 00.

Nantes
Le Change Graslin,
17 rue Jean-Jacques
Rousseau.
█ 02 40 69 24 64.

Orléans
Banque de France,
30 rue de la République.
█ 02 38 77 78 78.

Crédit Lyonnais,
7 pl du Martroi.
█ 02 38 75 63 33.

Tours
20 pl Jean Jaurès.
("Change 24/24" automatic
24-hour exchange machine)

Société Générale,
3 bd Heurteloup.
█ 02 47 70 57 00.

LOST CARDS AND TRAVELLER'S CHEQUES

Visa/MasterCard/Carte Bleue.
█ 08 92 70 57 05.

American Express Paris (Cards)
█ 01 47 77 70 00.

American Express (Cheques)
█ 0800 90 86 00.

THE EURO

THE EURO (€), the single European currency, is now operational in 12 of the 15 member states of the EU. Austria, Belgium, Finland, France, Germany, Greece, Ireland, Italy, Luxembourg, Netherlands, Portugal and Spain all chose to join the new currency; Denmark, the UK and Sweden chose to stay out, with an option to review their decision. France's Overseas Departments (Réunion etc) also all now use the euro.

Euro notes are identical throughout all 12 countries, bearing architectural drawings of fictitious monuments. The coins, however, have one side identical (the value side), and one side unique to each country. Both notes and coins are valid and interchangeable within each of the 12 countries.

Bank Notes

Euro bank notes have seven denominations. The 5€ note (grey in colour) is the smallest, followed by the 10€ note (pink), 20€ note (blue), 50€ note (orange), 100€ note (green), 200€ note (yellow) and 500€ note (purple). All notes show the stars of the European Union.

5 euros

10 euros

20 euros

50 euros

100 euros

200 euros

500 euros

2 euros   1 euro   50 cents   20 cents   10 cents

Coins

The euro has eight coin denominations: 1€ and 2€; 50 cents, 20 cents, 10 cents, 5 cents, 2 cents and 1 cent. The 1€ and 2€ coins are both silver and gold in colour. The 50-, 20- and 10-cent coins are gold. The 5-, 2- and 1-cent coins are bronze.

5 cents

2 cents

1 cent

Communications

Sign for public telephone

FRENCH TELECOMMUNICATIONS are among the most advanced in the world. The national agency is France Télécom, while postal services are run by La Poste. Public telephones are well distributed throughout the Loire Valley. Most take a telephone card *(télécarte)*, which can be purchased at local shops. Post offices, or *bureaux de postes*, are identified by the blue-on-yellow La Poste sign. Road signs may still say PTT, as La Poste was formerly known. Foreign newspapers are available in most large towns, and some TV channels broadcast English-language programmes.

Mail boxes throughout France are a distinctive yellow

USING A PHONECARD TELEPHONE

1 Lift the receiver and wait for the dialling tone.

2 Insert the *télécarte* with the arrow side facing up.

3 The screen displays the number of units still available, then gives you instructions to key in the phone number.

4 Key in the phone number and wait to be connected.

5 If you want to make another call, do not replace the receiver: simply press the green follow-on call button.

6 Replace the receiver after the call. When card re-emerges, remove it.

French phonecards

NE LAISSEZ PAS UN RHUME VOUS GACHER LA VIE !

Télécarte 50

SENDING A LETTER

POSTAGE STAMPS *(timbres)* are sold at La Poste singly or in *carnets* of ten. Common postage stamps are also sold at tobacconists. There are eight different price zones for international mail.

Post office hours vary. The minimum hours are around 9am to 5pm from Monday to Friday with a two-hour lunch break from noon to 2pm. On Saturdays they are open from 9am until noon. In larger towns, the main post office may remain open on weekdays from 8am until 7pm.

Letters and parcels can be sent worldwide. Letters are dropped into yellow mail boxes, which often have three slots – one for the town you are in; one for the surrounding *département* (the Loire Valley is divided into eleven *départements*, each with its own postcode); and one for other destinations *(autres destinations)*.

For a small collection fee, you can also receive or send mail care of post offices in France *(poste restante)*. The sender should write the recipient's name in block letters, followed by "Poste Restante", then the postcode and the name of the town to which the letter is to be sent.

TELEPHONING IN FRANCE

ALL French public phone boxes now take phone cards *(télécartes)* and most take credit cards. The last few coin telephones vanished with the advent of the euro. Phone cards are sold in units of either 50 or 120, and are easy to use. They can be purchased at post offices, tobacconists *(tabacs)* and some newsagents.

The Home Direct call service, or *pays direct*, enables you to make a call via the operator in your country, paying by telephone chargecard, credit card or by reversing the charges. In some cases, you

can also call a third country (with AT&T, for example). Reverse charge calls are known as *PCV*.

Most phone boxes are able to receive incoming calls. The box telephone number is displayed above the telephone unit. Main post offices offer long distance calling facilities from booths, or *cabines*. You pay at the counter after the call. This system is considerably cheaper than making an international call from a hotel, as hotels tend to add a large surcharge to the bill. The Minitel electronic telephone directory can be used free in post offices (see How to Key in to Minitel).

LA POSTE AUTOCOLLANT
7 TIMBRES À VALIDITÉ PERMANENTE
(et un complément de 0,70 Fr.)
LETTRES DE 20 G, POUR LA 20 F
FRANCE ET LES DOM-TOM

Standard issue stamps and a small book of stamps called a *carnet*

OTHER SERVICES

AT POST OFFICES you can also consult telephone directories (annuaires), use Minitel and send or receive money orders (mandats). You can also make use of fax and telex.

A lot of information is available from the Minitel electronic directory, which is holding its own against the internet (the internet phone directory is available via www.pagesjaunes.fr). The service is free and can be found at many post offices.

TELEVISION AND RADIO

THE SUBSCRIPTION channel Canal+ broadcasts CBS American evening news at 7am daily. Sky News and CNN are available in many hotels. The Franco-German channel ARTE broadcasts programmes and films from all over the world, often in the original language with French subtitles.

Details for the BBC World Service are listed in Saturday's edition of *The Times*.

HOW TO KEY IN TO MINITEL

Minitel provides a vast range of services through a screen and keyboard connected to the telephone line.

To use the system, press on/off button, then screen lights up to show a list of options, the first one being *3611 annuaire*. When beeping starts, press *Connexion/Fin*. Specify the service, the name of supplier, or the name of the individual required. Enter town or area and press *Envoi* to start. To disconnect, press *Veille* or *Connexion/Fin*. Charges payable are then displayed on the screen.

THE DÉPARTEMENTS OF THE LOIRE VALLEY

France is divided into 96 *départements*. Each *département* has its own two-digit number, and this is the first number of the postcode for any address in the *département*. If the postcode has three zeros at the end, the address lies within the *département's* main town.

Département	Postcode	Main Town
Cher	18	Bourges
Eure-et-Loir	28	Chartres
Indre	36	Châteauroux
Indre-et-Loire	37	Tours
Loir-et-Cher	41	Blois
Loire-Atlantique	44	Nantes
Loiret	45	Orléans
Maine-et-Loire	49	Angers
Mayenne	53	Laval
Sarthe	72	Le Mans
Vendée	85	La Roche-sur-Yon

FOREIGN NEWSPAPERS

IN MOST MAIN towns, English-language newspapers such as the *International Herald Tribune*, the *Guardian* and the *Financial Times* are often available for sale on the day of issue. Most other English newspapers as well as Swiss, Italian, German and Spanish titles are sold on the day of publication during the summer months and a day later out of season. *The European* magazine is published on Fridays.

A range of the newspapers available in the Loire Valley

USEFUL DIALLING CODES

- All French phone numbers have **ten digits** rather than eight. If you are using an old number, for the northwest (including the Loire Valley) prefix it with 02; Ile de France: 01; northeast: 03; southeast: 04; southwest: 05.
- To **call France**, dial: from the UK and US: 00 33; from Australia: 00 11 33. Omit the first 0 of the French area code.
- For **operator service**, dial 12.
- For **international information**, dial: 00 33 12, followed by the relevant country code.
- For **Home Direct** calls, dial 0800 99, then dial 00.
- To make direct **international calls**, dial 00 first.
- The **country codes** are: Australia, 61; Canada and US, 1; Eire, 353; New Zealand, 64; UK, 44.

TRAVEL INFORMATION

FORMING A BROAD BAND about 110 km (70 miles) south of Paris and stretching from the centre of France in the east to the Atlantic coast in the west, the Loire Valley is relatively well served by international motorway and rail links. The city of Nantes has an international airport with

flights to many major European cities. For travelling across the region, the TGV *(see pp242–4)* is swift; and for those who like travelling to be effortless, there is a weekly vehicle-only motorail service from Paris to Nantes. The motorways, however, are excellent, if a little crowded in summer.

Road sign to Nantes airport

ARRIVING BY AIR

NANTES-ATLANTIQUE airport has flights to most major European and Mediterranean cities, and Montreal and Toronto.
There are restaurants, bars, newsagents and a gift shop at the terminal, as well as a bank with a *bureau de change* (open during normal banking hours, *see p236*), and an information desk, which will make hotel reservations if necessary.

Parents travelling with young children and baggage can ask for help from airport staff, and there are fully equipped baby-changing facilities. Wheelchair access around the building is good, and assistance getting on and off the plane is available for disabled passengers .

Taxis to the town centre cost around 20€ (more at night and on Sundays). Airport buses to the centre are timed to coincide with most flight arrivals. Car-hire companies at the airport are Ada, Autop, Avis, Budget, Citer, Europcar, Hertz and Sixt.

AIRLINE DETAILS

CORSAIR (BOOK through Nouvelles Frontières) operate charter flights from Nantes to Montreal and Toronto on Tuesdays, from May to October. Air Transat also has charter flights to Montreal on Mondays and Toronto on Tuesdays. From the UK, Brit Air flies twice daily from London Gatwick

to Nantes, with an extra flight in July and August. Air France has six daily flights from Paris to Nantes. From other international departure points to Nantes, it is necessary to change planes in Paris. Passengers transferring in Paris or London to a connecting flight can ask to have their baggage sent on to Nantes when they check in. There are no direct flights to France from Australia or New Zealand, but Qantas Airways connects with British Airways and Air France in London.

Airport trolley slot machine

FARES AND DEALS

AIRLINE FARES to Nantes are at their highest over the Easter period and in the peak season in July and August. Different airlines, however, may have slightly different peak periods, so check with the airlines or an agent to find out which fares will apply when you travel.

For flights only, Advance Purchase Excursion fares (APEX) are relatively inexpensive but they have to be booked well in advance. They cannot be changed or cancelled without a penalty and contain minimum and maximum stay clauses. Note that children often travel

The interior of Nantes-Atlantique Airport

more cheaply than adults. The price of a standard fare ticket is often cheaper if your visit includes at least one Saturday overnight stay.

Competition between the airlines means that there are some very attractive deals on offer, both for charter and regular scheduled flights. It is worth taking the time to look around for the best deals.

If you book a cheap deal with a discount agent, check that the agent belongs to a recognized regulatory body. This may guarantee that you will get a refund if the agent should cease trading. Do not part with the full fare until you have seen the ticket. Check with the relevant airline to ensure that your seat has been confirmed, and reconfirm your return journey.

FLY-DRIVE AND FLY-RAIL PACKAGE HOLIDAYS

AIR FRANCE and the French railways offer combined fares for flight and train. You fly into Paris and then catch the train south. Very good deals are available to Angers, Nantes and Tours. There are also companies offering tailor-made package holidays in the Loire Valley with flight, car hire and accommodation all included in the cost.

A Boeing 737 jet belonging to the national airline, Air France

FLIGHT TIMES TO NANTES

ON LONG-HAUL flights you will need to change planes in Paris or London. Approximate flight times between major cities are as follows:

London: 1 hour, 25 mins.
Paris: 50 mins.
New York: 7 hours, 30 mins.

SAFETY IN THE AIR

PASSENGERS should make sure that their baggage is securely fastened and tagged and not left unattended at the airport. Never look after or check in baggage for somebody else. You are likely to be asked whether you are carrying any electrical goods, and it is advisable to keep these to a minimum.

If you are travelling with very young children, advise the airline as soon as possible in order to reserve a "skycot". If a child is not to occupy a separate seat, a special seat belt should be provided.

Pregnant women should check in advance with the airline to ensure they will be allowed to fly: most airlines have a cut-off date of 36 weeks. Between 28 and 36 weeks it is necessary to have a letter from your doctor stating that you are healthy enough to travel, and giving your estimated delivery date.

You should inform the airline in advance if you have any specific dietary needs.

Getting Around by Train

Travelling to the loire valley by train is fast and efficient. The French state railway, the Société Nationale des Chemins de Fer Français (SNCF), is one of Europe's best equipped and most comfortable. The train journey from Paris to Nantes or to Tours is very quick – the TGV *(Train à Grande Vitesse)* takes only 2 hours and 10 minutes to Nantes, and 75 minutes to Tours. With the Eurostar high-speed service running through the Channel Tunnel, travel to the Loire Valley from the UK is faster than before.

Automatic ticket machine

Main Routes

The main train routes to the Loire Valley from Northern Europe pass through Paris. The TGV network links the port of Calais with Paris Gare du Nord station. From there, passengers must transfer to Gare Montparnasse, before continuing their journey on the TGV Atlantique to the main towns in the Loire region. Corail express trains to Nantes also leave from Gare Montparnasse, while Corail express trains to all other Loire Valley destinations leave from Gare d'Austerlitz. Tickets from London to all the Loire Valley towns, travelling via the Eurostar, hovercraft or ferry, are available from Rail Europe and SNCF offices. From southern Europe, trains run to Nantes from Madrid in Spain (with a journey time of 16 hours) and Milan in Italy (with a journey time of 14 hours, 30 minutes).

Within the Loire Valley, the route along the River Loire via Nantes, Angers and Orléans is popular, so it is best to reserve tickets in advance on this and other *Grandes Lignes*.

Booking in the UK

French railways have UK postal and telephone contacts. Reservations made in the UK may be difficult to change in France, due to different computer booking systems. If you need to alter your return date you may have to pay for another reservation or, with Motorail, you will have to buy another ticket and then claim a refund on your return.

Booking in France

Ticket counters at all the stations are computerized. There are also automatic ticket and reservation machines (with English instructions) on the concourse of main stations. If you have a credit card with a PIN, you can check times and fares and make reservations using the Minitel system *(see p239)*. For travel by TGV, a ticket reservation is necessary, but can be made as little as five minutes before the train leaves. Ticket prices for all trains rise considerably at peak times, and reservations are compulsory during public holidays. The SNCF's international ticket and reservation system is connected by computer to most European travel agents and stations, allowing direct booking on services throughout Europe.

SNCF logo

Fares and Booking

TGV's have two price levels for 2nd class, normal and peak, and a single level for 1st class. The cost of the obligatory seat reservation is included in the ticket price. Tickets for other trains can be subject to a supplement and do not include the reservation charge (3€).

Discounts are available for people travelling with children *(Découverte Enfant+)*, for young people *(Découverte 12-25)*, for the over 60's *(Découverte Senior)*, for two people travelling together (must be a return trip – *Découverte à Deux)*, for return trips including a Saturday night *(Découverte Sejour)* and for advance booking *(Réductions Prem's)*. For those who use the railways a lot, up to 50 per cent discounts are available: *Carte Enfant+*, *Carte 12-25* and *Carte Senior*.

Rail passes purchased outside France include Eurodomino (3,5 or 10 days' travel in a month), Inter-Rail (unlimited travel in Europe), Eurail (for non-European residents) and France Railpass (for US citizens).

The ticket office at Chartres railway station

TIMES AND PENALTIES

TIMETABLES change twice a year, and leaflets for main routes are free. Trains in France are almost always on schedule. You must time-punch (*composter*) your ticket in the orange machine at the platform entrance or pay a penalty on the train.

MOTORAIL

MOTORAIL SERVICES (*trains autos*) carry cars, motorbikes and passengers to Paris overnight from Bologna or Milan in Italy (once or twice a week in the summer months only, with a journey time of 14 hours, 30 minutes). There are also daily services from Madrid in Spain (the journey takes 16 hours) and in the summer only from Düsseldorf (16 hours, 30 minutes) via

Frankfurt (journey takes 13 hours). From Paris, a motorail service runs to Nantes on Fridays (in summer it is daily) from the Gare Montparnasse. Note it only carries vehicles; passengers must travel on a separate TGV. Information and bookings are available

via French Railways in London or from any SNCF station in France. There are no motorail connections with the UK, but the **Eurotunnel** shuttle service carries cars and their passengers from Folkestone to Calais through the Channel Tunnel.

Departure and arrival dates and times

Ticket information, showing the route

Class, carriage number and seat number

Train number

Ticket issued by the **Société Nationale des Chemins de Fer (SNCF)**

Booking reference

Price per passenger

Total price paid

TGV RAIL SERVICE

Trains à Grande Vitesse, or high-speed trains, travel at up to 300 km/h (185 mph). Their speed and comfort make them relatively expensive. You must always reserve a seat in advance, the cost of which depends on your destination and on the time and date of your journey.

KEY TO TGV LINES

- Nord
- Atlantique
- Sud-Est

A high-speed TGV arriving at the station in Tours

MAIN LINE STATIONS

Nantes has two station exits, the Sortie Sud which brings you out in the new Cité des Congrès district, and the Sortie Nord, in the Jardin des Plantes district. Both are within walking distance of each other.

In Tours, most trains arrive at the suburban station of St-Pierre-des-Corps, from which a shuttle train *(navette)* takes passengers on to the town centre station in ten minutes. A similar shuttle service operates in Orléans, where many main line trains arrive at Les Aubrais station, 3 km (2 miles) outside the town centre. In both cases, the price of the shuttle is included in the cost of the ticket, and shuttles are timed so that they coincide with main line services. The departure time given on your ticket is the time at which the shuttle leaves the town centre and not the main line station.

EUROSTAR

Eurostar's striking yellow-and-white trains currently run 15 services per day between London's Waterloo International Station and the Gare du Nord in Paris. Each train has first- and second-class compartments, with the option of a waiter-service meal in first class. You can also buy refreshments from a trolley service or in the buffet car. The journey takes 3 hours. You must book tickets in

advance and check in at least 20 minutes before the departure time. To book, contact the **Rail Europe** office in London or ring the **Eurostar** bookings line.

EUROTUNNEL

The Eurotunnel shuttle-service carries cars and coaches and their passengers through the Channel Tunnel in 35 minutes. Tickets can be bought in advance from travel agents or by calling the **Eurotunnel** Customer Service Centre, but it is also possible to purchase a ticket for the next train when you arrive at the terminals in Folkestone or Calais. There are up to four trains an hour during peak times in the summer, and a minimum of one an hour at night. The terminals at each end have a range of restaurants and shops. Before boarding you go through passport and customs controls for both countries. This means you drive straight onto the motorway when you arrive at the other side.

DIRECTORY

TICKET RESERVATIONS

Rail Europe (for Eurostar and onward bookings, including motorail)
Call centre for telephone bookings/ ticket collection:
10 Leake Street, Waterloo, London SEI 7NN.
☎ (08705) 848 848.
For information/over-counter bookings:
179 Piccadilly, London WIV OBA (no phone).
W www.raileurope.co.uk

Eurostar
UK ☎ (01233) 617 575.
France ☎ 08 92 35 35 39.
☎ Minitel 3615/ 3616/ 3623 SNCF★Eurostar.
W www.eurostar.com

Eurotunnel
UK ☎ (0990) 353535.
France ☎ 03 21 00 61 00.
W www.eurotunnel.com

SNCF Information & Reservations
France ☎ 08 92 35 35 35.
W www.sncf.fr

DISCOUNT TICKETS

Wasteels
opposite Platform 2, Victoria Train Station, London SW1V 1JT
☎ (0207) 834 7066.

Usit Campus
52 Grosvenor Gardens, London SW1W OAG
☎ (0870) 240 1010

Usit Campus
14 Southampton St, Covent Garden, London WC2E 7HY.
☎ (020) 7836 3343.
W www.usitcampus.co.uk

The station forecourt in Tours

Getting Around by Road

FRANCE IS A MOTORIST'S PARADISE, and the main route to the Loire Valley is via an excellent, if expensive, autoroute (motorway) network. There are many beautiful roads in the Loire region, particularly those running along the banks of the rivers. Popular routes, especially the Atlantic coastal roads and the roads leading between the châteaux, can be busy in high season, but are clearer at other times of year.

WHAT TO TAKE

IF YOU ARE TAKING your own car to the Loire Valley, it is advisable to obtain a green card (a free extension of an existing policy from some insurers). Without it you only have third-party coverage in France, regardless of whether you have comprehensive cover in your own country. Drivers' organizations and most large insurance companies also offer special policies. It is compulsory to take the original registration document for your car, a current insurance certificate and a valid driving licence. You should also carry a passport or identification card. A sticker showing the country of registration should be displayed close to the rear number plate. The headlights of right-hand drive cars must be adjusted – kits for this are available at most ports. You must also carry a red warning triangle. Other recommended accessories include spare headlight bulbs, a first-aid kit and a fire extinguisher.

GETTING TO THE LOIRE VALLEY

UNLESS YOU ARE PREPARED TO take minor roads south from the western Channel ports through Normandy and Brittany, travellers from the UK and northern Europe will have difficulty avoiding Paris.

From Calais and Boulogne the A26 and A1 motorways lead to Paris and skirt the city centre, connecting with the southern A10 for Orléans, Blois and Tours and with the A11 for Chartres, Le Mans, Angers and Nantes. Avoid the Paris rush hour if you can.

From western Spain, take the A8 from San Sebastian to Bayonne, then the N10 to Bordeaux and the A10 to Tours and Orléans. From the eastern Spanish coast you can reach Bordeaux on the A7 and A61 and A62 passing via Narbonne and Toulouse. From Italy take the A7 and A8 or the A43 to Lyon, which is where the A72 and A71 head north to Bourges and Orléans. From anywhere in Germany, the quickest way to get to the Loire Valley is via Paris.

In high season, the motorways get crowded and, if you have time, it may be worth taking more minor (and more attractive) roads. Try not to travel over the first and last weekends in July and August, when thousands of French and foreign holiday-makers are on the roads.

USING THE AUTOROUTE TOLL

When you join an autoroute, take a ticket from the machine. This identifies your starting point on the autoroute. You do not pay until you reach an exit tollbooth. Charges are made according to the distance travelled and the type of vehicle.

Gare de Péage de Fresnes

2000 m

Motorway Sign
These signs indicate the name and distance to the next toll-booth. They are usually blue and white; some show the various tariff rates for cars, motorbikes, caravans and large trucks.

Tollbooth with Attendant
When you hand in your ticket at a staffed toll-booth, the attendant tells you the cost of your journey (péage) on the autoroute and the price will be displayed. You can pay with coins, notes or credit cards. A receipt is issued on request.

Automatic Machine
On reaching the exit tollbooth, insert your ticket into the machine and the price of your journey will be displayed in euros. You can pay either with coins or by credit card. The machine will give change and can issue a receipt.

Car Hire

IT IS WORTH contacting a number of car-hire firms before you go, as there are often special offers if you pre-pay. In France, **Rent a Car** is good value. Other options include Fly-drive packages, and the train and car-hire deals from the SNCF, with collection from main stations.

For more than three weeks, the best option may be TT Leasing, the short-term purchase and buy back service offered by Citroën, Peugeot and Renault.

Three of the most widely available car-hire firms in the Loire Valley

Rules of the Road

REMEMBER to drive on the right. The *priorité à droite* rule also applies, which means that you must give way to any vehicle coming out of a side turning on the right, unless signposting indicates otherwise. However, the *priorité à droite* rule no longer applies at roundabouts, so give way to cars already on the roundabout.

Seat belts are compulsory for both front and back seats. Overtaking when there is a single solid centre line is heavily penalized.

Be aware that instant fines are issued for speeding and drink-driving.

No entry for any vehicles

One-way system

VOUS N'AVEZ PAS LA PRIORITÉ

Give way at roundabouts

Right of way ends, give way to right

One of the motorways in the Loire Valley region

Fast Through Routes

THERE ARE three main motorways in the Loire Valley: the A11 *(L'Océane)* from Nantes to Chartres via Angers; the A10 *(L'Aquitaine)* from Tours to Orléans via Blois; and the A71 from Orléans to Bourges. There are police stations at motorway exits.

Country Routes

ONE OF THE pleasures of touring the Loire Valley is turning off the main routes onto small country roads. The RN and D (*Route Nationale* and *Départementale*) roads are often a good alternative to motorways.

The *Bison futé* ("crafty bison") signs will indicate alternative routes to avoid heavy traffic, and are particularly helpful during the French holiday periods, which are appropriately known as the *grands départs*. The worst weekends are in mid-July, and at the beginning and end of August when the French holidays start and finish.

Speed Limits

THE SPEED LIMITS in the Loire Valley are as follows:
• **Toll motorways** 130 km/h (80 mph) in dry weather, 110 km/h (68 mph) when it rains;
• **Dual carriageways and non-toll motorways** 110 km/h (68 mph), 100 km/h (60 mph) in the rain; 50 km/h (30 mph) in towns;
• **Other roads** 90 km/h (56 mph), 80 km/h (50 mph) in the rain;
• In **towns** 50 km/h (30 mph).
• In **fog**, 50 km/h (30 mph).

Maps

THE BEST GENERAL maps of the Loire Valley are the yellow Michelin regional maps (No. 232 for the Pays de la Loire and No. 238 for Centre Val de Loire) at a scale of 1:200 000. **IGN** (*Institut Géographique National*) maps are more detailed.

Town plans are usually provided free by local tourist offices. In large towns you may need a more detailed map, and these are published by Michelin or **Plans-Guides Blay**. In the UK, **Stanfords** in London is famous for its range of maps.

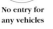

Some of the available maps of the Loire Valley

Petrol

PETROL *(essence)* is relatively expensive in France, especially on autoroutes. Large supermarkets and hypermarkets sell petrol at a discount. A map issued by French Government Tourist Offices *(see p231)* indicates the cheaper petrol stations situated up to 2 km (just over a mile) from motorway exits.

Many petrol stations in France are self-service (*libre

service), but if an attendant is on duty, it may be helpful to know that *faire le plein* means "to fill up the tank".

The grades of petrol to be found at most stations are premium *(super)*, regular *(essence)* and unleaded *(sans plomb)*. Diesel *(gasoil)* is also common and is the cheapest fuel on sale in France. LPG gas is also available, often at stations on motorways.

An *borodateur*, or pay-and-display parking meter

PARKING REGULATIONS

PARKING IN THE large towns is strictly regulated. If you are illegally parked, you may be towed away instantly to the police pound and face a fine of up to 150€. Loire Valley towns now have pay-and-display machines *(horodateurs)*. Many towns and villages offer free parking from noon to 2pm – ticket machines will automatically allow for this.

Even if you are legally parked, it is possible that you will find yourself hemmed in when you return: the French usually honk their horns to attract the guilty party.

COACH AND BUS TRAVEL

ALTHOUGH THE journey time to Nantes from London with Eurolines is almost 14 hours, compared to a 75-minute flight, the coach trip does cost less than half the price of the flight, which makes it good value. Coaches also depart from London to Tours on Wed, Sat and Sun, and there is a Wed and Sat service to Nantes and Angers, changing at Tours. In the

summer, the services are more frequent.

Local bus services in the region are good. In towns it is usually possible to take a bus from a rail station to the centre, and in the countryside, services are quite frequent and reliable.

There are also bus links between major tourist sites, as well as day trips to several châteaux, which are organized locally by some private coach companies.

For more information on bus routes and timetables, contact local town halls or tourist information offices.

TAXIS

PRICES VARY from one part of the region to another. The charges, predictably, are highest in the busy tourist areas. The pick-up charge is usually around 3€, and 50 cents or more for every kilometre. An extra charge will be made for any luggage. All taxis must use a meter *(compteur)*. Hailing a taxi is not customary in the Loire Valley – you must go to a taxi rank or book by phone.

A taxi meter showing the fare, or *prix à payer*

HITCHHIKING

HITCHHIKING is legal in France, although officially frowned upon. You will be cautioned by the police if you are hitching on motorways. **Allostop** can put you in touch with cars travelling in France and Europe. After paying an initial fee, which is determined by the length of the trip, hitchhikers pay the driver a minimal fixed rate per kilometre, which includes petrol costs and motorway tolls. The organization keeps records of drivers' and hitchhikers' details for security reasons.

DIRECTORY

CAR RENTAL

Avis
UK 【 *(020) 8848 8733.*
France 【 *0820 050505.*
Nantes (airport) 【 *02 40 84 81 01; (centre)* 【 *02 40 89 25 50.*
Orléans 【 *02 38 62 27 04.*

Budget
UK 【 *(0800) 181 181.*
France 【 *0825 00 35 64.*

Europcar
UK 【 *(01132) 422 233.*
Orléans 【 *02 38 73 00 40.*
Nantes 【 *02 40 29 05 10.*

Hertz
UK 【 *(0208) 679 1799.*
France 【 *0825 861 861.*

Rent a Car
Paris 【 *0836 694 695.*
Orléans 【 *02 38 62 22 44.*
Nantes 【 *02 40 20 09 09.*

TRAFFIC INFORMATION

Autoroute
【 *01 47 05 90 01.*

CRIR
【 *04 91 78 78 78.*

ESCOTA
【 *04 93 49 33 33 (24 hr) .*

MAPS

Espace IGN
107 rue la Boétie,
75008 Paris.
【 *01 43 98 85 00.*

Stanfords
12–14 Long Acre,
London WC2E 9LP.
【 *(020) 7836 1321.*

HITCHHIKING SERVICE

Allostop-Provoya
Paris 【 *01 53 20 42 42.*
W *www.allostop.fr*

COACH TRAVEL

Eurolines
UK 【 *(020) 7730 8235.*
Victoria Coach Station, London.
France 【 *08 92 69 52 52.*
28 av du Général de Gaulle,
93170 Bagnolet.
Minitel 3615 Eurolines

General Index

Page numbers in **bold** type refer to
main entries.

Acknowledgments

DORLING KINDERSLEY would like to thank the following people whose assistance contributed to the preparation of this book.

MAIN CONTRIBUTOR
Jack Tresidder has been living and writing in France since 1992. A former newspaper journalist and theatre critic, he has edited and written books on art, cinema and photography as well as travel.

EDITORIAL CONSULTANT
Vivienne Menkes-Ivry.

CONTRIBUTORS AND CONSULTANTS
Sara Black, Hannah Bolus, Patrick Delaforce, Thierry Guidet, Jane Tresidder.

ADDITIONAL PHOTOGRAPHY
Tony Gervis, Jason Lowe, Clive Streeter.

ADDITIONAL ILLUSTRATORS
Robert Ashby, Graham Bell, Stephen Conlin, Toni Hargreaves, The Maltings Partnership, Lee Peters, Kevin Robinson, Tristan Spaargaren, Ed Stuart, Mike Taylor.

CARTOGRAPHY
Lovell Johns Ltd, Oxford.

TECHNICAL CARTOGRAPHIC ASSISTANCE
David Murphy.

DESIGN AND EDITORIAL
Duncan Baird Publishers
MANAGING EDITOR Louise Bostock Lang
MANAGING ART EDITOR David Rowley
PICTURE RESEARCH Jill De Cet, Michèle Faram
RESEARCHER Caroline Mackenzie
DTP DESIGNER Alan McKee

Dorling Kindersley Limited
SENIOR EDITOR Fay Franklin
SENIOR MANAGING ART EDITOR Gillian Allan
DEPUTY EDITORIAL DIRECTOR Douglas Amrine
DEPUTY ART DIRECTOR Gaye Allen
MAP CO-ORDINATORS Michael Ellis, David Pugh
PRODUCTION David Proffit
PROOF READER Sam Merrell
INDEXER Brian Amos

Poppy Body, Sophie Boyack, John Grain, Richard Hansell, Matt Harris, Gail Jones, Nancy Jones, Ciaran McIntyre, Rebecca Milner, Emma O'Kelly, Lyn Parry, Philippa Richmond, Zoe Ross, Alison Verity.

SPECIAL ASSISTANCE
Mme Barthez, Château d'Angers; M Sylvain Bellenger, Château de Blois; M Bertrand Bourdin, France Télécom; M Jean-Paul and Mme Caroline Chaslus, Abbaye de Fontevraud; M Joël Clavier, Conseil Général du Loiret; Mme Dominique Féquet, Office de Tourisme, Saumur; M Gaston Huet, Vouvray; Mme Pascale Humbert, Comité Départemental du Tourisme de l'Anjou; M Alain Irlandes and Mme Guylaine Fisher, Atelier Patrimoine, Tours; Mme Sylvie Lacroix and M Paul Lichtenberg, Comité Régional du Tourisme, Nantes; M André Margotin, Comité Départemental du Tourisme du Cher; M Jean Méré, Champigny-sur-Veude, Touraine; Mme Marie-France de Peyronnet, Route Jacques-Cœur, Berry; M R Pinard, L'Ecole des Ponts et Chaussées, Paris; Père Rocher, Abbaye de Solesmes; M Loïc Rousseau, Rédacteur, *Vallée du Loir*; M Pierre Saboureau, Lochois; M de Sauveboeuf, Le Plessis-Bourré; M Antoine Selosse and M Frank Artiges, Comité Départemental du Tourisme de Touraine; Mme Sabine Sévrin, Comité Régional du Tourisme, Orléans; Mme Tissier de Mallerais, Château de Talcy.

PHOTOGRAPHY PERMISSIONS
Dorling Kindersley would like to thank the following for their assistance and kind permission to photograph at their establishments: M François Bonneau, Conservateur, Château de Valençay; M Nicolas de Brissac, Château de Brissac; Caisse Nationale des Monuments Historiques et des Sites; Conseil Général du Cher; Marquis and Marquise de Contades, Château de Montgeoffroy; M Robert de Goulaine, Château de Goulaine; Mme Jallier, Office de Tourisme, Puy-du-Fou; Château de Montsoreau, Propriété du Département de Maine-et-Loire; Musée Historique et Archéologique de l'Orléanais; M Jean-Pierre Ramboz, Sacristain, Cathédrale de Tours; M Bernard Voisin, Conservateur, Château de Chenonceau and all other churches, museums, hotels, restaurants, shops and sights too numerous to thank individually.

PICTURE CREDITS
t = top; tl = top left; tc = top centre; tr = top right; cla = centre left above; ca = centre above; cra = centre right above; cl = centre left; c = centre; cr = centre right; clb = centre left below; cb = centre below; crb = centre right below; bl = bottom left; b = bottom; bc = bottom centre; br = bottom right; bla = bottom left above; bca = bottom centre above; bra = bottom right above; blb = bottom left below; bcb = bottom centre below; brb = bottom right below.

Works of art have been reproduced with the permission of the following copyright holders:
© ADAGP, Paris and DACS, London 1996: 77ca, 102tl, 150b; © DACS, London 1996: 48cla; © DACS, London and SPADEM, Paris: 104c

The publisher would like to thank the following individuals, companies and picture libraries for permission to reproduce their photographs:

PHOTO AKG, London: 48br, Bibliothèque Nationale 51crb; *Catherine de Médicis* anon 16th-century 109tl; Stefan Diller 49bl; Galleria dell' Accademia *Saint Louis* Bartolomeo Vivarini 1477 50cl; Louvre, Paris *Charles VII* Jean Fouquet c.1450 47tl; Musée Carnavalet, Paris *George Sand* Auguste Charpentier 1839 22c; National Gallery, Prague *Self Portrait* Henri Rousseau 1890 23b; Samuel H Kress Collection, National Gallery of Art Washington *Diane de Poitiers in the Bath* François Clouet c.1571 108cla; ALLSPORT: Pascal Rondeau 59crb; ANCIENT ART AND ARCHITECTURE COLLECTION: 22b, 50br, 51tl, 54tr, 55b; ARCHIVES DU LOIRET: 58clb.

Y BERRIER: 77tl; BIBLIOTHÈQUE NATIONALE, DIJON: 149b; BIBLIOTHÈQUE NATIONALE, PARIS: 52–3c; BRIDGEMAN ART LIBRARY: Bibliothèque Nationale, Paris 47tc; British Library, London 46br, 52clb; Glasgow University Library 49br; Kress Collection, Washington DC 47tr; Kunsthistorisches Museum, Vienna 54br; Louvre, Paris *François I* Jean Clouet 44; Musée Condé, Chantilly 46bl, 135b; Prado, Madrid *The Vision of St Hubert* (detail) Jan Brueghal and Peter Paul Rubens 135t; Scottish National Potrait Gallery, Edinburgh *Mary Queen of Scots in White Mourning* François Clouet 23c; State Collection, France 54bl; Victoria & Albert Museum, London 19tr, 54bl; BRIDGEMAN ART LIBRARY/GIRAUDON: Château de Versailles 4br, 56cla, *Louis XIV as Jupiter Conquering La Fronde* anon 17th century 134tr; Galleria degli Uffizi, Florence 54cla; Louvre, Paris *Henry IV Receiving the Portrait of Marie de Médicis* Peter Paul Rubens 55tl, 74b; Musée des Antiquités Nationales, St-Germain 48cla; Musée des Beaux-Arts, Nantes *The Corn Sifters* Gustave Colbert 192b; Musée Condé, Chantilly 23t, 47bc, 47bl, 52tl, 93b, *Gabrielle d'Estrées in her Bath* French School 17th century 96c; Musée d'Orsay,

Paris *Marcel Proust* Jacques-Emile Blanche c.1891–2 22tc; Musée de la Venerie, Senlis *Diane de Poitiers as Diana the Hunter* Fontainebleau School 16th century 55crb; BRITISH MUSEUM 54–5; MICHAEL BUSSELL'S PHOTOGRAPHY: 29tl and br.

CAHIERS CIBA: 77crb; CAMERA PRESS: 77tr; CEPHAS: Stuart Boreham 63bl; Hervé Champollion 63cra, 152tr; Mick Rock 27crb; JEAN-LOUP CHARMET, Paris: 45b, 51b, 57cra; CHÂTEAU DE CHAMEROLLES: 137cbl; CHÂTEAU DE MONTGEOFFROY: 71cl; CHRISTIE'S IMAGES, LONDON: 53b; BRUCE COLEMAN: NG Blake: 71bc; Denis Green 185cr; Udo Hirsch 185bl; Hans Reinhard 28br, 184bl; Uwe Walz 71bl, 71br, 185br; COMITÉ DÉPARTEMENTAL DU TOURISME DU CHER: 25cra; COMITÉ RÉGIONAL DU TOURISME, NANTES: 226t and b, JP Guyonneau 227tl, J Lesage 225tr; COMITÉ DU TOURISME DE L'ANJOU: 84b, JP Guyonneau 84c.

DIATOTALE: Château de Chenonceau 106t.

EDITIONS GAUD: Château de Villandry *Jeune Infante* Pantoja de la Cruz 94tl; C ERRATH: 24br, 182tr, 183bl; ET ARCHIVE: 50bl, 100br; MARY EVANS PICTURE LIBRARY: 9inset, 22tl, 53cl, 61inset, 151tl, 195inset, 227inset; EXPLORER: F Jalain 56cl.

FÉDÉRATION NATIONALE DE LOGIS DE FRANCE: 197c; FONTENAY-LE-COMTE Office of TOURISME: 230cl; FONTEVRAUD ABBEY: 41b, 87b; FONTGOMBAULT ABBEY: Frère Eric Chevreau 147c.

GIRAUDON, Paris: 48tr and bl, 76tr and c, 135c; Archives Nationales, Paris 50tl; Bibliothèque Municipale, Laon 50–51cr; Château de Versailles *Louis XIII – Roi de France et de Navarre* after Vouet 47br, 56bl; Musée Antoine Lécuyer 134b; Musée Carnavalet, Paris 30tl, *Madame Dupin de Francueil* 109tr; Musée Condé, Chantilly 52br, 108b; Musée d'Histoire et des Guerres de Vendée, Cholet *Henri de la Rochejaquelein au Combat de Cholet le 17 Octobre 1793* Emile Boutigny 69cl; Musée de Tessé, Le Mans 166tr; Musée des Beaux-Arts, Blois 169crb; Musée du Vieux Château, Laval 160b (all rights reserved); Telarci 51cla; Victoria & Albert Museum, London 95tl; GÎTES DE FRANCE: 199ct; LA GOÉLETTE: JJ Derennes *The Three Graces* Charles-André Van Loo 106br.

SONIA HALLIDAY PHOTOGRAPHS: 53tl; ROBERT HARDING: 37br; Paolo Koba 17br; Sheila Terry 102b; D HODGES: 167b; KIT HOUGHTON: 38c; HULTON-DEUTSCH COLLECTION: 46tr, 111tc, 134cla.

IMAGE BANK: 34clb; DAVID W HAMILTON 32; IMAGE DE MARC 14b, 90c, 103b, 117b; INVENTAIRE GÉNÉRAL: Musée du Grand-Pressigny 48cla, 104c.

JERRICAN/BERENGUIER: 11bl. FRANK LANE PICTURE AGENCY: R Wilmshurst 94t.

MAIRIE DE BLOIS: J-Philippe Thibaut 42b; MANSELL COLLECTION: 30b; T MEZERETTE: 26t, 27tl; MUSÉES D'ANGERS: 16t, 51clb, 57crb, 77cra; COLLECTION MUSÉE D'ART ET D'HISTOIRE DE CHOLET: 57b, Studio Golder, Cholet *Jacques Cathelineau* Anne-Louis Girodet-Trioson 1824 187b; MUSÉE D'ARTS DÉCORATIFS ET MUSÉE DU CHEVAL, CHÂTEAU DE SAUMUR: 82cr; MUSÉE

DES BEAUX-ARTS DE RENNES: Louis Deschamps *Bal à la Cour des Valois* 109cbr; MUSÉE DES BEAUX-ARTS, TOURS: *Vue Panoramique de Tours en 1787* Pierre-Antoine Demachy 8–9; P Boyer *Christ in the Olive Grove* Andrea Mantegna 114b; MUSÉE DE BLOIS: J Parker 126c, 127br; MUSÉES DE BOURGES: Musée des Arts Décoratifs, Hôtel Lallemant *Concert Champêtre Instrumental* French-Italian School 150t; MUSÉE DOBRÉE, NANTES: 55clb, 191tl; COLLECTION MUSÉE ESTÈVE © ADAGP/DACS: Dubout *Samsâra* Maurice Estève oil on canvas 150b; COURTESY, MUSEUM OF FINE ARTS BOSTON: *Valley of the Petite Creuse* Claude Monet 1889 oil on canvas Bequest of David P Kimball in Memory of his Wife, Clara Bertram Kimball (© 1995. All rights reserved) 147br; MUSÉE HISTORIQUE D'ORLÉANS: 48clb; MUSÉES DU MANS: 166c; MUSÉE DES MARAIS SALANTS, BATZ-LOIRE-ATLANTIQUE: G Buron 179cr; COLLECTION DU MUSÉE DE LA MARINE DE LOIRE, CHÂTEAUNEUF-SUR-LOIRE (LOIRET): 33bc.

NHPA: Manfred Danegger 185cl; M Garwood: 79b; BA Janes 28tl; Helio & Van Ingen 29bl, 182tl; Andy Rouse 29c; R Sorensen & JB Olsen 184br; Robert Thompson 29tr; NATIONAL MOTOR MUSEUM, BEAULIEU: 57tr.

PARC NATUREL RÉGIONAL DU POITEVIN: 185tr; JOHN PARKER: 1c, 18bc, 24bl, 25tl, 35crb, 36crb, 37cla and cl, 38bl, 51cra, 54clb, 55cra, 58tl, 63br, 72tl, 73c, 75bc, 87tc, 95bc, 106cla, 107cb, 110bl, 111br, 115c, 116tr, 117cr, 121br, 126cl, 127bl, 128tl, 130tl and bl, 131tc and bc, 132tl, cl, clb and br, 133tc, cr, bc and br, 144tr, 170br, 171br, 220cl; PHOTOGRAPHERS' LIBRARY: 28cla; 159b; 199b; By kind permission from PUY DU FOU: 43t.

RÉUNION DES MUSÉES NATIONAUX, Paris: Château de Versailles *Château de Chambord* PD Martin (© Photo RMN) 134crb; REX FEATURES/SIPA PRESS: Riclafe 59tr, Tall 58bl; ROUTE HISTORIQUE JACQUES CŒUR: 16b; DAVID ROWLEY: 83b.

THE SCIENCE MUSEUM/SCIENCE & SOCIETY PICTURE LIBRARY, LONDON: 56br; SCIENCE PHOTO LIBRARY/CNES: 11tr; SPECTRUM COLOUR LIBRARY: 137cr; TONY STONE WORLDWIDE: 63tl and tr, Charlie Waite 154t.

TELEGRAPH COLOUR LIBRARY: Jean-Paul Nacivet: 24cla; TRH PICTURES: 58tr.

VILLE D'AMBOISE: Musée de la Poste 33cb; ROGER-VIOLLET: 52bl, Bibliothèque Nationale 56clb, 137tr, Musée d'Orléans *Entrée de Jeanne d'Arc à Orléans* Jean-Jacques Sherrer 137br.

J WARMINSKI: 79t; C WATIER: 67t, 70b; WILDLIFE MATTERS: 94tr, 95c and br.

Front endpaper: all commissioned photography.

JACKET: Front - DK PICTURE LIBRARY: Paul Kenward cl; John Parker cr; Kim Sayer bl. Masterfile UK: Miles Ertman main image. Back - DK PICTURE LIBRARY: Paul Kenward tl; Kim Sayer br. SPINE - Masterfile UK: Miles Ertman.

All other images © Dorling Kindersley. For further information, see: www.dkimages.com

DORLING KINDERSLEY SPECIAL EDITIONS

Dorling Kindersley books can be purchased in bulk quantities at discounted prices for use in promotions or as premiums. We are also able to offer special editions and personalized jackets, corporate imprints, and excerpts from all of our books, tailored specifically to meet your own needs.

To find out more, please contact: (in the United Kingdom) – Sarah.Burgess@dk.com or SPECIAL SALES, DORLING KINDERSLEY LIMITED, 80 STRAND, LONDON WC2R 0RL;

(in the United States) – SPECIAL MARKETS DEPARTMENT, DK PUBLISHING, INC., 375 HUDSON STREET, NEW YORK, NEW YORK 10014.

Phrase Book

IN EMERGENCY

Help!	**Au secours!**	oh se**koor**
Stop!	**Arrêtez!**	aret-**ay**
Call a	**Appelez un**	apuh-**lay** uñ
doctor!	**médecin!**	med**sañ**
Call an	**Appelez une**	apuh-**lay** oon
ambulance!	**ambulance!**	oñboo-**loñs**
Call the	**Appelez la**	apuh-**lay** lah
police!	**police!**	poh-**lees**
Call the fire	**Appelez les**	apuh-lay leh
brigade!	**pompiers!**	poñ-**peeyay**
Where is	**Où est le**	oo ay luh
the nearest	**téléphone le**	tehleh**fon** luh
telephone?	**plus proche?**	ploo **prosh**
Where is the	**Où est l'hôpital**	oo ay l'**opee**tal luh
nearest hospital?	**le plus proche?**	ploo **prosh**

COMMUNICATION ESSENTIALS

Yes	**Oui**	wee
No	**Non**	noñ
Please	**S'il vous plaît**	seel voo **play**
Thank you	**Merci**	mer-**see**
Excuse me	**Excusez-moi**	exkoo-**zay** mwah
Hello	**Bonjour**	boñ**zhoor**
Goodbye	**Au revoir**	oh ruh-**vwar**
Good night	**Bonsoir**	boñ-**swar**
Morning	**Le matin**	ma**tañ**
Afternoon	**L'après-midi**	l'apreh-**meedee**
Evening	**Le soir**	swar
Yesterday	**Hier**	eeyehr
Today	**Aujourd'hui**	oh-zhoor-**dwee**
Tomorrow	**Demain**	duh**mañ**
Here	**Ici**	ee-**see**
There	**Là**	lah
What?	**Quel, quelle?**	kel, kel
When?	**Quand?**	koñ
Why?	**Pourquoi?**	poor-**kwah**
Where?	**Où?**	oo

USEFUL PHRASES

How are	**Comment**	kom-moñ
you?	**allez-vous?**	tal**ay** voo
Very well,	**Très bien,**	treh byañ,
thank you.	**merci.**	mer-**see**
Pleased to	**Enchanté de**	oñshoñ-**tay** duh
meet you.	**faire votre**	fehr votr
	connaissance.	kon-ay-**sans**
See you soon.	**A bientôt.**	Ah byañ-**toh**
That's fine.	**Voilà qui est**	vvwalah kee ay
	parfait	par**fay**
Where is/are...?	**Où est/sont...?**	oo ay/soñ
How far	**Combien de**	kom-**byañ** duh
is it to...?	**kilomètres**	keelo-**metr**
	d'ici à...?	d'ee-**see** ah
Which	**Quelle est la**	kel ay lah **deer**-
way to...?	**direction pour...?**	ek-**syoñ** poor
Do you speak	**Parlez-vous**	par-**lay** voo
English?	**anglais?**	oñg-**lay**
I'm sorry.	**Excusez-moi.**	exkoo-**zay** mwah

I don't	**Je ne**	zhuh nuh kom-
understand.	**comprends pas.**	**proñ** pah
Could you	**Pouvez-vous**	poo-**vay** voo
speak slowly	**parler moins**	par-**lay** mwañ
please?	**vite s'il vous plaît?**	veet seel voo play

USEFUL WORDS

big	**grand**	groñ
small	**petit**	puh-**tee**
hot	**chaud**	show
cold	**froid**	frwah
good	**bon**	boñ
bad	**mauvais**	moh-**veh**
enough	**assez**	as**say**
well	**bien**	byañ
open	**ouvert**	oo-**ver**
closed	**fermé**	fer-**meh**
left	**gauche**	gohsh
right	**droite**	drwah
straight on	**tout droit**	too drwah
near	**près**	preh
far	**loin**	lwañ
up	**en haut**	oñ oh
down	**en bas**	oñ bah
early	**de bonne heure**	duh bon **urr**
late	**en retard**	oñ ruh-**tar**
entrance	**l'entrée**	l'on-**tray**
exit	**la sortie**	sor-**tee**
toilet	**les toilettes, les WC**	twah-let, vay-**see**
free, unoccupied	**libre**	leebr
free, no charge	**gratuit**	grah-**twee**

MAKING A TELEPHONE CALL

I'd like to	**Je voudrais**	zhuh voo-dreh
place a long-	**faire un**	fehruñ
distance call.	**interurbain.**	añter-oorbañ
I'd like to	**Je voudrais**	zhuh voo**dreh**
make a	**faire une**	fehr oon **syoñ**
reverse charge	**communication**	komoonikah-
call.	**PCV.**	peh-seh-veh
I'll try again	**Je rappelerai**	zhuh rapel-
later.	**plus tard.**	**eray** ploo tar
Can I leave a	**Est-ce que je peux**	es-**keh** zhuh puh
message?	**laisser un**	leh-**say** uñ
	message?	meh**sazh**
Hold on.	**Ne quittez pas,**	nuh kee-**tay** pah
	s'il vous plaît.	seel voo play
Could you	**Pouvez-vous**	poo-**vay** voo
speak up a	**parler un peu**	par-**lay** uñ puh
little please?	**plus fort?**	ploo for
local call	**la communication**	komoonikah-
	locale	**syoñ** low-**kal**

SHOPPING

How much	**C'est combien**	say kom-**byañ**
does this cost?	**s'il vous plaît?**	seel voo play
I would like ...	**je voudrais...**	zhuh voo-**dray**
Do you have?	**Est-ce que**	es-**kuh** voo
	vous avez?	zav**ay**

I'm just looking.	Je regarde seulement.	zhuh ruh**gar** suhl**moñ**
Do you take credit cards?	Est-ce que vous acceptez les cartes de crédit?	es-**kuh** voo zaksept-**ay** leh kart duh kreh-**dee**
Do you take traveller's cheques?	Est-ce que vous acceptez les chèques de voyage?	es-**kuh** voo zaksept-**ay** leh shek duh vwayazh
What time do you open?	A quelle heure vous êtes ouvert?	ah kel urr voo zet oo-**ver**
What time do you close?	A quelle heure vous êtes fermé?	ah kel urr voo zet fer-**may**
This one.	Celui-ci.	suhl-wee-**see**
That one.	Celui-là.	suhl-wee-**lah**
expensive	cher	shehr
cheap	pas cher, bon marché	pah shehr, boñ mar-**shay**
size, clothes	la taille	tye
size, shoes	la pointure	pwañ-**tur**
white	blanc	bloñ
black	noir	nwahr
red	rouge	roozh
yellow	jaune	zhohwn
green	vert	vehr
blue	bleu	bluh

TYPES OF SHOP

antique shop	le magasin d'antiquités	maga-**zañ** d'oñteekee-**tay**
bakery	la boulangerie	booloñ-**zhuree**
bank	la banque	boñk
book shop	la librairie	lee-**brehree**
butcher	la boucherie	boo-**shehree**
cake shop	la pâtisserie	patee-**sree**
cheese shop	la fromagerie	fromazh-**ree**
chemist	la pharmacie	farmah-**see**
dairy	la crémerie	krem-**ree**
department store	le grand magasin	groñ maga-**zañ**
delicatessen	la charcuterie	sharkoot-**ree**
fishmonger	la poissonnerie	pwasson-**ree**
gift shop	le magasin de cadeaux	maga-**zañ** duh kadoh
greengrocer	le marchand de légumes	mar-**shoñ** duh lay-**goom**
grocery	l'alimentation	alee-moñta-**syoñ**
hairdresser	le coiffeur	kwa**fuhr**
market	le marché	marsh-**ay**
newsagent	le magasin de journaux	maga-**zañ** duh zhoor-**no**
post office	la poste, le bureau de poste, le PTT	pohst, booroh duh pohst, peh-teh-teh
shoe shop	le magasin de chaussures	maga-**zañ** duh show-**soor**
supermarket	le supermarché	soo pehr-**marshay**
tobacconist	le tabac	tabah
travel agent	l'agence de voyages	l'azhoñs duh vwayazh

SIGHTSEEING

abbey	l'abbaye	l'abay-**ee**
art gallery	le galerie d'art	galer-**ree** dart
bus station	la gare routière	gahr roo-tee-**yehr**
cathedral	la cathédrale	katay-**dral**
church	l'église	l'ayg**leez**
garden	le jardin	zhar-**dañ**
library	la bibliothèque	beeb**leeo**-tek
museum	le musée	moo-**zay**
railway station	la gare (SNCF)	gahr (es-en-say-ef)
tourist information office	les renseignements touristiques, le syndicat d'initiative	roñsayn-**moñ** too-rees-**teek**, sañdee-syndeek d'eenee-syat**eev**
town hall	l'hôtel de ville	l'oh**tel** duh veel
private mansion	l'hôtel particulier	l'oh**tel** partikoo-**lyay**
closed for public holiday	fermeture jour férié	fehrmeh-**tur** zhoor fehree-**ay**

STAYING IN A HOTEL

Do you have a vacant room?	Est-ce que vous avez une chambre?	es-kuh voo-**zavay** oon shambr
double room	la chambre à deux personnes	shambr ah duh pehr-**son**
with double bed	avec un grand lit	avek un gronñ lee
twin room	la chambre à deux lits	shambr ah duh lee
single room	la chambre à une personne	shambr ah oon pehr-**son**
room with a bath, shower	la chambre avec salle de bains, une douche	shambr avek sal duh bañ, oon doosh
porter	le garçon	gar-**soñ**
key	la clef	klay
I have a reservation.	J'ai fait une réservation.	zhay fay oon rayzehrva-**syoñ**

EATING OUT

Have you got a table?	Avez-vous une table libre?	avay-**voo** oon tahbl leebr
I want to reserve a table.	Je voudrais réserver une table.	zhuh voo-**dray** rayzehr-**vay** oon tahbl
The bill please.	L'addition s'il vous plaît.	l'adee-**syoñ** seel voo **play**
I am a vegetarian.	Je suis végétarien.	zhuh swee vezhay-**tehryañ**
Waitress/ waiter	Madame, Mademoiselle/ Monsieur	mah-**dam**, mah-demwah**zel**/ muh-**syuh**
menu	le menu, la carte	men-**oo**, kart
fixed-price menu	le menu à prix fixe	men-**oo** ah pree feeks
cover charge	le couvert	koo-**vehr**
wine list	la carte des vins	**kart**-deh vañ
glass	le verre	vehr
bottle	la bouteille	boo-**tay**
knife	le couteau	koo-**toh**
fork	la fourchette	for-**shet**

PHRASE BOOK

English	French	Pronunciation
spoon	la cuillère	kwee-**yehr**
breakfast	le petit déjeuner	puh-**tee** deh-**zhuh-nay**
lunch	le déjeuner	deh-**zhuh-nay**
dinner	le dîner	dee-**nay**
main course	le plat principal	plah prañsee-**pal**
starter, first course	l'entrée, le hors-d'œuvre	l'oñ-**tray**, or-duhvr
dish of the day	le plat du jour	plah doo zhoor
wine bar	le bar à vin	bar ah vañ
café	le café	ka-**fay**
rare	saignant	**say**-noñ
medium	à point	ah **pwañ**
well done	bien cuit	byañ **kwee**

MENU DECODER

French	Pronunciation	English
l'agneau	l'an**yoh**	lamb
l'ail	l'eye	garlic
la banane	ba**nan**	banana
le beurre	burr	butter
la bière	bee-**yehr**	beer
la bière à la pression	bee-**yehr** ah lah pres-**syoñ**	draught beer
le bifteck, le steack	beef-**tek**, stek	steak
le bœuf	buhf	beef
bouilli	boo-**yee**	boiled
le café	kah-**fay**	coffee
le canard	ka**nar**	duck
le chocolat	**shoko**-lah	chocolate
le citron	see-**troñ**	lemon
le citron pressé	see-**troñ** press-**eh**	fresh lemon juice
les crevettes	kruh-**vet**	prawns
les crustacés	**kroos**-ta-**say**	shellfish
cuit au four	kweet oh foor	baked
le dessert	deh-**ser**	dessert
l'eau minérale	l'oh **meeney**-ral	mineral water
les escargots	leh zes-kar-**goh**	snails
les frites	freet	chips
le fromage	from-**azh**	cheese
le fruit frais	frwee freh	fresh fruit
les fruits de mer	frwee duh mer	seafood
le gâteau	gah-**toh**	cake
la glace	glas	ice, ice cream
grillé	gree-**yay**	grilled
le homard	om**ahr**	lobster
l'huile	l'weel	oil
le jambon	zhoñ-**boñ**	ham
le lait	leh	milk
les légumes	lay-**goom**	vegetables
la moutarde	moo-**tard**	mustard
l'œuf	l'uf	egg
les oignons	leh zon**yoñ**	onions
les olives	leh zo**leev**	olives
l'orange	l'oroñzh	orange
l'orange pressée	l'oroñzh press-**eh**	fresh orange juice
le pain	pan	bread
le petit pain	puh-**tee** pañ	roll
poché	posh-**ay**	poached
le poisson	pwah-**ssoñ**	fish
le poivre	pwavr	pepper
la pomme	pom	apple

French	Pronunciation	English
les pommes de terre	pom-duh tehr	potatoes
le porc	por	pork
le potage	poh-**tazh**	soup
le poulet	poo-**lay**	chicken
le riz	ree	rice
rôti	row-**tee**	roast
la sauce	sohs	sauce
la saucisse	soh**sees**	sausage, fresh
sec	sek	dry
le sel	sel	salt
la soupe	soop	soup
le sucre	sookr	sugar
le thé	tay	tea
le toast	toast	toast
la viande	vee-**yand**	meat
le vin blanc	vañ **bloñ**	white wine
le vin rouge	vañ **roozh**	red wine
le vinaigre	vee**naygr**	vinegar

NUMBERS

	French	Pronunciation
0	zéro	zeh-**roh**
1	un, une	uñ, oon
2	deux	duh
3	trois	trwah
4	quatre	katr
5	cinq	sañk
6	six	sees
7	sept	set
8	huit	weet
9	neuf	nerf
10	dix	dees
11	onze	oñz
12	douze	dooz
13	treize	trehz
14	quatorze	ka**torz**
15	quinze	kañz
16	seize	sehz
17	dix-sept	dees-**set**
18	dix-huit	dees-**weet**
19	dix-neuf	dees-**nerf**
20	vingt	vañ
30	trente	tront
40	quarante	karoñt
50	cinquante	sañk**oñt**
60	soixante	swas**oñt**
70	soixante-dix	swasoñt-**dees**
80	quatre-vingts	katr-**vañ**
90	quatre-vingts-dix	katr-vañ-**dees**
100	cent	soñ
1,000	mille	meel

TIME

English	French	Pronunciation
one minute	une minute	oon mee-**noot**
one hour	une heure	oon urr
half an hour	une demi-heure	oon **duh-mee** urr
Monday	lundi	luñ-**dee**
Tuesday	mardi	mar-**dee**
Wednesday	mercredi	mehrkruh-**dee**
Thursday	jeudi	zhuh-**dee**
Friday	vendredi	voñdruh-**dee**
Saturday	samedi	sam-**dee**
Sunday	dimanche	dee-**moñsh**